The New York Times

BOOK OF
POLITICS

167 YEARS OF COVERING
THE STATE OF THE UNION

Edited by ANDREW ROSENTHAL

Foreword by MAUREEN DOWD

STERLING
New York

STERLING
New York

An Imprint of Sterling Publishing Co., Inc.
1166 Avenue of the Americas
New York, NY 10036

ISBN 978-1-4549-3126-3

Distributed in Canada by Sterling Publishing Co., Inc.
^{c}/o Canadian Manda Group, 664 Annette Street
Toronto, Ontario, Canada M6S 2C8
Distributed in the United Kingdom by GMC Distribution Services
Castle Place, 166 High Street, Lewes, East Sussex, England BN7 1XU
Distributed in Australia by NewSouth Books
45 Beach Street, Coogee, NSW 2034, Australia

For information about custom editions, special sales, and premium and
corporate purchases, please contact Sterling Special Sales at 800-805-5489 or
specialsales@sterlingpublishing.com.

Manufactured in the United States of America

2 4 6 8 10 9 7 5 3 1

www.sterlingpublishing.com

Interior design by Ashley Prine, Tandem Books

Picture credits—see page 352

CONTENTS

PRESIDENTS AND THEIR ELECTIONS

CHAPTER 2

WAR

CHAPTER 3

THE ECONOMY

CHAPTER 4

RACE AND CIVIL RIGHTS

CHAPTER 6

THE RISE OF THE RIGHT

CHAPTER 7

POLITICAL SCANDALS

FOREWORD

By MAUREEN DOWD

BEFORE MIKE PENCE CALLED HIS WIFE "MOTHER," Ronald Reagan called his wife "Mommy." Before Donald Trump wooed the "forgotten" Americans in the middle, Bill Clinton wooed the "forgotten" Americans in the middle. Before the bank panic of 2008, there was the bank panic of 1933. Before our tragically misbegotten war in Iraq, there was our tragically misbegotten war in Vietnam. Before large crowds thrilled to the sight of a young and handsome Barack Obama on the campaign trail, they thrilled to the sight of a young and handsome J.F.K. on the campaign trail. Before the soul-crushing assassination of Martin Luther King Jr., there was the soul-crushing assassination of Abraham Lincoln. Before Donald Trump twisted the truth and created dangerous illusions, there were many other powerful men who twisted the truth and created dangerous illusions.

History rhymes, as the saying goes. And often in perverse ways.

This collection of remarkable work from *The New York Times*'s archives tells the story of America—how we formed an identity and how we lost it. Our correspondents traveled the world, living through history and recording and interpreting it for our readers.

This book begins with a scalding scene: a riven country and President Lincoln taking his last breaths.

"The pistol ball entered the back of the president's head and penetrated nearly through the head," Edwin M. Stanton, President Lincoln's secretary of war, wrote in a special dispatch to the paper headlined "Awful Event; Lincoln Shot by an Assassin." As the Cabinet hovered around the president's deathbed, Stanton wrote, "The wound is mortal. The president has been insensible ever since it was inflicted and is now dying."

The sometimes-morose Lincoln had been "cheerful and hopeful" about "a speedy peace" at a cabinet meeting with Gen. Grant earlier that evening, Stanton revealed, "and spoke very kindly of Gen. Lee and others of the Confederacy."

The book ends with another scalding scene: a riven country, as Donald Trump rails about fake news and fires F.B.I. Chief James Comey, sparking a special investigation into Russia's attempt to besmirch our democracy.

The devolution from Lincoln to Trump is jarring enough, but the Statue of Liberty surely laments the sad fact that a century and a half after the Civil War, we are once more bitterly at odds over existential questions about who we are and who we want to be.

Flash back to election night, November 9, 1932, a time when our leaders had respect for a free press. "The people could not have arrived at this result if they had not been informed properly of my views by an independent press," Franklin Delano Roosevelt said in his victory statement, "and I value particularly the high service of *The New York Times* in its reporting of my speeches and its enlightened comment."

Our election-night story explained that the country was voting a "national grouch" against three years of Depression, rejecting the argument by President Herbert Hoover's side that "things could have been worse."

When F.D.R. died at Warm Springs, *The Times* described the sadness that swept the nation's capital, as crowds filled up Lafayette Square adjacent to the White House. "The men's hats were off," Arthur Krock wrote, "and the tears that were shed were not to be seen only on the cheeks of women."

Krock wrote this about Eleanor Roosevelt: "A lesser human being would have been prostrated by the sudden and calamitous tidings, but Mrs. Roosevelt entered at once upon her responsibilities. . . . When Mr. Truman arrived and asked what he could do for her, Mrs. Roosevelt rejoined calmly, 'Tell us what we can do. Is there any way we can help you?'"

In a story from 1946 with particular relevance for America in 2018, Winston Churchill appeared with President Truman at Westminster College and warned that Moscow would seek the indefinite expansion of its power and policies. The United States was at the "pinnacle of world power," Churchill said, and must not fritter away its "clear and shining" opportunity, or it would "bring upon us all the long reproaches of the after-time." He named war and tyranny as the twin evils threatening the world and said nothing could stop an "age of plenty" except "human folly or subhuman crime."

Scrolling through the liquid history of journalism, you feel a shiver sometimes, knowing what is to come.

On November 7, 1960, Harrison E. Salisbury vividly described Senator John F. Kennedy's final boisterous marathon campaign trip up and down the East Coast.

In Teaneck, N.J., "the crowd stampeded when the candidate appeared, overturning press tables and breaking down barriers. Shrieks of women filled the air." When he got to the Naugatuck River Valley, "lights blazed in windows of homes along the way, and families rushed out and stood on their front steps as he passed. Not a few men were in pajamas, and there were women in nightdresses."

And then Salisbury writes this sentence, which tugs at the heart to read it now: "Motorists parked along Route 110 blinked their lights and honked their horns at the motorcade. Mr. Kennedy rode in an open car, bareheaded as usual, despite the cold night air."

The next story is dated November 23, 1963. James Reston wrote: "America wept tonight, not alone for its dead young president, but for itself. The grief was general, for somehow the worst in the nation had prevailed over the best. The indictment extended beyond the assassin, for something in the nation itself, some strain of madness and violence, had destroyed the highest symbol of law and order." Reston added that "the irony of the president's death is that his short administration was devoted almost entirely to various attempts to curb this very streak of violence in the American character" and "to restrain[ing] those who wanted to be more violent in the Cold War overseas and those who wanted to be more violent in the racial war at home."

Reston concluded that "the unexpected death of President Kennedy has forced Washington to meditate a little more on the wild element of chance in our national life."

Sometimes the headlines alone make you shake your head. Consider the one on Robert B. Semple Jr.'s story about Richard Nixon's win in 1968: "Goal Is Harmony— President-Elect Vows His Administration Will Be 'Open.'" It is frustrating how often we are hostages to the vagaries of politicians' gremlins.

There are descriptions of our racist history that are hard to read, like Roy Reed's 1965 story headlined "Alabama Police Use Gas and Clubs to Rout Negroes."

"Alabama state troopers and volunteer officers of the Dallas County sheriff's office tore through a column of Negro demonstrators with tear gas, nightsticks and whips here today to enforce Gov. George C. Wallace's order against a protest march from Selma to Montgomery." Other painful stories include 1973's "Firing Stepped Up at Wounded Knee" and a 1992 account of the riots in Los Angeles after four white police officers were acquitted of charges in the beating of a black motorist.

And there are times you will want to throw this book at the wall in fury. When, in 1970, the National Guard fires into a crowd of students at Kent State, killing four, and claims it was necessary because of a phantom sniper. Or when, in 1964, Congress approves a resolution requested by President Johnson to "strengthen his hand in dealing with Communist aggression in Southeast Asia."

In 1967, five years before the Vietnam War officially ended, Lyndon B. Johnson sent 50,000 more men to fight in the doomed jungle. R. W. "Johnny" Apple Jr., embedded with our troops, wrote a searing story that exposed it as a lost cause: "1.2 million allied troops have been able to secure only a fraction of a country less than one and a half times the size of New York State."

"It is galling work," Apple wrote, describing a firefight that could have killed him, along with several soldiers. "Because the enemy can fade into redoubts or across borders where the Americans cannot follow him, the same unit must be smashed again and again."

In inimitable Apple style, Johnny summed up the stalemate in Vietnam (and foreshadowed Afghanistan and Iraq) with some lines by Lewis Carroll:

If seven maids with seven mops
Swept it for half a year,
"Do you suppose," the Walrus said,
"That they could get it clear?"
"I doubt it," said the Carpenter,
And shed a bitter tear.

A story dated January 14, 2001, by Stephen Engelberg, is equally prescient about another horror for America: Osama bin Laden.

"His strategy is aptly captured by one of his many code names: The Contractor," Engelberg wrote. "The group he founded 13 years ago, Al Qaeda, Arabic for 'The Base,' is led by masterful opportunists who tailor their roles to the moment, sometimes teaching the fine points of explosives, sometimes sending in their own operatives, sometimes simply supplying inspiration."

While it's clear to see that *The Times* loosened up its style over the years—and hired more women—there is wonderful writing and reporting throughout its history.

In a 1980 story headlined "From Film Star to Candidate," Howell Raines profiled Ronald Reagan, noting that his family was so poor when he was growing up that Reagan's older brother, Neil, was "sometimes dispatched to the butcher shop to ask for the free liver given out as cat food," even though there was no cat.

"Mr. Reagan's background as a movie actor has been both a blessing and a curse," Raines wrote. "Political critics who characterize him as banal and shallow, a mouther of right-wing platitudes, delight in recalling that he costarred with a chimpanzee in *Bedtime for Bonzo*. Even now, 24 years after his last film role, he stews about being typed as the nice guy who didn't get the girl. 'I always got the girl,' he sometimes assures supporters."

This book chronicles the rise of the good, the bad and the ugly: suffragettes, the civil rights movement, Joe McCarthy, the Moral Majority, the Tea Party, the movement to let women in combat, gays in the military, the Parkland kids, #MeToo. And it chronicles some falls, because, as we know, Washington breeds arrogance, insecurity, self-pity and self-destructive tendencies.

In a story dated August 10, 1974, James T. Wooten describes Richard Nixon's farewell, "his face wet with tears" and his speech to his staff: "Always remember, others may hate you, but those who hate you don't win unless you hate them—and then you destroy yourself."

Which is exactly what happened to Nixon, who was eaten alive by his demons.

"Mr. Nixon's day began in the mist and rain of a humid Washington morning, when Manolo Sanchez, his longtime valet, laid out the clothes he would wear during the final hours of his tenure as president," Wooten wrote, adding: "While he spoke, Mr. Nixon's eyes brimmed with tears that glistened in the glare of the television lights, and although he occasionally smiled, his remarks were tinted with the sadness his friends say now plagues him.

"There was also a moment of irony, while, in discussing vocational integrity, he said that among other craftsmen, the country needs 'good plumbers.'"

Political reporting doesn't get much better than that.

INTRODUCTION

By ANDREW ROSENTHAL

POLITICS—THE JOURNALISM OF POLITICS, and the politics of journalism—have been in the lifeblood of *The New York Times* since its very inception. The newspaper, originally called *The New-York Daily Times*, was first published on Sept. 18, 1851, and for the early years of its existence it was a distinctly Republican organ. Its cofounder Henry Raymond was a deeply political man—one of the founding members of the Republican Party, and in fact a lieutenant governor of New York and a member of Congress while he was publishing *The Times*.

Under Raymond (who installed a Gatling gun in his office window to fend off protesters against the racist and classist draft laws of the Civil War era), *The Times* unabashedly supported the Northern cause during the war, as well as Abraham Lincoln's two elections. Thus, the first article in this collection is about the 1860 election, which Raymond called an "Astounding Triumph of Republicanism." Raymond's casual combination of political activity and electoral politics would be unthinkable at today's *Times*, as it would be in any other independent news organization.

Sold for $75,000 in 1896, when it had a circulation of some 9,000 and was losing money daily, the paper was acquired by the Tennessee publisher Adolph S. Ochs, who transformed it into a politically independent publication (albeit conservative in its approach to what was, as Ochs famously put it, "fit to print").

While the harsher critics of modern-day journalism might disagree, *The Times* tried to stay dispassionate about partisan politics in its news columns, although its editorial page and its Op-Ed columnists have always been clearly opinionated and often partisan. That is not to say that the newspaper's inclinations and preferences have always been hidden. In 1967, *The Times* ran an article by its rising star, R. W. Apple Jr.—known to one and all as "Johnny"—that had a clear agenda about the makings of a stalemate in Vietnam.

As you will read in these pages, *The Times*'s position on the civil rights moment was clear—it believed that equal rights for African Americans was a constitutional guarantee and did not really attempt to give the "other side" of that story any credibility. (Although, as you will see, the white men who ran *The Times* in the 1960s sometimes reflected a casual racism in their language, and they were most definitely not similarly supportive of women's rights.)

Today, *The Times* does not cover climate change as a scientifically disputed problem. While the paper largely ignored or disparaged concerns over the AIDS crisis and gay rights in its early coverage of those issues, *The Times*'s modern coverage of the struggle over the rights of gay, lesbian, bisexual and transgender Americans leaves no doubt about where the organization stands. The same is true generally for gun control.

Still, overall, the independent *Times* of today bears as little resemblance to the Republican-supporting *Times* of Raymond's day as the Republican Party of modern times bears to the Republican Party of Lincoln's age—which is to say almost none besides the name. (By the way, *The Daily New-York Times* dropped the "Daily" in 1857, and the hyphen was dropped from the city name in 1896.)

Because politics is everything and everything is politics, trying to assemble a few dozen articles from the 167 years of political coverage by *The New York Times* is like trying to pick the best five pieces of music of all time, or the best five artworks. It is, perhaps, a fool's errand. The selection of the articles in this book is an attempt to give readers a sense of the scope and breadth of the newspaper's political reportage and opinion writing, and not a truly comprehensive list of the best or most important political articles. Also, some articles have been condensed for space.

Some of the articles, especially the older ones, are almost comically deadpan in the Joe Friday "just the facts, ma'am" sense. Newspapers in the late 1800s and early 1900s were more like almanacs than today's publications are, and *The Times* more so than many. Hence, the epithet "paper of record," which today's *Times* editors reject.

If you read *The Times*'s coverage of the Battle of Gettysburg, which was simply too voluminous to include in the limited space of a book like this one, you will find a series of dispatches—from journalists, of course, but also from officers and men who fought on the bloody Pennsylvania field. They are simply strung together from one side of a page to the other, snaking down and up and down, without any transitions, context, analysis or the graphics and typographical tricks of modern times that are intended to make a newspaper page more pleasing to the eye and easier to read.

Today, of course, *The Times* publishes only a fraction of its coverage in printed form, but this anthology includes only articles from modern times that ran both in print and online, a perhaps Quixotic attempt to maintain some continuity. You won't find podcasts, interactive graphics, videos or any other multimedia that grace *The Times* coverage today because, well, this is a book.

The articles I have chosen include those that are directly about electoral politics— the election of presidents and members of Congress—and their behavior, good and bad, while in office. The collection also includes articles that profoundly affected politicians and their actions—the civil rights movement, war, the economy, battles over social issues like civil rights, race and racism—because they are part of American politics.

I've tried to include many of the seminal events in American political history, such as the atomic bombing of Japan in World War II, the assassinations of Lincoln, Kennedy and King, the rise of the hard right in modern times that led to the ascendancy of religious politics, the Tea Party and ultimately Donald Trump.

I've chosen some examples of *The Times*'s greatest strengths—its writers and its fearlessness about exposing the doings and wrongdoing of politicians. These include Maureen Dowd's iconic portrayal of President George H. W. Bush as he ran for reelection in 1992 and Howell Raines's portrait of Ronald Reagan in 1980 (perfect examples of the news profiles that were for decades a hallmark of *Times* political coverage); Johnny Apple's dispatch from a firefight in Vietnam (an example of the way the paper led American news organizations in its on-the-spot coverage of the world); the first article on the Pentagon Papers, by Neil Sheehan; the paper's exposé of President George W. Bush's illegal wiretapping of American citizens after the 9/11 attacks, by James Risen and Eric Lichtblau.

Many of these writers had an enormous impact on me as a journalist. I joined *The Times* in March 1987 as part of its political team in Washington. I covered the 1988 and 1992 presidential elections as a reporter, and almost every one since then as an editor, first in the newsroom and then, after September 2003, in the editorial department. I learned about sharp political reporting from Johnny Apple, about fearless coverage of the White House and other powerful institutions from Howell Raines, about the sheer joy of writing from the inimitable Maureen Dowd, and how to write editorials from Gail Collins. *The Times* is part of my DNA, I should note. My father, A. M. Rosenthal, was a *Times* reporter, foreign correspondent, editor, executive editor and columnist for almost all of his adult life.

There have been periods in its history when *The Times* was a magnet for great journalistic movements, and you will find in these pages bylines you may recognize. The Southern writers of the '60s and '70s, like Howell Raines; the legendary Roy Reed, who phoned in the story of the attack on the marchers in Selma, Ala.; Russell Baker, and Tom Wicker were the flames that lit *The Times*'s coverage of domestic politics in their day.

It has also attracted pioneers of more modern forms of journalism, like Maureen Dowd, who perfected the living portrait of politicians with her soaring and sometimes biting prose; Johnny Apple, who practically discovered the Iowa caucuses; and Michael Barbaro, who turned from writing to podcasting in recent years with enormous success.

But there are also articles in these pages from lesser-known writers, and some news articles without any byline at all, which was the convention in newspapers for many years.

My hope is that readers will find these selections informative, interesting, sometimes surprising and perhaps even inspiring. And I hope they will serve not just as a monument to great journalism of the past, but also as an appetizer for the main course, which is the vital, ongoing, ever-changing and expanding work of *The Times* and others in the sadly dwindling cadre of great American news organizations.

CHAPTER 1
PRESIDENTS
AND THEIR ELECTIONS

"I realize keenly the responsibility I shall assume, and I mean to serve with my utmost capacity the interest of the nation. The people could not have arrived at this result if they had not been informed properly of my views by an independent press."

—President Franklin Delano Roosevelt, November 9, 1932

THE 46 PRESIDENTS OF THE UNITED STATES are about as nondiverse a group as you could assemble. Forty-five men (Grover Cleveland was technically the 22nd and 24th president since he was elected to nonconsecutive terms), 44 of them white and 1 African American. All but 3 of them professed Protestant Christianity—Abraham Lincoln and Thomas Jefferson defied denominational labels and John F. Kennedy was the only Roman Catholic, even though it is the largest religious denomination in the country. All of them were of Western European ancestry; even Barack Obama was born to a woman of mostly English descent. Four of them were assassinated, all by firearms. Despite the power of incumbency, only 13 of them served two full terms in office (Franklin Roosevelt died in his fourth term). Some served with little distinction, such as Howard Taft and Grover Cleveland. Others lent their names to the most significant periods of our history, namely Lincoln, Roosevelt, Reagan, Clinton, Obama and perhaps Donald Trump.

OPPOSITE: The crowd on the National Mall in Washington, D.C., as Barack Obama is sworn in as the 44th president of the United States, January 20, 2009.

ASTOUNDING TRIUMPH OF REPUBLICANISM

NOVEMBER 7, 1860

The canvas for the presidency of the United States terminated last evening, in all the States of the Union, under the revised regulation of Congress, passed in 1845, and the result, by the vote of New York, is placed beyond question at once. It elects Abraham Lincoln of Illinois, president, and Hannibal Hamlin of Maine, vice president of the United States, for four years, from the 4th March next, directly by the people: these Republican candidates having a clear majority of the 309 electorial votes of the 33 states, over all three of the opposing tickets.

Being 19 over the required majority, without wasting the returns from the 2 Pacific states of Oregon and California. The election, so far as the city and state of New York are concerned, will probably stand, hereafter as one of the most remarkable in the political contests of the country; marked, as it is, by far the heaviest popular vote ever cast in the city, and by the sweeping, and almost uniform, Republican majorities in the country.

> *It elects Abraham Lincoln of Illinois, president, and Hannibal Hamlin of Maine, vice president of the United States.*

The state of Pennsylvania, which virtually decided her preference in October, has again thrown an overwhelming majority for the Republican candidates. And New Jersey, after a sharp contest has, as usual in nearly all the presidential elections, taken her place on the same side. The New England majorities run up by tens of thousands.

The Congressional elections which took place yesterday in this state have probably confirmed the probability of an anti-Republican preponderance in the next House of Representatives, by displacing several of the present Republican members.

AWFUL EVENT; PRESIDENT LINCOLN SHOT BY AN ASSASSIN

By EDWIN M. STANTON, APRIL 15, 1865

This evening at about 9:30 p.m., at Ford's Theatre, the president, while sitting in his private box with Mrs. Lincoln, Mrs. Harris and Major Rathburn, was shot by an assassin, who suddenly entered the box and approached behind the president.

The assassin then leaped upon the stage, brandishing a large dagger or knife, and made his escape in the rear of the theatre.

The pistol ball entered the back of the president's head and penetrated nearly through the head. The wound is mortal. The president has been insensible ever since it was inflicted and is now dying.

About the same hour an assassin, whether the same or not, entered Mr. Seward's apartments, and under the pretense of having a prescription, was shown to the secretary's sick chamber. The assassin immediately rushed to the bed and inflicted two or three stabs on the throat and two on the face. It is hoped the wounds may not be mortal. My apprehension is that they will prove fatal.

The nurse alarmed Mr. Frederick Seward, who was in an adjoining room, and hastened to the door of his father's room, when he met the assassin, who inflicted upon him one or more dangerous wounds. The recovery of Frederick Seward is doubtful.

It is not probable that the president will live throughout the night.

Gen. Grant and wife were advertised to be at the theatre this evening, but he started to Burlington at six o'clock this evening.

At a cabinet meeting at which Gen. Grant was present, the subject of the state of the country and the prospect of a speedy peace was discussed. The president was very cheerful and hopeful, and spoke very kindly of Gen. Lee and others of the Confederacy, and of the establishment of government in Virginia.

All the members of the cabinet except Mr. Seward, are now in attendance upon the president.

I have seen Mr. Seward, but he and Frederick were both unconscious.

View up Broadway from 13th Street in New York City during the funeral procession for President Abraham Lincoln, April 25, 1865.

SWEEP IS NATIONAL; DEMOCRATS WIN SENATE

By ARTHUR KROCK, NOVEMBER 9, 1932

Roosevelt Statement

President-elect Roosevelt gave the following statement to *The New York Times* early this morning:

"While I am grateful with all my heart for this expression of the confidence of my fellow Americans, I realize keenly the responsibility I shall assume, and I mean to serve with my utmost capacity the interest of the nation.

"The people could not have arrived at this result if they had not been informed properly of my views by an independent press, and I value particularly the high service of *The New York Times* in its reporting of my speeches and in its enlightened comment."

A political cataclysm, unprecedented in the nation's history and produced by three years of depression, thrust President Herbert Hoover and the Republican power from control of the government yesterday, elected Governor Franklin Delano Roosevelt president of the United States, provided the Democrats with a large majority in Congress and gave them administration of the affairs of many states of the Union.

Fifteen minutes after midnight, Eastern Standard Time, the Associated Press flashed from Palo Alto this line: "Hoover concedes defeat."

It was then 15 minutes after 9 in California, and the president had been in his residence on the Leland Stanford campus only a few hours, arriving with expressed confidence of victory.

> *"The people could not have arrived at this result if they had not been informed properly of my views by an independent press."*

A few minutes after the flash from Palo Alto the text of Mr. Hoover's message of congratulation to his successful opponent was received by *The New York Times*, though it was delayed in direct transmission to the president-elect. After offering his felicitations to Governor Roosevelt on his "opportunity to be of service to the country," and extending wishes for success, the president "dedicated" himself to "every possible helpful effort . . . in the common purpose of us all."

This language strengthened the belief of those who expect that the relations between the victor and the vanquished, in view of the exigent condition of the country, will be more than perfunctory, and that they may soon confer in an effort to arrive at a mutual program of stabilization during the period between now and March 4, when Mr. Roosevelt will take office.

The president-elect left his headquarters shortly before 2 a.m. without having received Mr. Hoover's message.

As returns from the Mountain States and the Pacific Coast supplemented the early reports from the Middle West and the Eastern Seaboard, the president was shown to have surely carried only 5 states with a total of 51 electoral votes. It is probable that Mr. Roosevelt has capture 42 states and 472 electoral votes. With 2 states in doubt he has taken 40 states and 448 votes. Only 266 are required for the election of a president. It also appeared certain that the Congress elected by the people yesterday will be wet enough not only to modify the Volstead Act, as pledged in the Democratic platform, but to submit flat repeal of national prohibition.

President Franklin D. Roosevelt gives his first inaugural address, March 3, 1933.

Republican Strongholds Fall

The states carried by the president, after weeks of strenuous appeal for reelection on his record, seemed early this morning to have been Delaware, Maine, New Hampshire, Pennsylvania and Vermont. It is possible that complete returns may deprive him of one or more of these, but Connecticut seems to have returned to the Republican standard.

In 1928 Mr. Hoover defeated Alfred E. Smith by a popular plurality of more than 6,300,000 and with a tally of 444 electoral votes to 87. Not only will this equation be more than reversed, according to all indications, but in the final accounting it may be shown that Mr. Smith, who aided powerfully in Governor Roosevelt's cause with especial effects in Massachusetts, Rhode Island, New York and New Jersey was a much less badly defeated candidate than his successful rival of four years ago.

Late returns indicate that such Republican fortresses as Michigan, Ohio, Indiana, Illinois, Kansas, New Jersey, Oregon, Utah, Wisconsin and Wyoming—and even the president's birth state of Iowa and resident commonwealth of California—will join New York and the eleven Southern states which led the van of Governor Roosevelt's overwhelming victory.

Votes National Grouch

The country was voting a "national grouch" against three years of business stagnation, against farm foreclosures, bank failures, unemployment, and the Republican argument that "things could have been worse." The president's single-handed fight to sustain his record, his warnings against Democratic changes in the Hawley-Smoot Tariff and efforts to impress the country with fear of a change of administration were as futile in the final analysis as straw votes and the reports of newspaper observers indicated that it would be.

Mr. Hoover joins in history Benjamin Harrison and William Howard Taft as the only Republican presidents who sought and were denied reelection. In the sum, his defeat was greater even than Mr. Taft's in 1912, for while his electoral and popular vote will be greater, he had a united party organization behind him and Mr. Taft was opposed by Theodore Roosevelt and the Bull Moose Party.

Defeat Privately Conceded

Before nine o'clock, following the discouraging news from New York, Connecticut, Illinois, Massachusetts and Indiana, Republican leaders privately conceded their defeat, although they withheld official acknowledgments. President-elect Roosevelt came early to his headquarters at the Biltmore Hotel, in New York City, where, surrounded by a happy and confident group, he heard the returns and smiled when his campaign and pre-nomination manager, National Chairman James A. Farley, reiterated his often-asserted but now disproved claim that Mr. Hoover would not carry one state.

The president was at his home in Palo Alto for the news. He had reached there this afternoon, weary after thousands of miles and active days and nights of campaigning, but expressing confidence that the people would give him a vote of confidence.

Business as represented by Wall Street has already discounted the result of the election and has expressed its confidence in the future by a general rise in stocks on Monday of this week. When the rise came, the betting was as high as seven to one on Governor Roosevelt and few important members of the financial community doubted that the odds were accurate.

END COMES SUDDENLY AT WARM SPRINGS

By ARTHUR KROCK, APRIL 13, 1945

F ranklin Delano Roosevelt, war president of the United States and the only chief executive in history who was chosen for more than two terms, died suddenly and unexpectedly at 4:35 p.m. today at Warm Springs, Ga., and the White House announced his death at 5:48 o'clock. He was 63.

The president, stricken by a cerebral hemorrhage, passed from unconsciousness to death on the 83rd day of his fourth term and in an hour of high triumph. The armies and fleets under his direction as commander in chief were at the gates of Berlin and the shores of Japan's home islands as Mr. Roosevelt died, and the cause he represented and led was nearing the conclusive phase of success.

Less than two hours after the official announcement, Harry S. Truman of Missouri, the vice president, took the oath as the 32nd president. The oath was administered by the chief justice of the United States, Harlan F. Stone, in a one-minute ceremony at the White House. Mr. Truman immediately let it be known that Mr. Roosevelt's cabinet is remaining in office at his request, and that he had authorized Secretary of State Edward R. Stettinius Jr. to proceed with plans for the United Nations conference on international organization at San Francisco, scheduled to begin April 25. A report was circulated that he leans somewhat to the idea of a coalition cabinet, but this is unsubstantiated.

Funeral Tomorrow Afternoon

It was disclosed by the White House that funeral services for Mr. Roosevelt will take place at 4 p.m. (E.W.T.) Saturday in the East Room of the Executive Mansion. The Rev. Angus Dun, Episcopal bishop of Washington; the Rev. Howard S. Wilkinson of St. Thomas's Church in Washington, and the Rev. John G. McGee of St. John's in Washington will conduct services.

The body will be interred at Hyde Park, N.Y., Sunday, with the Rev. George W. Anthony of St. James Church officiating. The time has not yet been fixed.

Jonathan Daniels, White House secretary, said Mr. Roosevelt's body would not lie in state. He added that, in view of the limited size of the East Room, which holds only about 200 persons, the list of those attending the funeral services would be limited to high government officials, representatives of the membership of both houses of Congress, heads of foreign missions, and friends of the family.

President Truman, in his first official pronouncement, pledged prosecution of the war to a successful conclusion. His statement, issued for him at the White House by press secretary Jonathan Daniels, said:

"The world may be sure that we will prosecute the war on both fronts, East and West, with all the vigor we possess to a successful conclusion."

News of Death Stuns Capital

The impact of the news of the president's death on the capital was tremendous. Although rumor and a marked change in Mr. Roosevelt's appearance and manner had brought anxiety to many regarding his health, and there had been increasing speculation as to the effects his death would have on the national and world situation, the fact stunned the government and the citizens of the capital.

It was not long, however, before the wheels of government began once more to turn. Mr. Stettinius, the first of the late president's ministers to arrive at the White House, summoned the cabinet to meet at once. Mr. Truman, his face gray and drawn, responded to the first summons given to any outside Mr. Roosevelt's family and official intimates by rushing from the Capitol.

Mrs. Roosevelt had immediately given voice to the spirit that animated the entire government, once the first shock of the news had passed. She cabled to her four sons, all on active service:

"He did his job to the end as he would want you to do. Bless you all and all our love. Mother."

Those who have served with the late president in peace and in war accepted that as their obligation. The comment of members of Congress unanimously reflected this spirit.

"He did his job to the end as he would want you to do."

Those who supported or opposed Mr. Roosevelt during his long and controversial years as president did not deviate in this. And all hailed him as the greatest leader of his time.

No president of the United States has died in circumstances so triumphant and yet so grave. The War of the States had been won by the Union when Abraham Lincoln was assassinated, and though the shadow of postwar problems hung heavy and dark, the nation's troubles were internal. World War II, which the United States entered in Mr. Roosevelt's third term, still was being waged at the time of his death, and in the Far East the enemy's resistance was still formidable. The United States and its chief allies, as victory nears, were struggling to resolve differences of international policy on political and economic issues that have arisen and will arise. And the late president's great objective—a league of nations that will be formed and be able to keep the peace—was meeting obstacles on its way to attainment.

Mr. Roosevelt died also in a position unique insofar as the history of American statesmen reveals. He was regarded by millions as indispensable to winning the war and making a just and lasting peace. On the basis of this opinion, they elected him to a fourth term in 1944. He was regarded by those same millions as the one American qualified to deal successfully and effectively with the leaders of other nations—particularly Prime Minister Winston Churchill and Marshal Joseph Stalin—and this was another reason for his reelection.

Yet the constitutional transition to the presidency of Mr. Truman was accomplished without a visible sign of anxiety or fear on the part of any of those responsible for waging war and negotiating peace under the chief executive. Though the democratic process has never had a greater shock, the human and official machines withstood it, once the first wave of grief had passed for a leader who was crushed by the burdens of war.

President Truman entered upon the duties imposed by destiny with a modest and calm, and yet a resolute, manner. Those who were with him through the late afternoon and evening were deeply impressed with his approach to the task.

"He is conscious of limitations greater than he has," said one. "But for the time being that is not a bad thing for the country."

How unexpected was President Roosevelt's death despite the obvious physical decline of the last few months is attested by the circumstances that no member of his family was with him at Warm Springs, no high-ranking associate or longtime intimate, and that his personal physician, Rear Admiral Ross McIntyre, was in Washington, totally unprepared for the news.

Personal Physician Surprised

The admiral, in answer to questions from the press today, said "this came out of a clear sky," that no operations had been performed recently on Mr. Roosevelt and that there had never been the slightest indication of cerebral hemorrhage. His optimistic reports of the late president's health, he declared, had been completely justified by the known tests.

This ease of mind is borne out by the fact that Mrs. Roosevelt was attending a meeting of the Thrift Club near Dupont Circle when Stephen Early, the president's secretary, telephoned her to come to the White House as soon as possible. Mrs. John Boettiger, the only daughter of the family, was visiting her slightly ailing son at the naval hospital at Bethesda, Md., some miles away.

While these simple offices were being performed by those nearest and dearest, the president lay in the faint room from which he never roused. A lesser human being would have been prostrated by the sudden and calamitous tidings, but Mrs. Roosevelt entered at once upon her responsibilities, sent off her message to her sons and told Mr. Early and Admiral McIntyre, "I am more sorry for the people of the country and the world than I am for us." When Mr. Truman arrived and asked what he could do for her, Mrs. Roosevelt rejoined calmly, "Tell us what we can do. Is there any way we can help you?"

Flag at Capitol Lowered

As soon as the news became a certainty the White House flag was lowered to half-staff—the first time marking the death of an occupant since Warren G. Harding died at the Palace Hotel in San Francisco, Aug. 2, 1923, following a heart attack that succeeded pneumonia. The flag over the Capitol was lowered at 6:30 p.m. Between these two manifestations of the blow that had befallen the nation and the world, the news had spread throughout the city and respectful crowds gathered on the Lafayette Square pavement across from the executive mansion. They made no demonstration. But the men's hats were off, and the tears that were shed were not to be seen only on the cheeks of women. Some presidents have been held in lukewarm esteem here, and some have been disliked by the local population, but Mr. Roosevelt held a high place in the rare affections of the capital.

The spoken tributes paid by members of Congress, a body with which the late president had many encounters, also testified to the extraordinary impression Mr. Roosevelt made on his times and the unparalleled position in the world he had attained. The comment of Senator Robert A. Taft of Ohio, a constant adversary on policy, was typical. "The greatest figure of our time," he called him, who had been removed "at the very climax of his career," who died "a hero of the war, for he literally worked himself to death in the service of the American people." And Senator Arthur H. Vandenberg of Michigan, another Republican and frequent critic, said that the late president has "left an imperishable imprint on the history of America and of the world."

THE 22ND AMENDMENT

FEBRUARY 28, 1951

A sudden rush of activity on the part of the state Legislatures has added a new amendment to the Constitution of the United States. This is the 22nd Amendment, which declares that after Mr. Truman (who is specifically exempted) no president shall be elected for more than two terms, or elected more than once if he has served in excess of two years of his predecessor's term. The amendment was approved by Congress and referred to the states in the spring of 1947. The first 18 of the necessary 36 ratifications by the states were obtained that year. Only 6 additional states

> *No president shall be elected for more than two terms.*

added their ratifications in the three succeeding years. But 12 states have voted favorably within the last few weeks, and with their approval the amendment now becomes a part of the basic law of the United States.

The strongest argument made against the amendment at the time of its adoption by Congress was that it might tie the hands of the electorate in some grave future national emergency and prevent the voters from exercising a free choice in their own best interest. Undoubtedly this argument had considerable force. The nation might find itself in a state of war, or approaching a state of war, when the second term of a president in office expired, and the case for continuing that president in office could be very strong indeed. Such a situation did arise, in fact, in 1940, and again (after a third term) in 1944.

The persuasive answer to this argument is that, with the new amendment in force, any president who happens to be in office when such an emergency arises will henceforth find it necessary, and will surely find it possible, to do what Mr. Roosevelt failed to do in 1940 and 1944—namely, develop within his own administration, or elsewhere within his party, an alternative leadership to his own, fully capable of presenting his policies adequately to the electorate. In such circumstances, the voters, if they so desired, would be able to achieve a continuity of policy in the White House.

For the rest: the strong arguments which established the century-and-a-half-old tradition against a third term still prevail, and have gained increasing force from the fact of the enormously larger powers of the presidency and the obvious hazards of too-long-continued centralization of these powers in the hands of any individual, however worthy. We welcome the adoption of the amendment.

FORECASTS UPSET—
PRESIDENT TAKES LEAD OVER DEWEY

By ARTHUR KROCK, NOVEMBER 3, 1948

At 6 a.m. today, after a night in which his political fortunes waxed and waned with every passing hour, President Harry S. Truman took an impressive lead over his Republican opponent, Gov. Thomas E. Dewey of New York, in both the popular and electoral vote of the nation which went to the polls yesterday in the 48 states of the Union to choose a president, a vice president, the 81st Congress and 32 governors.

Ahead in the popular vote at all times during the counting, the president gained the electoral lead when Illinois was conceded to him at 5 a.m. and his chance of gaining Ohio steadily improved. At 6 a.m. the division of electoral votes between him and Governor Dewey that appeared to be established was as follows:

Truman, 227; Dewey, 176; doubtful, 88.

The remaining 40 of the total of 531 electoral votes apparently had been won by the presidential candidate of the Democratic States' Rights Party, Gov. J. Strom Thurmond of South Carolina.

Truman Needs 39 More

Only 39 electoral votes were needed by the president to attain the majority of 266 that would give him a full term in the White House in his own right. And 53 were in sight—in the doubtful states of Iowa, Montana, Nevada, Washington, Iowa and California. However, in the last named, with a block of 25, Governor Dewey was holding the lead.

If California ends with a Dewey victory, Ohio, with 25 electors, can overcome that loss, and Ohio went definitely into the doubtful column in the early hours of today. Therefore the possibility that the election would end without a decision, and the choice of a president would devolve on the House of Representatives in the 81st Congress, remained within the area of strong possibility, with the Senate empowered to choose the next vice president. But Governor Dewey's chances to win the election were fading fast at dawn today.

The possibility of an election by the House is the consequence of the capture of 40 electors in the South by the States' Rights Democratic Party, whose nominees were Govs. J. Strom Thurmond of South Carolina and Fielding Wright of Mississippi. And, if this is the eventual outcome, the president will have been defeated by the revolt of Southern Democrats against his "civil rights" program of federal laws to enforce anti-segregation and a "fair employment practices" act in the states.

The returns at 6 a.m. however, further upset the earlier indication that the Progressive Party candidacy of Henry A. Wallace had not proved as costly to the president, or more so, than the Southern Democratic insurrection. For if Mr. Dewey's pluralities in New York and in Ohio are as narrow as was indicated early today, Mr. Truman can attribute his failure to carry them both to the Wallace vote that was subtracted from the normal Democratic following.

The Congressional returns were more definite. Democratic candidates for the Senate appear certain to win the four crucial contests that will give the two wings of the party a numerical Senate majority over the Republican in the 81st Congress. And the new House was moving toward a Democratic majority also.

But with late returns from Republican counties in New York adjacent to the metropolis, Governor Dewey was assured of the 47 electoral votes of the Empire State and those of New Jersey, Indiana and Maryland, in which the president had been leading. These developments halted Mr. Truman short of the goal of 266 electoral votes which any candidate must have to be elected president.

In these states and many others the president confounded the forecasters by the size of his popular vote, attained over a party split in two directions and the public attempts of party leaders to deny him the nomination on the ground that he was the weakest candidate that could be chosen.

President Harry S. Truman laughs as he holds an early edition of *The Chicago Tribune* on November 3, 1948. The newspaper famously jumped to an erroneous conclusion as early election returns came in.

But even if they fail to regain majorities in Congress, the Democrats are sure to be a powerful minority in Congress on those occasions when their sections can come together to make a party front. And they may end up with a majority of both houses, which would provide difficulties for either a Republican or a Democratic president despite the deep division in the Democratic ranks.

The states which seemed at 6 a.m. certain or likely to be carried by Mr. Dewey were: Connecticut, Kansas, Indiana, Maine, Maryland, Michigan, Nebraska, New Hampshire, New Jersey, New York, North Dakota, Oregon, Pennsylvania, Vermont—a total of 186.

The states in a similar category for Mr. Truman were: Arizona, Arkansas, Florida, Georgia, Illinois, Kentucky, Massachusetts, Minnesota, Missouri, New Mexico, North Carolina, Oklahoma, Rhode Island, Tennessee, Texas, Utah, Virginia, West Virginia and Wisconsin—a total of 221.

The States' Rights Democrats carried Alabama, Louisiana, Mississippi, South Carolina and two of Tennessee's 12 electors—a total of 40.

In doubt were California, Colorado, Idaho, Iowa, Montana, Nevada, Ohio, Washington, Delaware and Wyoming, with a total of 78 electors.

But in the early hours of today it was apparent that, whatever the decision would prove to be, the president had confounded all the forecasters and demonstrated that there was real foundation to his conviction that he had a "good fighting chance" to win despite the effort of Democratic Party bosses in the East, Midwest, Pacific Coast and the South to deny him the nomination on the ground that he would be overwhelmingly defeated.

Not for 12 years has the outcome of a presidential election been so confidently forecast by so many trained observers.

Also, organized labor, it was clear, had demonstrated tremendous power at the polls and would wield it effectively in the next Congress and administration no matter what party controls the one, or the other, or both.

Not for 12 years has the outcome of a presidential election been so confidently forecast by so many trained observers and sample polltakers arriving at the same conclusion. And even in 1936 the general expectation that Franklin D. Roosevelt would be overwhelmingly reelected over Alf M. Landon was somewhat restrained by a *Literary Digest* poll, which, up to the end of the campaign, indicated Mr. Landon would be chosen.

Except for President Truman himself, and some devoted persons around him who were infected by his certainty that he could overcome the reported trend, almost no politicians in either party at any point in the campaign believed he could do so. The voters went to the polls yesterday in an atmosphere resembling that in 1912.

In 1912, the Republican split that produced the independent candidacy of Theodore Roosevelt made Woodrow Wilson's first election a mathematical certainty, and yesterday the Democratic national ticket was weakened by two independent parties that splintered off from it—the States' Rights Party of the South, under Govs. J. Strom Thurmond of South Carolina and Fielding Wright of Mississippi, and the Progressives, whose standard-bearers were Henry A. Wallace, elected as vice president on the Democratic ticket in 1940, and Glen Taylor, an incumbent Democratic senator from Idaho.

Historically, since the end of the Reconstruction period in the South the percentages by which the two major parties have divided the popular vote have been so close that very seldom did the result merit the description of a "landslide." Except in 1904, 1920, 1936 and 1928 (in this latter year the defection of the Democratic South from that party's presidential candidate also assured a large margin of Republican victory), the division has been such that if an average of a dozen voters per precinct changed their intentions because of some campaign developments, the winner would have been the loser.

There have been in the same period, of course, many "landslides" in terms of electoral votes, the reason being that, no matter how small the margin of popular votes by which any state is won, its entire bloc of electoral votes is delivered by that margin.

Yesterday, therefore, while the forecasters were generally agreed on an electoral landslide for Governor Dewey, few expected it to be reflected in the division of the popular vote, calculated to reach a point between 51 million and 52 million. If the victor, however, attains a popular majority of 3 million and a plurality of 4 million to 5 million, the term can be accurately applied to the entire result.

At stake were the offices of president and vice president; of 32 senators in 31 states (Maine filled its vacancy in September by electing Mrs. Margaret Smith, Republican, to succeed Wallace H. White Jr., Republican); of 432 representatives in Congress out of a total of 435, and of 32 governors. In 8 states various types of referenda on how to deal with the liquor traffic, including a proposal for outright prohibition repeal in Kansas, were at issue; new labor laws were before the people in 3 more; GI benefits were to be settled by 8 more, and Massachusetts voters were passing on legalizing birth control in certain circumstances.

The campaign was put down by reporters and other observers as one of the dullest in history, and various reasons for this were assigned by analysts. Among them were:

Apathy was the direct consequence of a foregone conclusion.

It was the result of Mr. Dewey's tactics in declining to be drawn out by the president's personal and political attacks and conducting a "holding action" to maintain his lead. Mr. Truman's lack of personal color in contrast with that of the late President Roosevelt and his lack of fire in delivering fiery speeches were responsible. The American people are becoming more and more cynical about the fate predicted for them by one set of politicians if the other takes office, and about the promises each makes to them contingent on the victory of that side.

But for whatever reason the campaign was listless from the end of the extra session of Congress which President Truman called last summer. The defiant and angry speech of acceptance to the convention that nominated him, in which Mr. Truman announced his plan for the call, created popular excitement, and the extra session became an arena of sharp party combat. But after that adjourned the campaign soon resembled a debating society where opposing academic positions were asserted and defended before a yawning audience.

Mr. Wallace's experience with barrages of eggs and tomatoes in the South, and the brief turmoil which followed the revelation that Mr. Truman wanted to send the chief justice of the United States to Moscow as his personal peace intermediary with Marshal Stalin, were about the only incidents of the campaign that created any stir at all.

The president assailed the Republicans as a party, and their majority in the 80th Congress in terms of unusual harshness, and he spoke scornfully of his opponent's unwillingness to debate with him on specific charges. But only once did Mr. Truman indulge in personalities of a disagreeable character; and that was when he said that there was always a personable "front man" for groups in evil conspiracy against the people and, by using Hitler and the fuehrer's original backers for his comparison, deliberately left the inference that this history was repeating itself with Mr. Dewey.

But the president, despite efforts to persuade him to do so, declined to discuss his opponent's draft status during World War II and those of some of his principal assistants in Albany. And he refused to attack the governor on the report that in 1944 he planned to make it known that the navy had broken the Japanese code before Pearl Harbor without ascertaining whether or not that fact was still unknown to the Japanese. (In two letters, Gen. George C. Marshall informed Mr. Dewey that it was and successfully appealed to him not to make the revelation.)

Though Mr. Dewey generally maintained his strategy of saying little that was controversial and concentrating on generalities with popular appeal, he breached this strategy toward the end of the campaign in the East. Apparently fearing that Mr. Truman had made some headway in that region, the governor at Boston repeated most of his Los

Angeles speech of 1944 in endorsing the Social Security thesis of the New Deal. This— and a kind of matching game with the president on Palestine—was the only concession he made to an appearance of political necessity.

Mr. Truman, however, shifted his major strategy fundamentally toward the end of the campaign by reiterating his 10-point federal program to enforce civil rights which, after he offered it to Congress Feb. 2, 1948, cost him the support of the States' Rights Democrats. At the Philadelphia convention his spokesmen unsuccessfully attempted to soft-pedal this issue, avoiding all mention of the program in the platform and of Mr. Truman's relation to it. Until he spoke in Harlem last week the president made only vague and casual references to the subject, vaguer and even more casual during his trips through Texas and North Carolina.

But last week he and his managers apparently concluded they could not keep the South unbroken by this means and might lose essential support in the East and Midwest. Accordingly, the president specifically repeated his message to Congress in an area where Mr. Wallace made much of the issue.

Aside from the two obvious goals of active forces in yesterday's election—the Republicans to gain the presidency and hold control of Congress, the National Democrats to hold the presidency and regain a majority in Congress—there were three others.

Organized labor was out to demonstrate that its opposition can be fatal to national and local candidates. Mr. Wallace was intent on showing such strength for his American-Russian policy and his domestic program that the Democratic Party in defeat will move toward his views and accord him an important voice in its future. And the States' Rights Democrats were determined to defeat the major items in the civil rights program as well as to reestablish the influence of the Southern Democracy in the national party.

SENATOR CHEERED—
KENNEDY STEPS UP CAMPAIGN IN EAST

By HARRISON E. SALISBURY, NOVEMBER 7, 1960

Senator John F. Kennedy drew unusually large crowds in predawn hours today. Large turnouts continued during the day and most of the night as he brought his drive for the presidency near an end.

Some political observers said they had never seen anything quite like the Democratic candidate's schedule for the final hours before an election.

Mr. Kennedy was concentrating his last bid for votes in New England, Long Island and New Jersey.

Just before taking off tonight from Newark Airport for Lewiston, Me., and Providence, R.I., where he had appearances scheduled for later tonight, Mr. Kennedy told a roaring crowd in Jersey City's Journal Square:

20,000 Out at 3 a.m.

"We shall not slumber. We shall not sleep. We shall keep on working for the next 36 hours until election time."

From his record of almost around-the-clock campaigning yesterday and today it seemed that Mr. Kennedy proposed to take his words literally.

Wherever he went, whether it was 3:30 a.m. in Waterbury, Conn., or 3:30 p.m. in heavily Republican Suffolk County on Long Island, he drew large crowds.

The Waterbury turnout in the main square at 3 a.m. was estimated by newsmen at 20,000 and by the police at 26,000.

On New Haven's green today at about noon, Mr. Kennedy had a crowd that the police estimated at 45,000 to 50,000. The green was filled last month when Vice President Nixon appeared there. The police said then that the crowd was about 20,000.

At the railroad station plaza in Bridgeport, Conn., Mr. Kennedy drew a crowd estimated by the police at 55,000 to 60,000. The figure was probably high, but the crowd jammed almost two square blocks.

In Suffolk County, Mr. Kennedy was seen by 50,000 to 60,000. His appearance at the Long Island Arena at Commack attracted 8,000 to 9,000 inside and 5,000 to 10,000 others outside. It was the biggest political crowd ever assembled in the county, police officials said.

Senator John F. Kennedy acknowledges cheers as he greets well-wishers outside the Concourse Plaza Hotel in the Bronx, New York, November 5, 1960.

A crowd estimated by the police at 50,000 swamped Mr. Kennedy's motorcade when it finally arrived just before 8 p.m. at Broad Street in Newark, nearly two hours late. The police said it had started to assemble about 11 a.m.

More than 5,000 persons were inside the Mosque Theatre in Newark to hear Mr. Kennedy. The throng outside was so dense that reporters were trapped inside their motorcade buses for nearly 10 minutes.

"This is a very close election," Mr. Kennedy told the Newark crowd. "It will be decided by 1 to 2 percent of the votes in most of the close states."

Sixty-five thousand persons were at Journal Square in Jersey City to see the candidate. The police said there had been 80,000, but Mr. Kennedy was then two hours and 10 minutes late.

Before going to Jersey City, the senator addressed 10,000 persons at the Teaneck armory, a hall with a normal capacity of 8,000. Five thousand other persons were outside.

The crowd stampeded when the candidate appeared, overturning press tables and breaking down barriers. Shrieks of women filled the air, but the police reported no serious injuries.

New Day at 10:30 p.m.

Mr. Kennedy has been campaigning virtually without stopping for a week. However, his weekend drive was even greater.

After motorcading for hours in the New York area through downpours in an open car on Saturday, Mr. Kennedy appeared at a rally in the New York Coliseum. Leaving the Coliseum at about 10:30 p.m. he began what was in effect and entirely new day of campaigning.

He addressed two outdoor crowds in New York, then flew to the Stratford, Conn., airport outside Bridgeport. He arrived shortly before 1 a.m. and found 2,500 persons, a brass band and a girls' drill corps awaiting him.

He told the crowd that on Tuesday Mr. Nixon would be listening to the radio in California and that it would be "nice for Connecticut to send him the first news of how the election is going." Connecticut's returns are among the first in the nation.

Men in Pajamas

The senator then started on one of the most unusual political motorcades in history, traveling up the Naugatuck River Valley. At each of the small communities he found crowds ranging into the thousands.

Lights blazed in windows of homes along the way, and families rushed out and stood on their front steps as he passed. Not a few men were in pajamas, and there were women in nightdresses.

Motorists parked along Route 110 blinked their lights and honked their horns at the motorcade. Mr. Kennedy rode in an open car, bareheaded as usual, despite the cold night air.

At Stratford, there was a crowd of 1,500. At Shelton at 1:30 a.m., there was another, 1,500 persons. "I don't know what you're doing up at this hour, but on Tuesday we're going to need you," Mr. Kennedy said.

At Derby at 1:40 a.m. there were 2,000 people, many of them with red flares. Mr. Kennedy said: "I'm not accompanied by the president, the vice president, or Governor Rockefeller. I have been traveling alone through New York. No other candidate for president can make that claim."

Mr. Kennedy said he was sorry to be late but added, "I wasn't out playing golf—I was out carrying the message."

Mr. Kennedy's motorcade was two or more hours late all along the route.

There were 4,000 to 5,000 persons waiting for him at Ansonia at 1:45 a.m. He noted a sign in the crowd saying, "Click with Dick."

"The door at the White House is going to click on Dick on Tuesday night," he quipped. The crowd cheered.

There were 300 people at Beacon Falls and 1,500 in Naugatuck's main street.

Mr. Kennedy's motorcade approached the outskirts of Waterbury about 2:35 a.m. There were people standing two and three deep at many places.

Mr. Kennedy's cars were halted by the throng on Waterbury's green.

Scores of state troopers forced a passage for Mr. Kennedy, Gov. Abraham A. Ribicoff of Connecticut and John Bailey, Democratic state chairman in Connecticut and one of Mr. Kennedy's close political associates.

The crowds at New Haven were four to six deep along the city route.

The senator made his way to the second-floor balcony of the Roger Smith Hotel. "I'm going to make this election worth winning by doing something for our country," he said.

He told the crowd he had promised the mayor that he would have them all in bed by 3 a.m. "No," the crowd roared. The hour was then five minutes of 3 a.m. and it was after 4 o'clock before he was able to retire.

By 10 a.m., fresh, smiling and chipper, he emerged through a crowd of several thousand well-wishers who had reassembled in the square. He went from the hotel to the Roman Catholic Church of the Immaculate Conception next door and attended mass. The church was jammed. Mr. Kennedy's cavalcade pushed off in bright autumn sunshine at 11:40. By this time the crowd in the square had grown to 10,000.

There were crowds at every populated point as the motorcade went south on Route 69.

Confetti trailed from Mr. Kennedy's shoulders as he spoke to 1,000 persons at Prospect. He stood in his open car against a backdrop of scarlet sumac and here and there a maple that had not lost its autumn color.

The crowds at New Haven were four to six deep along the city route. The cavalcade then moved through the Yale University campus, where some of the dormitories had Nixon signs and banners.

Adlai E. Stevenson, the Democratic nominee four years ago, encountered a hostile crowd at Yale. However, nothing like that marked Mr. Kennedy's appearance.

There were 45,000 to 50,000 persons massed on the New Haven green.

Soviet Grains Seen

By 1970, Mr. Kennedy said, the Soviet Union will be ahead of the United States in science, military power and economic strength—unless new policies are pursued. "How many countries will follow a leader who is not able to maintain the lead?" he asked.

As Mr. Kennedy's motorcade entered Bridgeport, one of the banners in the crowd read, "The election of Kennedy will be the greatest thing for the world since Christ was born."

Mr. Kennedy flew to MacArthur Airport on Long Island, where 3,000 persons awaited him. He drove the 12 miles to the Commack arena with traffic backed up for 3 miles.

Eight thousand or 9,000 persons packed the arena. At one point a table on which number of mothers and fathers were holding up children collapsed. No one was injured.

"On Tuesday," Mr. Kennedy said, "I believe the people will not take the tired old road but will turn into the wind and vote Democratic."

Mr. Kennedy rode back to the airport. He was forced to leave his scheduled route through Smithtown and make a short detour because the narrow streets were so jammed.

He flew then to Teterboro, N.J., where he was met by a crowd of 3,000.

Mr. Kennedy will campaign Monday in New England, with rallies scheduled for Providence, R.I.; Springfield, Mass.; Hartford, Conn.; Burlington, Vt., and Manchester, N. H. Tomorrow night will be climaxed with a parade and rally in Boston.

Mr. Kennedy will vote in Boston Tuesday and then fly to Hyannis, Mass., to await the election returns.

WHY AMERICA WEEPS—KENNEDY VICTIM OF VIOLENT STREAK HE SOUGHT TO CURB IN THE NATION

By JAMES RESTON, NOVEMBER 23, 1963

America wept tonight, not alone for its dead young president, but for itself. The grief was general, for somehow the worst in the nation had prevailed over the best. The indictment extended beyond the assassin, for something in the nation itself, some strain of madness and violence, had destroyed the highest symbol of law and order.

Speaker John McCormack, now 71 and, by the peculiarities of our politics, next in line of succession after the vice president, expressed this sense of national dismay and self-criticism: "My God! My God! What are we coming to?"

The irony of the president's death is that his short administration was devoted almost entirely to various attempts to curb this very streak of violence in the American character.

When the historians get around to assessing his three years in office, it is very likely that they will be impressed with just this: his efforts to restrain those who wanted to be more violent in the Cold War overseas and those who wanted to be more violent in the racial war at home.

He was in Texas today trying to pacify the violent politics of that state.

He was in Texas today trying to pacify the violent politics of that state. He was in Florida last week trying to pacify the businessmen and appealing to them to believe that he was not "antibusiness." And from the beginning to the end of his administration, he was trying to damp down the violence of the extremists on the Right.

It was his fate, however, to reach the White House in a period of violent change, when all nations and institutions found themselves uprooted from the past. His central theme was the necessity of adjusting to change and this brought him into conflict with, those who opposed change.

Thus, while his personal instinct was to avoid violent conflict, to compromise and mediate and pacify, his programs for taxation, for racial equality, for medical care, for Cuba, all raised sharp divisions with the country. And even where his policies of adjustment had their greatest success—in relations with the Soviet Union—he was bitterly condemned.

The president somehow always seemed to be suspended between two worlds—between his ideal conception of what a president should be, what the office called for, and a kind of despairing realization of the practical limits upon his power.

He came into office convinced of the truth of Theodore Roosevelt's view of the president's duties—"the president is bound to be as big a man as he can."

And his inaugural—"now the trumpet summons us again"—stirred an echo of Wilson in 1913 when the latter said: "We have made up our minds to square every process of our national life with the standards we so proudly set up at the beginning and have always carried at our hearts."

This is what the president set out to do. And from his reading, from his intellectual approach to the office, it seemed, if not easy, at least possible.

But the young man who came to office with an assurance vicariously imparted from reading Richard Neustadt's *Presidential Power* soon discovered the two truths which all dwellers on that lonely eminence have quickly learned.

The first was that the powers of the president are not only limited but hard to bring to bear. The second was that the decisions—as he himself so often said—"are not easy."

What He Set Out to Do

Since he was never one to hide his feelings, he often betrayed the mood brought on by contemplating the magnitude of the job and its disappointments. He grew fond of quoting Lord [John] Morley's dictum—"Politics is one long second-best, where the choice often lies between two blunders."

Did he have a premonition of tragedy—that he who had set out to temper the contrary violences of our national life would be their victim?

Last June, when the civil rights riots were at their height and passions were flaring, he spoke to a group of representatives of national organizations. He tolled off the problems that beset him on every side and then, to the astonishment of everyone there, suddenly concluded his talk by pulling from his pocket a scrap of paper and reading the famous speech of Blanche of Spain in Shakespeare's *King John*:

> The sun's o'ercast with blood: Fair day, adieu!
> Which is the side that I must go withal?
> I am with both; each army hath a hand,
> And in their rage, I having hold of both,
> They whirl asunder and dismember me.

There is, however, consolation in the fact that while he was not given time to finish anything or even to realize his own potentialities, he has not left the nation in a state of crisis or danger, either in its domestic or foreign affairs.

World More Tolerable

A reasonable balance of power has been established on all continents. The state of truce in Korea, the Taiwan Strait, Vietnam and Berlin is, if anything, more tolerable than when he came to office.

Europe and Latin America were increasingly dubious of his leadership at the end, but their capacity to indulge in in dependent courses of action outside the alliance was largely due to the fact that he had managed to reach a somewhat better adjustment of relations with the Soviet Union.

Thus, President Johnson is not confronted immediately by having to take any urgent new decisions. The passage of power from one man to another is more difficult in other countries, and Britain, Germany, Italy, India and several other allies are so preoccupied by that task at the moment that drastic new policy initiatives overseas are scarcely possible in the foreseeable future.

At home, his tasks lie in the Congress, where he is widely regarded as the most skillful man of his generation. This city is in a state of shock tonight and everywhere, including Capitol Hill, men are of a mind to compose their differences and do what they can to help the new president.

Accordingly, the assumption that there will be no major agreements on taxes or civil rights this year will probably have to be revived. It is, of course, too early to tell. But it is typical and perhaps significant that the new president's first act was to greet the Congressional leaders of both parties when he arrived in Washington and to meet with them at once in the White House.

Today's events were so tragic and so brutal that even this city, which lives on the brutal diet of politics, could not bear to think much about the political consequences of the assassination.

Yet it is clear that the entire outlook has changed for both parties, and the unexpected death of President Kennedy has forced Washington to meditate a little more on the wild element of chance in our national life.

This was quietly in the back of many minds tonight, mainly because President Johnson has sustained a severe heart attack, and the constitutional line of succession places directly back of him, first Speaker McCormack, and then the president pro tempore of the Senate, 86-year-old Senator Carl Hayden of Arizona.

Again a note of self-criticism and conscience has touched the capital. Despite the severe illnesses of President Eisenhower just a few years ago, nothing was done by the Congress to deal with the problem of presidential disability.

For an all too brief hour today, it was not clear again what would have happened if the young president, instead of being mortally wounded, had lingered for a long time between life and death, strong enough to survive but too weak to govern.

These, however, were fleeting thoughts, important but irritating for the moment. The center of the mind was on the dead president, on his wife, who has now lost both a son and a husband within a few months, and on his family which, despite all its triumphs, has sustained so many personal tragedies since the last war.

He was, even to his political enemies, a wonderfully attractive human being, and it is significant that, unlike many presidents in the past, the people who liked and respected him best, were those who knew him the best.

He was a rationalist and an intellectual, who proved in the 1960 campaign and in last year's crisis over Cuba that he was at his best when the going was tough. No doubt he would have been reelected, as most one-term presidents are, and the subtle dualism of his character would have had a longer chance to realize his dream.

But he is gone now at 46, younger than when most presidents have started on the great adventure. In his book, *Profiles in Courage*, all his heroes faced the hard choice either of giving in to public opinion or of defying it and becoming martyrs.

He had hoped to avoid this bitter dilemma, but he ended as a martyr anyway, and the nation is sad tonight, both about him and about itself.

There is one final tragedy about today: Kennedy had a sense of history, but he also had an administrative technique that made the gathering of history extremely difficult. He hated organized meetings of the cabinet or the National Security Council, and therefore he chose to decide policy after private meetings, usually with a single person.

The result of this is that the true history of his administration really cannot be written now that he is gone.

He had a joke about this. When he was asked what he was going to do when he retired, he always replied that he had a problem. It was, he said, that he would have to race two other members of his staff, McGeorge Bundy and Arthur Schlesinger Jr., to the press.

Unfortunately, however, he was the only man in the White House who really knew what went on there during his administration, and now he is gone.

TURNOUT IS HEAVY—JOHNSON VICTOR BY WIDE MARGIN

By TOM WICKER, NOVEMBER 4, 1964

Lyndon Baines Johnson of Texas compiled one of the greatest landslide victories in American history yesterday to win a four-year term of his own as the 36th president of the United States.

Senator Hubert H. Humphrey of Minnesota, Mr. Johnson's running mate on the Democratic ticket, was carried into office as vice president.

Mr. Johnson's triumph, giving him the "loud and clear" national mandate he had said he wanted, brought 44 states and the District of Columbia, with 486 electoral votes, into the Democratic column.

Senator Barry Goldwater, the Republican candidate, who sought to offer the people "a choice, not an echo" with a strongly conservative campaign, won only 5 states in the Deep South and gained a narrow victory in his home state of Arizona. Carrying it gave him a total of 52 electoral votes.

Senator Plans Statement

A heavy voter turnout favored the more numerous Democrats.

In Austin, Tex., Mr. Johnson appeared in the Municipal Auditorium to say that his victory was "a tribute to men and women of all parties."

"It is a mandate for unity for a government that serves no special interest," he said.

The election meant, he said, that "our nation should forget our petty differences and stand united before all the world."

Mr. Goldwater did not concede. A spokesman announced that the senator would make no statement until 10 a.m. today in Phoenix.

Johnson Carries Texas

But the totals were not the only marks of the massive Democratic victory. Traditionally Republican states were bowled over like tenpins—Vermont, Indiana, Kansas, Nebraska, Wyoming, among others.

In New York, both houses of the legislature were headed for Democratic control for the first time in years. Heralded Republicans like Charles H. Percy, the gubernatorial candidate in Illinois, went down to defeat.

Former attorney general Robert F. Kennedy, riding Mr. Johnson's long coattails, overwhelmed Senator Kenneth B. Keating in New York.

But ticket splitting was widespread. And in the South, Georgia went Republican; never in its history had it done so. Into the Goldwater column, too, went Mississippi. Alabama, Louisiana and South Carolina—all part of the once solidly Democratic South.

But Mr. Johnson carried the rest of the South, including Virginia, Tennessee and Florida—states that went Republican in 1960. He carried his home state of Texas by a large margin and won a majority of the popular vote in the Old Confederacy.

Nationwide, the president's popular vote margin apparently would reach 60 percent or more. His popular vote plurality had risen early this morning to more than 13 million.

The president was clearly carrying into office with him a heavily Democratic Congress, with a substantially bigger majority in the House.

The vote poured in, through the high-speed counting system of the Network Election Service, at such a rate that the leading television broadcasters were calling it a Johnson victory about 9 p.m.

But the only time the Republican candidate ever was in front was early yesterday morning when Dixville Notch, N.H., traditionally the earliest-reporting precinct in the nation, gave him eight votes to none for Mr. Johnson.

Nationwide, the president's popular vote margin apparently would reach 60 percent or more.

After that, in the president's own slogan, it was "L.B.J. all the way."

Election analysts thought that would be the case when the first significant returns came in from rural Kansas, where partial counts of incomplete boxes are allowed. They showed Mr. Johnson running strongly in this traditionally Republican territory.

Their early judgments were strengthened when the president swept early-reporting Kentucky, an important border state that had not gone Democratic in a presidential election since 1948, and rolled to victory in Indiana, a Republican stronghold since 1936.

Ohio, a state counted upon as a vital part of the Goldwater victory strategy, fell to the president next, with Mr. Johnson compiling a massive lead in populous Cuyahoga County (Cleveland). One Negro precinct there went for the president by 99.9 percent of its vote.

In sharp contrast, Mr. Johnson at one point in the evening was carrying only 8.9 percent of the vote in Jackson, Miss., where his civil rights stand was unpopular. Mr. Goldwater compiled an overwhelming victory in that state, winning more than 80 percent of its vote.

But as victory after victory rolled in for the president—all New England, the big Middle Atlantic states of New Jersey and Pennsylvania, Southern states like Texas, Tennessee and North Carolina, the Western states of Oklahoma, Colorado and Kansas— Mr. Johnson's mounting total became a triumphant march across the nation.

There was nothing spotty or regional about it, and long before midnight it was apparent that the president would have the "loud and clear" national mandate.

It was one of the most significant victories in presidential history. The Goldwater campaign had posed a sharp challenge to almost the entire trend of national policy, domestic and foreign, since the Great Depression and World War II.

What He Proposed

He had proposed a sharp curtailment of federal government activities, particularly in the welfare field and in matters affecting the economy. He had called for a foreign policy of "brinkmanship," in which the nation's military might would be used as a threat against the Communist-bloc nations.

And he had raised doubts whether he would continue to lend federal influence and authority to the drive for Negro equality in the United States.

Mr. Johnson, in head-on conflict with Mr. Goldwater on almost every campaign issue, thus received decisive endorsement from the nation for the general line of policy pursued by the nation for more than a quarter-century, through administrations of both parties.

For himself, he won the distinction of being the first candidate from a Southern state to be elected to the White House in more than a hundred years.

And he won a massive vote of approval for the manner in which he had conducted its business since taking over the presidency when John F. Kennedy was assassinated last Nov. 22.

Morality In Government

Mr. Goldwater charged that there was "moral decay" in the nation and lawlessness in the streets; whether his reference was to hoodlums and juvenile delinquency or to Negro demonstrations was never made clear.

When Mr. Johnson's top assistant, Walter W. Jenkins, was arrested on a morals charge last month, and it was subsequently disclosed that he had been arrested on a similar charge in 1959, the Republicans added his case to the others. Mr. Goldwater, however, charged only that the Jenkins case had jeopardized national security.

Mr. Goldwater's thesis was that "moral decay" in the Johnson administration "trickled down" to the people and was affecting the fiber of the nation itself. Mr. Johnson seldom replied to these charges although he did defend Mr. Jenkins as an able public servant whose personal misconduct had not endangered the national security.

These were the main themes of the campaign—but there were others. Mr. Johnson spoke frequently of his "Great Society" concept, a plan that envisioned massive new federal programs in education, medical care, conservation of natural resources and urban renewal in the cities.

Mr. Goldwater criticized the Democratic tax cut of 1964 as politically inspired "gimmickry" and offered his own five-year program of tax reduction. He also called Mr. Johnson's "war on poverty" a "cruel hoax" designed only to win the votes of the less fortunate.

Mr. Johnson, however, attributed the nation's rising prosperity to the 1964 tax cut and promised even greater efforts to eliminate poverty, illiteracy and discrimination.

Most Democratic strategists believe, however, that the most telling argument on their side was the widespread belief that Mr. Goldwater would be careless in the use of nuclear weapons, belligerent in his foreign policy and thus would endanger the peace. This accounted, they believe, for the high percentage of women in both parties who indicated to polltakers that they feared to back Mr. Goldwater.

NOTE: *Johnson used his political capital, including decades in Congress, to enact his Great Society programs and push through major legislation on civil rights and voting rights. But he was ultimately ensnared by the Vietnam War, partly because of his insecurity in matters of foreign affairs, and was compelled to withdraw from the 1968 presidential campaign.*

GOAL IS HARMONY—PRESIDENT-ELECT VOWS HIS ADMINISTRATION WILL BE "OPEN"

By ROBERT B. SEMPLE JR., NOVEMBER 7, 1968

President-elect Richard M. Nixon turned yesterday from the business of winning elections to the business of assembling an administration.

Weary but thankful, he appeared before an elated band of supporters gathered in the ballroom of the Waldorf Astoria at 11:35 a.m. He expressed his gratitude for their efforts and his admiration for the "gallant and courageous fight" of his opponent. He also extended the hand of friendship to the disappointed partisans of Mr. Humphrey's cause—particularly the young. Near the end of his eight-minute talk, Mr. Nixon took note of the division in the nation and pledged, in these words, to bend every effort to restore racial peace and social harmony:

"I saw many signs in this campaign. Some of them were not friendly and some were very friendly. But the one that touched me the most was one that I saw in Deshler, Ohio, at the end of a long day of whistle-stopping, a little town, I suppose five times the population was there in the dusk, almost impossible to see—but a teenager held up a sign, 'Bring Us Together.'

"And that will be the great objective of this administration at the outset, to bring the American people together. This will be an open administration, open to new ideas, open to men and women of both parties, open to the critics as well as those who support us.

"We want to bridge the generation gap. We want to bridge the gap between the races. We want to bring America together. And I am confident that this task is one that we can undertake and one in which we will be successful."

Several hours later the campaign entourage began to disassemble, its members heading home for a brief but long-overdue rest. The candidate himself flew southward for a three-day vacation in Key Biscayne, a peninsula just south of Miami where he rested occasionally during the campaign.

Although he has been urged by his campaign manager, John Mitchell, to "soak up the sun and clear from his mind the campaign cobwebs," he is not likely to take the advice. Like most politicians, Mr. Nixon is rarely capable of keeping his mind off public matters for any length of time, and besides, the problems that confront him now require sustained attention.

Front page of *The New York Times* on November 7, 1968, announcing Richard Nixon's win by a thin margin and his pledge for an "open" administration.

Foremost is Vietnam. Mr. Nixon has offered to work with President Johnson and Secretary of State Rusk to help present a united front to Hanoi and, in his words, "to help get the negotiations in Paris off dead center."

The offer has yet to be accepted. But even if it is not, Mr. Nixon must begin now to prepare carefully his own diplomatic posture toward North Vietnam, and to think seriously about the new men whom he has said he will send to the Paris negotiations after January.

Preparing for Transition

No less pressing is the sprawling and often troublesome problem of preparing for a change of government in Washington. He has only 10 weeks in which to find the men, devise the machinery and prepare the ideas that will insure not only a successful transition but also a competent administration.

"Between Nov. 5 and Jan. 1," he recently told a news conference, "that is the time to get going and get it done. . . . The decisions made between Nov. 5 and the time of the inauguration will probably be the most important decisions that the new president will make insofar as determining the success of his administration over four years. Because if he makes poor decisions with regard to the selection of his cabinet, with regard to his budget and with regard [to the issues] . . . it's going to be very hard to correct them."

While both Mr. Nixon and his staff had refused to talk about the shape of a new administration in any but the most general terms, many prominent names have already surfaced in public speculation about cabinet posts.

Often-Mentioned Names

Among the most frequently mentioned are those of McGeorge Bundy, Ford Foundation president; Douglas Dillon, and Governor Rockefeller.

Each has been mentioned as a possible secretary of state; Mr. Rockefeller as secretary of defense as well.

Yet Nixon aides refused to say whether any of them has been considered, let alone approached. They will acknowledge only that Mr. Nixon regards Mr. Bundy well, that his relations with Mr. Rockefeller have greatly improved and that the likelihood of Mr. Dillon's reemergence in the Nixon administration is rather small.

"Nixon has never quite gotten over the fact that Dillon gave a lot of money to the Kennedy campaign in 1960," one aide asserted today.

Former Gov. William W. Scranton of Pennsylvania, who made a fact-finding tour of European capitals for Mr. Nixon during the campaign and who advised him on foreign policy, has also been mentioned as a possible secretary of state. But he has publicly insisted that he would not take the job, preferring to accept only "special missions" for the new president.

All that anyone can be certain of now are the criteria: Nixon aides, and the candidate himself, have made it plain that the next secretary of state must share the president's own convictions and must be prepared to work under a president who clearly intends to boss his own foreign policy.

NOTE: *Nixon swept to easy wins in 1968 and 1972 and enacted major expansions of social programs. Yet like a figure in a Greek tragedy, his paranoia and fundamental dishonesty led to the Watergate break-in, his cover-up of the events, and ultimately his resignation in disgrace (see pages 324–333).*

FROM FILM STAR TO CANDIDATE

By HOWELL RAINES, JULY 17, 1980

Like most good Ronald Reagan crowds, they brought their autograph pads and their Instamatics. Some had come in pickup trucks with "America: Repent or Perish" signs and others in Mercedes. There were stout women in their Sunday church dresses and slender ones who clearly had done their shopping in the stylish shops down in Atlanta. Almost all of them were white, and all of them were pleased on that drizzly April night in Greensboro, N.C., to applaud wildly when Senator Jesse Helms said that the Reagan candidacy had cosmic significance.

Man in the News

"That is why I am standing with him in this crucial election," the senator said in introducing Mr. Reagan, "because it may very well be that the Lord is giving all of us just one more chance to save this country."

Fervor of Supporters

For the 16 years of his political career, the former governor of California has evoked such responses, and it was the fervor of these conservative supporters that swept him past his Republican primary opponents and to the presidential nomination tonight. Mr. Reagan, demonstrating an innate grasp of the source of his appeal, has never hesitated to refer to his quest for the presidency in evangelical terms. "It isn't a campaign," he likes to say. "Let's make it a crusade."

The first battle of Mr. Reagan's crusade for the presidency ended here tonight amid the applause of the Joe Louis Arena. His nomination marked an impressive political comeback. He lost the Republican nomination four years ago in what was assumed to be his last hurrah, for he was then 65 years old. But this year, at 69, he defeated both the "age question" and an array of younger, vigorous Republican primary opponents in his campaign to become the oldest man ever nominated for the nation's highest office by a major political party.

Now he faces the second and decisive battle of his crusade—the contest of born-again candidates. President Carter, the Democratic incumbent, and John B. Anderson, the independent candidate, both refer to themselves as born-again Christians. Mr.

Ronald Reagan accepts the cheers of delegates after delivering his address at the Republican National Convention in Detroit, July 17, 1980.

Reagan, too, says that he is devoutly religious, but he was born-again in another sense. Once a "hemophiliac liberal" Democrat, he switched political philosophies in midlife to become born-again Republican.

The two main themes in Mr. Reagan's life, in fact, have to do with conversion from liberalism to conservatism and from the profession of acting to that of politics.

Significance of Acting Career

Mr. Reagan's background as a movie actor has been both a blessing and a curse. Political critics who characterize him as banal and shallow, a mouther of right-wing platitudes, delight in recalling that he costarred with a chimpanzee in *Bedtime for Bonzo*. Even now, 24 years after his last film role, he stews about being typed as the nice guy who didn't get the girl. "I always got the girl," he sometimes assures supporters.

Mr. Reagan got something else from the movie business—the oratorical skill that carried his campaign when its staff was in disarray and its treasury almost drained. At times, Mr. Reagan's fondness for simple answers and statistics memorized from the *Reader's Digest* led him into rhetorical excess. But no one has ever questioned that his ability to stir Middle American audiences like the one in Greensboro is his campaign's indispensable asset. "The most effective thing we can do," says Lyn Nofziger, a top aide, "is put him on television whenever we can."

Ronald Wilson Reagan is a product of Middle America, spiritually, intellectually and geographically. He was born Feb. 6, 1911, in Tampico, Ill., the second son of Nelle Wilson Reagan and John Edward Reagan, a first-generation Irish American who loved the shoe business, the Democratic Party and whisky. One of the searing memories of Ronald Reagan's youth was coming home at the age of 11 to find his father passed out on the front porch.

A Cultural Conservative

But it was, on balance, a happy boyhood now remembered with deep nostalgia. Mr. Reagan's biographers have noted that he reversed the small-town Middle West that Sinclair Lewis satirized. Long before he became a political conservative, Mr. Reagan was a cultural conservative—loyal to family, trusting of businessmen and critical of those who did not hold the same values.

The Reagans were poor enough so that the older son, Neil, was sometimes dispatched to the butcher shop to ask for the free liver given out as cat food. There was no cat. The Reagans ate the liver themselves. In the Depression, John Reagan lost his job and found work with the Works Progress Administration, one of Franklin D. Roosevelt's make-work agencies. In those days, Ronald Reagan recalled recently, "I was an enthusiastic New Deal Democrat."

But World War II, most of which Mr. Reagan spent in relaxed soldiering as a captain at "Fort Roach," an Army Air Corps studio in Hollywood, brought disenchantment with the laziness of civil service workers. About this time, Mr. Reagan underwent a political epiphany described in his autobiography, *Where's the Rest of Me?*

"I was truly so naive I thought the nearest Communists were fighting in Stalingrad," he wrote. "Finally, I was a near-hopeless hemophiliac liberal. I bled for 'causes.' I had voted Democratic, following my father, in every election. I had followed F.D.R. blindly. The story of my disillusionment with big government is linked fundamentally with the ideals that suddenly sprouted and put forth in the war year."

Turning Point in Life

The turning point came on a postwar holiday at Lake Arrowhead, a California resort. "One of the first impulses was to rent a speedboat 24 hours a day. The rental proprietor thought I was crazy. 'It's all right,' I assured him. 'I just want to know that the boat is there at the dock any time I want to take a drive on the water. I can't walk on it anymore.' In the end, the rental cost was more than the total cost of the boat. It was worth it." For on his boat rides, Mr. Reagan related, he resolved to use "my thoughts, my speaking abilities, my reputation as an actor" to change the world.

From that time, Mr. Reagan moved steadily to the right. Angry that the government took so much of the $3,500 weekly salary he was making in 1946, he seethed about "this evil day of progressive taxation." As president of the Screen Actors Guild, he fought against what he believed was a Communist plot to take over the movie industry and, fearful that leftists would try to kill him, he began carrying a pistol that he found difficult to give up. "The very night you take it off," Mr. Reagan recalled, "may be the night you need it on."

Mr. Reagan was not the joyless fellow this might indicate. After his divorce in 1948 from Jane Wyman, the actress, Mr. Reagan ran up nightclub bills of $750 a month.

The year 1952 brought two events of great importance in Mr. Reagan's political development. He married Nancy Davis, a conservative young actress whose father, Dr. Loyal Davis, was known for his skills as a surgeon and his unbending political attitudes.

Also, Mr. Reagan was getting too old to play leading-man roles, a fact cruelly driven home when he was cast as Shirley Temple's lover and a screening room audience groaned, "Oh, no." By 1954, he had become the $150,000-a-year television spokesman for the General Electric Company.

In his eight years with the company, Mr. Reagan's political philosophy solidified into its final shape. He was an exponent of traditional social values and militantly pro-business and antigovernment. One favorite target was the Tennessee Valley authority, or "government power octopus," as Mr. Reagan called it until he discovered that the government-owned corporation was a $50 million customer of General Electric.

By 1962, Mr. Reagan was a nationally recognized and increasingly controversial spokesman for conservative causes. When General Electric nervously tried to cut back on his speaking engagements, he left the company and joined the Republican Party.

> *By 1962, Mr. Reagan was a nationally recognized and increasingly controversial spokesman for conservative causes.*

Two years later, supporting Senator Barry Goldwater, he made a speech that some commentators have called the most brilliant national political debut since William Jennings Bryan's Cross of Gold speech in 1896.

In California, it set off a wave of enthusiasm that swept Mr. Reagan toward a candidacy in the 1966 gubernatorial race.

Aided by Wealthy Friends

At first he was reluctant, but a small circle of wealthy Southern Californians led by Holmes Tuttle, a multimillionaire automobile dealer from Los Angeles, organized a draft movement that in short order raised the seed money for a campaign.

In the gubernatorial race, Mr. Reagan defeated Edmund G. Brown, the politically seasoned incumbent and father of the present California governor, by almost a million votes. The Tuttle group became part of the new governor's "kitchen cabinet" and key advisers in Mr. Reagan's plan to "cut and squeeze and trim" state spending. But Mr. Reagan found that Mr. Brown had left too little money in the treasury to run the nation's largest state.

So the man who had campaigned as a hardline tax-cutter, in the first major act of his governorship, put through a $1 billion tax increase that was at that time the largest state-government tax increase in American history. Later, however, over the next eight years, he sponsored property tax rebates totaling $4.7 billion.

Doubled University Budget

While blustering at student militants, he doubled the state university budget over eight years. The state budget had grown by $6 billion when he left office at the end of 1974.

Two years after Mr. Reagan took office as governor, Mr. Nofziger and the "political hawks" on the staff were pushing Mr. Reagan for the 1968 presidential nomination, arguing that both Richard M. Nixon and Nelson A. Rockefeller were too liberal and that Mr. Reagan could be the champion of a conservative revolt.

Mr. Nixon, of course, crushed the Reagan effort.

"I think the governor suffered from that experience," said Mike Deaver, one of the few close advisers who is also close to the Reagans socially. "He also grew from it, because after that he was much more cautious about pols coming up to him and saying it's easy to run for president."

Caution, in the form of a belated and sporadic challenge of President Ford, cost Mr. Reagan the nomination in 1976. So this year, when John P. Sears, his campaign director, devised a cautious front-runner strategy that kept Mr. Reagan under wraps, Mr. Sears was dismissed, and Mr. Reagan took to the stump, unlimbered the heavy artillery of his conservative rhetoric and banged through to victory.

Values His Privacy

As much as he loves to fire up the crowds with red-meat oratory, Mr. Reagan is a deeply private man. Aides call him "kind to a fault" and perhaps too undemanding of his staff. But some who have worked with him for years know virtually nothing of his personal life.

They do know that his private life centers on his 58-year-old wife, whom Mr. Reagan calls "Mommy." In Sacramento, he eschewed the bars and other political haunts for dinner at home, where he liked to don his pajamas and work through his briefcase while watching television with Mrs. Reagan.

Staff members recall that Mr. Reagan often quit work at five or six in the evening, and as he left the Capitol, he frequently urged late-working aides to go home to their wives and families, too.

Mr. Reagan has a flash-fire temper that sometimes leads him to dash his reading glasses against his desk before the anger departs, often as quickly as it arrived. He also has, Mr. Deaver said, a secret humanitarian streak that leads to such private acts as hand-delivering two dozen roses to the wife of a serviceman who had written to Mr. Reagan about the pain of being in Vietnam on his wedding anniversary.

While family bonding is a favorite theme, the ties that bind Mr. and Mrs. Reagan seem wound much more loosely around his four children. Maureen, his 39-year-old daughter by Miss Wyman, and Michael, 35, the adoptive son of that marriage, recalled being raised mostly in boarding schools. The children of the second marriage are Patricia, 27, and Ronald, 22. Patricia Reagan, a songwriter whose professional name is Patricia Davis, is once again living at her parents' Pacific Palisades home after having lived with a rock musician in a period that severely strained her relationship with her parents. Ronald dropped out of Yale to apprentice himself to the Joffrey Ballet "farm team" in New York. The Reagan campaign staff has responded awkwardly to his new career, apparently fearful of the image that his choice of profession sometimes raises.

Becomes a Millionaire

With his high salaries from the movies and General Electric, Mr. Reagan invested in the California real estate that made him a wealthy man. He became a millionaire by selling a Malibu Canyon ranch for $1.9 million in 1966, far more than the $65,000 that he paid for the property in 1951.

The ranch is Mr. Reagan's favorite place. It is there that he relaxes with his horses and indulges his taste for, and broad knowledge of, good wines.

Unlike some politicians, Mr. Reagan is not one to trade political gossip with his staff or reporters. After an ethnic joke that he told in an unguarded moment wound up in print, Mr. Reagan became even more guarded and distant. Reporters, parodying the description of Mr. Reagan as "the oldest and wisest" candidate, dubbed him "the oldest and coldest."

But if Mr. Reagan is distant, he is also genial in a practiced way, and the combination of his manner and his age has infected the campaign press corps with a curious and uncharacteristic courtesy. It is a rare press conference at which anyone really presses him to explain his sweeping generalities about economic and military policy.

Support from Wife

Those who do are likely to draw an icy look from Mrs. Reagan, the quiet, precisely groomed woman who is in her way an indefatigable campaigner. Her eyes seldom leave her husband during a speech, and she laughs at his standard jokes and claps at the same applause lines a half dozen times a day, each time as if for the first time.

The Reagans make much of saying that Mrs. Reagan will not sit in on cabinet meetings, in the fashion of Rosalynn Carter, the first lady. But Mrs. Reagan does not hesitate to assert herself if her husband seems threatened, as he seemed to be by a female reporter demanding to know why he did not support the proposed federal equal rights amendment. "May I speak to that?" Mrs. Reagan said, stepping firmly between her husband and the microphone.

Friends and foes alike say that Mr. Reagan's ideas have not changed in two decades. But in the Reagan camp, there is a strong belief in the historical inevitability of a Reagan presidency.

This is based on the belief that the American electorate has moved sharply to the right, duplicating the shift that Mr. Reagan himself made many years ago.

In the matter of inevitability, Mr. Deaver likes to recall a remark that Senator Strom Thurmond, one of the few active politicians older than Mr. Reagan, made in 1968, when it became clear that Mr. Nixon would be the nominee. "You ought to be president, son," Mr. Thurmond said, "but not this year."

NOTE: *Reagan's election was the start of a major shift rightward in American politics. While he didn't embrace the religious right's narrow and often bigoted philosophy, he sowed the seeds that led to the rise of the movement, which ultimately hijacked his party. Though he is often still cited as the intellectual father of Republican conservatism, his party bears no real resemblance in the 21st century to the one he inherited in the late 20th.*

BIOGRAPHY OF A CANDIDATE: GEORGE HERBERT WALKER BUSH

By MAUREEN DOWD, AUGUST 20, 1992

It was torture, in 1988, for George Bush to try to explain who he was. Plucking at his chest, as though he could pull his soul out of a buttoned-down shirt, he told campaign aides, "We got to get me out there; we got to get more of me out there."

Throughout his presidency, he has known, as he once put it, that people were "trying to figure out what makes this crazy guy tick" and wondering whether "there was some there there—if not in me then in others" around him.

Perhaps there has never been a politician who has labored so long, and so reluctantly, to define and redefine, explain and explain yet again, who he is. Four years after pledging to reveal his "heartbeat" in a convention speech, he was frantically working until the last minute on a speech intended to show "what is in my heart."

George Herbert Walker Bush is an existential Yankee—born in Milton, Mass., reared in Greenwich, Conn., and now living in the moment—who never seems to understand why he cannot just be. He draws strength from his title. He is president, and therefore he is doing something right, he will tell those who challenge him.

But the problem is this: George Bush has projected many different versions of George Bush over the years, trying to court and hold a disparate coalition. His image now is not so much like his bold bronze statue in the Astrodome, with gaze fixed and body standing firm against the wind. It is more like a hologram that changes depending on the angle from which you look at it. He can be charming. He can be whiny. He can be passive. He can be hyperactive. He can be conservative. He can be moderate. He can be firm. He can be, as an aide once said, a victim of his last conversation. He bashes Democrats in Congress. He eats barbecue at the White House with Democrats in Congress.

With his mother's voice in one ear, reminding him not to gloat, he can be modest. With his own voice in the other ear, reminding him that he has completed many important missions, he can be proud and confident.

He can be principled, seeming unconcerned about the political cost, as he was when he stood up to Saddam Hussein and when he insisted that Israel freeze settlements in the West Bank as a condition for $10 billion in loan guarantees.

But more often, as with his shifting stands on abortion, taxes and civil rights, political costs seem to determine his principles.

In the most revealing comment ever made about Mr. Bush, the late C. Fred Chambers, a Texas oil executive and a close friend, explained why Mr. Bush, as a young politician in Houston, had changed to a more progressive position on civil rights. "George understands that you have to do politically prudent things to get in a position to do what you want," he said.

Democrats, predictably, put it less kindly. "You can't find an issue in the last 30 years that George Bush hasn't been on both sides of, with the exception of cutting the capital gains tax," said James Carville, a strategist for Gov. Bill Clinton.

Indeed, Mr. Bush's strongest conviction has been born of his class. The boy nicknamed "Poppy" who rode out the Depression in a chauffeured sedan that ferried him to Greenwich Country Day School, the boy whose father was a pillar of the Wall Street establishment, grew up believing that what fuels America is capital and that its preservation is of paramount importance.

"He thinks Bill Clinton would be a disaster as president because he doesn't understand capitalism, as we perceive it," said Jonathan Bush, the president's younger brother.

Political Chameleon Eager to Please

Ever since he began his political career in Houston in the early 1960s, when he appalled his moderate supporters by soothing the John Birch Society–types in the Goldwater movement, Mr. Bush has been making one Faustian bargain after another, veering between the right wing he needed and the moderate Republican wing that was his heritage. He was brought up in a world that valued public service, internationalist goals and noblesse oblige, the responsibility of the powerful to help the less powerful.

It is the worst fear of some friends that he may have sold off too many pieces of himself, in the mistaken belief he could someday get them back; that in his boyish eagerness to avoid conflict, to knit together opposing groups, to please everyone, he may have lost the ability to project a simple, coherent set of political ideas.

Mr. Bush's friend, Thomas Ludlow Ashley, a Washington lobbyist who was a Democratic congressman from Ohio, said the president "finds it hard to get emotionally involved in passionate dislike of one side or another."

NOTE: *Bush's inability to express himself and rally anything like a true political coalition behind him ultimately led to his defeat in 1992 when he tried for reelection—his candidacy a relic of the Cold War era and of the age of gentlemanly public service by the nation's wealthy class.*

THE 1992 ELECTIONS: PRESIDENT—THE OVERVIEW; CLINTON CAPTURES PRESIDENCY WITH HUGE ELECTORAL MARGIN; WINS A DEMOCRATIC CONGRESS

By ROBIN TONER, NOVEMBER 4, 1992

G ov. Bill Clinton of Arkansas was elected the 42nd president of the United States yesterday, breaking a 12-year Republican hold on the White House.

Mr. Clinton shattered the Republicans' political base with a promise of change to an electorate clearly discontented with President Bush.

Ross Perot, the Texas billionaire who roiled this race throughout, finished third, drawing roughly equally from both major-party candidates, according to Voter Research & Surveys, the television polling consortium. His share of the popular vote had the potential to exceed any third-party candidate's in more than half a century.

Bill Clinton greets backers on Election Day in Little Rock, Ark., November 3, 1992.

Faithful Are Won Back

The president-elect, capping an astonishing political comeback for the Democrats over the last 18 months, ran strongly in all regions of the country and among many groups that were key to the Republicans' dominance of the 1980s: Catholics, suburbanites, independents, moderates and the Democrats who crossed party lines in the 1980s to vote for Ronald Reagan and Mr. Bush.

The governor from Arkansas won such big, closely contested states as Michigan, Missouri, Pennsylvania, New Jersey and Illinois. As polls closed across the nation, networks announced projected winners based on voter surveys. It was Ohio that put him over the top shortly before 11 p.m., followed closely by California. Based on those projections, Mr. Bush prevailed in his adopted state of Texas and other pockets of Republican states around the country.

"In massive numbers, the American people have voted to make a new beginning."

With 83 percent of the nation's precincts reporting by 3 a.m. today, Mr. Clinton had 43 percent to 38 percent for Mr. Bush and 18 percent for Mr. Perot.

A state-by-state breakdown of those returns gave the president-elect more than 345 electoral votes, a commanding victory in the Electoral College, which requires 270 for election. His victory also provided coattails for Democrats running for Congress in the face of tough Republican challenges: Democrats, who control both chambers, appeared likely to gain in the Senate and suffer manageable losses in the House.

"With High Hopes"

In a victory speech to a joyous crowd in Little Rock, Mr. Clinton declared, "On this day, with high hopes and brave hearts, in massive numbers, the American people have voted to make a new beginning."

He described the election as a "clarion call" to deal with a host of domestic problems too long ignored and to "bring our nation together." He paid tribute to the voters he had met along the campaign trail, saying they had simply demanded that "we want our future back." The president-elect, who looked euphoric and seemed to savor every cheer, added, "I intend to give it to you."

He also hailed his longtime rival, Mr. Bush, for "his lifetime of public service" and the "grace with which he conceded this election."

"Not very long ago I received a telephone call from President Bush," the president-elect said. "It was a generous and forthcoming telephone call, of real congratulations and an offer to work with me in keeping our democracy running in an effective and important transition."

The crowd hailed the victor repeatedly with cries of "We love you, Bill," especially when he paid tribute to his home state, the object of Republican ridicule throughout the campaign.

Mr. Clinton credited much of his success to his wife, Hillary, who was also a target of Republican attacks. The Clintons and their daughter, Chelsea, were joined by Vice President–elect Al Gore and his family, creating once again the tableau of youth and generational change that they projected throughout the campaign. Mr. Gore and Mr. Clinton embraced in a jubilant bear hug.

Bush Gives Concession

Mr. Bush, looking weary but composed, made his concession speech shortly after 11 p.m. in Houston. "The people have spoken and we respect the majesty of the Democratic system," he said. Mr. Bush congratulated Mr. Clinton, but did not mention Mr. Perot and promised that his own administration would "work closely with his team to insure the smooth transition of power."

Vice President Dan Quayle made his concession speech in Indianapolis a few minutes later and like Mr. Bush congratulated Mr. Clinton and hushed the boos. "We must all pull together now. If he runs the country as well as he ran the campaign, we'll be all right."

Congressional leaders said they welcomed the new era beyond divided government. "We welcome the challenge and the responsibility," said Senator George Mitchell of Maine, the majority leader.

There were other signs of change: California elected two women to the Senate, in Representative Barbara Boxer and the former San Francisco mayor Dianne Feinstein. Illinois also elected a woman, Carol Moseley Braun, to the Senate, as did Washington State, which chose Patty Murray.

Mr. Perot made his concession speech in remarkably good spirits and seemed intent on signaling that he was not leaving the political stage. "This is not the time to get discouraged," he said. "This is the time to redouble our efforts, to make sure we live in alabaster cities undimmed by human tears."

Mr. Clinton's campaign represented the culmination of years of effort by centrist Democrats to redefine their party and reconnect with the middle class. It also represented an extraordinary turnaround for a party that for much of 1991 seemed destined to lose to a president soaring in the approval ratings in the aftermath of the war in the Persian Gulf.

Brown Sees "Watershed"

"It was a watershed election for America," said Ronald H. Brown, the chairman of the Democratic National Committee. "The case for change was made, and it resonated so much that it broke down traditional political lines. It's a new day." In fact, the voter surveys showed that economic discontent and a hunger for change were two of the engines of the Democratic victory.

Republicans sadly watched Mr. Bush become the third one-term president in 20 years. "He was a good man, he was a good president," said Representative Vin Weber of Minnesota, a cochairman for the Bush campaign. "But he thought that if he simply did the right thing, people would understand. Whereas I think Reagan understood the need to communicate your vision."

Lynn Martin, the secretary of labor, said of the voters last night, "They understand about world affairs, but they were worried about their own."

But there was also Republican anger; Mary Matalin, deputy manager of the Bush campaign, accused the news media of bias last night in their coverage of the 1992 election. Ahead, many Republicans feared, was a round of soul-searching, finger-pointing and a struggle to recast their party for an era beyond the Cold War, an era that seems relentlessly focused on domestic needs.

A Grueling Comeback

The voting capped a grueling campaign in which Mr. Clinton came back from seeming disaster in the New Hampshire primary, where questions were raised about how he avoided the draft in the Vietnam War, setting off a round of attacks from his political opponents on his trustworthiness. Mr. Clinton survived with a remarkably disciplined campaign that stayed focused on the economy and what he often called "the forgotten middle class."

Mr. Bush, at the same time, fell from great heights as the economy continued to falter. He spent much of the year trying to convince the voters that the country was in better shape than they thought. Still, the voter surveys showed that 7 in 10 voters considered the economy either poor or "not so good," and Mr. Clinton ran strongly among them.

Mr. Clinton also ran strongly among young voters, working women and a variety of other groups that showed the strains in the Republican coalition, which had been held together for years by economic growth and a fierce anti-Communism. And his Southern roots, like those of Jimmy Carter in 1976, made him a formidable challenger to the Republicans in the heart of their political base in the South. The big states of Florida and Texas stayed fiercely competitive until the end.

Mr. Clinton's careful strategy to appeal to suburban residents, independent voters and moderates clearly paid off. Nearly half of the suburban voters backed Mr. Clinton, compared with about a third who were supporting Mr. Bush. Mr. Clinton also carried 4 in 10 of the independent voters, with Mr. Bush splitting the rest with Mr. Perot.

Here, and in several other demographic categories, Mr. Clinton broke into groups that for the past decade were clear parts of the Republican presidential majority—the swing voters drawn to the Republicans by the promise of fiscal responsibility and economic growth. In 1980 and 1988, for example, independents went heavily for Mr. Reagan and Mr. Bush.

The president-elect also won more than half of the voters who consider themselves moderates, suggesting that he had succeeded in his goal of recasting the Democratic Party in a more centrist image. Only 3 in 10 of the moderates backed Mr. Bush, who was widely thought to be hurt by the backlash to the "family values" appeal at the Republican National Convention. Again, that was a far poorer showing than Mr. Bush had in 1988.

Mr. Clinton also succeeded in bringing home many of the Democrats who persistently crossed party lines in presidential elections in the 1980s: more than half of the Democrats who voted for Mr. Bush in 1988 voted for Mr. Clinton this time around.

Mr. Bush essentially ran even with Mr. Clinton among white voters, but the Democratic nominee, as is the case with most recent Democratic nominees, did far better with black voters.

Mr. Bush ran better than Mr. Clinton among white Protestants, but the Democrat carried about half of the Catholic votes and an even bigger majority among Jewish voters.

"Way Beyond Abortion"

Mr. Bush and Mr. Clinton fared about the same among men, but Mr. Clinton had an edge among women, particularly among working women. Only 3 in 10 of the working women voted for Mr. Bush, according to the poll.

"It goes way beyond abortion," said Ann F. Lewis, a former Democratic strategist and commentator. "George Bush campaigned four years ago on the promise of a kinder, gentler nation, and women are keenly aware that he provided neither."

There was also a distinct generational cast to this election. Mr. Clinton, who carefully courted MTV viewers, carried half of the 18- to 29-year-olds, after a decade in which

Bush's appeal of last Friday's Florida Supreme Court ruling and by granting him a stay of the recount on Saturday afternoon, just hours after the vote counting had begun.

"None are more conscious of the vital limits on judicial authority than are the members of this court," the majority opinion said, referring to "our unsought responsibility to resolve the federal and constitutional issues the judicial system has been forced to confront."

The dissenters said nearly all the objections raised by Mr. Bush were insubstantial. The court should not have reviewed either this case or the one it decided last week, they said.

Justice John Paul Stevens said the court's action "can only lend credence to the most cynical appraisal of the work of judges throughout the land."

His dissenting opinion, also signed by Justices Breyer and Ruth Bader Ginsburg, added: "It is confidence in the men and women who administer the judicial system that is the true backbone of the rule of law. Time will one day heal the wound to that confidence that will be inflicted by today's decision. One thing, however, is certain. Although we may never know with complete certainty the identity of the winner of this year's presidential election, the identity of the loser is perfectly clear. It is the nation's confidence in the judge as an impartial guardian of the rule of law."

What the court's day and a half of deliberations yielded tonight was a messy product that bore the earmarks of a failed attempt at a compromise solution that would have permitted the vote counting to continue. It appeared that Justices Souter and Breyer, by taking seriously the equal protection concerns that Justices Kennedy and O'Connor had raised at the argument, had tried to persuade them that those concerns could be addressed in a remedy that would permit the disputed votes to be counted.

Justices O'Connor and Kennedy were the only justices whose names did not appear separately on any opinion, indicating that one or both of them wrote the court's unsigned majority opinion, labeled only *per curiam*, or "by the court." Its focus was narrow, limited to the ballot counting process itself. The opinion objected not only to the varying standards used by different counties for determining voter intent, but to aspects of the Florida Supreme Court's order determining which ballots should be counted.

"We are presented with a situation where a state court with the power to assure uniformity has ordered a statewide recount with minimal procedural safeguards," the opinion said. "When a court orders a statewide remedy, there must be at least some assurance that the rudimentary requirements of equal treatment and fundamental fairness are satisfied."

Three members of the majority—the chief justice, and Justices Scalia and Thomas— raised further, more basic objections to the recount and said the Florida Supreme Court had violated state law in ordering it.

The fact that Justices O'Connor and Kennedy evidently did not share these deeper concerns had offered a potential basis for a coalition between them and the dissenters. That effort apparently foundered on the two justices' conviction that the midnight deadline of Dec. 12 had to be met.

The majority said that "substantial additional work" was needed to undertake a constitutional recount, including not only uniform statewide standards for determining a legal vote, but also "practical procedures to implement them" and "orderly judicial review of any disputed matters that might arise." There was no way all this could be done, the majority said.

The dissenters said the concern with Dec. 12 was misplaced. Justices Souter and Breyer offered to send the case back to the Florida courts "with instructions to establish uniform standards for evaluating the several types of ballots that have prompted differing treatments," as Justice Souter described his proposed remand order. He added: "unlike the majority, I see no warrant for this court to assume that Florida could not possibly comply with this requirement before the date set for the meeting of electors, Dec. 18."

Justices Stevens and Ginsburg said they did not share the view that the lack of a uniform vote-counting standard presented an equal protection problem.

In addition to joining Justice Souter's dissenting opinion, Justice Breyer wrote one of his own, signed by the three other dissenters, in which he recounted the history of the deadlocked presidential election of 1876 and of the partisan role that one Supreme Court justice, Joseph P. Bradley, played in awarding the presidency to Rutherford B. Hayes.

"This history may help to explain why I think it not only legally wrong, but also most unfortunate, for the court simply to have terminated the Florida recount," Justice Breyer said. He said the time problem that Florida faced was "in significant part, a problem of the court's own making." The recount was moving ahead in an "orderly fashion," Justice Breyer said, when "this court improvidently entered a stay." He said: "As a result, we will never know whether the recount could have been completed."

"As a result, we will never know whether the recount could have been completed."

There was no need for the court to have involved itself in the election dispute this time, he said, adding: "Above all, in this highly politicized matter, the appearance of a split decision runs the risk of undermining the public's confidence in the court itself. That confidence is a public treasure. It has been built slowly over many years, some of which were marked by a Civil War and the tragedy of segregation. It is a vitally necessary ingredient of any successful effort to protect basic liberty and, indeed, the rule of law itself."

"We do risk a self-inflicted wound," Justice Breyer said, "a wound that may harm not just the court, but the nation."

Justice Ginsburg also wrote a dissenting opinion, joined by the other dissenters. Her focus was on the implications for federalism of the majority's action. "I might join the chief justice were it my commission to interpret Florida law," she said, adding: "The extraordinary setting of this case has obscured the ordinary principle that dictates its proper resolution: federal courts defer to state high courts' interpretations of their state's own law. This principle reflects the core of federalism, on which all agree."

"Were the other members of this court as mindful as they generally are of our system of dual sovereignty," Justice Ginsburg concluded, "they would affirm the judgment of the Florida Supreme Court."

Unlike the other dissenters, who said they dissented "respectfully," Justice Ginsburg said only: "I dissent."

Nothing about this case, *Bush v. Gore*, No. 00-949, was ordinary: not its context, not its acceptance over the weekend, not the enormously accelerated schedule with argument on Monday and not the way the decision was released to the public tonight.

When the court issues an opinion, the justices ordinarily take the bench and the justice who has written for the majority gives a brief oral description of the case and the holding.

Today, after darkness fell and their work was done, the justices left the Supreme Court building individually from the underground garage, with no word to dozens of journalists from around the world who were waiting in the crowded pressroom for word as to when, or whether, a decision might come. By the time the pressroom staff passed out copies of the decision, the justices were gone.

OBAMA ELECTED PRESIDENT AS RACIAL BARRIER FALLS

By ADAM NAGOURNEY, NOVEMBER 4, 2008

Barack Hussein Obama was elected the 44th president of the United States on Tuesday, sweeping away the last racial barrier in American politics with ease as the country chose him as its first black chief executive.

The election of Mr. Obama amounted to a national catharsis—a repudiation of a historically unpopular Republican president and his economic and foreign policies, and an embrace of Mr. Obama's call for a change in the direction and the tone of the country.

But it was just as much a strikingly symbolic moment in the evolution of the nation's fraught racial history, a breakthrough that would have seemed unthinkable just two years ago.

Mr. Obama, 47, a first-term senator from Illinois, defeated Senator John McCain of Arizona, 72, a former prisoner of war who was making his second bid for the presidency.

To the very end, Mr. McCain's campaign was eclipsed by an opponent who was nothing short of a phenomenon, drawing huge crowds epitomized by the tens of thousands of people who turned out to hear Mr. Obama's victory speech in Grant Park in Chicago.

Mr. McCain also fought the headwinds of a relentlessly hostile political environment, weighted down with the baggage left to him by President Bush and an economic collapse that took place in the middle of the general election campaign.

A jubilant President Barack Obama with his wife, Michelle, and daughters Sasha and Malia, on *The New York Times* front page of November 5, 2008.

"If there is anyone out there who still doubts that America is a place where all things are possible, who still wonders if the dream of our founders is alive in our time, who still questions the power of our democracy, tonight is your answer," said Mr. Obama, standing before a huge wooden lectern with a row of American flags at his back, casting his eyes to a crowd that stretched far into the Chicago night. "It's been a long time coming," the president-elect added, "but tonight, because of what we did on this date in this election at this defining moment, change has come to America."

Mr. McCain delivered his concession speech under clear skies on the lush lawn of the Arizona Biltmore, in Phoenix, where he and his wife had held their wedding reception. The crowd reacted with scattered boos as he offered his congratulations to Mr. Obama and saluted the historical significance of the moment.

"This is a historic election, and I recognize the significance it has for African Americans and for the special pride that must be theirs tonight," Mr. McCain said, adding, "We both realize that we have come a long way from the injustices that once stained our nation's reputation."

Not only did Mr. Obama capture the presidency, but he led his party to sharp gains in Congress. This puts Democrats in control of the House, the Senate and the White House for the first time since 1995, when Bill Clinton was in office.

The day shimmered with history as voters began lining up before dawn, hours before polls opened, to take part in the culmination of a campaign that over the course of two years commanded an extraordinary amount of attention from the American public.

As the returns became known, and Mr. Obama passed milestone after milestone— Ohio, Florida, Virginia, Pennsylvania, New Hampshire, Iowa and New Mexico—people rolled spontaneously into the streets to celebrate what many described, with perhaps overstated if understandable exhilaration, a new era in a country where just 143 years ago, Mr. Obama, as a black man, could have been owned as a slave.

For Republicans, especially the conservatives who have dominated the party for nearly three decades, the night represented a bitter setback and left them contemplating where they now stand in American politics.

Mr. Obama and his expanded Democratic majority on Capitol Hill now face the task of governing the country through a difficult period: the likelihood of a deep and prolonged recession, and two wars. He took note of those circumstances in a speech that was notable for its sobriety and its absence of the triumphalism that he might understandably have displayed on a night when he won an Electoral College landslide.

"The road ahead will be long, our climb will be steep," said Mr. Obama, his audience hushed and attentive, with some, including the Rev. Jesse Jackson, wiping tears from their eyes. "We may not get there in one year or even one term, but America, I have never been more hopeful than I am tonight that we will get there. I promise you, we as a people will get there." The roster of defeated Republicans included some notable party moderates, such as Senator John E. Sununu of New Hampshire and Representative Christopher Shays of Connecticut, and signaled that the Republican conference convening early next year in Washington will be not only smaller but more conservative.

Mr. Obama will come into office after an election in which he laid out a number of clear promises: to cut taxes for most Americans, to get the United States out of Iraq in a fast and orderly fashion, and to expand health care.

In a recognition of the difficult transition he faces, given the economic crisis, Mr. Obama is expected to begin filling White House jobs as early as this week.

Mr. Obama defeated Mr. McCain in Ohio, a central battleground in American politics, despite a huge effort that brought Mr. McCain and his running mate, Gov. Sarah Palin of Alaska, back there repeatedly. Mr. Obama had lost the state decisively to Senator Hillary Rodham Clinton of New York in the Democratic primary.

Mr. McCain failed to take from Mr. Obama the two Democratic states that were at the top of his target list: New Hampshire and Pennsylvania. Mr. Obama also held on to Minnesota, the state that played host to the convention that nominated Mr. McCain; Wisconsin; and Michigan, a state Mr. McCain once had in his sights.

The apparent breadth of Mr. Obama's sweep left Republicans sobered, and his showing in states like Ohio and Pennsylvania stood out because officials in both parties had said that his struggles there in the primary campaign reflected the resistance of blue-collar voters to supporting a black candidate.

"I always thought there was a potential prejudice factor in the state," Senator Bob Casey, a Democrat of Pennsylvania who was an early Obama supporter, told reporters in Chicago. "I hope this means we washed that away."

Mr. McCain called Mr. Obama at 10 p.m., Central time, to offer his congratulations. In the call, Mr. Obama said he was eager to sit down and talk; in his concession speech, Mr. McCain said he was ready to help Mr. Obama work through difficult times.

"I need your help," Mr. Obama told his rival, according to an Obama adviser, Robert Gibbs. "You're a leader on so many important issues."

Mr. Bush called Mr. Obama shortly after 10 p.m. to congratulate him on his victory.

"I promise to make this a smooth transition," the president said to Mr. Obama, according to a transcript provided by the White House. "You are about to go on one of the great journeys of life. Congratulations, and go enjoy yourself."

For most Americans, the news of Mr. Obama's election came at 11 p.m., Eastern Time, when the networks, waiting for the close of polls in California, declared him the victor. A roar sounded from the 125,000 people gathered in Hutchison Field in Grant Park at the moment that they learned Mr. Obama had been projected the winner.

The scene in Phoenix was decidedly more sour. At several points, Mr. McCain, unsmiling, had to motion his crowd to quiet down—he held out both hands, palms down—when they responded to his words of tribute to Mr. Obama with boos.

Mr. Obama, who watched Mr. McCain's speech from his hotel room in Chicago, offered a hand to voters who had not supported him in this election, when he took the stage 15 minutes later. "To those Americans whose support I have yet to earn," he said, "I may not have won your vote, but I hear your voices, I need your help and I will be your president, too."

Initial signs were that Mr. Obama benefited from a huge turnout of voters, but particularly among blacks. That group made up 13 percent of the electorate, according to surveys of people leaving the polls, compared with 11 percent in 2006.

In North Carolina, Republicans said that the huge surge of African Americans was one of the big factors that led to Senator Elizabeth Dole, a Republican, losing her reelection bid.

Mr. Obama also did strikingly well among Hispanic voters; Mr. McCain did worse among those voters than Mr. Bush did in 2004. That suggests the damage the Republican Party has suffered among those voters over four years in which Republicans have been at the forefront on the effort to crack down on illegal immigrants.

The election ended what by any definition was one of the most remarkable contests in American political history, drawing what was by every appearance unparalleled public interest.

Throughout the day, people lined up at the polls for hours—some showing up before dawn—to cast their votes. Aides to both campaigns said that anecdotal evidence suggested record-high voter turnout.

Reflecting the intensity of the two candidates, Mr. McCain and Mr. Obama took a page from what Mr. Bush did in 2004 and continued to campaign after the polls opened.

Mr. McCain left his home in Arizona after voting early Tuesday to fly to Colorado and New Mexico, two states where Mr. Bush won four years ago but where Mr. Obama waged a spirited battle.

These were symbolically appropriate final campaign stops for Mr. McCain, reflecting the imperative he felt of trying to defend Republican states against a challenge from Mr. Obama.

"Get out there and vote," Mr. McCain said in Grand Junction, Colo. "I need your help. Volunteer, knock on doors, get your neighbors to the polls, drag them there if you need to."

By contrast, Mr. Obama flew from his home in Chicago to Indiana, a state that in many ways came to epitomize the audacity of his effort this year. Indiana has not voted for a Democrat since President Lyndon B. Johnson's landslide victory in 1964, and Mr. Obama made an intense bid for support there. He later returned home to Chicago to play basketball, his Election Day ritual.

DONALD TRUMP IS ELECTED PRESIDENT IN STUNNING REPUDIATION OF THE ESTABLISHMENT

By MATT FLEGENHEIMER AND MICHAEL BARBARO, NOVEMBER 9, 2016

Donald John Trump was elected the 45th president of the United States on Tuesday in a stunning culmination of an explosive, populist and polarizing campaign that took relentless aim at the institutions and long-held ideals of American democracy.

The surprise outcome, defying late polls that showed Hillary Clinton with a modest but persistent edge, threatened convulsions throughout the country and the world, where skeptics had watched with alarm as Mr. Trump's unvarnished overtures to disillusioned voters took hold.

The triumph for Mr. Trump, 70, a real estate developer–turned–reality television star with no government experience, was a powerful rejection of the establishment forces that had assembled against him, from the world of business to government, and the consensus they had forged on everything from trade to immigration.

> *It was a decisive demonstration of power by a largely overlooked coalition.*

The results amounted to a repudiation, not only of Mrs. Clinton, but of President Obama, whose legacy is suddenly imperiled. And it was a decisive demonstration of power by a largely overlooked coalition of mostly blue-collar white and working-class voters who felt that the promise of the United States had slipped their grasp amid decades of globalization and multiculturalism.

In Mr. Trump, a thrice-married Manhattanite who lives in a marble-wrapped three-story penthouse apartment on Fifth Avenue, they found an improbable champion.

"The forgotten men and women of our country will be forgotten no longer," Mr. Trump told supporters around 3 a.m. on Wednesday at a rally in New York City, just after Mrs. Clinton called to concede.

In a departure from a blistering campaign in which he repeatedly stoked division, Mr. Trump sought to do something he had conspicuously avoided as a candidate: Appeal for unity.

"Now it's time for America to bind the wounds of division," he said. "It is time for us to come together as one united people. It's time."

That, he added, "is so important to me."

He offered unusually warm words for Mrs. Clinton, who he has suggested should be in jail, saying she was owed "a major debt of gratitude for her service to our country."

Bolstered by Mr. Trump's strong showing, Republicans retained control of the Senate. Only one Republican-controlled seat, in Illinois, fell to Democrats early in the evening. And Senator Richard Burr of North Carolina, a Republican, easily won reelection in a race that had been among the country's most competitive. A handful of other Republican incumbents facing difficult races were running better than expected.

Mr. Trump's win—stretching across the battleground states of Florida, North Carolina, Ohio and Pennsylvania—seemed likely to set off financial jitters and immediate unease among international allies, many of which were startled when Mr. Trump in his campaign cast doubt on the necessity of America's military commitments abroad and its allegiance to international economic partnerships.

From the moment he entered the campaign, with a shocking set of claims that Mexican immigrants were rapists and criminals, Mr. Trump was widely underestimated as a candidate, first by his opponents for the Republican nomination and later by Mrs. Clinton, his Democratic rival. His rise was largely missed by polling organizations and data analysts. And an air of improbability trailed his campaign, to the detriment of those who dismissed his angry message, his improvisational style and his appeal to disillusioned voters.

He suggested remedies that raised questions of constitutionality, like a ban on Muslims entering the United States.

He threatened opponents, promising lawsuits against news organizations that covered him critically and women who accused him of sexual assault. At times, he simply lied.

But Mr. Trump's unfiltered rallies and unshakable self-regard attracted a zealous following, fusing unsubtle identity politics with an economic populism that often defied party doctrine.

His rallies—furious, entertaining, heavy on name-calling and nationalist overtones—became the nexus of a political movement, with daily promises of sweeping victory, in the election and otherwise, and an insistence that the country's political machinery was "rigged" against Mr. Trump and those who admired him.

He seemed to embody the success and grandeur that so many of his followers felt was missing from their own lives—and from the country itself. And he scoffed at the poll-driven word-parsing ways of modern politics, calling them a waste of time and money. Instead, he relied on his gut.

At his victory party at the New York Hilton Midtown, where a raucous crowd indulged in a cash bar and wore hats bearing his ubiquitous campaign slogan "Make

Trump supporter Thurston Yates of Louisiana stands in front of his home, displaying a Trump "Make America Great Again" sign.

America Great Again," voters expressed gratification that their voices had, at last, been heard.

"He was talking to people who weren't being spoken to," said Joseph Gravagna, 37, a marketing company owner from Rockland County, N.Y. "That's how I knew he was going to win."

For Mrs. Clinton, the defeat signaled an astonishing end to a political dynasty that has colored Democratic politics for a generation. Eight years after losing to President Obama in the Democratic primary—and 16 years after leaving the White House for the United States Senate, as President Bill Clinton exited office—she had seemed positioned to carry on two legacies: her husband's and the president's.

Her shocking loss was a devastating turn for the sprawling world of Clinton aides and strategists who believed they had built an electoral machine that would swamp Mr. Trump's ragtag band of loyal operatives and family members, many of whom had no experience running a national campaign.

On Tuesday night, stricken Clinton aides who believed that Mr. Trump had no mathematical path to victory, anxiously paced the Jacob K. Javits Convention Center as states in which they were confident of victory, like Florida and North Carolina, either fell to Mr. Trump or seemed in danger of tipping his way.

Mrs. Clinton watched the grim results roll in from a suite at the nearby Peninsula Hotel, surrounded by her family, friends and advisers who had the day before celebrated her candidacy with a champagne toast on her campaign plane.

But over and over, Mrs. Clinton's weaknesses as a candidate were exposed. She failed to excite voters hungry for change. She struggled to build trust with Americans who were baffled by her decision to use a private email server as secretary of state. And she strained to make a persuasive case for herself as a champion of the economically downtrodden after delivering perfunctory paid speeches that earned her millions of dollars.

The returns Tuesday also amounted to a historic rebuke of the Democratic Party from the white blue-collar voters who had formed the party base from the presidency of Franklin D. Roosevelt to Mr. Clinton's. Yet Mrs. Clinton and her advisers had taken for granted that states like Michigan and Wisconsin would stick with a Democratic nominee, and that she could repeat Mr. Obama's strategy of mobilizing the party's ascendant liberal coalition rather than pursuing a more moderate course like her husband did 24 years ago.

But not until these voters were offered a Republican who ran as an unapologetic populist, railing against foreign trade deals and illegal immigration, did they move so drastically away from their ancestral political home.

To the surprise of many on the left, white voters who had helped elect the nation's first black president, appeared more reluctant to line up behind a white woman.

From Pennsylvania to Wisconsin, industrial towns once full of union voters who for decades offered their votes to Democratic presidential candidates, even in the party's lean years, shifted to Mr. Trump's Republican Party. One county in the Mahoning Valley of Ohio, Trumbull, went to Mr. Trump by a 6-point margin. Four years ago, Mr. Obama won there by 22 points.

Mrs. Clinton's loss was especially crushing to millions who had cheered her march toward history as, they hoped, the nation's first female president. For supporters, the election often felt like a referendum on gender progress: an opportunity to elevate a woman to the nation's top job and to repudiate a man whose remarkably boorish behavior toward women had assumed center stage during much of the campaign.

Mr. Trump boasted, in a 2005 video released last month, about using his public profile to commit sexual assault. He suggested that female political rivals lacked a presidential "look." He ranked women on a scale of 1 to 10, even holding forth on the desirability of his own daughter—the kind of throwback male behavior that many in the country assumed would disqualify a candidate for high office.

On Tuesday, the public's verdict was rendered.

Uncertainty abounds as Mr. Trump prepares to take office. His campaign featured a shape-shifting list of policy proposals, often seeming to change hour to hour. His staff was in constant turmoil, with Mr. Trump's children serving critical campaign roles and a rotating cast of advisers alternately seeking access to Mr. Trump's ear, losing it and, often, regaining it, depending on the day.

Even Mr. Trump's full embrace of the Republican Party came exceedingly late in life, leaving members of both parties unsure about what he truly believes. He has donated heavily to both parties and has long described his politics as the transactional reality of a businessman.

Mr. Trump's dozens of business entanglements—many of them in foreign countries—will follow him into the Oval Office, raising questions about potential conflicts of interest. His refusal to release his tax returns, and his acknowledgment that he did not pay federal income taxes for years, has left the American people with considerable gaps in their understanding of the financial dealings.

But this they do know: Mr. Trump will thoroughly reimagine the tone, standards and expectations of the presidency, molding it in his own self-aggrandizing image.

He is set to take the oath of office on Jan. 20.

NOTE: *Donald Trump's ability to savor his narrow victory in the Electoral College was short-lived. Protests against his election erupted around the country, and the investigation into Russian meddling in the 2016 election became a focal point of his presidency. As of this writing, Trump is still trying to stymie the investigation of Robert Mueller, the special counsel appointed to look into the meddling, and is sometimes in open war with his own Justice Department. Plea bargains struck with some of his advisers and campaign aides, and criminal cases against others, continue to plague him.*

CHAPTER 2

WAR

"It was to spare the Japanese people from utter destruction that the ultimatum of July 26 was issued at Potsdam. Their leaders promptly rejected that ultimatum. If they do not now accept our terms, they may expect a rain of ruin from the air the like of which has never been seen on this earth."

—President Harry S. Truman, August 6, 1945

WARS ARE A THREAD through American presidencies; Jimmy Carter boasted that he was the only president who could say, "We never fired a bullet. We never dropped a bomb." Born in revolutionary war, the nation tore itself in two over slavery and states' rights issues before it was 100 years old, mended itself, at least to some degree, and then engaged in a wide range of skirmishes and periods of looking outward and cringing inward. The so-called "good wars"—World War I and World War II—ushered in periods of massive upheaval that in turn led to new and deadlier conflicts. Americans lost their innocence about being on the righteous side of war in Vietnam. They endured the Cold War, which dominated the foreign affairs of every president from Harry Truman to George H. W. Bush. In the post–Cold War world, they encountered a new kind of endless war against terrorism, which eroded American notions of exceptionalism, domestic safety and liberty like no other previous conflict had.

OPPOSITE: View of part of the utter devastation of Hiroshima in the aftermath of the August 6, 1945, atomic bomb blast there, June 26, 1946.

"GOOD" WARS

SELECTIVE DRAFT WINS MAJORITY IN HOUSE COMMITTEE

APRIL 18, 1917

The administration made such headway in the House Committee on Military Affairs today that the reporting of the Army Conscription Bill, with but one material amendment, became a practical certainty. The bill is expected to go into the House within 48 hours; indications favor its report tomorrow afternoon.

The recalcitrant on the committee gradually lost ground today until the proponents of the selective draft gained the majority. On the showdown in committee it is not believed more than half a dozen members, mostly Democrats, will oppose the bill.

A change in the ages of the classes to be called out by the president under the selective draft plan, is only material modification to receive the approval of the House committee. Instead of a draft of men between the ages of 19 and 25 the House committee is expected to vote, and the administration to accept, that the muster of men under the conscription plan shall be as follows: first call, eligible men between the ages of 20 and 25, inclusive; second call, ages 26 to 32; third, ages 33 to 37; fourth, ages 38 to 42. If a fifth class should be needed the ages would be between 43 and 48.

Consult Republican Leaders

The president summoned to the White House Chairman Dent of the House Military Affairs Committee and two Republican leaders—Mr. Mann of Illinois and Mr. Lenroot of Wisconsin. It was made plain at these conferences that the administration would not yield on the conscription issue.

Chairman Dent went to the White House with suggestions of a compromise bill providing for a tryout of the volunteer plan before conscription was put into effect. The same compromise was proposed while Secretary Baker was before the House committee. Both the president and the secretary of war flatly rejected the proposition for a volunteer army, or an army half-volunteer and half-conscript.

Newly drafted soldiers report for duty at Camp Meade outside Baltimore, 1917.

The secretary of war agreed to yield on certain minor features of the administration measure; he would not budge on the fundamentals. Mr. Baker was before the House committee in the morning and returned for a further conference and free discussion tonight. When the committee adjourned after 10 o'clock, the administration appeared for the first time to be in control of the situation and the Army Bill was on the way to a favorable report.

Secretary Baker told the House committee flatly tonight that the War Department's plan for the organization of an army by selective conscription was the only feasible way of meeting the emergency with Germany. After the committee adjourned, Chairman Dent called all the Democratic members together in conference. He expressed hope of getting a unanimous report, despite the division in the committee over the draft provision. The committee will meet tomorrow for the final vote on the draft issue.

Representative Quin of Mississippi is said to have been one of the recalcitrant Democrats who fell into line after Secretary Baker's visit to the committee. Representative

Fields of Kentucky, who voted "present" on the test vote, is expected to support the bill after the change relating to the ages of the men drafted for service. Mr. Fields objected to a bill providing for a call of men between the ages of 18 and 25 only.

In the House, the administration has been gaining recruits for the bill for a week.

Impatient at the Delay

The administration made it entirely clear today that it had no intention of yielding an inch on any essential part of its program for raising an army by conscription.

The subject was discussed at a brief cabinet meeting. There were many evidences that the president and his advisers were becoming impatient over congressional delay in giving the government support in its war program, and it was hinted that unless the House showed greater readiness to acquiesce in the president's policy it was possible that he would take means to tell the country who was holding up army preparations. It was recalled that on March 4 last, the day the 64th Congress ended, he publicly scored the "little group of willful men" who killed the armed neutrality bill in the Senate.

> *The administration . . . had no intention of yielding an inch.*

President Wilson and Secretary Baker take the position that further delay on the Army Bill will endanger the war plans against Germany. There were intimations that the president did not mince words in expressing his views of the seriousness of the present problem in talking with Mr. Dent this afternoon.

After the cabinet meeting, it was indicated that the full influence of the administration would be concentrated on the passage of the army measure.

ROOSEVELT PLEDGE

By FELIX BELAIR JR., SEPTEMBER 2, 1939

President Roosevelt pledged the nation today to make every effort to keep this country out of war. He said he hoped and believed it could be done.

Then he made a final checkup on the machinery already set up for preserving American neutrality, as well as for swinging military, naval and industrial forces into action in event of any unexpected emergency.

The president's promise to do all in his power to keep the nation at peace was given as he gravely faced his regular Friday morning press conference. There was little he could say at this critical period in the world's history, he remarked, except to appeal to the newspaper men present for their full cooperation in adhering as closely as possible to the facts, since this was best not only for this nation but for civilization as a whole.

Roosevelt pledged the nation today to make every effort to keep this country out of war.

In this regard, the president set an example for his auditors. He said what he had to say without attempting to minimize or exaggerate the gravity of the European situation. He appeared to be neither exuberant nor depressed by the turn of events that kept him from his bed for all but a few hours last night. Occasionally he was humorous, but throughout his manner was calm.

Would "Allay Anxiety"

Later in the day the president let it be known that he would address the nation over the three major broadcasting networks on Sunday night from 10 to 10:15 o'clock, Eastern daylight time, in an effort "to allay anxiety and relieve suspense." Stephen T. Early, his secretary, who hurried back to Washington from a brief vacation today, said Mr. Roosevelt would speak on international affairs in a manner that would "clearly state our position" and would be of international interest.

The president began his memorable press conference with the explanation that there was little if anything he could say on such anticipated questions as when he would call a special session of Congress and issue a neutrality proclamation. These things, he explained, would have to await developments "over there" during the day, and possibly tomorrow, which would have a direct bearing on any American action.

But if anyone had any questions that he was able to answer, Mr. Roosevelt said, he would answer gladly. A reporter observed that the question uppermost in every one's mind just now was: "Can we keep out of it?" The president cast his eyes downward for a moment as he pondered the request for comment. Then he replied:

"Only this—that I not only sincerely hope so, but I believe we can, and that every effort will be made by the administration to so do."

The president consented readily when permission was asked to quote him directly on his statement.

NOTE: *Roosevelt struggled to overcome the powerful isolationist and often anti-Semitic trends driving American politics—even in his own party—to enter a war he knew the Europeans could not win on their own. Finally, the Japanese attack on Pearl Harbor gave him the reason he needed to declare war.*

NEW AGE USHERED

By SIDNEY SHALETT, AUGUST 7, 1945

The White House and War Department announced today that an atomic bomb, possessing more power than 20,000 tons of a destructive force equal to the load of 2,000 B-29s and more than 2,000 times the blast power of what previously was the world's most devastating bomb, had been dropped on Japan.

The announcement, first given to the world in utmost solemnity by President Truman, made it plain that one of the scientific landmarks of the century had been passed, and that the "age of atomic energy," which can be a tremendous force for the. advancement of civilization as well as for destruction, was at hand.

At 10:45 o'clock this morning, a statement by the president was issued at the White House that 16 hours earlier—about the time that citizens on the Eastern Seaboard were

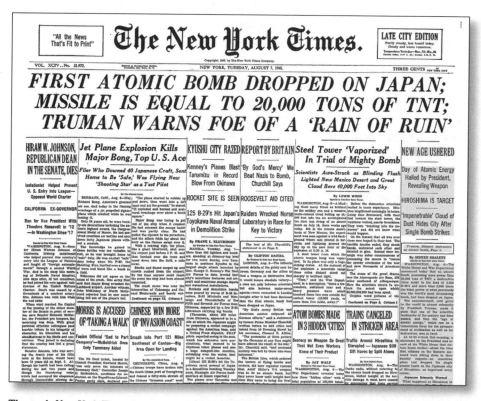

The stark *New York Times* front page of August 7, 1945.

sitting down to their Sunday suppers—an American plane had dropped the single atomic bomb on the Japanese city of Hiroshima, an important army center.

Japanese Solemnly Warned

What happened at Hiroshima is not yet known. The War Department said it "as yet was unable to make an accurate report" because "an impenetrable cloud of dust and smoke" masked the target area from reconnaissance planes. The secretary of war will release the story "as soon as accurate details of the results of the bombing become available."

But in a statement vividly describing the results of the first test of the atomic bomb in New Mexico, the War Department told how an immense steel tower had been "vaporized" by the tremendous explosion, how a 40,000-foot cloud rushed into the sky, and two observers were knocked down at a point 10,000 yards away. And President Truman solemnly warned:

"It was to spare the Japanese people from utter destruction that the ultimatum of July 26 was issued at Potsdam. Their leaders promptly rejected that ultimatum. If they do not now accept our terms, they may expect a rain of ruin from the air the like of which has never been seen on this earth."

Most Closely Guarded Secret

The president referred to the joint statement issued by the heads of the American, British and Chinese governments, in which terms of surrender were outlined to the Japanese and warning given that rejection would mean complete destruction of Japan's power to make war.

[The atomic bomb weighs about 400 pounds and is capable of utterly destroying a town, a representative of the British Ministry of Aircraft Production said in London, the United Press reported.]

What is this terrible new weapon, which the War Department also calls the *Cosmic Bomb*? It is the harnessing of the energy of the atom, which is the basic power of the universe. As President Truman said, "The force from which the sun draws its power has been loosed against those who brought war to the Far East."

"Atomic fission"—in other words, the scientists' long-held dream of splitting the atom— is the secret of the atomic bomb. Uranium, a rare, heavy metallic element, which is radio-active and akin to radium, is the source essential to its production. Secretary of War Henry L. Stimson, in a statement closely following that of the president, promised that "steps have been taken, and continue to be taken, to assure us of adequate supplies of this mineral."

The imagination-sweeping experiment in harnessing the power of the atom has been the most closely guarded secret of the war. America to date has spent nearly $2 billion in advancing its research. Since 1939, American, British and Canadian scientists have worked on it. The experiments have been conducted in the United States, both for reasons of achieving concentrated efficiency and for security; the consequences of having the material fall into the hands of the enemy, in case Great Britain should have been successfully invaded, were too awful for the Allies to risk.

All along, it has been a race with the enemy. Ironically enough, Germany started the experiments, but we finished them. Germany made the mistake of expelling, because she was a "non-Aryan," a woman scientist who held one of the keys to the mystery, and she made her knowledge available to those who brought it to the United States. Germany never quite mastered the riddle, and the United States, Secretary Stimson declared, is "convinced that Japan will not be in a position to use an atomic bomb in this war."

A Sobering Awareness of Power

Not the slightest spirit of braggadocio is discernible either in the wording of the official announcements or in the mien of the officials who gave out the news. There was an element of elation in the realization that we had perfected this devastating weapon for employment against an enemy who started the war and has told us she would rather be destroyed than surrender, but it was grim elation. There was sobering awareness of the tremendous responsibility involved.

Secretary Stimson said that this new weapon "should prove a tremendous aid in the shortening of the war against Japan," and there were other responsible officials who privately thought that this was an extreme understatement, and that Japan might find herself unable to stay in the war under the coming rain of atom bombs.

There was sobering awareness of the tremendous responsibility involved.

It was obvious that officials at the highest levels made the important decision to release news of the atomic bomb because of the psychological effect it may have in forcing Japan to surrender. However, there are some officials who feel privately it might have been well to keep this completely secret. Their opinion can be summed up in the comment by one spokesman: "Why bother with psychological warfare against an enemy that already is beaten and hasn't sense enough to quit and save herself from utter doom?"

The first news came from President Truman's office. Newsmen were summoned and the historic statement from the chief executive, who still is on the high seas, was given to them.

"That bomb," Mr. Truman said, "had more power than 20,000 tons of TNT. It had more than 2,000 times the blast power of the British Grand Slam, which is the largest bomb (22,000 pounds) ever yet used in the history of warfare."

Explosive Charge Is Small

No details were given on the plane that carried the bomb. Nor was it stated whether the bomb was large or small. The president, however, said the explosive charge was "exceedingly small." It is known that tremendous force is packed into tiny quantities of the element that constitutes these bombs. Scientists, looking to the peacetime uses of atomic power, envisage submarines, ocean liners and planes traveling around the world on a few pounds of the element. Yet, for various reasons, the bomb used against Japan could have been extremely large.

Hiroshima, first city on earth to be the target of the Cosmic Bomb, is a city of 318,000, which is—or was—a major quartermaster depot and port of embarkation for the Japanese. In addition to large military supply depots, it manufactured ordnance, mainly large guns and tanks, and machine tools, and aircraft-ordnance parts.

President Truman grimly told the Japanese that "the end is not yet."

"In their present form these bombs are now in production," he said, "and even more powerful forms are in development."

NOTE: *The dropping of the atomic bombs in Japan may have hastened the end of World War II, but it also ushered in a nuclear arms race that dominated international affairs—and still does. As it turns out, the atomic bombs used in Japan, as devastating and catastrophically deadly as they were, are mere firecrackers compared to the thermonuclear bombs of today.*

NUMBER 29

OCTOBER 26, 1945

While the London Conference of Foreign Ministers was in its last sad stages early this month, the Charter of the United Nations received its 29th ratification. Except for a formality, prescribed in paragraph 3 of article 110 of the charter, this made U.N.O. [United Nations Organization] a going concern. The formality was attended to on Wednesday, when First Secretary Fedor T. Orekhov of the Soviet Embassy in Washington deposited with the State Department the ratifications of the Ukrainian and White Russian Republics and, as the 29th, the ratification of the Union of Soviet Socialist Republics. Secretary Byrnes, following the procedure laid down at San Francisco, then issued a protocol reciting that the conditions for the charter's coming into effect had been met. This document is now, as he added in his brief statement to the public, "a part of the law of nations."

It must have been by intention—Russia's intention and our intention—that the U.S.S.R. was enabled to push the button that will make U.N.O. operative. Wednesday's informal formalities dramatized the fact that Russia is accepting serious international obligations. This drama in the State Department might not be so spectacular as some occurrences in Poland, in the Balkans, in Korea or even in the U.N.O.'s executive committee, which is trying

Russia is saying, with every sign of sincerity, that she wants to do her share.

to iron out procedural questions in preparation for the December meeting of the new assembly. But as of Wednesday, Russia is saying, with every sign of sincerity, that she wants to do her share "to maintain international peace and security . . . to develop friendly relations among nations . . . to achieve international cooperations in solving international problems . . . and in promoting and encouraging respect for human rights."

By this significant act, Russia, with 50 other nations, agrees to settle international disputes by peaceful means; to "refrain from the threat or use of force against the territorial integrity or political independence" of any state; to act in concert with other powers against aggressors; to discuss, in the General Assembly, the "principles of cooperation in the maintenance of international peace and security"; to maintain and respect an International Court of Justice; to commit to an economic and social council "international economic, social, health and related problems."

Some of the language of the charter is specific and some is vague. Secretary Byrnes wisely said that "the maintenance of peace depends not upon any document, but upon what is in the minds and hearts of men." There is no mechanism by which any great power can be brought to justice, though there is ample provision for the chastisement of erring lesser powers. The charter is an expression of good intentions, with agencies for making good intentions effective. It cannot create the good intentions, or of itself, perpetuate them.

But have we any reason to suppose that the level of good intentions in the world has declined since the charter was signed on June 26? We are pretty sure that we mean well now, as we did then—in fact, we are more desperately in earnest because we have been frightened by our own horrible toy, the atomic bomb. And certainly the other governments which last June took steps against war have not come to tolerate warfare because it can now be carried on with greater efficiency through atomic fission.

The four months that have passed since the June ceremonies at San Francisco have shown that it is possible for allies to quarrel. They have also shown that civilization is in dire peril if quarrels of this nature are not prevented or settled. We in America see this fact clearly. Are we to consider the people of other nations so stupid or so bloodthirsty that they can't or won't see it? The question ought to answer itself. We ought to assume that the people of other nations share in full sincerity our hatred for war. We ought to assume that they are as eager as we are to make U.N.O. a success. If this is what Wednesday's ceremonies signified we can be sure that various points of differences will in time be settled.

"BAD" WARS

CONGRESS BACKS PRESIDENT ON SOUTHEAST ASIA MOVES; RESOLUTION WINS

By E. W. KENWORTHY, AUGUST 8, 1964

The House of Representatives and the Senate approved today the resolution requested by President Johnson to strengthen his hand in dealing with Communist aggression in Southeast Asia.

After a 40-minute debate, the House passed the resolution, 416 to 0. Shortly afterward the Senate approved it, 88 to 2. Senate debate, which began yesterday afternoon, lasted 9 hours. The resolution gives prior Congressional approval of "all necessary measures" that the president may take "to repel any armed attack" against United States forces and "to prevent further aggression."

The resolution, the text of which was printed in *The New York Times*. Thursday, also gives advance sanction for "all necessary steps" taken by the president to help any nation covered by the Southeast Asia collective defense treaty that requests assistance "in defense of its freedom."

Johnson Hails Action

President Johnson said the Congressional action was "a demonstration to all the world of the unity of all Americans."

"The votes prove our determination to defend our forces, to prevent aggression and to work firmly and steadily for peace and security in the area," he said.

"I am sure the American people join me in expressing the deepest appreciation to the leaders and members of both parties in both houses of Congress for their patriotic, resolute and rapid action."

The debates in both houses, but particularly in the Senate, made clear, however, that the near-unanimous vote did not reflect a unanimity of opinion on the necessity or advisability of the resolution.

Except for Senators Wayne L. Morse, Democrat of Oregon, and Ernest Gruening, Democrat of Alaska, who cast the votes against the resolution, members in both houses uniformly praised the president for the retaliatory action he had ordered against North Vietnamese torpedo boats and their bases after the second torpedo boat attack on United States destroyers in the Gulf of Tonkin.

There was also general agreement that Congress could not reject the president's requested resolution without giving an impression of disunity and nonsupport that did not, in fact, exist.

There was no support for the thesis on which Senators Morse and Gruening based their opposition—that the resolution was "unconstitutional" because it was "a predated declaration of war power" reserved to Congress.

Nevertheless, many members said the president did not need the resolution because he had the power as commander in chief to order United States forces to repel attacks.

Several members thought the language of the resolution was unnecessarily broad and they were apprehensive that it would be interpreted as giving Congressional support for direct participation by United States troops in the war in South Vietnam.

Expansion Held Inevitable

Representative of these doubts and reservations were the brief remarks by Senator George D. Aiken, Republican of Vermont. Senator Aiken, a member of the Foreign Relations Committee, said:

"It has been apparent to me for some months that the expansion of the war in Southeast Asia was inevitable. I felt that it shouldn't occur, but the decision wasn't mine.

"I am still apprehensive of the outcome of the president's decision, but he felt that the interests of the United States required prompt action. As a citizen I feel I must support our president whether his decision is right or wrong.

"I hope the present action will prove to be correct. I support the resolution with misgivings."

In the House, Eugene Siler, Republican of Kentucky, who was absent, was paired against the resolution, but his opposition was not counted. His office said he regarded the resolution as "buck-passing" by the president with the intent of silencing any later criticism.

Reservations about the resolution took two principal forms. The first was that it might be interpreted as giving advance approval of a change in the United States mission in South Vietnam of providing a training cadre and matériel.

Senator Gaylord Nelson, Democrat of Wisconsin, made much of this question yesterday. Today he proposed an amendment to resolve all doubts about the meaning of the resolution.

Conflicting Views Noted

Mr. Nelson noted that some members had welcomed the resolution as authorizing the president "to act against the privileged sanctuary" of the Communists in North Vietnam while other members thought it did not envisage an extension of the present mission.

His amendment stated: "Our continuing policy is to limit our role to the provision of aid, training assistance and military advice, and it is the sense of Congress that, except when provoked to a greater response, we should continue to attempt to avoid a direct military involvement in the Southeast Asian conflict."

Mr. Nelson asked Senator J. W. Fulbright, Democrat of Arkansas, whether as chairman of the Foreign Relations Committee and floor manager of the resolution he would accept the amendment. If not, Mr. Nelson said, he could not support the resolution.

Mr. Fulbright replied that he could not accept the amendment because the House had already voted and adoption of the amendment would require that the resolution go to conference with resulting delay.

"An Accurate Reflection"

However, Mr. Fulbright added that the amendment was "unobjectionable" as a statement of policy and was "an accurate reflection of what I believe is the president's policy."

With this reassurance, Mr. Nelson was satisfied that he had made a "legislative record" of administration intent. He did not offer his amendment and voted for the resolution.

The second reservation arose from the possibility that Premier Nguyen Khanh of South Vietnam might extend the war into North Vietnam and that the United States would lose control of its freedom of action. Senator Jacob K. Javits, Republican of New York, asked Mr. Fulbright: "Suppose that South Vietnam should be jeopardized by its own extension of the struggle beyond its own capacity to wage a successful war in North Vietnam. Then what would happen in terms of our commitment and the commitment which the president is empowered to undertake?"

Mr. Fulbright declared that he did not believe South Vietnam "could involve us beyond the point where we ourselves wished to be involved."

.50-CALIBER ORDEAL ON A VIETNAM FIELD

By R. W. APPLE JR., FEBRUARY 1, 1966

The place has no name. It is a stretch of fine white sand, surrounded by palm trees, 285 miles northeast of Saigon and a few miles from the tranquil South China Sea. Today a little group of Americans—soldiers in the First Cavalry Division (Airmobile)—spent the most terrifying hours of their lives on it.

The company was ordered this morning to continue its push north through Binh Dinh Province. It had already overrun two enemy positions in two days, and its men were weary.

All went well until the company moved onto the sand "island" in the midst of the rice paddies—an "island" much like the one only four miles to the south where two other companies from the First Cavalry fought and bled all last Saturday.

It was 12:30 when Company A reached the edge of the sand, glittering under the bright Vietnamese midday sun.

First there was a single ping—the sound of a sniper firing. And then, as if by signal, the chatter of automatic weapons fire burst from the trees on the other side of the field of sand.

Everyone in the company, perhaps 150 men, flung himself to the ground. Then they began working their way toward the trees, firing their weapons, cursing, shouting and calling for help on their radios. Some of them were hit.

By the time they had crossed the 300 yards that separated them from the trees, Company A had suffered grievously. Platoon leaders were down, radio operators, riflemen. One of the platoons, which had started the day with 40 men, had 23 killed or wounded by 3 p.m.

The worst was yet to come.

Capt. Eugene Fox of Washington, the company commander, set up his headquarters in a thatched hut—what the riflemen call a *hootch*—and began to assess the damage. Suddenly, two 60-mm mortar rounds fell into the area. One struck the hut a direct blow and four more men were hit.

By now the enemy fire had slackened—many, no doubt, had been killed—and the area was considered safe for helicopters. A flight of UH-1Bs swept in and set down 150 fresh men from Company C.

Two medical evacuation helicopters also landed, kicking up great blinding swirls of sand that ripped at the faces of the men on the ground. I was a passenger on the first of these two choppers.

Helicopters airlift members of the 2nd Battalion, 14th Infantry Regiment during Operation Wahiawa, South Vietnam, May 16, 1966.

As I jumped out, I saw a score of dirty men, wearing bloody bandages, huddled on litters or squatting in the middle of the field of sand. There were not enough litter bearers, so I helped put several of the wounded onto the waiting helicopters.

Thus it happened that when the choppers lifted off I found myself almost alone, with snipers' bullets whizzing overhead.

Several other correspondents were nearby, and in one spot a lieutenant and two enlisted men were lying prone, their faces in the sand. I ran over to join them; we talked for a few minutes, kneeling during a lull in the shooting.

Then, without warning, from behind our backs came a volley of gunfire of tremendous intensity. None of us had any idea what was happening, because the Vietcong were in front of us beyond the command post.

Bullets Everywhere

We flattened our bodies on the sand. On my left was First Lieut. Paul H. Mobley of Rockville, Md., the company's executive officer, who had been supervising the loading of the wounded. On my right was Specialist Theodis Young, a 25-year-old rifleman from the Eastern Parkway section of Brooklyn.

Bullets—they were .50-caliber machine-gun bullets, we discovered later—smashed into the sand all around us. One series of six made a neat line four inches from my right arm.

We could not move, we could not take cover for there was none. We could not shoot back. We could not even tell who was shooting at us. We could only cringe and hope it would stop.

Lieutenant Mobley, his face contorted, screamed: "Dig, dig, you bastards, don't get up to do it! Use your elbows and knees! Use your pots [helmets] if you have to."

The incredible barrage of machine-gun fire, intermixed with the almost soft pop of M79 grenade launchers, kept up for 10 minutes. The sound of the M79's, an American weapon, gave Specialist Young the clue he needed. He turned his head, spat out some sand, and shouted: "Them's Arvins! Them's Arvins, lieutenant!"

> *We could not move, we could not take cover for there was none.*

When the fire let up, we craned our necks. There, not 50 yards behind us, were 12 box-like armored personnel carriers, manned by soldiers from the Army of the Republic of South Vietnam, which is known to the G.I.s as the Arvin.

After two or three minutes, they opened fire again. Lieutenant Mobley screamed over and over: "G.I., G.I., don't shoot!" The South Vietnamese were too far away to hear. Still the bullets whizzed overhead and ricocheted around us.

The lieutenant asked whether anyone had a smoke grenade, and the man on his left said he had one but could not get to it. It was lashed to the back of his pack.

Lieutenant Mobley crawled over and worked with frenzied energy to untie it. When he got it free, he threw it backward over his head. It began spewing purple smoke, a pre-arranged allied signal, almost at once.

At last the shooting stopped. We looked up and saw the South Vietnamese waving from their turrets. Specialist Young cursed.

As I got up, I almost lost my trousers. It took a moment or two to realize that a bullet had slit them open down the back without touching my skin.

Captain Fox's men, in a trench in front of his command post, had not been so lucky. He had shouted into his radio all during the barrage, begging the South Vietnamese to stop.

They had finally heard him, but not until an M79 grenade had burst near him.

Five Hurt by Shrapnel

Five American soldiers were hurt by pieces of flying shrapnel that struck them in the legs or torsos. A technician employed by the Columbia Broadcasting System, Vallop Rodboon of Bangkok, Thailand, was wounded in the abdomen.

Captain Fox puffed on a cigar and said he had never seen anything to compare with today, not even in the Ia Drang Valley in November. The company's first sergeant, William A. Standfield of Terre Haute, Ind., said he had seen no parallel to it in three wars.

"None of us will ever come any closer than this," he said.

Captain Fox explained that the personnel carriers had been sent to root out the Vietcong, that they had taken fire from the grove of trees as they had moved up, and that they had wheeled and fired back. They had not known that Lieutenant Mobley and his small group and Captain Fox's headquarters lay between them and the enemy.

Sgt. Carmine McClellan of Mount Carmel, Ill., an American adviser who was riding one of the personnel carriers, laughed as they drove up to the command post.

"Guess we shook you up a little," he said.

Someone told him what had happened. He clasped his head in disbelief and murmured "Oh, no. Oh, no."

VIETNAM:
THE SIGNS OF STALEMATE

By R. W. APPLE JR., AUGUST 7, 1967

A little more than two years ago, on July 28, 1965, President Johnson committed the United States more decisively than ever to the war in Vietnam by announcing the deployment of 50,000 more American troops to this stricken corner of Southeast Asia.

Last Thursday, in response to the urgent entreaties of his commanders, Mr. Johnson disclosed that he would send 45,000 to 50,000 more men, for a total of 525,000, by next June 30.

The war is not going well. Victory is not close at hand. It may be beyond reach.

Between these two benchmarks of the most frustrating conflict in American history, the fighting has careened along, week by bloody week, through wet seasons and dry, through two Christmas cease-fires, through peace feelers and escalations.

By this weekend, 12,269 Americans had been listed as killed and 74,818 as injured, millions of artillery shells and billions of rifle bullets had been fired, and 833 airplanes had fallen to enemy gunners.

The war costs the United States more than $2 billion each month.

And yet, in the opinion of most disinterested observers, the war is not going well. Victory is not close at hand. It may be beyond reach. It is clearly unlikely in the next year or even the next two years, and American officers talk somberly about fighting here for decades.

The official statements from Washington and Saigon seem optimistic, as they have been for almost five years. Gen. William C. Westmoreland, the American commander in Vietnam, said recently that his men had made "tremendous progress." Secretary of State Dean Rusk said the enemy was "hurting very badly."

Stalemate is a fighting word in Washington. President Johnson rejects it as a description of the situation in Vietnam. But it is the word used by almost all Americans here, except the top officials, to characterize what is happening. They use the word for many reasons, including the following:

The Americans and their allies, having killed by their own count 200,000 enemy troops, now face the largest enemy force they have ever faced: 297,000 men, again by their own count.

The enemy has progressed from captured rifles and skimpy supplies to rockets, artillery, heavy mortars, a family of automatic infantry weapons and flame throwers, most of which has been brought into South Vietnam in the face of American airpower.

1.2 million allied troops have been able to secure only a fraction of a country less than one and a half times the size of New York State.

The allies are reaching the bottom of their ready manpower pool, while the North Vietnamese have committed only one-fifth of their regular army.

Above all, if the North Vietnamese and American troops were magically whisked away, the South Vietnamese regime would almost certainly crumble within months, so little have the root problems been touched.

Enemy's Tenacity Defies Awesome U.S. Effort

It is true, as General Westmoreland has often said, that the United States has built an awesome logistical empire in Vietnam, that the enemy seldom wins a major battle, that more highways are open than before, that American bombers have severely hampered Hanoi's war effort, that the Vietcong are suffering.

But the enemy continues to fight with tenacity, imagination and courage, and no one knows when he will stop.

The goal of American policy, simply stated, is to defeat, together with the other allies, the Vietcong guerrillas and their backers, the North Vietnamese, so that South Vietnam's nationalists can transform their society into something strong and durable.

Originally, American troops were to form a series of dikes, or military shields, around critical areas, so that the South Vietnamese, sheltered from North Vietnam's regulars, could regroup and build.

This is still the role of the gallant marines along the demilitarized zone, facing the North Vietnamese homeland, who have lost 10,000 men killed or wounded since Jan. 1; of the Fourth Infantry Division, along the Cambodian border, and of other divisions that mount search-and-destroy operations in enemy base areas.

Americans Frustrated by Hit-and-Run Assaults

It is galling work. Because the enemy can fade into redoubts or across borders where the Americans cannot follow him, the same unit must be smashed again and again. General Westmoreland once conceded that he was unable to hurt any unit so badly that it could not be refitted in 90 days.

Frustrated, the allies have turned increasingly to the use of artillery and airpower to hurt the enemy, substituting F-100 fighter bombers and 155-mm howitzers for infantrymen. The natural tendency of a technological society is to spend its steel and its inventiveness rather than its men.

But in Vietnam, technology is no substitute for the man on the ground. Artillery does not keep the Vietcong from moving at night; patrolling does. The artillery, in fact, often hurts more than it helps. When a 155-mm shell, aimed almost at random into the gloom, crashes onto a sleeping hamlet, potential Vietcong are often created in an instant.

The most damaging fact is this: behind these dikes that have been manned at the cost of so much blood and treasure, almost nothing has improved. The North Vietnamese have been pushed back into their lairs, away from the hamlets and villages, but security in the countryside is as bad as ever.

"I've destroyed the division three times," a senior American general said the other day. "I've chased main-force units all over the country, and the impact was zilch: it meant nothing to the people."

So now the Americans, implicitly admitting that they despair of results from the South Vietnamese themselves, are moving into action against the guerrillas, while trying at the same time to keep the North Vietnamese off balance.

Of the 25 American units of regimental or brigade size deployed in Vietnam, 14 are committed to the grisly business of digging out the mines in roads and defending tiny hamlets.

"We are on the way to a policy of occupation in this country," a Washington official said not long ago. "We have found that unless we put enormous numbers of our own troops into a very small area, the thing doesn't go."

Where Big Units Manage, Smaller Ones Fail

Where large units have been committed—for example, the First Cavalry Division (Airmobile) on the Bong Son plain and the South Koreans in Phu Yen Province— progress has been made.

Where the same tactic has been tried with smaller units, it has not worked. The marines, stretched thin, have been trying to pacify the area around the Da Nang air base for two years, but they were unable to prevent the rocket attack on July 15 that took a heavy toll in men and machines.

Army units have been engaged for months in Operation Rang Dong, the struggle to secure the approaches to Saigon, but during the last two weeks the guerrillas have mined

Route 4, the main road to the Mekong Delta, have struck with mortars at the Nha Be naval complex within sight of the lights of Saigon, and have fired their rockets into key American bases.

In all 53 districts of the III Corps—the sector around Saigon where the earth has been scorched in Operations Junction City, Cedar Falls and Manhattan—there remains a virtually complete guerrilla structure: a 10-man squad for each hamlet, a 30-man platoon for each village, an 80-man company for each district and at the top a 350-man company for each of 12 provinces.

The Vietcong have the incalculable advantage of the tactical offensive. The allies must defend and build; the Vietcong serve their ends by attacking and falling back.

For a Complete Shield, 8 Million Troops

To repeat the pattern of Phu Yen and Binh Dinh in all the populous areas of South Vietnam, one ranking American official has estimated, the allies would require 8 million men. Even then, as General Westmoreland has acknowledged, the problem would not immediately be solved because if the Americans pulled back, the enemy would filter down from the hills.

The situation has reminded more than one American in South Vietnam of these lines by Lewis Carroll:

"If seven maids with seven mops
Swept it for half a year,
Do you suppose," the Walrus said,
"That they could get it clear?"
"I doubt it," said the Carpenter,
And shed a bitter tear.

The answer to the seeming impasse is pacification—reestablishing the government presence in the hamlets so that the peasants will want to defend themselves and will have the means to do so. To accomplish this, the United States has built schools, pigpens and marketplaces; the South Vietnamese have conducted village and hamlet elections; a total of 315,000 pacification workers, American and South Vietnamese soldiers and civil servants have been committed; the American command structure has been reorganized, and enormous sums are being spent this year: $400 million by the Americans, $135 million by the South Vietnamese.

Some American officials argue that progress is inevitable because of the resources involved, that if enough manpower and money are poured out of Saigon, some of it, somehow, will have an impact on the faraway peasant.

But the ground to be covered is enormous. According to the new system for evaluating hamlets, a total of 1,944 out of 12,537 are controlled by the government—a figure amounting to fewer than one in six. The rest are contested or, to some degree, controlled by the Vietcong.

Some of the most experienced Americans here consider a hamlet secure when its chief is willing to sleep in it. About 2,000 are thought to meet this criterion.

Pacification Runs Behind Schedule in 26 Areas

The modest goal for this year is the pacification of 1,100 hamlets, most of them in 26 priority areas; but even this seems beyond the present state of the art. Of the 44 provinces, 26 are behind schedule.

American officials concede that pacification is at best creeping ahead in three-quarters of the country and stopped cold in the northern part.

Competent pacification workers are becoming harder and harder to recruit; the goal of 41,000 by the end of 1967 will not be reached, and those already at work are being killed it a rate near 15 a week. The 53 South Vietnamese army battalions supposedly protecting the workers are not doing so. Morale is so bad that 13 of every 100 workers are expected to desert during 1967.

A senior American said recently, "There is at least a 2-to-1 chance that we will increase the momentum of pacification over the next 12 or 18 months."

But nothing better than this can be hoped for, in the opinion of many observers, without a thorough overhaul of South Vietnamese society—without a second revolution to counter the revolution, however bogus, that the Vietcong have promised for more than a decade.

The peasants, by and large, are apolitical. They stand by and watch as they are buffeted by the war. They want security more than anything else, but they can be rallied to an ideal, as the North Vietnamese and the Vietcong have sometimes shown.

The ideal is nowhere to be found in Saigon.

Unless a theme more positive and more stirring than simple anti-Communism can be found, the war appears likely to go on until someone gets tired and quits, which could take generations.

Central Fact in South: Lack of Commitment

Unless the central fact of the allied war effort—the critical lack of commitment of South Vietnamese society to work for its own survival—is changed, there can be no real victory because there can be no viable, democratic Vietnamese society, which is what the United States came here to help build. The Americans responsible for the war effort seem to have given relatively little thought to this problem, perhaps because it drives them up against the reality that the people they are fighting for are none too eager to fight for themselves.

Consider, for example, General Westmoreland's program for improving the South Vietnamese Army. It is contained in a thick booklet stamped "Secret," and it includes 44 subprograms—all of which relate to more equipment, better professional training, more advisers. None relate to what football coaches like to call "the will to win."

Commenting on this preoccupation with the material, *The Saigon Post* recalled the recent fate of the Egyptian Army, with its magnificent Soviet-made tanks and jets, and suggested that South Vietnamese's generals bear in mind Napoleon's dictum: "The moral is to the physical as three to one."

South Vietnamese Troops

Allowing for such exceptional units as the marines, the rangers and the paratroops, the performance of South Vietnam's forces has been shockingly bad, in the opinion of most advisers.

Commanders only reluctantly commit their units to battle, because they are afraid of losing men. Once in battle, they are often unable to rally their troops. South Vietnamese units broke and ran during the early fighting around Con Thien and again during recent fighting in the Mekong Delta.

One recent instance of inaction by government troops occurred in the middle of May. The Vietcong overran a battalion command post in the delta, killing 3 American advisers and 29 South Vietnamese. One enemy body was found after the attack. Three South Vietnamese companies sat out the action only 300 yards away.

"Need for Reinforcements a Measure of Our Failure"

After years of cajolery by their advisers, government units still operate ineffectively at night (as, indeed, some American units do). A visitor recently inspected three "night patrols" in three parts of the country. One was walking down a highway with transistor radios blaring, one was asleep in a house and the third was hiding in a cave.

The American advisers—whose superiors, including General Westmoreland, have refused to demand the removal of incompetent leaders—have had little impact. One former adviser described his role as that of "a glorified radio operator, tolerated only because I could call in air strikes."

"Every time Westy makes a speech about how good the South Vietnam Army is," another general has said, "I want to ask him why he keeps calling for more Americans. His need for reinforcements is a measure of our failure with the Vietnamese."

At the same time, paradoxically, the Americans have created a dependent psychology in which the South Vietnamese abdicate responsibility in combat only to reassert it later.

An experienced adviser tells of having led a government battalion in a ferocious all-night battle while its commander hid in a foxhole. The next morning, the commander emerged, shook himself and ordered his men to move out. When the American suggested that a less bunched-up formation might be better, the commander coldly ignored him.

At bottom, American officers say when they know that they will not be quoted by name, the trouble with the South Vietnamese army is a lack of leadership. The fighting men are tough, willing and courageous, but like soldiers everywhere, they are worthless if badly led and poorly motivated.

Most Talented Men Are Lost to the Cause

The lack of leaders is heartbreaking to those who would reform the army. The best talent in the current generation has long since been lost: thousands of men who might be leading South Vietnamese troops in combat are serving with the North Vietnamese or the Vietcong, heirs to the country's nationalist revolution against the French. Of all the government officers serving as lieutenant colonel or higher, only two fought on the side of the Vietminh in the war against the French.

Some potential leaders are languishing in exile as a result of the purges of the last decade. Countless others have been killed in battle. In their place stands a corps of young officers, often incompetent and more often corrupt. Weary of the war and cynical toward it, many of them work a four-and-a-half-day week, leaving their troops at noon Friday and repairing to Can Tho or Da Nang or Saigon in search of diversion. It is not uncommon to see two dozen off-duty army officers taking their ease of a Saturday night in Maxim's, a frightfully expensive Saigon nightclub.

Watching one such group drive through town in a long black car recently, a Vietnamese student commented, "Nguyen Huu Tho doesn't live like that." Mr. Tho is chairman of the National Liberation Front, the political arm of the Vietcong.

Saigon's army hardly seems a likely force to lead a revolution, and whatever can be said of the army can be said of the government as well, for the army is the government.

If the villagers resent soldiers who steal their rice and chickens, they resent far more the corrupt district and province officials, nearly all of them military men. They resent, for example, the delta province chief whose waterworks and electrical plant serve his headquarters and his house but not a single peasant hut, and they resent the highlands province chief who sold them diseased pigs, bought with American aid funds, at enormous profit to himself.

Tales of Corruption Abound in Saigon

The corruption—the sense of a diseased society—is most pervasive in Saigon. Many of the stories that float through the city's cafes are no doubt false; but in a sense, that does not matter because most of the people believe them.

This belief is a major political fact, contributing to cynicism and noncommitment. Conceivably General X's wife did not buy and sell draft deferments, but everyone said she did. The question has been asked: Is it reasonable to expect young men to volunteer eagerly to fight for their country in this kind of atmosphere?

La Thanh Nghe, a former cabinet minister, is accused of having sold antibiotics to the Vietcong and, at the same time of having earned almost a million dollars in kickbacks from American drug suppliers. Policemen on duty at night along Tu Do Street tell a journalist that they will need $3 to be sure his car is not towed away. Clerks on the piers, unable to locate the papers needed to clear a shipment through customs, suddenly find them when $10 passes across the counter.

Added to this is a civil service so weary, so undermanned, so bogged down in antique French techniques—18 seals and signatures are required on one car-ownership document—that the tiniest tasks require weeks.

This is the system through which the pacification campaign must be made to work, through which the army must be reformed, the economy must be managed, the hearts and minds of the people must somehow be won.

FOUR KENT STATE STUDENTS KILLED BY TROOPS

By JOHN KIFNER, MAY 5, 1970

F our students at Kent State University, two of them women, were shot to death this afternoon by a volley of National Guard gunfire. At least eight other students were wounded.

The burst of gunfire came about 20 minutes after the guardsmen broke up a noon rally on the Commons, a grassy campus gathering spot, by lobbing tear gas at a crowd of about 1,000 young people.

In Washington, President Nixon deplored the deaths of the four students in the following statement:

"This should remind us all once again that when dissent turns to violence it invites tragedy. It is my hope that this tragic and unfortunate incident will strengthen the determination of all the nation's campuses, administrators, faculty and students alike to stand firmly for the right which exists in this country of peaceful dissent and just as strong against the resort to violence as a means of such expression."

In Columbus, Sylvester Del Corso, adjutant general of the Ohio National Guard, said in a statement that the guardsmen had been forced to shoot after a sniper opened fire against the troops from a nearby rooftop and the crowd began to move to encircle the guardsmen.

> *"This should remind us all once again that when dissent turns to violence it invites tragedy."*

Frederick P. Wenger, the assistant adjutant general, said the troops had opened fire after they were shot at by a sniper.

"They were understanding orders to take cover and return any fire," he said.

This reporter, who was with the group of students, did not see any indication of sniper fire, nor was the sound of any gunfire audible before the guard volley. Students, conceding that rocks had been thrown, heatedly denied that there was any sniper.

Gov. James A. Rhodes called on J. Edgar Hoover, director of the Federal Bureau of Investigation, to aid in looking into the campus violence. A Justice Department spokesman said no decision had been made to investigate. At 2:10 this afternoon, after the shootings, the university president, Robert I. White, ordered the university closed for an indefinite time, and officials were making plans to evacuate the dormitories and bus out-of-state students to nearby cities.

Robinson Memorial Hospital identified the dead students as Allison Krause, 19 years old, of Pittsburgh; Sandra Lee Scheuer, 20, of Youngstown, Ohio, both coeds; Jeffrey Glenn Miller, 20, of 22 Diamond Drive, Plainview, L.I., and William K. Schroeder, 19, of Lorain, Ohio.

At 10:30 p.m. the hospital said that six students had been treated for gunshot wounds. Three were reported in critical condition and three in fair condition. Two others with superficial wounds were treated and released.

Students here, angered by the expansion of the war into Cambodia, have held demonstrations for the last three nights. On Saturday night, the Army Reserve Officers Training Corps building was burned to the ground and the guard was called in and martial law was declared.

Today's rally, called after a night in which the police and guardsmen drove students into their dormitories and made 69 arrests, began as students rang the iron victory bell on the Commons, normally used to herald football victories.

A National Guard jeep drove onto the Commons and an officer ordered the crowd to disperse. Then several canisters of tear gas were fired, and the students straggled up a hill that borders the area and retreated into buildings.

A platoon of guardsmen, armed—as they have been since they arrived here with loaded M1 rifles and gas equipment—moved across the green and over the crest of the hill, chasing the main body of protesters.

The youths split into two groups, one heading farther downhill toward a dormitory complex, the other eddying around a parking lot and girls' dormitory just below Taylor Hall, the architecture building.

COMMUNISTS TAKE OVER SAIGON; U.S. RESCUE FLEET IS PICKING UP VIETNAMESE WHO FLED IN BOATS

By GEORGE ESPER, MAY 1, 1975

C ommunist troops of North Vietnam and the Provisional Revolutionary Government of South Vietnam poured into Saigon today as a century of Western influences came to an end.

Scores of North Vietnamese tanks, armored vehicles and camouflaged Chinese-built trucks rolled to the presidential palace.

The president of the former non-Communist government of South Vietnam, Gen. Duong Van Minh, who had gone on radio and television to announce his administration's surrender, was taken to a microphone later by North Vietnamese soldiers for another announcement. He appealed to all Saigon troops to lay down their arms and was taken by the North Vietnamese soldiers to an undisclosed destination.

[Soon after, the Saigon radio fell silent, normal telephone and telegraph communications ceased and the Associated Press said its wire link to the capital was lost at 7 p.m., Wednesday, Saigon time (7 a.m. Wednesday, New York time).

[In Paris, representatives of the Provisional Revolutionary Government announced that Saigon had been renamed Ho Chi Minh City in honor of the late president of North Vietnam. Other representatives said in a broadcast monitored in Thailand that former government forces in eight provinces south of the capital had not yet surrendered, but no fighting was mentioned.]

A North Vietnamese tank rolls through the gates of the presidential palace in Saigon as the city falls, April 30, 1975.

The transfer of power was symbolized by the raising of the flag of the National Liberation Front over the presidential palace at 12:15 p.m. today, about two hours after General Minh's surrender broadcast.

Hundreds in Saigon Cheer

Hundreds of Saigon residents cheered and applauded as North Vietnamese military vehicles moved to the palace grounds from which the war against the Communists had been directed by President Nguyen Van Thieu, who resigned April 21, and by President Ngo Dinh Diem, who was killed in a coup in 1963.

Broadcasting today in the early hours of the Communist takeover, the Provisional Revolutionary Government's representatives said:

"We representatives of the liberation forces of Saigon formally proclaim that Saigon had been totally liberated. We accept the unconditional surrender of Gen. Duong Van Minh, president of the former government."

Colonel Shoots Himself

Meanwhile, many former soldiers sought to lose themselves in the populace. However, one police colonel walked up to an army memorial statue, saluted and shot himself. He died later in the hospital.

Shots rang out at one point around the City Hall. A North Vietnamese infantry platoon, dressed in olive-drab uniforms and black rubber sandals, took up defense positions in the square in front of the building. They exchanged shots with a few holdouts. Some people on motorbikes looked apprehensively to see where the firing was coming from. In a short while it subsided.

Coastal Ships Jammed

Between General Minh's surrender broadcast and the entry of the Communist forces into the city, South Vietnamese soldiers and civilians jammed aboard several coastal freighters tied up along the Saigon River, hoping to escape. They dejectedly left the ships as the Communist troops drove along the waterfront in jeeps and trucks, waving National Liberation Front flags and cheering.

As the Communist troops drove past, knots of civilians stood in doorways and watched without apparent emotion. Later, as more North Vietnamese troops poured into the city, many people began cheering.

Ky Nhan, a Vietnamese who had been submitting photographs to the Associated Press for three years, came to the agency's office with a Communist friend and two North Vietnamese soldiers and said, "I guarantee the safety of everybody here."

"I have been a revolutionary for 10 years," said Mr. Nhan. "My job in the Vietcong was liaison with the international press."

This correspondent served them Coca-Cola and some leftover cake.

One of the soldiers, a 25-year-old sergeant named Binh Huan Lam, said he was from Hanoi and had been a soldier for 10 years.

"I have not married because it was not necessary during the war," he said.

Arrival Described

After smoking a cigarette, Tran Viet Ca, a 24-year-old private, told the Americans he had served seven years in the North Vietnamese Army.

"Two days ago we attacked Bien Hoa," he said. "Today we drove down the highway past the United States Army base at Long Binh. Our forces were led by a brigade of tanks. There was a little resistance, but most Saigon soldiers had already run away. Then we drove into Saigon."

Loud explosions were heard in the late afternoon in Saigon. They were said to have taken place aboard an ammunition barge burning in the Saigon River, but no damage was reported in the city except at the United States Embassy and other American buildings, which Saigonese looted. At the embassy they took virtually everything, including the kitchen sinks and a machine to shred secret documents.

A bronze plaque with the names of five American servicemen who died in a 1968 attack by Communist guerrillas was torn from the lobby wall. An Associated Press correspondent retrieved it.

Another memento from the embassy that was saved was a color portrait of former president Richard M. Nixon and his family, inscribed "To Ambassador and Mrs. Graham Martin with appreciation for their service to the nation. From Richard Nixon."

A French businessman who said he was taking refuge in the New Zealand Embassy grabbed the picture.

"I know the ambassador," he said. "I will personally deliver it to him in the United States sometime in the future."

Outside the embassy, Thong Nhut Boulevard was littered with burned cars.

NIXON TRIED TO SPOIL JOHNSON'S VIETNAM PEACE TALKS IN '68, NOTES SHOW

By PETER BAKER, JANUARY 2, 2017

Richard M. Nixon told an aide that they should find a way to secretly "monkey wrench" peace talks in Vietnam in the waning days of the 1968 campaign for fear that progress toward ending the war would hurt his chances for the presidency, according to newly discovered notes.

In a telephone conversation with H. R. Haldeman, who would go on to become White House chief of staff, Nixon gave instructions that a friendly intermediary should keep "working on" South Vietnamese leaders to persuade them not to agree to a deal before the election, according to the notes, taken by Mr. Haldeman.

The Nixon campaign's clandestine effort to thwart President Lyndon B. Johnson's peace initiative that fall has long been a source of controversy and scholarship. Ample evidence has emerged documenting the involvement of Nixon's campaign. But Mr. Haldeman's notes appear to confirm longstanding suspicions that Nixon himself was directly involved, despite his later denials.

"There's really no doubt this was a step beyond the normal political jockeying, to interfere in an active peace negotiation given the stakes with all the lives," said John A. Farrell, who discovered the notes at the Richard Nixon Presidential Library for his forthcoming biography, *Richard Nixon: The Life,* to be published in March by Doubleday. "Potentially, this is worse than anything he did in Watergate."

Mr. Farrell, in an article in *The New York Times'* Sunday Review over the weekend, highlighted the notes by Mr. Haldeman, along with many of Nixon's fulsome denials of any efforts to thwart the peace process before the election.

Mr. Farrell's discovery, according to numerous historians who have written books about Nixon and conducted extensive research of his papers, finally provides validation of what had largely been surmise.

While overshadowed by Watergate, the Nixon campaign's intervention in the peace talks has captivated historians for years. At times resembling a Hollywood thriller, the story involves colorful characters, secret liaisons, bitter rivalries and plenty of lying and spying. Whether it changed the course of history remains open to debate, but at the very least it encapsulated an almost-anything-goes approach that characterized the nation's politics in that era.

95

As the Republican candidate in 1968, Nixon was convinced that Johnson, a Democrat who decided not to seek reelection, was deliberately trying to sabotage his campaign with a politically motivated peace effort meant mainly to boost the candidacy of his vice president, Hubert H. Humphrey. His suspicions were understandable, and at least one of Johnson's aides later acknowledged that they were anxious to make progress before the election to help Mr. Humphrey.

Through much of the campaign, the Nixon team maintained a secret channel to the South Vietnamese through Anna Chennault, widow of Claire Lee Chennault, leader of the Flying Tigers in China during World War II. Mrs. Chennault had become a prominent Republican fund-raiser and Washington hostess.

Nixon met with Mrs. Chennault and the South Vietnamese ambassador earlier in the year to make clear that she was the campaign's "sole representative" to the Saigon government. But whether he knew what came later has always been uncertain. She was the conduit for urging the South Vietnamese to resist Johnson's entreaties to join the Paris talks and wait for a better deal under Nixon. At one point, she told the ambassador she had a message from "her boss": "Hold on, we are gonna win."

> *The Nixon team maintained a secret channel to the South Vietnamese through Anna Chennault.*

Learning of this through wiretaps and surveillance, Johnson was livid. He ordered more bugs and privately groused that Nixon's behavior amounted to "treason." But lacking hard evidence that Nixon was directly involved, Johnson opted not to go public.

The notes Mr. Farrell found come from a phone call on Oct. 22, 1968, as Johnson prepared to order a pause in the bombing to encourage peace talks in Paris. Scribbling down what Nixon was telling him, Mr. Haldeman wrote, "Keep Anna Chennault working on SVN," or South Vietnam.

A little later, he wrote that Nixon wanted Senator Everett Dirksen, a Republican from Illinois, to call the president and denounce the planned bombing pause. "Any other way to monkey wrench it?" Mr. Haldeman wrote. "Anything RN can do."

Nixon added later that Spiro T. Agnew, his vice-presidential running mate, should contact Richard Helms, the director of the Central Intelligence Agency, and threaten not to keep him on in a new administration if he did not provide more inside information. "Go see Helms," Mr. Haldeman wrote. "Tell him we want the truth—or he hasn't got the job."

After leaving office, Nixon denied knowing about Mrs. Chennault's messages to the South Vietnamese late in the 1968 campaign, despite proof that she had been in touch with John N. Mitchell, Mr. Nixon's campaign manager and later attorney general.

Other Nixon scholars called Mr. Farrell's discovery a breakthrough. Robert Dallek, an author of books on Nixon and Johnson, said the notes "seem to confirm suspicions" of Nixon's involvement in violation of federal law. Evan Thomas, the author of *Being Nixon*, said Mr. Farrell had "nailed down what has been talked about for a long time."

Ken Hughes, a researcher at the Miller Center of the University of Virginia, who in 2014 published *Chasing Shadows*, a book about the episode, said Mr. Farrell had found a smoking gun. "This appears to be the missing piece of the puzzle in the Chennault affair," Mr. Hughes said. The notes "show that Nixon committed a crime to win the presidential election."

Still, as tantalizing as they are, the notes do not reveal what, if anything, Mr. Haldeman actually did with the instruction, and it is unclear that the South Vietnamese needed to be told to resist joining peace talks that they considered disadvantageous already.

Moreover, it cannot be said definitively whether a peace deal could have been reached without Nixon's intervention or that it would have helped Mr. Humphrey. William P. Bundy, a foreign affairs adviser to Johnson and John F. Kennedy who was highly critical of Nixon, nonetheless concluded that prospects for the peace deal were slim anyway, so "probably no great chance was lost."

Luke A. Nichter, a scholar at Texas A&M University and one of the foremost students of the Nixon White House secret tape recordings, said he liked more of Mr. Farrell's book than not, but disagreed with the conclusions about Mr. Haldeman's notes. In his view, they do not prove anything new and are too thin to draw larger conclusions.

"Because sabotaging the '68 peace efforts seems like a Nixon-like thing to do, we are willing to accept a very low bar of evidence on this," Mr. Nichter said.

Tom Charles Huston, a Nixon aide who investigated the affair years ago, found no definitive proof that the future president was involved but concluded that it was reasonable to infer he was because of Mr. Mitchell's role. Responding to Mr. Farrell's findings, Mr. Huston wrote on Facebook that the latest notes still do not fully answer the question.

The notes, he wrote, "reinforce the inference but don't push us over the line into a necessary verdict." Critics, he added, ignore that there was little chance of a peace deal, believing that "it is irrelevant that Saigon would have walked away without intervention by the Nixon campaign." In effect, he said, "they wish to try RN for thought crimes."

An open question is whether Johnson, if he had had proof of Nixon's personal involvement, would have publicized it before the election.

Tom Johnson, the notetaker in White House meetings about this episode, said that the president considered the Nixon campaign's actions to be treasonous but that no direct link to Nixon was established until Mr. Farrell's discovery.

"It is my personal view that disclosure of the Nixon-sanctioned actions by Mrs. Chennault would have been so explosive and damaging to the Nixon 1968 campaign that Hubert Humphrey would have been elected president," said Mr. Johnson, who went on to become the publisher of *The Los Angeles Times* and later chief executive of CNN.

Mr. Farrell found the notes amid papers that were made public by the Nixon library in July 2007 after the Nixon estate gave them back.

Timothy Naftali, a former director of the Nixon library, said the notes "remove the fig leaf of plausible deniability" of the former president's involvement. The episode would set the tone for the administration that would follow. "This covert action by the Nixon campaign," he said, "laid the ground for the skulduggery of his presidency."

COLD WAR

BRITON SPEAKS OUT

By HAROLD B. HINTON, MARCH 6, 1946

Afraternal association between the British Empire and the United States was advocated here today by Winston Churchill to stem "the expansive and proselytizing tendencies" of the Soviet Union.

Introduced by President Truman at Westminster College, Great Britain's wartime prime minister asserted that a mere balance of power in the world today would be too narrow a margin and would only offer "temptations to a trial of strength."

On the contrary, he added that the English-speaking peoples must maintain an overwhelming preponderance of power on their side until "the highroads of the future will be clear, not only for our time but for a century to come."

Says Curtain Divides Europe

Mr. Churchill painted a dark picture of postwar Europe, on which "an iron curtain has descended across the continent" from Stettin in the Baltic to Trieste in the Adriatic.

Warsaw, Berlin, Prague, Vienna, Budapest, Belgrade, Sofia and Bucharest are all being subjected to increasing pressure and control from Moscow, he said, adding:

Winston Churchill during his famous "Iron Curtain" speech at Westminster College, Fulton, Mo., March 5, 1946.

"This is certainly not the liberated Europe we fought to build up. Nor is it one which contains the essentials of permanent peace."

Even in front of the "iron curtain," he asserted, Italy was hampered in its efforts to return to a normal national existence by "Communist-trained Marshal Tito's claims to former Italian territory," and the reestablishment of a strong France was impeded by fifth columns working "in complete unity and absolute obedience to the directions they receive from the Communist center."

He strongly intimated a parallel between the present position of the Soviet Union with that of Germany in 1935, when, he said, "Germany might have been saved from the awful fate which has overtaken her and we might all have been spared the miseries Hitler let loose upon mankind without a single shot being fired."

But time is running short, he warned, if the world is not "to try to learn again, for a third time, in a school of war incomparably more rigorous than that from which we have just been released."

His words, he continued, were not offered in the belief that war with the Soviet Union was inevitable or imminent. He expressed the view that Russia does not desire war, but cautioned that Moscow does desire the fruits of war and the indefinite expansion of its power and policies.

Appeasement Is Opposed

The difficulties of the Western democracies, he said, will not be removed by closing their eyes to them, by waiting to see what happens or by a policy of appeasement.

Expressing admiration and regard for Marshal Stalin, Mr. Churchill asserted that the English-speaking peoples understood Russia's need to secure her western frontiers against renewed German aggression and welcomed Russia into her rightful place among the leading countries of the world.

From his experience with them, he said that he learned that Russians admired nothing so much as strength, and that they had no respect for military weakness.

Given an overwhelming show of strength on the side of upholding the principles of the United Nations Organization, Mr. Churchill asserted, the Soviet Union would be prepared to come to a settlement of outstanding differences with the Western world.

He suggested that the secret of the atomic bomb be kept in the hands of the United States, Great Britain and Canada, because "it would be imprudent and wrong" to confide it to the U.N.O., while that organization was "still in its infancy."

He said that no one in the world had slept less well because the atomic secret was in its present custody, but the people of the world would not rest so soundly if that secret were possessed by "some Communist or neo-Fascist state."

He also called for immediate establishment of a U.N.O. air force, to be made up of a number of squadrons from member countries capable of supplying them. These squadrons would be trained and equipped at home, but would be stationed abroad. They would not be required to go into action against their own country, but would otherwise be at the orders of the U.N.O. Although he expressed confidence in the ultimate ability of the U.N.O. to preserve the peace of the world, Mr. Churchill said that it must become "a true temple of peace" and not "merely a cockpit in the Tower of Babel."

Comparing its inception with that of the League of Nations, he regretted that he could not "see or feel the same confidence or even the same hopes in the haggard world at this time."

The fraternal association he advocated between the British Empire and the United States would include interchange of officers and cadets among the military schools of the associates, similarity of weapons and training manuals, common war plans, joint use of all naval and air bases and intimate relationships among high military advisers.

With this potential strength behind them, he said, the English-speaking peoples could reach "now, in 1946, a good understanding on all points with Russia."

The special relationships of the type he urged, Mr. Churchill argued, would be fully consistent with loyalty to the U.N.O. He recalled the special relations between the United States and Canada, the United States and the other American republics, and the 20-year treaty between Great Britain and Russia (he interjected that "I agree with Mr. Bevin [British Foreign Minister] that it might well be a 50-year treaty") as examples of international cooperation which serve to buttress, not undermine, the peace of the world.

The United States now stands at the pinnacle of world power, Mr. Churchill asserted, and shares with the other English-speaking peoples what he described as the overall strategic concept of "the safety and welfare, the freedom and progress of all the homes and families of all the men and women in all the lands."

For the United States to ignore or fritter away its "clear and shining" opportunity would be to "bring upon us all the long reproaches of the after-time," he added.

Turning to the Far East, Mr. Churchill called the outlook there "anxious," especially in Manchuria, despite the aspects of the Yalta agreement, to which he was a party.

He defended the agreement on the ground that the war with Germany was then expected to last until the autumn of 1945, with the war against Japan calculated to endure 18 months after that.

Mr. Churchill gave his listeners the impression that he and President Roosevelt would not have dealt so generously with Marshal Stalin, had they realized that collapse of the Axis was near at hand.

War and tyranny were the twin evils Mr. Churchill saw threatening the world today. He looked for the hunger and distress now afflicting so much of the world to pass fairly quickly, and for "the inauguration and enjoyment of an age of plenty."

"Nothing can stand in the way of such an outcome," he said, except "human folly or subhuman crime."

Mr. Churchill described himself as a "private visitor" with no official mission or status of any kind, and as a man whose early private ambitions had been satisfied beyond his wildest dreams.

He said that Mr. Truman had granted him full liberty "to give you my true and faithful counsel in these anxious and baffling times."

In his introduction, the president said that he and Mr. Churchill both believed in freedom of speech, adding:

"I know he will have something constructive to say."

When Mr. Truman later took the platform to acknowledge the doctorate of laws which Westminster conferred on him, as well as on Mr. Churchill, he told the audience that it was "your moral duty and mine to see that the Charter of the United Nations is implemented as the law of the land and the law of the world."

The president, however, made no direct reference to the "fraternal association" Mr. Churchill suggested.

"We are either headed for complete destruction or are facing the greatest age in history," Mr. Truman said, adding:

"It is up to you to decide, and up to me to see that we follow that path toward that great age and not toward destruction.

"The release of atomic energy has given us a force which means the happiness and welfare of every human being on Earth or the destruction of civilization.

"I prefer to think we have the ability, the moral stamina and the energy to see that the great age comes about, not destruction."

Churchill Drops Serious Note

When it came Mr. Churchill's turn to thank Dr. Franc Lewis McCluer, the faculty and trustees of Westminster College for the honor they conferred on him, he dropped the serious tenor of his earlier address and made the following remarks:

"Mr. President, President McCluer, members of the faculty: I am not sure that I may say fellow members of the faculty. I am most grateful, and through you to the authorities of the state of Missouri and to the college authorities, for their great kindness in that conferring upon me another of these degrees, which I value so highly and, as I was saying only the other day at Miami, which have a double attraction to me, that they do not require any preliminary examinations.

"I value very much this token of goodwill which comes from this center of education in the very heart of the United States and in the state which is so dear to the heart of the president of this great country.

"I also thank you all here for the great patience, indulgence, kindness and attention to listen to what I had to say, for I am quite sure it will have been right and wise to say at this juncture. I am very glad to have had this opportunity and am grateful to all who have come here and assisted me to discharge my task.

"I am, of course, unswerving in my allegiance to my own king and country, but I can never feel entirely a foreigner in the United States, which is my motherland and where my ancestors, forebears on that side of the family for five generations, have lived.

"I was, however, a little puzzled the other day when one branch of the Sons of the Revolution invited me to become a member, on the grounds that my forebears undoubtedly fought in Washington's armies.

"I felt on the whole that I was on both sides then, and therefore I should adopt as far as possible an unbiased attitude. But I may justly tell you how proud is my love for this great and mighty nation and empire of the United States."

This was a gala day in Fulton and Jefferson City, the state capital, where the president and Mr. Churchill left their train. In both towns the motor cavalcade drove slowly around the principal streets, which were lined with spectators.

Police estimated that the normal population of 8,000 turned out in Fulton and was augmented by some 20,000 visitors who had come from as far distant as St. Louis.

Dr. McCluer entertained the president and Mr. Churchill with the members of their immediate party at luncheon in his home on the campus before the ceremonies.

The president and Mr. Churchill marched into the gymnasium at the end of the long academic procession. Mr. Truman wore the hood indicating the honorary doctorate of laws conferred on him last summer by the University of Kansas City, while Mr. Churchill wore a scarlet hood indicating an Oxford degree.

Mr. Churchill's speech was received with marked applause in the passages where it dealt with the responsibility of this country to see that another World War was avoided, but the proposal for "fraternal association" brought only moderate handclapping.

U.S. AND SOVIET REACH ACCORD ON CUBA; CAPITAL HOPEFUL

By E. W. KENWORTHY, OCTOBER 29, 1962

President Kennedy and Premier Khrushchev reached apparent agreement today on a formula to end the crisis over Cuba and to begin talks on easing tensions in other areas.

Premier Khrushchev pledged the Soviet Union to stop work on its missile sites in Cuba, to dismantle the weapons and to crate them and take them home. All this would be done under verification of United Nations representatives.

President Kennedy, for his part, pledged the lifting of the Cuban arms blockade when the United Nations had taken the "necessary measures," and that the United States would not invade Cuba.

President John F. Kennedy signs the order for the Cuban blockade in the Oval Office, October, 23, 1962.

U.S. Conditions Met

Essentially this formula meets the conditions that President Kennedy set for the beginning of talks. If it is carried out, it would achieve the objective of the president in establishing the blockade last week: the removal of Soviet missile bases in Cuba.

While officials were gratified at the agreement reached on United States terms, there was no sense either of triumph or jubilation. The agreement, they realized, was only the beginning. The terms of it were not nailed down and Soviet negotiators were expected to arrive at the United Nations with a "bag full of fine print."

Although Mr. Khrushchev mentioned verification of the dismantling by United Nations observers in today's note, sources here do not consider it unlikely that the Russians may suggest that the observers be under the procedures of the Security Council.

This would make their findings subject to a veto by the Soviet Union as 1 of the 11 members of the Council.

No Big Gains Envisioned

United States officials did not expect a Cuban settlement, if it materialized, to lead to any great breakthroughs on such problems as inspection for a nuclear test ban and disarmament. On the other hand, it was thought possible that a Cuban settlement might set a precedent for limited reciprocal concessions in some areas.

The break in the crisis came dramatically early this morning after a night of steadily mounting fears that events were running ahead of diplomatic efforts to control them.

RAZE BERLIN WALL, REAGAN URGES SOVIET

By GERALD M. BOYD, JUNE 13, 1987

President Reagan sought today to undercut Europe's perception of Mikhail S. Gorbachev as a leader of peace, bluntly challenging the Soviet leader to tear down the Berlin Wall.

Speaking 100 yards from the wall that was thrown up in 1961 to thwart an exodus to the West, Mr. Reagan made the wall a metaphor for ideological and economic differences separating East and West.

"There is one sign the Soviets can make that would be unmistakable, that would advance dramatically the cause of freedom and peace," the president said.

"Secretary General Gorbachev, if you seek peace—if you seek prosperity for the Soviet Union and Eastern Europe—if you seek liberalization: come here, to this gate.

"Mr. Gorbachev, open this gate.

"Mr. Gorbachev, tear down this wall."

Mr. Reagan made the remarks with the Brandenburg Gate in East Berlin in the background. An East Berlin security post was in view.

The Berlin police estimated that 20,000 people had turned out to hear the president, but some observers thought the crowd was smaller than that.

The Soviet press agency TASS said that Mr. Reagan, by calling for destruction of the wall, had given an "openly provocative, war-mongering speech" reminiscent of the Cold War.

Reagan Peers into East Berlin

Before the speech, Mr. Reagan peered across the wall from a balcony of the old Reichstag building into East Berlin, where a patrol boat and a gray brick sentry post were visible. Later, when asked how he felt, he said, "I think it's an ugly scar."

Asked how he regarded a perception among some people in Europe that Mr. Gorbachev was more committed to peace, Mr. Reagan said, "They just have to learn, don't they?"

Administration officials had portrayed the speech as a major policy statement. But the main new initiative was a call to the Soviet Union to assist in helping Berlin become an aviation hub of Central Europe by agreeing to make commercial air service more convenient.

Some Reagan advisers wanted an address with less polemics but lost to those who favored use of the opportunity to raise East-West differences and questions about Mr. Gorbachev's commitment to ending the nuclear arms race and his internal liberalization policies.

President Ronald Reagan acknowledges the crowd after his speech in front of the Brandenburg Gate in West Berlin, on June 12, 1987, where he exclaimed "Mr. Gorbachev, tear down this wall!" Applauding Reagan are West German Chancellor Helmut Kohl (right) and West German Parliament President Philipp Jenninger (left).

"In Europe, only one nation and those it controls refuse to join the community of freedom," Mr. Reagan said. "Yet, in this age of redoubled economic growth of information and innovation, the Soviet Union faces a choice. It must make fundamental changes or it will become obsolete."

Shield of Bulletproof Glass

Speaking with two panes of bulletproof glass shielding him from East Berlin, Mr. Reagan stressed themes of freedom and a peaceful reunification of Berlin.

These were points made by President Kennedy in his "Ich bin ein Berliner" speech two years after the wall was built.

"Standing before the Brandenburg Gate, every man is a German, separated from his fellow men," Mr. Reagan said. "Every man is a Berliner, forced to look upon a scar."

Using this speech to portray Moscow as the villain in the arms race, Mr. Reagan said 10 years ago it had challenged the Western alliance with a "grave new threat" by deploying SS-20 nuclear missiles that could strike West European capitals. But, Mr. Reagan said, the alliance remained strong and had deployed Pershing II and cruise missiles, so the prospects for eliminating such nuclear weapons is "within the reach of possibility."

"While we pursue these arms reductions, I pledge to you that we will maintain the capacity to deter Soviet aggression at any level at which it might occur," he said.

Mr. Reagan, whose speech was broadcast to West European countries, said it was unclear whether Mr. Gorbachev's campaign of liberalization represented "profound changes" or "token changes."

The wall has been an attractive symbol to American presidents, including Mr. Kennedy and Jimmy Carter.

Taking note of that pattern, Mr. Reagan said, "We come to Berlin, we American presidents, because it is our duty to speak in this place of freedom."

The trip, in which Mr. Reagan also took part in a ceremony celebrating Berlin's 750th anniversary, provided the president with a lift at the end of the economic summit meeting in Venice of the seven major industrialized democracies.

At the end of a second event in Berlin, at Tempelhof Airport, miniature parachutes rained down as symbols of the 1948–49 airlift that kept the city alive during a Soviet land blockade.

Greeted by Kohl

Chancellor Helmut Kohl of West Germany greeted the president and then flew aboard Air Force One to Bonn to receive him there.

Speaking before the president, Mr. Kohl said that the countries of the Soviet bloc's Warsaw Pact "must abandon their conventional superiority and their aggressive military doctrine."

Suggesting Berlin as a start for cooperation between East and West, Mr. Reagan urged international meetings, summer exchanges of youngsters from West Berlin and East Berlin, culture exchanges and sports events, including Olympic Games jointly in the two countries.

Several times, Mr. Reagan addressed the Germans in their language. In one case, Mr. Reagan made a special appeal to East Berliners by saying, "Es gibt nur ein Berlin," or "There is only one Berlin."

He began his remarks by quoting from a popular old song: "I come here today because wherever I go, whatever I do: 'Ich hab', noch einen Koffer in Berlin,' or 'I still have a suitcase in Berlin.'"

NOTE: *Reagan's defiance of the Soviet Union, and his policy of spending trillions on American and West European defense programs, certainly hastened the fall of the Communist bloc. But these strategies also worsened the deficit spending that paid for such programs and led to decades of Americans struggling to get out of the hole Reagan dug.*

U.S. TO RESTORE FULL RELATIONS WITH CUBA, ERASING A LAST TRACE OF COLD WAR HOSTILITY

By PETER BAKER, DECEMBER 17, 2014

President Obama on Wednesday ordered the restoration of full diplomatic relations with Cuba and the opening of an embassy in Havana for the first time in more than a half century as he vowed to "cut loose the shackles of the past" and sweep aside one of the last vestiges of the Cold War.

The surprise announcement came at the end of 18 months of secret talks that produced a prisoner swap negotiated with the help of Pope Francis and concluded by a telephone call between Mr. Obama and President Raúl Castro. The historic deal broke an enduring stalemate between two countries divided by just 90 miles of water but oceans of mistrust and hostility dating from the days of Theodore Roosevelt's charge up San Juan Hill and the nuclear brinkmanship of the Cuban Missile Crisis.

"We will end an outdated approach that for decades has failed to advance our interests, and instead we will begin to normalize relations between our two countries," Mr. Obama said in a nationally televised statement from the White House. The deal, he added, will "begin a new chapter among the nations of the Americas" and move beyond a "rigid policy that is rooted in events that took place before most of us were born."

In doing so, Mr. Obama ventured into diplomatic territory where the last 10 presidents refused to go, and Republicans, along with a senior Democrat, quickly characterized the rapprochement with the Castro family as appeasement of the hemisphere's leading dictatorship. Republican lawmakers who will take control of the Senate as well as the House next month made clear they would resist lifting the 54-year-old trade embargo.

"This entire policy shift announced today is based on an illusion, on a lie, the lie and the illusion that more commerce and access to money and goods will translate to political freedom for the Cuban people," said Senator Marco Rubio, a Republican from Florida and son of Cuban immigrants. "All this is going to do is give the Castro regime, which controls every aspect of Cuban life, the opportunity to manipulate these changes to perpetuate itself in power."

For good or ill, the move represented a dramatic turning point in relations with an island that for generations has captivated and vexed its giant northern neighbor. From the 18th century, when successive presidents coveted it, Cuba loomed large in the American imagination long before Fidel Castro stormed from the mountains and seized power in 1959.

Mr. Castro's alliance with the Soviet Union made Cuba a geopolitical flash point in a global struggle of ideology and power. President Dwight D. Eisenhower imposed the first trade embargo in 1960 and broke off diplomatic relations in January 1961, just weeks before leaving office and seven months before Mr. Obama was born. Under President John F. Kennedy, the failed Bay of Pigs operation aimed at toppling Mr. Castro in April 1961 and the 13-day showdown over Soviet missiles installed in Cuba the following year cemented its status as a ground zero in the Cold War.

But the relationship remained frozen in time long after the fall of the Berlin Wall and the collapse of the Soviet Union, a thorn in the side of multiple presidents who waited for Mr. Castro's demise and experienced false hope when he passed power to his brother, Raúl. Even as the United States built relations with Communist nations like China and Vietnam, Cuba remained one of just a few nations, along with Iran and North Korea, that had no formal ties with Washington.

Students celebrated in Havana after news that Washington had released three Cuban spies in a prisoner exchange.

Mr. Obama has long expressed hope of transforming relations with Cuba and relaxed some travel restrictions in 2011. But further moves remained untenable as long as Cuba held Alan P. Gross, an American

> *Mr. Obama has long expressed hope of transforming relations with Cuba.*

government contractor arrested in 2009 and sentenced to 15 years in a Cuban prison for trying to deliver satellite telephone equipment capable of cloaking connections to the internet.

After winning reelection, Mr. Obama resolved to make Cuba a priority for his second term and authorized secret negotiations led by two aides, Benjamin J. Rhodes and Ricardo Zúñiga, who conducted nine meetings with Cuban counterparts starting in June 2013, most of them in Canada, which has ties with Havana.

Pope Francis encouraged the talks with letters to Mr. Obama and Mr. Castro and had the Vatican host a meeting in October to finalize the terms of the deal. Mr. Obama spoke with Mr. Castro by telephone on Tuesday to seal the agreement in a call that lasted more than 45 minutes, the first direct substantive contact between the leaders of the two countries in more than 50 years.

On Wednesday morning, Mr. Gross walked out of a Cuban prison and boarded an American military plane that flew him to Washington, accompanied by his wife, Judy.

While eating a corned beef sandwich on rye bread with mustard during the flight, Mr. Gross received a call from Mr. Obama. "He's back where he belongs, in America with his family, home for Hanukkah," Mr. Obama said later.

For its part, the United States sent back three imprisoned Cuban spies who were caught in 1998 and had become a cause célèbre for the Havana government. They were swapped for Rolando Sarraff Trujillo, a Cuban who had worked as an agent for American intelligence and had been in a Cuban prison for nearly 20 years, according to a senior American official. Mr. Gross was not technically part of the swap, officials said, but was released separately on "humanitarian grounds," a distinction critics found unpersuasive.

The United States will ease restrictions on remittances, travel and banking, while Cuba will allow more internet access and release 53 Cubans identified as political prisoners by the United States. Although the embargo will remain in place, the president called for an "honest and serious debate about lifting" it, which would require an act of Congress.

Mr. Castro spoke simultaneously on Cuban television, taking to the airwaves with no introduction and announcing that he had spoken by telephone with Mr. Obama on Tuesday.

"We have been able to make headway in the solution of some topics of mutual interest for both nations," he declared, emphasizing the release of the three Cubans. "President Obama's decision deserves the respect and acknowledgment of our people."

Only afterward did Mr. Castro mention the reopening of diplomatic relations. "This in no way means that the heart of the matter has been resolved," he said. "The economic, commercial and financial blockade, which causes enormous human and economic damages to our country, must cease." But, he added, "the progress made in our exchanges proves that it is possible to find solutions to many problems."

Mr. Obama is gambling that restoring ties with Cuba may no longer be politically unthinkable with the generational shift among Cuban Americans, where many younger children of exiles are open to change. Nearly 6 in 10 Americans support reestablishing relations with Cuba, according to a *New York Times* poll conducted in October. Mr. Obama's move had the support of the Catholic Church, the U.S. Chamber of Commerce, Human Rights Watch and major agricultural interests.

At a news conference in Washington, Mr. Gross said he supported Mr. Obama's move toward normalizing relations with Cuba, adding that his own ordeal and the injustice with which Cuban people had been treated were "a consequence of two governments' mutually belligerent policies."

"Five and a half decades of history show us that such belligerence inhibits better judgment," he said. "Two wrongs never make a right. This is a game changer, which I fully support."

But leading Republicans, including Speaker John A. Boehner and the incoming Senate majority leader, Senator Mitch McConnell, did not. In addition to Mr. Rubio, two other Republican potential candidates for president joined in the criticism. Senator Ted Cruz of Texas called it a "very, very bad deal," while former governor Jeb Bush of Florida said it "undermines the quest for a free and democratic Cuba."

A leading Democrat agreed. "It is a fallacy that Cuba will reform just because the American president believes that if he extends his hand in peace, that the Castro brothers suddenly will unclench their fists," said Senator Robert Menendez of New Jersey, the outgoing chairman of the Foreign Relations Committee and a Cuban American.

While the United States has no embassy in Havana, there is a bare-bones facility called an interests section that can be upgraded, currently led by a diplomat, Jeffrey DeLaurentis, who will become the chargé d'affaires pending the nomination and confirmation of an ambassador.

Mr. Obama has instructed Secretary of State John Kerry to begin the process of removing Cuba from the list of states that sponsor terrorism, and the president announced that he would attend a regional Summit of the Americas next spring that Mr. Castro is also to attend. Mr. Obama will send an assistant secretary of state to Havana next month to talk about migration, and Commerce Secretary Penny Pritzker may lead a commercial mission.

Mr. Obama's decision will ease travel restrictions for family visits, public performances and professional, educational and religious activities, among other things, but ordinary tourism will still be banned under the law. Mr. Obama will also allow greater banking ties, making it possible to use credit and debit cards in Cuba, and American travelers will be allowed to import up to $400 worth of goods from Cuba, including up to $100 in tobacco and alcohol products.

"These 50 years have shown that isolation has not worked," Mr. Obama said. "It's time for a new approach."

He added that he shared the commitment to freedom for Cuba. "The question is how we uphold that commitment," he said. "I do not believe we can keep doing the same thing for over five decades and expect a different result."

NOTE: *As he did with most of Barack Obama's policies, Donald Trump set out to reverse the thaw in relations with Cuba, enacting a series of executive orders that reimposed travel restrictions and threw the political and economic lives of Cubans into uncertainty.*

ENDLESS WAR

REAGAN TAKES OATH AS 40TH PRESIDENT; PROMISES AN "ERA OF NATIONAL RENEWAL"— MINUTES LATER, 52 U.S. HOSTAGES IN IRAN FLY TO FREEDOM AFTER 444-DAY ORDEAL

By BERNARD GWERTZMAN, JANUARY 21, 1981

The 52 Americans who were held hostage by Iran for 444 days were flown to freedom yesterday. Jimmy Carter, a few hours after giving up the presidency, said that everyone "was alive, was well and free."

The flight ended the national ordeal that had frustrated Mr. Carter for most of his last 14 months in office, and it allowed Ronald Reagan to begin his term free of the burdens of the Iran crisis.

The Americans were escorted out of Iran by Algerian diplomats, aboard an Algerian airliner, underscoring Algeria's role in achieving the accord that allowed the hostages to return home.

Transferred to U.S. Custody

The Algerian plane, carrying the former hostages, stopped first in Athens to refuel. It then landed in Algiers, where custody of the 52 Americans was formally transferred by the Algerians to the representative of the United States, former deputy secretary of state Warren M. Christopher. He had negotiated much of the agreement freeing them.

They then boarded two United States Air Force hospital planes and flew to Frankfurt, West Germany, early this morning. They will stay at an American military hospital in nearby Wiesbaden, where they will be visited by Mr. Carter, as President Reagan's representative, later today. They will stay in Wiesbaden for a week or less to "decompress," as one official described it.

Iran hostage returnees land at the Rhein-Main U.S. Air Force base in Frankfurt, West Germany, January 21, 1981.

The 52 Americans were freed as part of a complex agreement that was not completed until early yesterday morning, when the last snags holding up their release were removed by Mr. Carter and his aides, in the final diplomatic action of their administration. Under the terms of the accord, as the Algerian plane left Iranian air space, nearly

$3 billion of Iranian assets that had been frozen by the United States were returned to Iran, and many more billions of dollars were made available for Iranian repayment of debts.

The 52 Americans were freed only minutes after Ronald Reagan was sworn in as the 40th president of the United States. The concurrence in timing held millions of Americans at their radios and television sets, following the pageantry of Inauguration Day and the news of the hostages' release.

Negotiations Were Intense

The negotiators, who had worked around the clock for five days in an effort to bring the crisis to an end before Mr. Carter left office, said that they had no idea whether the Iranians had deliberately dragged out the talks so as to insure that the hostages were not actually in the air until Mr. Reagan was president.

Mr. Reagan was informed that the Algerian plane carrying the hostages had left Iranian airspace as he was about to have lunch with the Congressional leadership at the Capitol after the inauguration ceremony.

"With thanks to almighty God, I have been given a tag line, the get-off line, that everyone wants for the end of a toast or a speech, or anything else," the president said after brief remarks. "Some 30 minutes ago, the Algerian planes bearing our prisoners left Iranian airspace and they're now free of Iran." Ringing applause drowned out his final remarks, and Mr. Reagan responded by lifting a glass of white California wine to his lips and drinking to the end of the crisis.

Drama Seized World's Attention

The end of the drama that has seized American and world attention for nearly 15 months evoked a jumble of emotions from the families of the 52, ranging from exhilaration to disbelief.

Anita Schaefer, wife of Col. Thomas E. Schaefer, who was the senior military officer in the embassy in Teheran when it was seized on Nov. 4, 1979, was told that the plane carrying the hostages had left Teheran by Mr. Carter at Andrews Air Force Base, only minutes before the former president boarded his plane for the trip home to Plains, Ga.

"Tom is in the air," Mr. Carter told her as they embraced, both crying. Mr. Carter, at Plains, said that while he was on Air Force One, "I had received word, officially, for the first time, that the aircraft carrying the 52 American hostages had cleared Iranian airspace on the first leg of the journey home and that every one of the 52 hostages was alive, was well and free."

He had hoped to fly to West Germany Monday, his last full day in office. But at Mr. Reagan's invitation, Mr. Carter, together with other senior members of his administration, will make the trip today. Former secretary of state Cyrus R. Vance had already gone to Wiesbaden to be there when the Americans arrive.

"Throughout this time of trial, we Americans have stood as one, united in our prayers, steadfast in our concern for fellow Americans in peril," Mr. Carter said.

"I doubt that at any time in our history more prayers have reached heaven for any Americans than have those given to God in the last 14 months."

> *"Americans have stood as one, united in our prayers."*

Carter administration officials have been very sensitive to allegations that the arrangement amounted to "ransom." This charge has been made by some Republicans and columnists—but not by Mr. Reagan—because the United States agreed to return Iran's frozen assets, to drop claims against Iran and to help Iran seek to recover the property of the late shah in the United States.

Yesterday afternoon, four hours after they were out of office, former secretary of state Edmund S. Muskie and former treasury secretary G. William Miller, as well as several other outgoing officials, took part in a news conference at the State Department that had been permitted by the Reagan administration.

Mr. Muskie stressed that "the assets returned are Iranian property" and that the terms of the agreement "were determined to be fair and technically feasible."

Aides to Mr. Carter have maintained that Iran was "punished" for the seizure of the hostages by having had its billions of dollars worth of assets frozen for nearly 15 months, and by being isolated politically and economically as a result of the crisis.

The hostages themselves, a virtual cross-section of this country, ranging from Ivy League Foreign Service officers to teenage enlisted men, were described by the Swiss ambassador in Teheran, Eric Lang, as having been very emotional at the airport there prior to departure.

"They were laughing and crying and hugging each other," he said. "Many of them could not believe they were on their way to freedom." The Swiss have represented the United States in Teheran, but in recent weeks the most significant help given the hostages was provided by Algeria, which at the request of Iran became the intermediary in three months of protracted negotiations.

Americans Examined by Doctors

As part of the agreement, worked out through the Algerians, the American hostages were turned over to Algerian custody, and they and their belongings were flown out on two Algerian aircraft. A third, and smaller, Algerian plane carried six doctors who had examined the Americans before their release.

The Americans were taken to Algiers not only as part of the arrangement but to demonstrate the United States government's gratitude for the Algerian efforts, State Department officials said.

The negotiations, which last month seemed on the verge of collapse when Iran demanded that the United States provide $24 billion in financial guarantees, picked up momentum in the last two weeks. The last five days were particularly active as diplomats and financial experts in Washington, Algiers, Teheran, London and New York worked around the clock to conclude the accord.

Early Monday morning, Mr. Christopher signed the formal agreement in Algiers and Behzad Nabavi, the chief Iranian negotiator, signed it in Teheran. That led to a sense of anticipation that the hostages would be freed late Monday.

But the Iranians objected to a document sent to Iran by the United States to allow the complex agreement to be put into effect. American officials said that there were several other snags in the final hours, as messages went back and forth through Algiers.

It was uncertain Monday night whether Mr. Carter would be able to bring about the hostage release during his presidency, but at about 3 a.m. yesterday, Jody Powell, Mr. Carter's spokesman, told a crowd of reporters at the White House that a formula had been agreed upon by Washington and Teheran on removing the last obstacle to the carrying out of the accord.

Under terms of the agreement, the 12 American banks holding frozen Iranian assets funneled them to the Federal Reserve Bank of New York. At about 6 a.m. the Federal Reserve sent nearly $8 billion to the Bank of England for a special escrow account in the name of the Algerian central bank.

By 7 a.m. the Algerians were able to notify Iran that they had possession of the frozen assets and that Iran was now obligated to release the American hostages to them.

This happened in the morning hours Washington time, which is eight and a half hours behind Teheran time. The hostages were then put aboard one of the two Boeing 727s that Algeria had sent there Monday, and their belongings on the other.

AFTER THE WAR: THE OVERVIEW; TRUCE HOLDS, BUT U.S. VOWS TO STAY IN IRAQ UNTIL BAGHDAD MEETS ALLIES' PEACE TERMS

By ANDREW ROSENTHAL, MARCH 1, 1991

A s war subsided into isolated skirmishing, the Bush administration said today that it would keep United States forces in southern Iraq until it was satisfied that Iraq would comply with American terms for a permanent cease-fire.

Administration officials said it could be many months, and perhaps even as much as a year, before the American force would withdraw from the Persian Gulf region. They said that some kind of long-term American military presence in the gulf appeared inevitable but declined to be more specific.

At the same time, the Bush administration moved to get the United Nations Security Council to endorse a resolution as early as Friday that would embody the demands of the United States and its allies, including the prompt return of all prisoners of war and an Iraqi promise to provide the location of land and sea mines planted by Baghdad's forces in Kuwait and the Persian Gulf.

Smoke from burning oil wells blankets the sky in Kuwait, March 1991.

Destruction of Tanks

Apparently eager to obtain a political settlement as decisive as the military victory, the allies today also introduced a new element by linking the withdrawal of allied forces from Iraq to the destruction of the tanks and other military equipment left behind on the battlefield by Iraqi forces.

The Baghdad government agreed overnight to abide by the 12 United Nations resolutions on Kuwait, as required by Mr. Bush and the coalition.

At the United Nations, diplomats said today that the United States and its Persian Gulf war allies plan to retain the right to attack Iraq again if it breaks their peace terms under the provisions of a new Security Council resolution they are drafting that would eventually convert the present "pause" in the fighting into a formal cease-fire.

Iraq Agrees to Meeting

Today, Iraq moved steadily toward meeting more of the allied conditions. In the latest step toward that goal since President Bush ordered a suspension of allied offensive actions at midnight Wednesday, Mr. Bush announced today that Iraq had agreed to send military officers to a meeting with commanders of the allied forces. The time and location of the meeting were not clear.

It was also not clear whether the allies had a firm commitment from Iraq to two other conditions: that Iraq immediately release prisoners of war and detained civilians, and reveal the location of all land and sea mines.

But Mr. Bush said he expected the commanders' meeting to take place "very soon" and a senior aide said the White House was viewing the Iraqi agreement to hold the meeting "in the most hopeful terms."

Before a meeting with the Kuwaiti ambassador at the White House, the president said he expects a "prompt repatriation" of prisoners of war, an issue that has been at the top of the Bush administration's agenda as it tries to carry the strong domestic support for the fight against Iraq into the postwar period.

A Vow on P.O.W.s

"We are going to get back our P.O.W.s and we're going to do it fast," Mr. Bush said.

But the White House did not offer as optimistic a forecast on another potentially troublesome political question—how long it will take to withdraw allied forces from the gulf.

Marlin Fitzwater, the White House spokesman, said that even the first token withdrawals of American troops would not begin for many days.

Administration officials said the coalition would not begin addressing withdrawal schedules, or the composition of a peacekeeping force, until after Iraq and the coalition had worked out the terms of the cease-fire.

The United States also moved to capitalize on the convergence of interests that held the coalition against Iraq together during months of military buildup, sanctions and war, starting the process of addressing what the White House called the "trying and frustrating" problems of the Middle East as a whole.

Baker Heads to Region

Secretary of State James A. Baker III made plans to leave Washington next Wednesday for a weeklong trip to the Middle East that will include his first visit to Israel since he became secretary of state and a final stop in the Soviet Union, and was to focus on security arrangements in the gulf, arms control in the Middle East as a whole, the Arab-Israeli conflict and narrowing the gap between the region's oil-rich and poor.

Mr. Baker is to visit Saudi Arabia, Syria and Egypt and meet with Kuwaiti officials, but it was not clear if this would occur in Kuwait City.

After the fighting stopped, Mr. Fitzwater said, "there was some relief" in the White House. But he said, "There is not a sense of finality, because there's just too much left to be done."

As soon as war gave way to diplomacy, the Bush administration took a hardline position that seemed intended to prevent President Saddam Hussein of Iraq from stalling on the coalition's military and political terms for peace and from hanging onto his prisoners as bargaining chips.

War-Crimes Trials

Mr. Fitzwater said the president did not want to resume the fighting, but he clearly held out the threat of more war if Baghdad did not release the prisoners, along with tens of thousands of Kuwaiti detainees, or reneged on its commitment to abide by the United Nations' resolutions.

"We're still in this existing position where our forces are in place," Mr. Fitzwater said, describing Mr. Bush's offer of a cease-fire as a "lever" against Iraq. "We have suspension of hostilities, but essentially we're right there and prepared to respond in any way we need to."

The United States continued to hold out the possibility of war crimes trials for Iraqi officers who took part in reported atrocities in Kuwait during the occupation.

But a senior administration official suggested that Mr. Bush would probably not pursue war-crimes charges against Mr. Hussein himself. The official, who briefed reporters on condition of anonymity, said the threat of war-crimes charges had been intended primarily to discourage Mr. Hussein from mistreating American prisoners or using chemical and biological weapons on the battlefield.

Mr. Fitzwater would not say how long allied forces would remain in the large slice of southern Iraq they seized in the four-day land offensive. But he said, "They certainly would remain there for the duration of the suspension of hostilities." After that, when a permanent cease-fire is in place, he said, "it remains to be seen."

"Take Care of Civilians"

Mr. Fitzwater refused to describe the allied troops as "an occupying force," saying the coalition troops had no plans to install a civil administration of the territories under their control or otherwise "take care of civilians."

Mr. Fitzwater also suggested that any move to ease the economic sanctions imposed on Baghdad by the United Nations would be contingent on swift Iraqi compliance with the terms outlined by Mr. Bush.

And in slightly more explicit terms than he has used before, he renewed the United States' effort to encourage the Iraqis to remove Mr. Hussein from power. Mr. Fitzwater said the Iraqi leader's continued presence in Baghdad "causes us to want to be extremely conservative" about postwar security arrangements and about how long the United Nations might keep economic sanctions in place against Baghdad.

"It would be much easier to look upon Iraq's problems if he were not in power," he said.

Margaret D. Tutwiler, spokeswoman for the State Department, repeated that the United States would like to leave in place an embargo on arms trade with Iraq as part of the administration's effort to prevent the rearming of Baghdad's army.

Outlining the provisions of the resolution, Miss Tutwiler said the Security Council would "demand implementation" of the resolutions that Iraq has not yet fulfilled, including one that requires the Iraqi Revolutionary Council, Baghdad's ruling council, to rescind a law passed last August that made Kuwait the 19th province of Iraq.

But Mr. Fitzwater made it clear that there would be no significant immediate withdrawal. He noted that some news reports had quoted him as saying some withdrawals might begin in a "few days," but said "the stories made that sound a little faster than it probably should."

"I'm sure it's going to be double digits before we're able to see troops come out," Mr. Fitzwater said. "It's clear that the president has indicated that he wants our forces to be coming out as soon as possible, and that's what it will be. But by the same token, we won't be withdrawing troops until it's fully realistic."

NOTE: *After Iraq invaded Kuwait on August 2, 1990, President George H. W. Bush worked slowly and skillfully to assemble an international coalition to drive Saddam Hussein's forces out. The war was brief, well managed and later seen as a stark contrast with his son's invasion of Iraq.*

ONE MAN AND A GLOBAL WEB OF VIOLENCE

By STEPHEN ENGELBERG, JANUARY 14, 2001

I n 1987, several years after he began training Arab volunteers to oust Soviet forces from Afghanistan, Osama bin Laden had a vision. The time had come, he told friends, to start a global jihad, or Islamic holy war, against the corrupt secular governments of the Muslim Middle East and the Western powers that supported them.

Mr. bin Laden, the Saudi millionaire, would use his camps in Afghanistan to take holy warriors from around the world—who had always pursued local goals—and shape them into an international network that would fight to bring all Muslims under a militant version of Islamic law.

Some of his comrades in arms warned him that the goal was unattainable.

"I talked to Osama one day and asked him what was he doing," recalled Abdullah Anas, an Algerian who was fighting in Afghanistan at the time and provided a rare personal narrative of the formation of Mr. bin Laden's organization. "Imagine after five years a guy from Malaysia goes back to his country. How can he remember you are his leader? He will get married, have children, engage in work in his country. How can you establish one camp for jihad in the world?"

But he and other doubters watched as Mr. bin Laden, who is now America's most wanted terror suspect, set about doing just that. Mr. Anas's account and those of other witnesses, along with intelligence from United States, the Middle East and Europe, draw a vivid and newly detailed portrait of the birth of a modern jihad movement. What began as a holy war against the Soviet Union took on a new dimension, Mr. Anas said, when Mr. bin Laden broke away and established a new corps of militant Muslims whose ambitions reached far beyond the borders of Afghanistan.

From his Afghan camps, Mr. bin Laden created a kind of clearinghouse for Islamic terrorism, which American officials say not only conducts its own operations but trains and underwrites local militants, connecting homegrown plots to a global crusade.

His strategy is aptly captured by one of his many code names: The Contractor. The group he founded 13 years ago, Al Qaeda, Arabic for "The Base," is led by masterful opportunists who tailor their roles to the moment, sometimes teaching the fine points of explosives, sometimes sending in their own operatives, sometimes simply supplying inspiration.

The group has become a beacon for Muslim Malaysians, Algerians, Filipinos, Palestinians, Egyptians, even Americans who have come to view the United States as

Osama bin Laden during a 1996 interview in Afghanistan with the Arabic newspaper *Al-Quds Al-Arab*.

their enemy, an imperial power propping up corrupt and godless governments. Mr. bin Laden has tried to bridge divisions in a movement long plagued by doctrinal, ethnic and geographic differences. "Local politics drives what they're doing, but it's much more visionary," said Robert Blitzer, a former F.B.I. counterterrorism official. "This is worldwide. This is, 'We want to be somewhere in a hundred years.'"

According to a recent Central Intelligence Agency analysis, Al Qaeda operates about a dozen Afghan camps that have trained as many as 5,000 militants, who in turn have created cells in 50 countries. Intelligence officials say the group is experimenting with chemical weapons, including nerve gas, at one of its camps.

Mr. bin Laden and his supporters use centuries-old interpretations of the Koran to justify violence in the name of God against fellow Muslims or bystanders—a vision on the furthest extremes of one of the world's largest religions. But their operations are thoroughly modern—encrypted email, bomb-making recipes stored on CD-ROMs, cell phones and satellite communications.

The group plans attacks months or years in advance, investigators say. A former United States Army sergeant, Ali A. Mohamed—who worked for Mr. bin Laden and is now a government witness—has told prosecutors that Al Qaeda trains "sleeper" agents, or "submarines," to live undetected among local populations.

Mr. bin Laden has not achieved his more ambitious goals. He has not brought more Muslims under the rule of Islamic law, toppled any of the Arab governments he took aim at or driven the United States out of the Middle East. His violence has repulsed many believers and prompted severe crackdowns in Arab states that already have limited political freedoms.

Nonetheless, he and his small inner circle have preoccupied American officials, paralyzing embassies, thwarting military exercises and making Americans abroad feel anxious and vulnerable. Earlier this month, the United States closed its Rome embassy for nearly two days after intelligence officials warned of a possible attack.

American officials have charged Mr. bin Laden with masterminding the 1998 bombings of two embassies in Africa that killed more than 200 people, and suspect him of involvement in the October bombing of the destroyer *Cole* in Yemen, which killed 17 sailors. Four men went on trial this month in lower Manhattan in the African bombings.

American authorities are also examining Al Qaeda's role in three plots timed to millennium celebrations in 1999—attacks directed at another American ship, a so-far unknown target in the United States, and tourist sites and a hotel in Jordan.

Mr. bin Laden's group has recently attempted operations against Israel—a significant departure, American and Middle Eastern officials say. They acknowledge that he has ensured his organization's survival, in the event of his capture or death, by designating a successor: his longtime aide, Abdulaziz abu Sitta, an Egyptian known as Muhammad Atef or Abu Hoffs al-Masri. Last week, according to Al Jazeera, an Arab satellite channel, his son married Mr. Masri's daughter in Kandahar, Afghanistan.

"His arrest, which we dearly hope for, is only one step along the road of the many things we need to do to eliminate the network of organizations," said Richard A. Clarke, the top White House counterterrorism official.

THE CAUSE
Afghan War Draws Young Arab Fighters

Al Qaeda grew out of the jihad inspired by Muslim scholars to combat the Soviet Union's 1979 invasion of Afghanistan. They issued religious rulings, known as *fatwas*, which exhorted Muslims everywhere to defend the Islamic land of Afghanistan from infidels. Over the next few years, several thousand young Arab men joined the Afghan resistance.

One of the first to answer the call was a young Algerian named Boujema Bounouar, who went by the nom de guerre Abdullah Anas. In recent interviews in London, where he now lives, Mr. Anas recounted how Mr. bin Laden went to Afghanistan to fight the Soviets and was drawn to a group of Egyptians who wanted to start a global jihad.

Mr. Anas, who is now a leader of an Algerian Islamic political party, is not a dispassionate observer. He acknowledges that he opposed Mr. bin Laden, whose program of terrorism, he says, has tarred the reputations of thousands of Arabs who fought honorably for the Afghan cause. But his firsthand account, which conforms with Western intelligence analysis, provides one of few portraits of Mr. bin Laden's evolution as a militant leader.

The two men were defined by many of the same forces. Mr. Anas said his journey from teacher of the Koran to holy warrior began in 1984, when he was 25 and living with his family in Western Algeria. Visiting the local library, he read in a news weekly about a religious ruling that waging war against the Soviets was every Muslim's duty.

"After a few days, everyone heard about this fatwa and started talking," he recalled. "Where is this Afghanistan? Which people are they? How can we go there? How much is the ticket?"

That year, Mr. Anas was among the million Muslims who participated in the hajj, the annual pilgrimage to Mecca, Saudi Arabia. "You feel very holy," he said. "People from all over the world. From Zimbabwe to New Delhi. Everyone is wearing just two pieces of white cotton. Everybody. You can't describe who is the minister, who is the president. No jewelry. No good suit."

In Mecca, he said, prayer leaders spoke emotionally about the jihad in Afghanistan.

He was standing in the marble expanse of the Great Mosque with 50,000 others when, he said, a friend pointed out a radical Palestinian scholar who was organizing the Arab support for the Afghans. His name was Abdullah Azzam, and his writings, which would help spur the revival of the jihad movement in the 20th century, were just becoming widely known.

Mr. Anas introduced himself and asked whether the magazine article he had seen in the library was correct. Had the religious leaders agreed that fighting in Afghanistan was a duty of all Muslims?

"He said, 'Yes, it's true.'"

"'O.K.,' I said. 'If I want to go to Afghanistan, what do I do now?'"

Mr. Azzam gave him a business card with a telephone number in Islamabad, Pakistan, where he was a university professor. A week later, Mr. Anas was on a flight from Saudi Arabia to Pakistan.

He had no idea where he was going, or what he would do. He dialed the only phone number he knew in Pakistan, reaching Mr. Azzam, who offered him a place to stay in his own house, a bustling salon frequented by students and scholars.

It was there that he first caught sight of Mr. Azzam's youngest daughter, whom he would marry five years later. And Mr. Azzam introduced him to a Saudi visitor identified in the traditional Arabic way, as Abu Abdullah, the father of his eldest son, Abdullah. The visitor was Osama bin Laden.

The two men exchanged pleasantries. Mr. bin Laden's name was well known. He was said to be the youngest of 24 brothers in a family that ran one of the largest construction companies in the Arab world.

Mr. bin Laden seemed no different from the other Arab volunteers who were starting to arrive in Pakistan, Mr. Anas recalled. The conversation turned to how the volunteers could help the Afghans win their jihad and teach them more about Islam.

The Soviet forces had a considerable advantage in the Afghan conflict. Their helicopter gunships controlled the air, and their troops held the main roads. But the rebels had powerful friends. The United States and Saudi Arabia were spending millions funneling arms to the Afghans through Pakistan's intelligence service.

Mr. Anas began by teaching the Koran to the Afghan rebels, who did not speak Arabic and learned the verses by rote. He also led prayers at a "guest house" set up in Pakistan for Arab volunteers. At the time, he said, there were no more than a few dozen Arabs in the country, working with the rebels. None spoke the Afghan languages.

After a few months, Mr. Anas said, he trekked into Afghanistan to join a combat unit, one of three Arabs traveling with a caravan of 600 Afghan soldiers. He learned Farsi and took on the role of mediator, traveling among the feuding rebel camps. He spent most of each year inside Afghanistan.

Mr. Anas became a top aide to Commander Ahmed Shah Massoud, whose troops controlled northern Afghanistan and are now fighting the Taliban rulers—who support Mr. bin Laden.

Like many Muslims who joined the rebels, Mr. Anas expected to die in the Afghan jihad and earn the special status designated in the Koran for martyrs, which includes forgiveness of sins and the enjoyment in Paradise of beautiful virgins. "It's not the main idea to be a *shahid*," or martyr, he said. "But it's part of my plan."

In the mid-1980s, American and Middle Eastern intelligence officials say, Mr. bin Laden moved to Peshawar, a Pakistani city near the border with Afghanistan. The city was a staging ground for the war against the Soviets; American, French and Pakistani intelligence officers intrigued and competed there to manipulate the Afghan cause to their countries' advantage.

Mr. bin Laden's fortune of several hundred million dollars gained him immediate popularity.

"He was one of the guys who came to jihad in Afghanistan," Mr. Anas said. "But unlike the others, what he had was a lot of money. He's not very sophisticated politically or organizationally. But he's an activist with great imagination. He ate very little. He slept very little. Very generous. He'd give you his clothes. He'd give you his money."

Mr. Anas, who returned annually to Pakistan from the Afghan battlefields to visit with Mr. Azzam, said Mr. bin Laden at first slept in the guest house in Peshawar on a cushion on the floor. He recalled that Mr. Azzam liked to say: "You see, this man has everything in his country. You see he lives with all the poor people in this room."

At about this time, in 1984, Mr. Azzam set up the organization that would play a pivotal role in the global jihad over the next decade. It was called the Makhtab al Khadimat, the Office of Services, and its goal was to recruit and train Muslim volunteers for the Afghan fronts. Mr. Azzam raised money for the organization in countries overseas including the United States and gave impassioned speeches promoting the Afghan cause. Mr. bin Laden embraced the idea from its inception and became Mr. Azzam's partner, providing financial support and handling military affairs.

Mr. bin Laden worked best with small groups, Mr. Anas said. "When you sit with Osama, you don't want to leave the meeting," he said. "You wish to continue talking to him because he is very calm, very fluent."

A main goal of the Office of Services, Mr. Anas said, was to prevent the increasing number of outside volunteers from taking sides in the rebels' factional struggles. "We are in Afghanistan to help the jihad and all the Afghan people," Mr. Azzam told him.

But there was increasing frustration from many of the disaffected young Muslims over Mr. Azzam's insistence that the Office of Services support only the Afghan cause—when many were agitated about the plight of their own homelands. Some approached Mr. bin Laden.

"They told him: 'You shouldn't be staying with Abdullah Azzam. He doesn't do anything about the regimes—Saudi, Egyptian, Algerian. He's just talking about Afghanistan,'" Mr. Anas said. "These people are always saying to Osama: 'You should establish something. Have a clear idea to use these people after Afghanistan for other wars.'"

Among those most ardently courting Mr. bin Laden was a group of Egyptian radicals called the Egyptian Islamic Jihad, which helped assassinate President Anwar el-Sadat in 1981.

The Egyptian group advocated the overthrow of governments by terrorism and violence, and one of its key figures, Ayman al-Zawahiri, had taken shelter in Afghanistan. Mr. Anas said—and Western intelligence agencies agree—that Dr. Zawahiri was a commanding early influence on Mr. bin Laden. Today he is part of Al Qaeda's leadership, according to intelligence officials.

But Mr. Azzam quarreled bitterly with the Egyptians.

Mr. Anas said he once witnessed a heated argument between Mr. Azzam and Sheik Omar Abdel Rahman, a radical religious scholar, who argued that the flouting of Islamic law had turned Presidents Mohammed Zia ul-Haq of Pakistan and

> *The Egyptian group advocated the overthrow of governments by terrorism and violence.*

Hosni Mubarak of Egypt into infidels who could therefore be killed. Sheik Abdel Rahman later moved to Brooklyn, where he was associated with an Office of Services branch. In 1995 he was convicted of plotting to blow up New York landmarks.

In 1986, according to Mr. Anas and Middle Eastern intelligence officials, Mr. bin Laden began to chart a separate course. He established his own training camp for Persian Gulf Arabs, a group of about 50 who lived in tents set apart from the other Afghan fighters. He called the camp Al Masadah—The Lion's Den.

Within little more than a year the movement divided, as Mr. bin Laden and the Egyptians founded Al Qaeda—the "base" for what they hoped would be a global crusade.

Mr. Anas said Mr. Azzam confided to him that Egyptian ideologues had wooed Mr. bin Laden away, gaining access to his money. "He told me one time: 'I'm very upset about Osama. This heaven-sent man, like an angel. I am worried about his future if he stays with these people.'"

The differences between Mr. Azzam and Mr. bin Laden were largely tactical, Mr. Anas said, noting that the two men remained friends. A committed enemy of Israel, Mr. Azzam believed the Arab warriors should focus on creating an Islamic state in Afghanistan, a process that could take decades. Mr. bin Laden, according to Mr. Anas, came to believe that such a war could be fought in many countries simultaneously.

"The arguments were very secret," Mr. Anas said. "Only three to four people knew about them at the time." Mr. Azzam saw little difference between the United States and the Soviet Union, contending in his articles and speeches that both were hostile to Islam. But Mr. Azzam opposed terrorism against the West, Mr. Anas said.

By the late 1980s, Peshawar had become a magnet for disaffected young Muslims who shared Mr. bin Laden's views. "Ten people would open a guest house and start issuing fatwas," Mr. Anas recalled. "'We are going to make revolution in Jordan, in Egypt, in Syria.' And they haven't got any contact with the real jihad in Afghanistan."

The tide of the Afghan war was turning. Stinger missiles, provided through the American covert program, had forced Soviet aircraft to fly far above the battlefields. Afghanistan had become Moscow's Vietnam. By February 1989, the Soviets had withdrawn.

A C.I.A. official said that the agency, aware of the changing nature of the jihad, had taken some steps he would not specify to counter the threat. But Milt Bearden, the former C.I.A. station chief in Islamabad, who coordinated the agency's anti-Soviet effort in Afghanistan, disagreed.

"The Soviet Union, armed to the teeth, was falling apart," he said. "A shooting war then erupted in the Persian Gulf. Afghanistan was off the front burner."

When the war ended, he said, "we got the hell out of there."

The Afghan rebels' war continued, first against the Soviet-backed government and then within their own ranks. On Nov. 24, 1989, Mr. Azzam and two sons were killed by a car bomb in Peshawar as they drove to Friday prayers. The murders were never solved.

Mr. Anas said he tried to take over leadership of the Office of Services. According to the C.I.A., the group split; the extremist faction took control, siding with Mr. bin Laden.

"They loved the ideas of Osama and the person of Abdullah Azzam," Mr. Anas said wistfully. "They don't love me."

THE BASE
From Many Lands, Under One Banner

Fired by their triumph over the Soviets, the Arabs who had fought in Afghanistan returned home, eager to apply the principles of jihad to their native lands.

The Koran sets strict limits on when and how holy war is to be undertaken. But Gilles Kepel, a leading French scholar of contemporary Islam, said the Afghan veterans were guided by their own radical interpretation of sacred Muslim texts. "Intoxicated by the Muslim victory in Afghanistan," he said, "they believed that it could be replicated elsewhere—that the whole world was ripe for jihad, which is contrary to Islamic tradition."

They called themselves the Arab Afghans.

In Jordan some founded a group, Jaish Muhammad, that officials say took aim at King Hussein, whose family claims descent from the Prophet Muhammad.

In Algeria, the Arab Afghans were among the founders of the Armed Islamic Group, the most radical to emerge after the military government canceled the 1991 elections. Known by its French initials, G.I.A., it began by blowing up military targets and escalated to wholesale massacres of Algerians who did not believe in the jihad.

According to Mr. Anas, one of its founding members was an Algerian who had initially fought with him in Afghanistan but joined Al Qaeda in the late 1980s. Mr. Anas says he has been told that Mr. bin Laden provided some of the seed money for the G.I.A.

The early 1990s proved difficult for Mr. bin Laden. He was enraged by King Fahd's decision to let American troops wage the Persian Gulf war from Saudi Arabia, site of the two holiest shrines in Islam. He began to focus his wrath on the United States and the Saudi government. After the conflict ended, he moved to Afghanistan.

But his stay was brief. Within months he fled, telling associates that Saudi Arabia had hired the Pakistani intelligence service to kill him. There is no confirmation that such a plot existed. Nonetheless, in 1991, Mr. bin Laden moved to Sudan, where a militantly Islamic government had taken power.

Over the next five years, Mr. bin Laden built a group that combined legitimate business with support for world holy war.

He also set out to accomplish his overriding goal of gathering the leading Islamic extremist groups under one banner. According to Middle Eastern officials, Mr. bin Laden and his envoys met with radicals from Pakistan and Egypt to propose an international Islamic front, led by Afghan veterans, that would fight Americans and Jews.

Al Qaeda began training its own operatives. Ali Mohamed, the government witness who has said he arranged Mr. bin Laden's move to Sudan, told investigators that he taught group members about weapons, explosives, kidnapping, urban fighting, counterintelligence and other tactics at camps in Afghanistan and Sudan. He said he showed some of the trainees how to set up cells "that could be used in operations."

The dispatch of American troops to Somalia in late 1992 and 1993 as part of a United Nations mission was another affront to Mr. bin Laden. The Bush administration presented it as a relief operation. American officials say a defector from Al Qaeda told them it viewed the deployment as a dangerous expansion of American influence in the region and a step toward undermining the Islamic government of Sudan.

Al Qaeda privately issued fatwas that directed members to attack American soldiers in Saudi Arabia, Yemen and the Horn of Africa, according to American prosecutors.

They said he also sent his military chief, an Egyptian who had been with him at the formation of Al Qaeda, to find the vulnerabilities of United Nations forces in Africa.

Al Qaeda created a cell in Kenya as a "gateway" to its operations in Somalia, the prosecutors assert. Members of the group blended into Kenyan society, opening legitimate businesses that sold fish and dealt in diamonds, and operating an Islamic charity.

Federal prosecutors say at least five group members crossed the border to Somalia, where they trained some of the fighters involved in an Oct. 3, 1993, battle with United States special forces that left 18 Americans and several hundred Somalis dead.

The battle, one of the most widely publicized setbacks for American forces in recent memory, cast a shadow over every subsequent Clinton administration debate on the possible uses of ground troops. American intelligence did not learn of Al Qaeda's role in the ambush until several years later.

Prosecutors say the group also considered attacking Americans in Kenya to retaliate for the Somalia mission. Mr. Mohamed testified that Mr. bin Laden sent him to Nairobi in late 1993 to look over possible American, French, British and Israeli targets for a bomb attack, including the American Embassy. He said he took photos, drew diagrams and wrote a report, which he delivered to his boss in Khartoum. "Bin Laden looked at the picture of the American Embassy and pointed to where a truck could go as a suicide bomber," he said.

American prosecutors say Al Qaeda had more grandiose plans: a leading member, an Iraqi who Mr. Anas said had first gravitated to Mr. bin Laden in Afghanistan, tried to buy enriched uranium in Europe.

The Iraqi, Mamdouh Mahmud Salim, forged links between Mr. bin Laden's group and others supported by Iran. Mr. Salim met with an Iranian religious official in Khartoum, and soon afterward, the prosecutors say, Al Qaeda members got training from Hezbollah, the Iranian-backed Shiite group in Lebanon skilled in making car bombs. American officials said this alliance was notable because it marked the first time radicals from the minority Shiite branch of Islam collaborated with extremists from the dominant Sunni branch.

Mr. bin Laden's business ventures in Sudan—including a tannery, a transportation company and a construction concern—raised money and served as cover for the travels of Mr. Salim and others, according to American officials. They said that his companies cornered Sudan's exports of gum, sunflower and sesame products—and that he invested $50 million of his family money in a new Islamic bank in Khartoum.

THE NETWORK
As in Afghanistan, So in the World

The new jihad movement was fueled by the civil war that consumed Afghanistan in the early 1990s. The training camps that had once schooled soldiers to battle the Soviet enemy now attracted militants more interested in fomenting holy war back home—in America, Europe or the Middle East—than in the struggle for control of Afghanistan.

The Office of Services, the Pakistan-based group founded in the 1980s by Mr. Azzam to recruit soldiers for the anti-Soviet cause, arranged the travels of some of these new jihadists, according to European and American officials.

Many of those associated with the office, Mr. Anas said, shared Mr. bin Laden's vision of a global movement. American officials suspect they were acting under his instructions, though this remains a subject of debate among intelligence analysts.

American investigators stumbled across the first signs of the new global phenomenon in 1993, when they began to examine the bombing at the World Trade Center.

They discovered that the four men who carried out the attack, which killed 6 and wounded more than 1,000, had ties to Sheik Omar Abdel Rahman, whom they charged with leading a worldwide "jihad organization" that had begun plotting to kill Americans as early as 1989.

Mr. Abdel Rahman was later convicted of conspiring to blow up New York landmarks, including the United Nations. But in the years since, American intelligence officials have come to believe that he and the World Trade Center bombers had ties to Al Qaeda.

The evidence is suggestive, but not conclusive. Several of those convicted in the World Trade Center case were associated with the Brooklyn refugee center that was a branch of the Office of Services, the Pakistan-based organization that Mr. bin Laden helped finance and lead. The Brooklyn center was headed for a time by Mustafa Shalabi, an Egyptian murdered in 1991 in a case that remains unsolved. Federal prosecutors recently disclosed that it was Mr. Shalabi whom Mr. bin Laden called in 1991 when he needed help moving to Sudan, according to Mr. Mohamed, the federal witness.

One of the men convicted of bombing the World Trade Center, Ahmad M. Ajaj, spent four months in Pakistan in 1992, returning to the United States with a bomb manual later seized by the United States government. An English translation of the document, entered into evidence in the World Trade Center trial, said that the manual was dated 1982, that it had been published in Amman, Jordan, and that it carried a heading on the front and succeeding pages: The Basic Rule.

Those appear to be errors. Two separate translations of the document, one done at the request of *The New York Times*, show that the heading said "Al Qaeda"—which translates as "The Base," the name of Mr. bin Laden's group. In addition, the document lists a publication date of 1989, a year after Mr. bin Laden founded his organization. And the place of publication is Afghanistan, not Jordan.

Steven Emerson, a terrorism expert who first pointed out the errors, said they deprived investigators of a subtle early clue to the existence of Mr. bin Laden's group.

While the trade center trial ended in 1994, federal prosecutors did not open their grand jury investigation of Mr. bin Laden and Al Qaeda until 1996.

"Had the government correctly translated the material," Mr. Emerson said, "it might have understood that the men who blew up the World Trade Center and Mr. bin Laden's group were linked."

Asked about the mistranslation, an official in the United States Attorney's office, who declined to be identified, said only that Mr. Ajaj had been carrying "voluminous material printed by various organizations." He added that their titles referred to international conspiracy, commando operations and engineering of explosives.

The jihad movement also took root in Europe. In August 1994, three young French Muslims of North African descent, wearing hoods and brandishing machine pistols, opened fire on tourists in a hotel lobby in Marrakesh, Morocco, killing two Spaniards and wounding a third. The French police investigating the attack learned that it had been planned by two Moroccan veterans of the Afghan war, who had recruited commandos for the attack in Paris and Orleans and sent more than a dozen of them to Afghanistan for training.

The indoctrination of the young Muslims began with religion, according to French court papers and testimony. An Orleans mathematics professor and interpreter of the Koran, Mohamed Zinedine, gathered around him a group of men from the slums of Orleans who wanted to learn how to pray. Later, French court papers say, he instructed them in the concept of waging jihad against corrupt governments, saying it was a higher stage of Islamic observance.

One young Moroccan testified that Mr. Zinedine—who is now a fugitive—showed him a videotape of Muslim victims of "torture in Bosnia, of babies with their throats cut, of pregnant women disemboweled, and fingernails torn off." The young man added, "He told me there was a way of helping them and that I must help them." Prayers for people like the Muslims in Bosnia, he quoted Mr. Zinedine as saying, were not enough. He must become an "armed humanitarian."

European investigators tracing the Afghan network in France, Belgium and Germany found records of phone calls between local extremists and the Office of Services in Pakistan. In March 1995, Belgian investigators came across another clue: A CD-ROM in the car of another Algerian, who had been trained in Afghanistan in 1992 and was part of the G.I.A. cell in Brussels. The CD was initially ignored, Belgian officials say.

Months later, the Belgians began translating its contents and discovered several different versions of a manual for terrorism that had begun circulating among Islamic militants in the early 1990s. The voluminous manual covered diverse subjects, from "psychological war in Islam" to "the organizational structure of Israeli intelligence" to "recruiting according to the American method."

The manual also offered detailed recipes for making bombs, including instructions on when to shake the chemicals and how to use a wristwatch as a detonator. In addition, there were instructions on how to kill with toxins, gases and drugs. The preface included a dedication to the new hero of the holy war: Osama bin Laden. Versions of the manual circulated widely and were seized by the police all over Europe.

Reuel Gerecht, a former C.I.A. official, said he was told that the agency did not obtain its own copy of the manual before the end of 1999. "The truth is," he said, "they missed for years the largest terrorist guide ever written." The omission, he asserted, reflects the agency's reluctance to scrutinize the fallout from its support of the anti-Soviet jihad.

> *"The truth is they missed for years the largest terrorist guide ever written."*

A C.I.A. official said that the agency had had "access to versions" of the manual since the late 1980s. "It's not the Holy Grail that Gerecht reports it to be," he said, adding that the terrorist-related parts were fairly recent additions.

By the mid-1990s, American officials had begun to focus on Mr. bin Laden and his entourage in Sudan. They saw him as the embodiment of a dangerous new development: a stateless sponsor of terrorism who was using his personal fortune—which one Middle Eastern official estimated at $270 million—to bankroll extremist causes.

American officials pressed Sudan to eject Mr. bin Laden, and in 1996 they succeeded, forcing him into exile. It was a diplomatic triumph, but one that many American officials would come to rue. Mr. bin Laden made his way back to Afghanistan, where a new group of young Islamic militants, the Taliban, was taking control.

American and Middle Eastern officials said some of the cash that the Taliban used to buy off local warlords came from Mr. bin Laden. Soon the new, hardline rulers of Afghanistan allowed him to use their country to pursue his goal of creating "one jihad camp for the world," as Mr. Anas put it.

THE EDICT
A Sacred Muslim Duty to Kill All Foes

Two years after he arrived in Afghanistan, in February 1998, Mr. bin Laden publicly announced his intentions. At a camp in Khost, in eastern Afghanistan, he and several other leaders of militant groups declared that they had founded the International Islamic Front for Jihad Against Jews and Crusaders, an umbrella entity that included Al Qaeda and groups from Egypt, Pakistan and Bangladesh, among others.

The front issued the following fatwa: "To kill Americans and their allies, both civil and military, is an individual duty of every Muslim who is able, in any country where this is possible."

On Aug. 7, 1998, eight years to the day after the first American troops set foot in Saudi Arabia, Mr. bin Laden delivered on the threat, American prosecutors say. Bombs exploded hours apart at the American Embassies in Kenya and Tanzania.

The plot, as described by federal prosecutors, was truly international. Prosecutors assert that the attacks were carried out by Muslims from Tanzania, Saudi Arabia and Jordan, most of whom were trained in Afghanistan. The Kenyan plotters, they say, spoke directly with Mr. bin Laden by satellite telephone as they developed their plans.

The plot, as described by federal prosecutors, was truly international.

The attacks were costly for Al Qaeda. Less than two weeks after the embassy bombings, the United States conducted air strikes against Mr. bin Laden's camps in Afghanistan. Over the next two years, police and intelligence agencies around the world, many prodded by the United States, arrested more than 100 militants in some 20 countries.

Almost every month, authorities detain or question people with ties to Al Qaeda. Late last year, in what American officials described as one of the more alarming cases, the Kuwaiti police arrested a local man, an Afghan veteran, who said he was associated with Mr. bin Laden's group and planning to bomb American and Kuwaiti targets. American officials say he ultimately led the police to a weapons cache of almost 300 pounds of explosives and more than 1,400 detonators.

And in addition to the two-day closure of the American Embassy in Rome, officials say, recent warnings of a possible Al Qaeda attack prompted the United States to divert an entire carrier battle group scheduled to dock in Naples.

American officials acknowledge that Al Qaeda and Mr. bin Laden have proven resourceful, resilient adversaries. Much of his personal wealth has now been spent, or is in bank accounts that are now frozen. But officials say he is raising money through a network of charities and businesses. His group reconstitutes its networks in many countries as quickly as they are disrupted.

And failure can breed success. In late 1999, American officials say, a group of Yemenis botched an attempt to blow up an American ship, *The Sullivans*, as it passed through Yemen. Their boat, loaded with explosives, sank a few feet off shore.

This year, American officials say, a Saudi operative of Mr. bin Laden's who helped organize that attack worked with some of the same people on the bombing of the *Cole* in Yemen.

Internal crackdowns on Muslim militants, like the Algerian government's largely successful attempts to stamp out the G.I.A. in the mid-1990s, have in several instances fueled the international jihad.

American officials said the most radical Algerians were now collaborating with Mr. bin Laden. In 1999, Algerians were for the first time implicated in plots against the United States, when Ahmed Ressam was arrested crossing the border from Canada with a carload of explosives. Mr. Ressam goes on trial later this year in Los Angeles.

American and Middle Eastern officials say Al Qaeda has now expanded its jihad to include Israel, which until recently had regarded Mr. bin Laden as an American problem. The officials say Al Qaeda has financed and trained an anti-Israel group, Asbat al Ansar, that operates from a Palestinian refugee camp in Lebanon.

Last June, Israel charged in a sealed indictment that a Hamas member who was plotting to attack targets within Israel, including settlers and the army, had been trained in one of Mr. bin Laden's Afghan camps. "Al Qaeda wants in on the action—the new intifada against Israel," said one American official.

Olivier Roy, a French scholar who follows Islamic activities, says Al Qaeda's biggest asset is the thousands of jihadists around the world who no longer see their struggle in strictly local or even national terms, which makes them impervious to normal political or military pressure. Mr. bin Laden's actions, he said, are "not the continuation of politics by other means. Osama bin Laden doesn't want to negotiate."

NOTE: *Despite his declaration of war against terrorists and those who protected them, President George W. Bush missed a chance to capture or kill bin Laden at the battle of Tora Bora in late 2001; it was not until May 2, 2011, that a team of Navy S.E.A.L.s dispatched by President Barack Obama finally killed the master terrorist in the Pakistani city of Abbottabad, where he had been holed up in plain sight of the country's military.*

A NATION CHALLENGED: NEWS ANALYSIS; HOME FRONT: EDGY SUNDAY

By R. W. APPLE JR., OCTOBER 8, 2001

When the word came that the waiting had ended, first from Kabul, then from officials at the Pentagon and finally from President Bush, it came on a pristine fall Sunday, "a perfect day for football," as the announcers like to say, just as many people were sitting down in front of their television sets for their weekly dose of gridiron glory.

The president looked stern and sounded resolute as he told the American people that "the battle is now joined on many fronts" and promised "sustained, comprehensive and relentless operations" to bring to justice those responsible for the Sept. 11 attacks. But it was not easy to grasp all the implications, even as the generals and the politicians talked of precision munitions and the suppression of enemy air defenses in Afghanistan, a little-known country 7,000 miles away.

So a superficial sort of normality quickly reasserted itself, as it did after the shocking news that came on another Sunday—Dec. 7, 1941. Shoppers resumed shopping, and the football telecasts went on as scheduled.

But as Americans turned their attention back to watching football this afternoon, much of the country was unsettled. No matter how hard they try not to, no matter how steadfast they may consider themselves, millions of Americans fear retaliation. Even before the bombs burst all across Afghanistan, they were busy buying gas masks and antibiotics. Promising to take every precaution, Mr. Bush still made the remarkable concession that "many Americans feel fear today."

Never before has the United States launched a military campaign against such an elusive and hydra-headed foe, with so little clarity about precisely how it will prevail. And not since the War of 1812 has a foreign threat to the American homeland been quite so palpable. It was "a moment of utmost gravity," as Prime Minister Tony Blair of Great Britain said, a moment for the tablets of history, a moment without real parallel in the nation's past.

Washington braced for the worst. A State Department warning was cast in unusually dire terms, cautioning that the bombing "may result in strong anti-American sentiment and retaliatory actions against United States citizens and interests."

Richard Shelby of Alabama, the ranking Republican on the Senate Intelligence Committee, was blunter: he said on the ABC News program *This Week* this morning that he expected "more attempts, more attacks."

Senator Bob Graham, Democrat of Florida, the committee chairman, agreed that "the threat level" was likely to increase once American military forces went into action.

Mr. Bush said with ample justification that the United States was "supported by the collective will of the world"; his administration has assembled a coalition significantly broader than the one assembled by his father for the Persian Gulf war. But it is a fragile alliance, the preservation of which will dictate a degree of policy ambiguity that makes military people uncomfortable.

Nor is long-term support at home assured. The present national unity may last; it may not. Two related factors that will shape opinion are how much progress is made (and how quickly) in the pursuit of terrorists, and how much further punishment the terrorists can inflict on the United States.

The word *war* has been widely used in the last three weeks, by ordinary folk as well as politicians. War, whether conventional or unconventional, is an enterprise in which one side kills members of the other, and the other side does likewise, until one cannot continue, but it is by no means clear that the country has thought this through in its first reaction to Sept. 11.

Osama bin Laden, the suspected terrorist leader, made it clear once again, on videotape, that he would not back off. The tape, date uncertain, was broadcast on Arabic satellite television. He challenged the allied efforts to picture him as a renegade who has corrupted the teaching of his faith, describing the American war against him as a war against Afghanistan and Islam. As long as it continues, he promised, Americans "will never taste security."

Clearly, Mr. Bush understands that defeating Mr. bin Laden, unraveling his terrorist network and then moving on to other countries that harbor terrorists will test the capacity of the American people to stay focused on the task at hand and to put up with setbacks over an extended period of time.

He appealed for "patience with the long waits that will result from tighter security, patience and understanding that it will take time to achieve our goals, patience in all the sacrifices that may come." Only "the patient accumulation of successes," he continued, will bring victory.

But how will success be defined? If Mr. bin Laden is captured or killed, will that be enough? Many moderate Arab states will insist that it is, Pakistan probably among them; already, a senior State Department official said tonight, the Pakistani government has risked a conservative Muslim uprising merely by granting the United States overflight rights.

If the Taliban is ousted or disintegrates, what will replace it? For centuries the various peoples in Afghanistan have found it difficult to work together in a stable government, and continued instability would provide a rich breeding ground for terrorists and terrorism. Yet the White House insists military action is "not designed to replace one regime with another."

Clearly the United States has put tremendous pressure on some countries, particularly in the Middle East, in its quest for intelligence-sharing, bases for its ships and planes, and so on. This has succeeded, for the most part, but many of the arrangements have not been made public. One thing unknown is whether they apply just to this first phase or the whole campaign.

They will no doubt be sorely tested as the campaign unfolds.

Defense Secretary Donald H. Rumsfeld reiterated today that "our aim remains much broader" than Afghanistan, and said of terrorism, "We intend to oppose it wherever it is." The objective of military missions tends gradually to grow broader and timetables slip; if that happens here, nations like Saudi Arabia, Egypt and even Jordan will be hard to keep onboard.

Still, the coalition is remarkable, and in certain ways it seems to have the makings of the New World Order about which George Bush the elder used to speak. Germany, one of the main adversaries of the United States in World War II, has promised to send armed forces to fight alongside Americans this time. Russia, the great Cold War adversary, issued a statement once the bombing had started that said terrorist actions "must be countered by all means."

Mr. Bush called President Vladimir V. Putin a half hour before the attacks began to inform him of the plans. Mr. Putin, many diplomats say, sees the current conflict not only as an opportunity to justify his own battle against Chechen rebels but also as a means of reasserting his country's entitlement, not to its former superpower status but to a place at the head table of nations.

Likewise, Mr. Blair. His stout support of the United States, whatever else it accomplishes, will reinforce London's special relationship with Washington—something British prime ministers are always eager to do, given their country's anomalous relationship with Europe. Mr. Blair's eloquent, almost Churchillian speeches have resonated powerfully in Washington.

A NATION CHALLENGED: CONGRESS; HOUSE PASSES TERRORISM BILL MUCH LIKE SENATE'S, BUT WITH FIVE-YEAR LIMIT

By ROBIN TONER AND NEIL A. LEWIS, OCTOBER 13, 2001

The House of Representatives approved legislation today to give the government broad new powers for the wiretapping, surveillance and investigation of terrorism suspects.

But, in recognition of many lawmakers' fears of the potential for government over-reaching and abuse, the House also included a five-year limit after which many of those powers would expire.

Passage of the bill, by a vote of 337 to 79, was the climax of a remarkable 18-hour period in which both the House and the Senate adopted complex, far-reaching anti-terrorism legislation with little debate in an atmosphere of edgy alarm, as federal law enforcement officials warned that another attack could be imminent. Many lawmakers said it had been impossible to truly debate, or even read, the legislation that passed today.

President Bush gestures to congressman to gather around as he prepares to sign the Patriot Act, October 26, 2001.

Civil liberties advocates implored Congress to slow down and consider the legislation's impact, which they said could be a dangerous infringement on Americans' privacy and constitutional rights. But the drive to send an antiterrorism bill to the president—it was called the Patriot Act in the House, the U.S.A. Act in the Senate—was strong. With lopsided votes in both houses, enactment of the measure, perhaps in a matter of days, is now seen as a fait accompli.

The bill passed by the House is essentially the legislation approved by the Senate on Thursday night, although with a few key changes, including the five-year sunset provision. It was the product of last-minute negotiations between top House Republicans and the Bush administration, and was suddenly substituted this morning for a more cautious antiterrorism bill that had strong bipartisan support. Many Democrats were furious, and even some Republicans voiced dismay.

Still, Republican leaders said it was critical to minimize differences with the Senate legislation and avert the need for lengthy negotiations between the two chambers.

"The attorney general has been quite plain that as soon as the president signs the bill, law enforcement will begin using these new powers," said the House judiciary chairman, Representative F. James Sensenbrenner Jr., Republican of Wisconsin. "Time is of the essence in light of the increased threat the F.B.I. has announced against the United States and its citizens."

In a reflection of the sense of crisis, after casting their votes the lawmakers remained in the House chamber for a closed briefing on bioterrorism.

Still, unlike the Senate, which passed its antiterrorism legislation by a vote of 96 to 1, the House had many Democrats who remained opposed to the bill; all but 4 of the votes against it were from Democrats. "We need to do everything in our power to end the blight of terrorism everywhere around the world," said Representative John Conyers Jr. of Michigan, ranking Democrat on the Judiciary Committee. "But we must remember that just as this horrendous act could destroy us from without, it could also destroy us from within."

Mr. Conyers cited a variety of past government infringements on civil liberties during times of crisis, including the internment of Japanese Americans during World War II and the adoption of the Alien and Sedition Acts of 1798, which among other things broadly proscribed criticism of the president or Congress.

The legislation, produced in response to Attorney General John Ashcroft's demand for immediate action, would give the government new powers to monitor email among terrorism suspects and, with a single warrant, wiretap any phones a suspect might use. It would increase penalties for those who support terrorist groups and encourage greater sharing of information—including information obtained by grand juries—among intelligence and law enforcement agencies.

The bill passed by the Senate also includes measures to fight money laundering—an important source of support for terrorism, many lawmakers said. The House bill does not include those provisions, and the Senate majority leader, Tom Daschle of South Dakota, said today that the Senate would not give final approval to a bill unless it had them.

Another difference between the two bills is the sunset provision, which does not exist in the Senate's version but is considered to have wide support there. The House bill would allow the president to reauthorize the new powers after three years; after an additional two years, Congress would have to review and decide whether to extend them.

Neither version incorporates the administration's proposal to allow, without the filing of charges, indefinite detention of foreigners suspected of involvement in terrorism. Instead, the attorney general would be permitted to detain such suspects up to seven days, after which they would have to be charged with a criminal or immigration violation or be released. But Timothy Edgar, a legal counsel at the American Civil Liberties Union, argued that the wording of the bills still left the possibility of indefinite detention of anyone certified as a terrorist suspect even if not charged.

The bill also allows the authorities to carry out search warrants in people's homes, for example, without notifying them until afterward if officials assert that prior notification would obstruct an investigation. And the bill makes it a crime to harbor terrorists, and defines that crime broadly; one could be guilty simply by having "reasonable grounds to believe" that the person being harbored was a terrorist.

Many lawmakers were outraged that a bipartisan bill, which had passed the Judiciary Committee by a unanimous vote, was set aside for legislation negotiated at the last minute by a very small group. Members rose to say that almost no one had read the new bill, and pleaded for more time and more deliberation.

Representative David R. Obey, Democrat of Wisconsin, described the new bill as a "backroom quick fix." He added bitterly: "Why should we care? It's only the Constitution."

Asked about complaints that lawmakers were being asked to vote on a bill that they had not read, the chairman of the Rules Committee, Representative David Dreier, Republican of California, replied, "It's not unprecedented."

NOTE: *Regardless of the obvious flaws in the Patriot Act and the secretive way in which it was rushed through Congress, lawmakers later reauthorized the bill in July 2005, complete with the deliberately created loopholes that allowed the second Bush administration to wiretap Americans without warrants.*

JUSTICES, 5 TO 4, BACK DETAINEE APPEALS FOR GUANTÁNAMO

By LINDA GREENHOUSE, JUNE 13, 2008

T he Supreme Court on Thursday delivered its third consecutive rebuff to the Bush administration's handling of the detainees at Guantánamo Bay, ruling 5 to 4 that the prisoners there have a constitutional right to go to federal court to challenge their continued detention.

The court declared unconstitutional a provision of the Military Commissions Act of 2006 that, at the administration's behest, stripped the federal courts of jurisdiction to hear habeas corpus petitions from the detainees seeking to challenge their designation as enemy combatants.

Writing for the majority, Justice Anthony M. Kennedy said the truncated review procedure provided by a previous law, the Detainee Treatment Act of 2005, "falls short of being a constitutionally adequate substitute" because it failed to offer "the fundamental procedural protections of habeas corpus."

> *"The laws and Constitution are designed to survive, and remain in force, in extraordinary times."*

Justice Kennedy declared: "The laws and Constitution are designed to survive, and remain in force, in extraordinary times."

The decision, left some important questions unanswered. These include "the extent of the showing required of the government" at a habeas corpus hearing in order to justify a prisoner's continued detention, as Justice Kennedy put it, as well as the handling of classified evidence and the degree of due process to which the detainees are entitled.

Months or years of continued litigation may lie ahead, unless the Bush administration, or the administration that follows it, reverses course and closes the prison at Guantánamo Bay, which now holds 270 detainees. Chief Judge Royce C. Lamberth of the federal district court here said the court's judges would meet in the next few days with lawyers for both sides to decide "how we can approach our task most effectively and efficiently."

There are some 200 habeas corpus petitions awaiting action in the district court, including those filed by the 37 detainees whose appeals were before the Supreme Court in the case decided on Thursday, *Boumediene v. Bush*, No. 06-1195.

A guard mans the tower at Camp Delta, located at the Guantánamo Bay Naval Base in Cuba, October 4, 2007.

Despite the open questions, the decision, which was joined by Justices John Paul Stevens, David H. Souter, Ruth Bader Ginsburg, and Stephen G. Breyer, was categorical in its rejection of the administration's basic arguments. Indeed, the court repudiated the fundamental legal basis for the administration's strategy, adopted in the immediate aftermath of the attacks of Sept. 11, 2001, of housing prisoners captured in Afghanistan and elsewhere at the United States naval base in Cuba, where Justice Department lawyers advised the White House that domestic law would never reach.

In a concurring opinion on Thursday, Justice Souter said the ruling was "no bolt out of the blue," but rather should have been anticipated by anyone who read the court's decision in *Rasul v. Bush* in 2004. That decision, part of the initial round of Supreme Court review of the administration's Guantánamo policies, held that because the long-term lease with Cuba gave the United States unilateral control over the property, the base came within the statutory jurisdiction of the federal courts to hear habeas corpus petitions.

Congress responded the next year, in the Detainee Treatment Act, by amending the statute to remove jurisdiction, and it did so again in the Military Commissions Act to make clear that it wanted the removal to apply to cases already in the pipeline. The decision on Thursday went beyond the statutory issue to decide, for the first time, the underlying constitutional question.

President Bush, appearing with Prime Minister Silvio Berlusconi of Italy at a news conference in Rome, said he was unhappy with the decision. "We'll abide by the court's decision—that doesn't mean I have to agree with it," the president said, adding that "it was a deeply divided court, and I strongly agree with those who dissented."

The dissenting opinions, one by Chief Justice John G. Roberts Jr. and the other by Justice Scalia, were vigorous. Each signed the other's, and the other two dissenters, Justices Clarence Thomas and Samuel A. Alito Jr., signed both.

Of the two dissenting opinions, Justice Antonin Scalia's was the more apocalyptic, predicting "devastating" and "disastrous consequences" from the decision. "It will almost certainly cause more Americans to be killed," he said. "The nation will live to regret what the court has done today." He said the decision was based not on principle, "but rather an inflated notion of judicial supremacy."

Chief Justice Roberts, in somewhat milder tones, said the decision represented "overreaching" that was "particularly egregious" and left the court open to "charges of judicial activism." The decision, he said, "is not really about the detainees at all, but about control of federal policy regarding enemy combatants." The public will "lose a bit more control over the conduct of this nation's foreign policy to unelected, politically unaccountable judges," he added.

The focus of the chief justice's ire was the choice the majority made to go beyond simply ruling that the detainees were entitled to file habeas corpus petitions. Under two unrelated Supreme Court precedents, formal habeas corpus procedures are not necessarily required, as long as Congress provides an "adequate substitute."

Congress in this instance did provide an alternative procedure that might be viewed as a substitute. The Detainee Treatment Act gave detainees access to the federal appeals court here to challenge their designation as enemy combatants, made by a military panel called a Combatant Status Review Tribunal.

The detainees' lawyers argued that because this process fell far short of the review provided by traditional habeas corpus, it could not be considered an adequate substitute. The appeals court itself never decided that question, because it ruled in February 2007 that the detainees had no right to habeas corpus in the first place, and that all their petitions must be dismissed. It was this ruling that the Supreme Court reviewed on Thursday.

Justice Kennedy said the Supreme Court, having decided that there was a right to habeas corpus, would "in the ordinary course" send the case back to the appeals court for it to consider "in the first instance" whether the alternative procedure was an adequate substitute.

But he said "the gravity of the separation-of-powers issues raised by these cases and the fact that these detainees have been denied meaningful access to a judicial forum for a period of years render these cases exceptional" and required the justices to decide the issue for themselves rather than incur further delay.

The majority's conclusion was that the alternative procedure had major flaws, mostly because it did not permit a detainee to present evidence that might clear him of blame but was either withheld from the record of the Combatant Status Review Tribunal or was learned of subsequently. The tribunals' own fact-finding ability was so limited as to present "considerable risk of error," thus requiring full-fledged scrutiny on appeal, Justice Kennedy said.

Eric M. Freedman, a habeas corpus expert at Hofstra University Law School, said the court was "on the right side of history" to reject what he called "habeas lite." Calling the decision "a structural reaffirmation of what the rule of law means," Professor Freedman, who was a consultant to the detainees' lawyers, said it was as important a ruling on the separation of powers as the Supreme Court has ever issued.

Mr. Bush, in his statement in Rome, said the administration would decide whether to ask Congress to weigh in once more. Success at such an effort would appear unlikely, given that the Supreme Court decision was praised not only by the Democratic leadership, but also by the ranking Republican on the Senate Judiciary Committee, Arlen Specter of Pennsylvania. Senator Specter had voted for the jurisdiction-stripping measure, but then filed a brief at the court arguing that the law was unconstitutional.

In addition to removing habeas corpus jurisdiction, the Military Commissions Act also provided authority for the military commissions that the court's 2006 decision in *Hamdan v. Rumsfeld* said was lacking. The case the court decided on Thursday did not directly concern military commissions, which are due to conduct trials of the several dozen detainees who have been charged with war crimes. The Justice Department said on Thursday that the decision would not delay those trials.

Divided as the Supreme Court was in this case, the justices were unanimous, surprisingly so, in a second habeas corpus ruling on Thursday. Again rejecting the Bush administration's position, the court held in an opinion by Chief Justice Roberts that two civilian United States citizens being held in American military custody in Iraq were entitled to file habeas corpus petitions.

Proceeding to the merits of the petitions, the court then ruled against the two men, Mohammad Munaf and Shawqi Ahmad Omar, who are facing criminal charges under

Iraqi law. Their release through habeas corpus "would interfere with the sovereign authority of Iraq to punish offenses against its laws committed within its borders," Chief Justice Roberts said.

The administration had argued in the case, *Munaf v. Geren*, No. 06-1666, that because the men were technically held by the 26-nation multinational force in Iraq, federal courts did not have jurisdiction to hear their habeas corpus petitions. Chief Justice Roberts said that, to the contrary, what mattered was that the men were held by "American soldiers subject to a United States chain of command."

NOTE: *Although the Supreme Court ruled that Guantánamo Bay fell under the rule of law, Congress threw up huge obstacles to removing the prisoners from the illegal detention camp and it continues to be a source of domestic political upheaval and international scorn as well as a recruiting point for terrorists. Barack Obama was unsuccessful in his push to close the prison; in January 2018, President Trump signed an executive order to keep the prison open indefinitely.*

BUSH LETS U.S. SPY ON CALLERS WITHOUT COURTS

By JAMES RISEN AND ERIC LICHTBLAU, DECEMBER 16, 2005

Months after the Sept. 11 attacks, President Bush secretly authorized the National Security Agency to eavesdrop on Americans and others inside the United States to search for evidence of terrorist activity without the court-approved warrants ordinarily required for domestic spying, according to government officials.

Under a presidential order signed in 2002, the intelligence agency has monitored the international telephone calls and international email messages of hundreds, perhaps thousands, of people inside the United States without warrants over the past three years in an effort to track possible "dirty numbers" linked to Al Qaeda, the officials said. The agency, they said, still seeks warrants to monitor entirely domestic communications.

The previously undisclosed decision to permit some eavesdropping inside the country without court approval was a major shift in American intelligence-gathering practices, particularly for the National Security Agency, whose mission is to spy on communications abroad. As a result, some officials familiar with the continuing operation have questioned whether the surveillance has stretched, if not crossed, constitutional limits on legal searches.

"This is really a sea change," said a former senior official who specializes in national security law. "It's almost a mainstay of this country that the N.S.A. only does foreign searches."

Nearly a dozen current and former officials, who were granted anonymity because of the classified nature of the program, discussed it with reporters for *The New York Times* because of their concerns about the operation's legality and oversight.

According to those officials and others, reservations about aspects of the program have also been expressed by Senator John D. Rockefeller IV, the West Virginia Democrat who is the vice chairman of the Senate Intelligence Committee, and a judge presiding over a secret court that oversees intelligence matters. Some of the questions about the agency's new powers led the administration to temporarily suspend the operation last year and impose more restrictions, the officials said.

The Bush administration views the operation as necessary so that the agency can move quickly to monitor communications that may disclose threats to the United States, the officials said. Defenders of the program say it has been a critical tool in helping disrupt terrorist plots and prevent attacks inside the United States.

Administration officials are confident that existing safeguards are sufficient to protect the privacy and civil liberties of Americans, the officials say. In some cases, they said, the

Justice Department eventually seeks warrants if it wants to expand the eavesdropping to include communications confined within the United States. The officials said the administration had briefed Congressional leaders about the program and notified the judge in charge of the Foreign Intelligence Surveillance Court, the secret Washington court that deals with national security issues.

The White House asked *The New York Times* not to publish this article, arguing that it could jeopardize continuing investigations and alert would-be terrorists that they might be under scrutiny. After meeting with senior administration officials to hear their concerns, the newspaper delayed publication for a year to conduct additional reporting. Some information that administration officials argued could be useful to terrorists has been omitted.

Dealing with a New Threat

While many details about the program remain secret, officials familiar with it say the N.S.A. eavesdrops without warrants on up to 500 people in the United States at any given time. The list changes as some names are added and others dropped, so the number monitored in this country may have reached into the thousands since the program began, several officials said. Overseas, about 5,000 to 7,000 people suspected of terrorist ties are monitored at one time, according to those officials.

Several officials said the eavesdropping program had helped uncover a plot by Iyman Faris, an Ohio trucker and naturalized citizen who pleaded guilty in 2003 to supporting Al Qaeda by planning to bring down the Brooklyn Bridge with blowtorches. What appeared to be another Qaeda plot, involving fertilizer bomb attacks on British pubs and train stations, was exposed last year in part through the program, the officials said. But they said most people targeted for N.S.A. monitoring have never been charged with a crime, including an Iranian American doctor in the South who came under suspicion because of what one official described as dubious ties to Osama bin Laden.

The eavesdropping program grew out of concerns after the Sept. 11 attacks that the nation's intelligence agencies were not poised to deal effectively with the new threat of Al Qaeda and that they were handcuffed by legal and bureaucratic restrictions better suited to peacetime than war, according to officials. In response, President Bus significantly eased limits on American intelligence and law enforcement agencies and the military.

But some of the administration's antiterrorism initiatives have provoked an outcry from members of Congress, watchdog groups, immigrants and others who argue that the measures erode protections for civil liberties and intrude on Americans' privacy.

Opponents have challenged provisions of the USA Patriot Act, the focus of contentious debate on Capitol Hill this week, that expand domestic surveillance by giving the Federal Bureau of Investigation more power to collect information like library lending lists or internet use. Military and F.B.I. officials have drawn criticism for monitoring what were largely peaceful antiwar protests. The Pentagon and the Department of Homeland Security were forced to retreat on plans to use public and private databases to hunt for possible terrorists. And last year, the Supreme Court rejected the administration's claim that those labeled "enemy combatants" were not entitled to judicial review of their open-ended detention.

Mr. Bush's executive order allowing some warrantless eavesdropping on those inside the United States—including American citizens, permanent legal residents, tourists and other foreigners—is based on classified legal opinions that assert that the president has broad powers to order such searches, derived in part from the September 2001 Congressional resolution authorizing him to wage war on Al Qaeda and other terrorist groups, according to the officials familiar with the N.S.A. operation.

The National Security Agency, which is based at Fort Meade, Md., is the nation's largest and most secretive intelligence agency, so intent on remaining out of public view that it has long been nicknamed "No Such Agency." It breaks codes and maintains listening posts around the world to eavesdrop on foreign governments, diplomats and trade negotiators as well as drug lords and terrorists. But the agency ordinarily operates under tight restrictions on any spying on Americans, even if they are overseas, or disseminating information about them.

What the agency calls a "special collection program" began soon after the Sept. 11 attacks, as it looked for new tools to attack terrorism. The program accelerated in early 2002 after the Central Intelligence Agency started capturing top Qaeda operatives overseas, including Abu Zubaydah, who was arrested in Pakistan in March 2002. The C.I.A. seized the terrorists' computers, cell phones and personal phone directories, said the officials familiar with the program. The N.S.A. surveillance was intended to exploit those numbers and addresses as quickly as possible, they said.

In addition to eavesdropping on those numbers and reading email messages to and from the Qaeda figures, the N.S.A. began monitoring others linked to them, creating an expanding chain. While most of the numbers and addresses were overseas, hundreds were in the United States, the officials said.

Under the agency's longstanding rules, the N.S.A. can target for interception phone calls or email messages on foreign soil, even if the recipients of those communications are in the United States. Usually, though, the government can only target phones and email messages in the United States by first obtaining a court order from the Foreign Intelligence Surveillance Court, which holds its closed sessions at the Justice Department.

Traditionally, the F.B.I., not the N.S.A., seeks such warrants and conducts most domestic eavesdropping. Until the new program began, the N.S.A. typically limited its domestic surveillance to foreign embassies and missions in Washington, New York and other cities, and obtained court orders to do so.

Since 2002, the agency has been conducting some warrantless eavesdropping on people in the United States who are linked, even if indirectly, to suspected terrorists through the chain of phone numbers and email addresses, according to several officials who know of the operation. Under the special program, the agency monitors their international communications, the officials said. The agency, for example, can target phone calls from someone in New York to someone in Afghanistan.

Warrants are still required for eavesdropping on entirely domestic-to-domestic communications, those officials say, meaning that calls from that New Yorker to someone in California could not be monitored without first going to the Federal Intelligence Surveillance Court.

A White House Briefing

After the special program started, Congressional leaders from both political parties were brought to Vice President Dick Cheney's office in the White House. The leaders, who included the chairmen and ranking members of the Senate and House intelligence committees, learned of the N.S.A. operation from Mr. Cheney, Lt. Gen. Michael V. Hayden of the air force, who was then the agency's director and is now a full general and the principal deputy director of national intelligence, and George J. Tenet, then the director of the C.I.A., officials said.

It is not clear how much the members of Congress were told about the presidential order and the eavesdropping program. Some of them declined to comment about the matter, while others did not return phone calls.

Later briefings were held for members of Congress as they assumed leadership roles on the intelligence committees, officials familiar with the program said. After a 2003 briefing, Senator Rockefeller, the West Virginia Democrat who became vice chairman of the Senate Intelligence Committee that year, wrote a letter to Mr. Cheney expressing concerns about the program, officials knowledgeable about the letter said. It could not be determined if he received a reply. Mr. Rockefeller declined to comment. Aside from the Congressional leaders, only a small group of people, including several cabinet members and officials at the N.S.A., the C.I.A. and the Justice Department, know of the program.

Some officials familiar with it say they consider warrantless eavesdropping inside the United States to be unlawful and possibly unconstitutional, amounting to an improper search. One government official involved in the operation said he privately complained to a Congressional official about his doubts about the program's legality. But nothing came of his inquiry. "People just looked the other way because they didn't want to know what was going on," he said.

A senior government official recalled that he was taken aback when he first learned of the operation. "My first reaction was, 'We're doing what?'" he said. While he said he eventually felt that adequate safeguards were put in place, he added that questions about the program's legitimacy were understandable.

Some of those who object to the operation argue that is unnecessary. By getting warrants through the foreign intelligence court, the N.S.A. and F.B.I. could eavesdrop on people inside the United States who might be tied to terrorist groups without skirting longstanding rules, they say.

The standard of proof required to obtain a warrant from the Foreign Intelligence Surveillance Court is generally considered lower than that required for a criminal warrant—intelligence officials only have to show probable cause that someone may be "an agent of a foreign power," which includes international terrorist groups—and the secret court has turned down only a small number of requests over the years. In 2004, according to the Justice Department, 1,754 warrants were approved. And the Foreign Intelligence Surveillance Court can grant emergency approval for wiretaps within hours, officials say.

Administration officials counter that they sometimes need to move more urgently, the officials said. Those involved in the program also said that the N.S.A.'s eavesdroppers might need to start monitoring large batches of numbers all at once, and that it would be impractical to seek permission from the Foreign Intelligence Surveillance Court first, according to the officials.

The N.S.A. domestic spying operation has stirred such controversy among some national security officials in part because of the agency's cautious culture and longstanding rules.

Widespread abuses—including eavesdropping on Vietnam War protesters and civil rights activists—by American intelligence agencies became public in the 1970s and led to passage of the Foreign Intelligence Surveillance Act, which imposed strict limits on intelligence gathering on American soil. Among other things, the law required search warrants, approved by the secret F.I.S.A. court, for wiretaps in national security cases. The agency, deeply scarred by the scandals, adopted additional rules that all but ended domestic spying on its part.

After the Sept. 11 attacks, though, the United States intelligence community was criticized for being too risk-averse. The National Security Agency was even cited by the independent 9/11 Commission for adhering to self-imposed rules that were stricter than those set by federal law.

Concerns and Revisions

Several senior government officials say that when the special operation began, there were few controls on it and little formal oversight outside the N.S.A. The agency can choose its eavesdropping targets and does not have to seek approval from Justice Department or other Bush administration officials. Some agency officials wanted nothing to do with the program, apparently fearful of participating in an illegal operation, a former senior Bush administration official said. Before the 2004 election, the official said, some N.S.A. personnel worried that the program might come under scrutiny by Congressional or criminal investigators if Senator John Kerry, the Democratic nominee, was elected president.

In mid-2004, concerns about the program expressed by national security officials, government lawyers and a judge prompted the Bush administration to suspend elements of the program and revamp it.

For the first time, the Justice Department audited the N.S.A. program, several officials said. And to provide more guidance, the Justice Department and the agency expanded and refined a checklist to follow in deciding whether probable cause existed to start monitoring someone's communications, several officials said.

A complaint from Judge Colleen Kollar-Kotelly, the federal judge who oversees the Federal Intelligence Surveillance Court, helped spur the suspension, officials said. The judge questioned whether information obtained under the N.S.A. program was being improperly used as the basis for F.I.S.A. wiretap-warrant requests from the Justice Department, according to senior government officials. While not knowing all the details of the exchange, several government lawyers said there appeared to be concerns that the Justice Department, by trying to shield the existence of the N.S.A. program, was in danger of misleading the court about the origins of the information cited to justify the warrants.

One official familiar with the episode said the judge insisted to Justice Department lawyers at one point that any material gathered under the special N.S.A. program not be used in seeking wiretap warrants from her court. Judge Kollar-Kotelly did not return calls for comment.

A related issue arose in a case in which the F.B.I. was monitoring the communications of a terrorist suspect under a F.I.S.A.-approved warrant, even though the National Security Agency was already conducting warrantless eavesdropping.

According to officials, F.B.I. surveillance of Mr. Faris, the Brooklyn Bridge plotter, was dropped for a short time because of technical problems. At the time, senior Justice Department officials worried what would happen if the N.S.A. picked up information that needed to be presented in court. The government would then either have to disclose the N.S.A. program or mislead a criminal court about how it had gotten the information.

Several national security officials say the powers granted the N.S.A. by President Bush go far beyond the expanded counterterrorism powers granted by Congress under the USA Patriot Act, which is up for renewal. The House on Wednesday approved a plan to reauthorize crucial parts of the law. But final passage has been delayed under the threat of a Senate filibuster because of concerns from both parties over possible intrusions on Americans' civil liberties and privacy.

Under the act, law enforcement and intelligence officials are still required to seek a F.I.S.A. warrant every time they want to eavesdrop within the United States. A recent agreement reached by Republican leaders and the Bush administration would modify the standard for F.B.I. wiretap warrants, requiring, for instance, a description of a specific target. Critics say the bar would remain too low to prevent abuses.

Bush administration officials argue that the civil liberties concerns are unfounded, and they say pointedly that the Patriot Act has not freed the N.S.A. to target Americans. "Nothing could be further from the truth," wrote John Yoo, a former official in the Justice Department's Office of Legal Counsel, and his coauthor in a *Wall Street Journal* opinion article in December 2003. Mr. Yoo worked on a classified legal opinion on the N.S.A.'s domestic eavesdropping program.

At an April hearing on the Patriot Act renewal, Senator Barbara A. Mikulski, Democrat of Maryland, asked Attorney General Alberto R. Gonzales and Robert S. Mueller III, the director of the F.B.I., "Can the National Security Agency, the great electronic snooper, spy on the American people?"

"Generally," Mr. Mueller said, "I would say generally, they are not allowed to spy or to gather information on American citizens."

President Bush did not ask Congress to include provisions for the N.S.A. domestic surveillance program as part of the Patriot Act and has not sought any other laws to authorize the operation. Bush administration lawyers argued that such new laws were unnecessary, because they believed that the Congressional resolution on the campaign against terrorism provided ample authorization, officials said.

The Legal Line Shifts

Seeking Congressional approval was also viewed as politically risky because the proposal would be certain to face intense opposition on civil liberties grounds. The administration also feared that by publicly disclosing the existence of the operation, its usefulness in tracking terrorists would end, officials said.

The legal opinions that support the N.S.A. operation remain classified, but they appear to have followed private discussions among senior administration lawyers and other officials about the need to pursue aggressive strategies that once may have been seen as crossing a legal line, according to senior officials who participated in the discussions.

For example, just days after the Sept. 11, 2001, attacks on New York and the Pentagon, Mr. Yoo, the Justice Department lawyer, wrote an internal memorandum that argued that the government might use "electronic surveillance techniques and equipment that are more powerful and sophisticated than those available to law enforcement agencies in order to intercept telephonic communications and observe the movement of persons but without obtaining warrants for such uses."

Mr. Yoo noted that while such actions could raise constitutional issues, in the face of devastating terrorist attacks "the government may be justified in taking measures which in less troubled conditions could be seen as infringements of individual liberties."

The next year, Justice Department lawyers disclosed their thinking on the issue of warrantless wiretaps in national security cases in a little-noticed brief in an unrelated court case. In that 2002 brief, the government said that "the Constitution vests in the president inherent authority to conduct warrantless intelligence surveillance (electronic or otherwise) of foreign powers or their agents, and Congress cannot by statute extinguish that constitutional authority."

Administration officials were also encouraged by a November 2002 appeals court decision in an unrelated matter. The decision by the Foreign Intelligence Surveillance Court of Review, which sided with the administration in dismantling a bureaucratic "wall" limiting cooperation between prosecutors and intelligence officers, cited "the president's inherent constitutional authority to conduct warrantless foreign intelligence surveillance."

But the same court suggested that national security interests should not be grounds "to jettison the Fourth Amendment requirements" protecting the rights of Americans against undue searches. The dividing line, the court acknowledged, "is a very difficult one to administer."

NOTE: The Times *came under heavy criticism for delaying the publication of this article for about a year, until after Bush was reelected, but insisted that the decision was not political and that the article had not been ready for publication earlier.*

CHAPTER 3
THE ECONOMY

"I don't think we're in a recession, but no question we're in a slowdown. . . . One way Congress, if they really want to make a substantial difference in creating certainty during uncertain times, is to make the tax cuts we passed permanent."

—President George W. Bush, February 28, 2008

LIKE WAR, ECONOMIC ISSUES have dominated every president's attentions, fears, failures and occasional triumphs—so much so that Bill Clinton's team adopted the internal admonition, "It's the economy, stupid." The New Deal tested the constitutional limits of presidential power, while Lyndon Johnson's War on Poverty redrew the boundaries of government involvement in people's economic lives. Richard Nixon's price controls strained the ideological unity of his Republican Party; Americans tittered over Gerald Ford's "Whip Inflation Now" (W.I.N.) program; the 2008 financial collapse brought George W. Bush's tenure to an ignominious ending and gave Barack Obama a mammoth challenge for his historic presidency. All along, Americans hotly debated Republican notions of low taxation and small government versus Democratic ideals of government activism and social safety nets.

OPPOSITE: A house for sale in Detroit, December 30, 2008. Detroit was one of six U.S. cities with record one-month declines in home prices during the 2008 collapse.

BANK BILL IS ENACTED

MARCH 10, 1933

A record for executive and legislative action was written today in the effort of the nation to end its banking difficulties, but progress was partly checked tonight by the inability of an administrative arm of the government to keep pace.

After Congress had passed emergency legislation designed to affect a wholesale resumption of banking activities throughout the United States and the measure had been signed by the executive, all within 8 hours and 37 minutes, President Roosevelt was forced to issue a proclamation at 10:10 o'clock tonight, extending the bank holiday and gold embargo indefinitely until the Treasury Department could make regulations to meet the new conditions. This may be as late as Monday.

The President last night had said that a large number of banks could open tomorrow.

Keen disappointment at the outcome was apparent at the White House, where President Roosevelt and his associates had worked almost incessantly since his inauguration last Saturday to bring about the reopening of the banks of the country.

On Michigan's second "bankless" day, Chrysler workers line up in Detroit at a special disbursing office on February 16, 1933, to cash their paychecks.

Sense of Disappointment Felt

The president's sense of disappointment was radiated to leaders of Congress.

The president had told them that enactment of the emergency banking law would bring about the opening of a large number of banks tomorrow, and they had held out this statement to their colleagues as the reason for haste, resulting in such action as the House passing the bill unanimously after 40 minutes' debate and the Senate following within 3 hours.

Undismayed by the turn of affairs, the president and his Congressional advisers went into conference tonight to work out the task for the remainder of the present extraordinary session.

It was expected that the president would send up a message urging two other legislative enactments, one to provide for unemployment relief and the other carrying out the economy program which the president's party has promised.

After the White House conference ended, Senator Glass said that the bank holiday had been continued, first, to permit the state banks to come under the shelter of the Federal Reserve System, and second, to give the Federal Reserve and regional banks opportunity to ascertain more accurately than the Controller of the Currency had been able to do, what banks should be opened when the holiday ended.

Congress Moves with Speed

The new Congress moved with a speed that dazzled the veteran members of that assembly. Within less than seven hours and a half, the Congress convened in special season, organized, received the message from President Roosevelt asking a measure to "reopen all sound banks," passed that measure and sent it to the White House.

Barely an hour and fifteen minutes after the Senate passed the act by a vote of 73 to 7, the House having adopted it unanimously, it became law by the signature of Franklin D. Roosevelt.

This deferment of the reopening of banks already rated as sound by tests which national bank examiners have been making during the last two days was made necessary, by the fact that there was no time before tomorrow morning to issue the necessary regulations.

It was expected that possibly by Saturday, and certainly by Monday, those banks which have demonstrated their soundness to the inspectors of the Federal Reserve System will be permitted to open.

Officials were besieged all day with applications from state banks to enter the protective zone of the Federal Reserve System as expanded by today's legislation.

The new banking law was designed to provide both the authority and the currency with which to reopen all the solvent national banks and Federal Reserve members, and indirectly, their correspondents.

Briefly, the act provided:

· Issuance of new Federal Reserve Bank notes in an amount necessary to meet the present situation, such notes to bear an interest tax to assure their retirement when no longer needed.

· A grant to the president of practically dictatorial powers to stop hoarding, retrieve gold from hoarding and embargo gold.

· Extension of power to the executive branch for such control over all national banks as may be necessary for the protection of depositors and creditors, including creation of a "conservator" system for these institutions.

· Validation of what already has been done by the president and what may hereafter be done under the Trading with the Enemy Act to deal with the present emergency.

The bill made a peacetime record in Congress. It was passed unanimously in the House after forty minutes of debate, without a completed copy being available to a member. It was approved by the Senate three hours later by a vote of 73 to 7. Opposing the measure were Senators Borah, Carey, Dale, La Follette, Nye, Costigan and Shipstead.

The new Treasury banknotes "shall be receivable at par in all parts of the United States" for the same purposes are national bank notes and shall be direct obligations of the Federal Reserve Banks issuing them.

> *Issuance of national banknotes is limited to the amount of the capital stock of the bank of issue.*

Issuance of national banknotes is limited to the amount of the capital stock of the bank of issue, but this restriction does not apply to Federal Reserve Bank notes. Various estimates have been made as to the amount of additional currency which might be quickly available under the various provisions of the bill, one government expert putting the total at $2.8 billion or more, with much depending upon rulings by the Reserve System as to eligible collateral.

The bill was not amended in a single particular from the form in which it was received from Secretary Woodin and Attorney General Cummings, who drafted it.

The bill was a mere restatement in legislative form of the message sent by President Roosevelt to Congress on the subject.

"Our task," the president's message said, "is to reopen all sound banks."

And with that he proceeded to ask for particular provisions. He wanted immediate legislation giving the executive branch control over banks for the protection of depositors; he wanted authority to open such banks as "have already been ascertained to be in sound condition and other such banks as rapidly as possible."

He asked authority, too, to reorganize and reopen banks that may be found to require reorganization. He asked last of all for amendments to the Federal Reserve Act that would provide such additional currency, "adequately secured," as might be necessary to issue to meet "all demands for currency" in the present situation without increasing the unsecured indebtedness of the government.

Party Lines Are Forgotten

The president expressed the belief that the legislation requested not only would lift immediately all unwarranted doubts and suspicions as to the soundness of the banking system but also would "mark the beginning of a new relationship between the banks and the people of the country."

The president urged action, and he got action. Senators who for years had held unswervingly to certain convictions on banking and currency swallowed them in the urge for speed in the banking crisis. Leaders of the opposition party laid down a plea for the support of President Roosevelt with as much feeling as if he had been the champion of their own band.

Mr. Roosevelt indicated in his message that he would ask still other things of this extra session. He mentioned "two other measures" which he regarded as of immediate urgency. Congressional leaders believed that one of them would be a $500 million public works bond issue as an aid to unemployment, and the other a reorganization order in the interest of public economy.

Glass Supports the Measure

The only delay in meeting the president's request for legislation was the time it took to explain the measure to the Senate Banking and Currency Committee. Senator Glass, author of the Federal Reserve Act, who later told the Senate that under ordinary circumstances the measure would be a "shock" to his convictions, performed the task of explaining it.

The Virginian later took the floor and espoused it as a "great piece of legislation," great because it met so paralyzing an emergency. He considered his support of the measure a patriotic duty.

As for the House, it did not delay. It did not even wait for a copy of the bill. Drafted as it was in an all-night conference of Congressional leaders and administration officials, it was still in an unfinished form this afternoon and was corrected from time to time in the type forms at the Government Printing Office.

Impatient at the delay, the House leaders brought up the subject under unanimous consent. They used a first draft of the bill, corrected by pencil. They allowed only forty minutes' debate and not all of this actually was used, as the 435 members demanded as with one voice, "Vote! Vote! Vote!"

No Roll Call in the House

Democratic and Republican members alike agreed that "this is no time to argue," and within less time than it takes to tell it on paper the House passed the bill without a single dissenting vote—without even asking a roll call—and sent it along to the Senate, several hundred of its members following it over to the other side of the Capitol.

NOTE: *This act of Congress, also known as the Glass-Steagall Act, represented the first real attempt to regulate the banking industry, by separating banks from firms that dealt in stock and bond trading, and insuring depositors' accounts through the new Federal Deposit Insurance Corporation. Opposition from the political right and the financial industry emerged almost immediately, but it was not until 1999 that Congress essentially repealed it and President Bill Clinton, a Democrat, signed off. Predictably, banks immediately moved into the business of stock speculation, which many economists said was a root cause of the 2008 Great Recession.*

THE N.I.R.A. DECISION

MAY 28, 1935

Two incidental reasons for satisfaction with the decision of the United States Supreme Court in the case of the National Industrial Recovery Act must catch every eye. The first is that Chief Justice Hughes spoke for a unanimous court. There can be no question now of asserting that the minority was right in a 5-to-4 decision; nor can there be invidious remarks about the Tories among the judges outvoting the Liberals. All are united in upholding the view that most of the provisions of N.I.R.A. are invalid under the Constitution. The second cause for gratification is that the judgment of the court came so long after the enactment of the law. Had it fallen near the time when the nation was enthusiastic about N.I.R.A. it would have been bad both for the court and the country. Now it follows closely upon a marked change of public sentiment. The Recovery Act had done its work, the chief benefit of which was to stir the people into hopeful activity and had come to be almost universally regarded as a piece of legislation now obsolete and ineffective. Nowhere will the opinion of the Supreme Court in the matter now provoke angry resentment. The judges simply pronounce to be dead a statute which the great mass of the people had already decided to be dead.

Taking the instance of codes under N.I.R.A., we find the Supreme Court making a complete end of them. It decides that Congress had no constitutional power to delegate to the president authority to impose codes upon private business. Especially repugnant to the court was

> *Especially repugnant to the court was the grant of authority to [the president] to make changes in the codes as he might please.*

the grant of authority to him to make changes in the codes as he might please. The Constitution does not permit delegation of power to the president to do "whatever he thinks desirable." Going still further, the Supreme Court holds that no group in any industry may frame a code for itself through which the attempt is made to give the force of law. In other words, violation of the code, even when it is voluntary, cannot be punished by the courts. This seems to make the case against the codes complete. A large number of them had already been extinguished. The rest of them were ended by Mr. Richberg's announcement last night.

More striking and penetrating is the decision of the court that the federal government has no constitutional right to go into the states and fix hours and wages in industries which are not clearly and exclusively engaged in interstate commerce. Transactions, declares the court, which merely affect intrastate commerce, are not subject to federal legislation and must remain within the control of the states. Otherwise, affirm the judges, we should soon have everything brought within federal jurisdiction, with the result of setting up a "centralized government" never contemplated by the Constitution. This part of the decision seems to do away with section 3 of the Recovery Act and leaves it only a thing of shreds and patches. Congress may attempt to piece the fragments together, but it is now evident that if any revision of N.I.R.A. is to be made, it will have to be an entirely new law. Perhaps the old one will now be allowed to expire on its appointed date of June 16.

Great significance attaches to the ruling out by the court of business which merely "affects interstate commerce." That same clause, it will be noted, occurs in the Wagner Labor Bill. If it remains there and another judicial test is made, the consequence will be expected to be the same as in the rejection of N.I.R.A. as unconstitutional. It is a nice point to decide whether an industry is frankly engaged in interstate commerce, or merely affects it indirectly. Yet it was deemed vitally important by the government, since the solicitor general argued in this very case that intrastate transactions are frequently so interwoven with interstate commerce that the latter cannot be "effectively regulated without control over the former." That control the Supreme Court has declared to be unconstitutional.

There will be more to say of this Supreme Court decision, as Congress may seek to gather up the fragments of N.I.R.A. The action of the court seems so far to have met with general approval. Senator Borah says that by it the Constitution is reestablished. Two years ago Congress was ready to take great chances with the supreme law. Hereafter it may be more careful, since the evidence is now clear that the Supreme Court will not permit the federal government to usurp or encroach upon the constitutional rights of "indestructible states."

THE CHOICE OF A CANDIDATE

SEPTEMBER 19, 1940

The *New York Times* supported Franklin D. Roosevelt for the presidency in 1932 and again in 1936. In 1940 it will support Wendell Willkie.

It has made its choice, as all Americans must make their choice, in one of the great crises of this nation's history. The liberties of the American people are in danger. A hostile power, openly proclaiming its hatred of the democratic way of life, has swept across Europe and is now battering it at the gates of England, seeking to grasp the eastern approaches to that Atlantic world in which our own democracy has lived and prospered.

Both Mr. Roosevelt and Mr. Willkie understand the critical nature of this threat to the United States. Both are citizens of the world. Both know that it is impossible to isolate ourselves from the consequences of a world revolution. Both know that we must take sides morally or count for nothing. Both are opposed to actual intervention in the war, but short of war both favor every possible aid that can be given to the one democracy in Europe that still stands in Hitler's path.

This agreement between the two presidential candidates on the fundamentals of a foreign policy is a deeply fortunate fact for the American people. Without it we might now be involved in a bitter controversy which would wreck our unity. As matters stand, the choice before us has been narrowed to this question: In whose hands, Mr. Roosevelt's or Mr. Willkie's, is the safety of the American people likely to be more secure during the critical test that lies ahead?

We give our own support to Mr. Willkie primarily for these reasons: Because we believe that he is better equipped than Mr. Roosevelt to provide this country with an adequate national defense; because we believe he is a practical liberal who understands the need of increased production; because we believe that the fiscal policies of Mr. Roosevelt have failed disastrously; because we believe that at a time when the

Wendell Willkie preparing to give a speech at the National Press Club, Washington, D.C., June 12, 1940.

traditional safeguards of democracy are failing everywhere it is particularly important to honor and preserve the American tradition against vesting the enormous powers of the presidency in the hands of any man for three consecutive terms of office.

Our readers are entitled to a statement of the reasons which, upon mature consideration, have led us to these opinions.

Defense of the United States

In the field of national defense, we recognize that Mr. Roosevelt has taken a number of necessary steps, all of which have had our wholehearted endorsement, both before he was ready to take them and later, when he had acted. He has recreated the Defense Advisory Commission and called some able men to Washington. He has recommended that Congress appropriate large funds for defense equipment. He has succeeded in negotiating leases for new naval and air bases which are of great potential importance to the defense of the whole North American continent. He strongly urged Congress to adopt a system of compulsory selective military service.

But there are a number of other equally important steps which Mr. Roosevelt has not taken. He has withheld power from the Advisory Commission and made it a mere consultative agency, unable on its own authority to cut the endless red tape in Washington. He has kept power for himself, tried to be his own defense administrator and retained in his own hands control over too many details of a defense program which still lacks central planning. He has seemed to regard the whole business of defense as a sideshow to the ordinary activities of the country, requiring no fundamental change in the habits of the American people and no revision of any of the policies of his administration. We find Mr. Willkie's early call for sacrifice, for hard work, "sweat and toil," more reassuring than Mr. Roosevelt's cheerful confidence that we need not let ourselves become "discomboomerated" by the task that lies before us.

But all these points, important as they are, only touch the surface of the matter. At bottom, adequate national defense means much more than airplanes, tanks and cannon, even when all of these are actually on hand and not just "on order." It means a nation strong in its economic health and power, with a thriving industry, full employment, both of manpower and of money, new capital flowing vigorously into new channels of production. It means, in short, a nation with gigantic industrial force behind its army and its navy.

The record shows that Mr. Roosevelt has achieved least success in the solution of this very problem. He has failed to create the conditions for a confident and expanding business. It is a reasonable assumption that this same problem can be managed better by a man who understands business, who has the confidence of business, who has himself been a part of business, whose interest in business problems has been firsthand and continuous rather than casual and intermittent, and whose experience includes a successful personal record in stimulating business and expanding industrial production.

In this field Mr. Willkie is the professional and Mr. Roosevelt is the amateur.

Liberalism and Reform

In the field of domestic policy, this newspaper has recognized the need of the sound social and economic reforms of the two Roosevelt administrations. It has given its support to these reforms. Specifically, it has endorsed the purpose and the principle of the Social Security Act, the National Housing Act of 1934, the Slum Clearance Act of 1936, the Wagner Housing Act of 1937, the Soil Conservation Act, the Securities Act of 1933, the regulation of the stock exchanges, the supervision of investment trusts. The reforms at which every one of these measures aimed were long overdue.

Mr. Willkie has affirmed his own belief in the necessity of reform and his own support of the major reforms of the Roosevelt administrations. Because of this he has been attacked by the president's friends as a mere plagiarist who is now attempting to steal the New Deal's thunder, and an impostor who is trying to run "on the president's own program." This is a curious attitude for the president's friends to take. It is a curious attitude, because it suggests a belief that the New Deal has a monopoly on reform and wants nobody else to share in it. But the truth is that no faction and no party has a monopoly on reform in the United States; many men have shared in it and will continue to share in it. "Plagiarism" is beside the point. For seven years Mr. Roosevelt himself has been making daily use of important reforms introduced by Republican administrations— among them the Sherman Antitrust Law, the Pure Food and Drug Act, the Children's Bureau, the executive budget, the Reconstruction Finance Corporation.

For ourselves, we welcome the fact that Mr. Willkie stands pledged to conserve rather than to destroy what is best in Mr. Roosevelt's reforms. We believe that these reforms would be safe in Mr. Willkie's hands, not only because Mr. Willkie is a man of goodwill, but because his approach to the problems now before us shows him to be a liberal. He is enough of a student and enough of a realist to know that we are living in a changing time and that it is both necessary and desirable that the government should take an increasingly active part in policing the financial markets, in safeguarding labor's right to bargain collectively and in achieving social justice for underprivileged people.

More than this, we believe that Mr. Willkie could be relied upon not to make some of the mistakes and not to take some of the risks which Mr. Roosevelt has made and taken. For we believe that while Mr. Roosevelt has helped enormously to awaken the social conscience of this country, and that while he deserves lasting credit for this leadership, Mr. Roosevelt has also put his own reforms in peril. He has put them in peril by ignoring or by failing to understand the fundamental problem of increased production; by encouraging great numbers of Americans to believe that it is possible to grow richer by working less and producing less; by fostering the idea that there exists somewhere a great fund of wealth which has only to be divided more equitably in order to make everybody prosperous; by permitting important members of his administration to preach the doctrines of class jealousy and class hatred.

Mr. Willkie stated the case accurately when he said that "American liberalism does not consist merely in reforming things; it consists also in making things." It consists in expanding the production of the necessities and the good things of life. Wealth is only another word for production, and in the long run there is no other way to achieve a higher standard of living for the whole people of a nation than to produce in abundance.

We believe that Mr. Willkie understands this crucial point better than Mr. Roosevelt, and that he would be more likely to succeed in putting this principle into practice.

"The Road to Bankruptcy"

In the field of fiscal policy our dissent from the course pursued by Mr. Roosevelt dates from his first year in office. We expressed this dissent in 1936, even while supporting him for reelection, and ventured then to express the hope that he would pursue a more responsible fiscal policy during his second term in office. Unfortunately, his course during his second term has become still more reckless. We cite evidence at three points to support this statement.

(1) The fantastic silver policy of the Roosevelt administration, scarcely begun in 1936, has now grown to almost incredible proportions. More than 2 billion ounces of a metal for which our government has no earthly use—approximately a hundred times as much silver as all the silver mines in the United States produced in the year before this policy began—have been bought by the Treasury at overvalued prices in an artificial market. This policy makes no sense, except as a political maneuver to win the support of the so-called silver bloc. Otherwise its only visible results have been to drive off the silver standard the one important country which had previously been on it and to take from other nations useless silver in exchange for our own good wheat and oil and motor cars

and other exports. There is only one way to describe such a policy as this. It leads over the hills to the poorhouse.

(2) The national budget, which was originally to be balanced so courageously, has been continuously out of balance since Mr. Roosevelt entered office. The national debt has more than doubled in seven years. It is true that the new defense program has now made a balanced budget hopeless at the moment. But even before this program was proposed, the administration was operating under a gigantic deficit and spending far more money annually than had ever been raised by taxation in any year in the whole history of the United States. Moreover, the problem of the budget is not less serious, but far more serious, because of the new difficulties presented by the defense program. For the sake of conserving the national credit in a time of danger, expenditures other than those for defense ought now to be cut to a point at which they balance tax yields. But the administration, with whom borrowing has become a habit, has not proposed a single important economy as an offset against its huge defense spending.

(3) The fundamental trouble is that the administration has thrown overboard the central fiscal theory in which it professed to believe, even as late as 1936. It has abandoned the idea that the best contribution it could make to reemployment and recovery is to put its own fiscal house in order. It now believes, and the president frankly says this in his budget messages, that when business is lagging, the government ought to go in debt deliberately in order to "create purchasing power" and "energize private enterprise." This is the perfect politician's paradise—a paradise in which public money is spent on a gigantic scale without any responsibility of raising an equivalent amount of money by taxation. We believe that the results of a continuation of this policy will be precisely what Mr. Roosevelt himself said they would be in 1932—"If, like a spendthrift, a nation throws discretion to the winds and is willing to make no sacrifice at all in spending . . . it is on the road to bankruptcy." We believe that there is no real possibility whatever of checking the present trend toward bankruptcy so long as Mr. Roosevelt remains in office. It will be a desperately hard task at best. The only present hope lies in a change of administrations.

The Third-Term Issue

We come, finally, in the choice before us, to an issue which has been defined by more than a hundred years of American history, by the deliberate decision of some of our greatest presidents and by the reluctance of many Americans today to surrender what they believe to be a safeguard of the democratic system the issue of the third term.

From Mr. Roosevelt's own statement in his radio acceptance speech to the Democratic National Convention, the country knows that even as late as a year ago he had no intention of challenging the tradition against a third term: "Last September it was still my intention to announce clearly and simply at an early date that under no conditions would I accept re-election." This announcement was never made; when the president finally declared his intentions regarding the third term he did not say that "under no conditions would he accept reelection," but merely that he "had no wish to be a candidate again"—a very different statement. The practical effect of the postponement was to lessen greatly the chance of any other Democrat to receive his party's nomination. The practical effect of the change in the character of the president's announcement was to encourage the "draft," which some of the highest officials of his own Administration had long favored and long worked to bring about. From these facts it seems to us that only one conclusion can be drawn. As the situation created by the war developed, the president came to regard his own personal leadership as indispensable and to believe that there was no other member of his party, however trusted, however close to him, however deeply in accord with his own convictions about the war or about domestic issues, who could safely take his place.

The doctrine of one man's indispensability is a new doctrine for this country. It is a doctrine which less scrupulous men in Europe have used to root themselves in power. It is a doctrine which we in the United States have good reason to question, particularly when we consider how the powers of the presidency have grown, what immense patronage, what gigantic expenditures, what enormous power to perpetuate himself in office is now within the grasp of any president of the United States.

These considerations are especially relevant when the particular president who now chooses to remain in office for a third term is the same president who has never sur-rendered voluntarily a single one of the vast "emergency" powers which Congress has given him. He is the same president who has shown himself so impatient of constitutional restraints that he was willing to circumvent the Supreme Court itself by adding enough members to it to give his own opinions a majority.

In the defeat of Mr. Roosevelt and the election of Mr. Willkie there is an opportunity to safeguard a tradition with the wisdom of long experience behind it.

NOTE: *The primary objections that* The Times *had to Roosevelt's reelection seem rather odd in retrospect—that his policies were going to bankrupt the country, and that he was not tough enough to face up to the threat from Nazi Germany, which of course they did not, and he certainly was. The third concern—that three terms was too many for a president—proved to be prophetic. The Constitution was later amended to allow only two presidential terms.*

NIXON ORDERS 90-DAY WAGE-PRICE FREEZE, ASKS TAX CUTS, NEW JOBS IN BROAD PLAN

By JAMES M. NAUGHTON, AUGUST 16, 1971

President Nixon charted a new economic course tonight by ordering a 90-day freeze on wages and prices, requesting federal tax cuts and making a broad range of domestic and international moves designed to strengthen the dollar.

In a 20-minute address, telecast and broadcast nationally, the president appealed to Americans to join him in creating new jobs, curtailing inflation and restoring confidence in the economy through "the most comprehensive new economic policy to be undertaken in this nation in four decades."

Some of the measures Mr. Nixon can impose temporarily himself and he asked for tolerance as he does. Others require Congressional approval and—although he proposed some policies that his critics on Capitol Hill have been urging upon him—will doubtless face long scrutiny before they take effect.

Two Tax Reductions

Mr. Nixon imposed a ceiling on all prices, rents, wages and salaries—and asked corporations to do the same voluntarily on stockholder dividends—under authority granted to him last year by Congress but ignored by the White House until tonight.

The president asked Congress to speed up by one year the additional $50 personal income tax exemption scheduled to go into effect on Jan. 1, 1973, and to repeal, retroactive to today, the 7 percent excise tax on automobile purchases.

He also asked for legislative authority to grant corporations a 10 percent tax credit for investing in new American-made machinery and equipment and pledged to introduce in Congress next January other tax proposals that would stimulate the economy.

Combined with new cuts in federal spending, the measures announced by Mr. Nixon tonight represented a major shift in his administration's policy on the economy.

Cuts Ruled Out Earlier

Only seven weeks ago, after an intensive cabinet-level study of economic policy, the president announced that he would not seek any tax cuts this year and would hew to his existing economic "game plan," confident of success.

Eleven days ago, Mr. Nixon reasserted his opposition to a wage and price review board—a less stringent method of holding down prices and wages than the freeze he ordered—and said only that he was more receptive to considering some new approach to curtailing inflation.

The program issued tonight at the White House thus came with an unaccustomed suddenness, reflecting both domestic political pressures on the president to improve the economy before the 1972 elections, and growing international concern over the stability of the dollar.

The changes represented an internal policy victory for Paul W. McCracken, chairman of the Council of Economic Advisers, and Arthur F. Burns, chairman of the Federal Reserve Board, both of whom had pushed over a number of months for a wage price curtailment. It marked the first major defeat for George P. Schultz, Mr. Nixon's director of management and budget, who has vigorously opposed such an incomes policy.

The president adopted the new tactics following a weekend of meetings at the presidential retreat at Camp David, Md. With him there were Dr. Burns, Mr. McCracken, Mr. Shultz and John B. Connally, the secretary of the Treasury.

"Action on three Fronts"

"Prosperity without war requires action on three fronts," Mr. Nixon declared in explaining his new policies. "We must create more and better jobs; we must stop the rise in the cost of living; we must protect the dollar from the attacks of international money speculators.

"We are going to take that action—not timidly, not halfheartedly and not in piecemeal fashion," he said. As a corollary to his tax cut proposals, the president announced that he would slash $64.7 billion from the current federal budget to produce stability as well as stimulation, the budget cutback would come from a 5 percent reduction in the number of federal employees, a 10 percent cut in the level of foreign aid and through postponement of the effective dates of two costly domestic programs—federal revenue sharing with states and localities and reform of the federal welfare system.

Mr. Nixon's sudden adoption of a wage and price freeze represented his most drastic reversal of form. He established an eight-member Cost of Living Council to monitor a program under which management and labor must keep wages and prices at the same levels that existed in the 30 days prior to tonight.

Wage or price increases that had been scheduled to go into effect during the next 90 days, such as a 5 percent raise for the nation's rail workers due to take effect on Oct. 1, must he postponed at least until the 90 days expire. But wage improvements that took effect before tonight, including the 50-cent-an-hour increase won by the steelworkers on Aug. 2, will not be affected.

The White House did not include interest rates in the freeze on the theory that they cannot properly be kept under a fixed ceiling. Although describing the freeze as "voluntary," officials noted there was a provision for court injunctions and fines as high as $5,000 for failure to adhere to the ceiling.

The freeze could be extended after 90 days if Mr. Nixon should decide it still is needed. This authority to impose a ceiling will expire on April 30.

Political pressures for some form of an incomes policy have been building for weeks. Public opinion polls have certified concern over unemployment and prices as the number one domestic issue. Democratic presidential hopefuls have singled out the economy as the primary area for criticizing Mr. Nixon.

At a White House briefing just before the president's address, Secretary Connally said that the changes had been "long in the making." But he conceded in response to questions that he had left last week on vacation without any expectation that Mr. Nixon would put the program into effect tonight.

Why Strategy Changed

In explaining why the White House had shifted its economic strategy since he expressed confidence on June 30 that "we're on the right path." Mr. Connally cited tonight an "unacceptable" level of unemployment—currently running at an annual rate of 5.3 percent—as well as continued inflation, a deteriorating balance of trade and an "unsatisfactory" balance of payments in dealings abroad.

Congress, which is in recess until after the Labor Day weekend, must approve the president's request for new consumer tax breaks and investment credits.

The individual income tax exemption, currently $650 for each member of a family, is scheduled to rise to $700 next Jan. 1, and $750 a year later. Mr. Nixon asked that it go to $750 in one step next January.

"Every action I have taken tonight is designed to nurture and stimulate [the] competitive spirit, to help snap us out of the self-doubt, the self-disparagement that saps our energy and erodes our confidence in ourselves," the president said.

In calling for repeal of the tax on automobiles, the president said it would represent an average drop of about $200 in the price of a new car. "I shall insist that the American auto industry pass this tax reduction on to the nearly 8 million customers who are buying automobiles this year," he emphasized, but did not say how he would keep that pledge.

APRIL 30 WINDUP OF MOST CONTROLS URGED BY SHULTZ

By EDWARD COWAN, FEBRUARY 7, 1974

The Nixon administration recommended to Congress today that it let all wage-price controls expire on April 30 except for health care and petroleum products.

Secretary of the Treasury George P. Shultz said the administration opposed even standby controls because they "can become an inflationary force in and of themselves." He explained that the expectation that they would be used could accelerate price and wage increases.

Some members of the Senate banking subcommittee who heard Mr. Shultz and John T. Dunlop, director of the Cost of Living Council, thought standby authority should be extended beyond the scheduled expiration on April 30 of the Economic Stabilization Act, the enabling authority for controls.

To Seek Commitments

No senator present, however, said that controls themselves should be kept in effect beyond April 30. Mr. Dunlop testified that in the 83 days until then he would seek price-restraint commitments from more industries in exchange for suspensions of controls.

The reluctance of some members of Congress in this election year to appear to be leaving consumers without a shield from an inflation that the administration forecasts at 7 percent was expressed by Senator J. Bennett Johnston Jr., Democrat of Louisiana, who is chairman of the Subcommittee on Production and Stabilization.

"I am searching for a middle ground," he said, "a meeting place for those who see total decontrol as a sublime but perilous experiment as well as those for whom controls are a nightmare of economic inefficiency and inequity."

Senator Johnston introduced yesterday a bill that he said would provide "orderly transition to selective controls."

Senator William Proxmire of Wisconsin, the ranking Democrat on the Banking Committee, backed the administration, but for his own reasons.

"This wage-price act has to go," he said. "The working people of this country are really being hurt badly by this program. Wages are being held down. Prices are going through the roof."

The two Republicans at the hearing, Senators John G. Tower of Texas and Bill Brock of Tennessee, endorsed the administration position.

Later, at a news conference, Mr. Dunlop echoed the view of many on Capitol Hill that the legislative situation was wide open.

"I haven't the slightest idea what Congress will do," he said.

Mr. Shultz explained that no action by Congress was necessary to keep crude oil and refinery products under price controls because the Emergency Petroleum Allocation Act signed in November does that until March 1, 1975.

The fact was thought to give the administration a slight advantage in pressing Congress for a separate bill along the lines proposed today. Some observers expect the key issue will be whether President Nixon signs standby controls authority, as he did reluctantly in 1970, when he said he would not use it.

Arthur F. Burns, chairman of the Federal Reserve Board, generally supported the administration proposal. As for credit policy, he acknowledged that the central bank was coming under "a great deal of pressure" to "step up the rate of growth of the money supply" and bring down interest rates to ward off an economic "recession." Dr. Burns used that term, then moments later changed his usage to "slowdown or recession."

"I haven't the slightest idea what Congress will do."

"We will not open up the spigot and permit the money supply to increase rapidly," he said. To do so, he added, would make no significant dent in unemployment and would add to inflation.

The Banking Committee hearing room was packed to overflowing as Mr. Shultz, who is also chairman of the Cost of Living Council, Mr. Dunlop and James W. McLane, Mr. Dunlop's deputy, made their way to the witness table.

Business and labor lobbyists stood in the back row and waited in the corridor to learn what the administration proposed to do about the price-wage controls program Mr. Nixon announced with startling suddenness two and a half years ago, on Aug. 15, 1971. Mr. Dunlop submitted a loosely bound volume of 63 pages of testimony and 157 pages of graphs, charts and statistics, largely written by him. Running through it was his strongly held view that inflation over the years has been a many-faceted problem that must be examined afresh in each context and dealt with in highly specific, flexible ways.

Various studies have indicated that wage-price controls have moderated the rate of inflation by perhaps 1 or 2 percent, he testified.

Nevertheless, he said, the effectiveness of direct wage-price restraints is short-lived. "They tend to run down and wear out," he added.

Mr. Dunlop recommended that Congress enact legislation to keep health care under controls until enactment of national health insurance legislation. He said a great deal of the inflationary pressure in the health field resulted from the infusion of large sums of federal money for Medicare and Medicaid in recent years.

Dr. James H. Sammons of Baytown, Tex., chairman of the board of trustees of the American Medical Association, recommended that all controls be allowed to lapse on April 30. He criticized controls on hospital fees as a "capricious and unwise" attempt "to restructure health care." He accused the Cost of Living Council of having "attempted to dictate medical practice patterns under the guise of price control."

The administration asked that Congress extend the life of the council so that it could press for anti-inflationary government policies, especially in agriculture, monitor performance by industry and labor under stabilization commitments given in exchange for early release from controls, keep an eye on potentially inflationary problem spots in the economy, promote productivity and watch for developing shortages.

Mr. Dunlop said the council should have authority to compel individual companies, industries or unions to explain "price and wage decisions" at public hearings. Dr. Burns in similar proposal would give a review board the power to delay increases pending the outcome of the hearing.

In response to a question, Secretary Shultz held out the possibility that "if they are way out of bounds for no good reason," the administration could ask Congress to intervene.

BIPARTISAN SPIRIT FALTERS IN FIGHTS ON DEBT RELIEF

By EDMUND L. ANDREWS, FEBRUARY 29, 2008

Just a month after President Bush and Democratic leaders hailed their bipartisan agreement on an economic stimulus plan, the two sides went to war on Thursday over how to prevent widening damage from the housing crisis.

Senate Republicans, lining up with President Bush, blocked a Democratic bill that would provide more money for homeowner counseling programs and let bankruptcy judges reduce the terms of a mortgage for people about to lose their houses through foreclosure.

Meanwhile, the Bush administration flatly rejected Democratic proposals to rescue hundreds of thousands of borrowers, as well as their mortgage lenders, by having the government buy up and restructure billions of dollars in delinquent home loans. Instead, the president called on Congress to extend indefinitely his 2001 and 2003 tax cuts, which expire at the end of 2010. With new data showing that the economy may be even weaker than previously thought, Republicans and Democrats plunged back into a partisan, ideological clash over whether the government should try to stabilize home prices, prevent foreclosures and perhaps even bail out lenders.

The battle played out as Ben S. Bernanke, chairman of the Federal Reserve, told the Senate Banking Committee on Thursday that he did not expect a recession or a return of stagflation. But he reiterated his prediction of very slow growth this year and rattled investors by warning that some smaller banks might fail.

"I expect there will be some failures," he told lawmakers. The Dow Jones industrial average declined 112 points.

In Congress, Democratic lawmakers have begun to push ahead with an agenda aimed at shoring up the housing market with federal money, giving delinquent homeowners more bargaining power with their lenders and having the government buy troubled mortgages.

About 20 percent of subprime mortgages, which are made to people with low credit scores or low incomes, are delinquent and in danger of default. Moody's Economy.com recently estimated that 3 million subprime borrowers were likely to default over the next several years.

Delinquencies are also climbing sharply among people with good credit who took out risky mortgages, often with no down payment, and are now watching the resale value of their homes sink to less than the amount of the outstanding mortgage.

The bill drafted by Senate Democrats would have provided $4 billion for state and local programs to rehabilitate abandoned housing; $10 billion for states to raise low-cost

A boarded-up house in Central Falls, R.I., where more than 100 homes were foreclosed by banks. December 27, 2008.

mortgage money through tax-free revenue bonds; and another $200 million for counseling services to help homeowners renegotiate their loans.

The Bush administration opposed most of those provisions, but the biggest fight was over allowing bankruptcy judges to reduce the total owed or the interest rate on mortgages as part of a broader debt restructuring.

That provision, supported by a wide range of consumer and civil rights groups, drew intense opposition from the mortgage industry, whose lobbyists argued that it would increase risks for lenders and drive up mortgage rates in the future.

Republican lawmakers blocked the bill, voting almost entirely along party lines to defeat a "motion to proceed" that required 60 votes.

Senator Mitch McConnell, the Senate Republican leader who is from Kentucky, called the Democratic bill a "hastily concocted political exercise."

But in presenting what they described as their own proposal to protect homeowners, Mr. McConnell and other Republican lawmakers resorted to a grab bag of longstanding Republican initiatives, like making Mr. Bush's tax cuts permanent and reducing "frivolous litigation," that had little direct connection to the mortgage mess.

Democrats, knowing that they could not muster 60 votes to pass their bill, charged that Mr. Bush and the Republicans were protecting banks and Wall Street firms while doing little for people trapped in mortgages they cannot afford and houses they cannot sell.

"Their do-nothing leadership will cause this crisis to spiral farther out of control," said Senator Richard J. Durbin, Democrat of Illinois. Mr. Durbin, who had drafted the provision to let bankruptcy judges modify mortgages on a person's primary residence, said his measure could have helped as many as 600,000 people avoid foreclosure and keep their homes.

Senator Harry Reid of Nevada, the Senate Democratic leader, promised to bring up the housing bill again but declined to say when. "The bankers on Wall Street and the big lenders are high-fiving tonight," Mr. Reid said after failing to get enough votes to bring the bill up on the Senate floor. "It is becoming increasingly clear that Republicans either have no interest in turning around our sinking economy, or no ideas on how to do so."

President Bush, who met with his top economic advisers at the Labor Department on Thursday, brushed aside the need for new government rescue efforts.

"I don't think we're in a recession, but no question we're in a slowdown," he told reporters at a news conference. "One way Congress, if they really want to make a substantial difference in creating certainty during uncertain times, is to make the tax cuts we passed permanent."

The next big fight could be over proposals, which the Bush administration strongly opposes, that would allow the federal government to buy up billions of dollars in troubled mortgages. Representative Barney Frank, Democrat of Massachusetts and chairman of the House Financial Services Committee, proposed a bill this week that would provide $10 billion for the Federal Housing Administration to help refinance as many as 1 million distressed subprime loans with cheaper government-insured loans.

Senator Christopher J. Dodd, Democrat of Connecticut, has proposed creating a government agency that would buy troubled mortgages at a discount and restructure them into more affordable loans.

Henry M. Paulson Jr., the Treasury secretary, said such proposals appeared to be a taxpayer-funded bailout and saw no need for them. "While some in Washington are proposing big interventions, most of the proposals I've seen would do more harm than good. I'm not interested in bailing out investors, lenders and speculators," Mr. Paulson said in prepared remarks to the Economic Club of Chicago.

But unlike other Democratic proposals, the idea of a government-funded mortgage buyout has considerable support among banks and mortgage lenders. Lobbyists for the mortgage bankers have circulated a detailed proposal, though company executives said they were merely providing "technical information" requested by Democratic lawmakers.

Stephen O'Connor, chief lobbyist for the Mortgage Bankers Association, which fought intensely to prevent bankruptcy judges from having the power to change mortgage terms, said this week that the administration and Congress should have a "conversation" about mortgage buyout proposals.

NOTE: *The financial disaster of 2008 hurt economies worldwide and led to the ruin of millions of American homeowners who found their mortgages were suddenly held on properties worth almost nothing. It spawned the Occupy Wall Street movement and helped lead to the election of Barack Obama—but also to the political backlash that swept the Tea Party, the hard right, and, ultimately, Donald Trump into office.*

IN TAX OVERHAUL, TRUMP TRIES TO DEFY THE ECONOMIC ODDS

By PATRICIA COHEN, DECEMBER 20, 2017

When President Trump adds his distinctive signature to the tax bill, he will also be making a huge bet that the Republican strategy of deep cuts for businesses and wealthy individuals will fuel extraordinary growth across the board.

Perhaps more than any other American political leader, Mr. Trump knows that long shots, like his own presidential bid, sometimes pay off. In that vein, he and congressional Republicans are arguing that their bitterly contested and expensive rewrite of the tax code will ultimately create more jobs and raise wages.

If they are proved correct, they will be repudiating not only historical experience, but most experts. From Congress's own prognosticators to Wall Street's virtuosos, scarcely any independent analyses project anything like the rosy forecasts offered by the president's top economic advisers.

To Mr. Trump and his allies, the normal models just do not fully capture the high-octane "rocket fuel" embedded in the tax plan. Mr. Trump intuitively understands just how much attitudes and expectations can shape economic decisions.

With a businessman in the White House, Mr. Trump argues that companies, large and small, have a renewed faith in the economy. And the corporate tax cut, combined with the rollback in regulation, will prompt waves of new investment and hiring, as middle-class Americans liberally spend the extra money in their pockets.

"We're going to easily see 4 percent growth next year," the National Economic Council director, Gary D. Cohn, said. Steven Mnuchin, the Treasury secretary, declared the tax plan would generate enough growth to more than pay for its $1.5 trillion cost.

But those pronouncements are at odds with estimates from the former employer of both men, Goldman Sachs. The bank projected that the tax bill will add just three-tenths of 1 percent of growth in the next two years, before its impact peters out.

The firm's annual growth estimate of 2.5 percent for 2018 matched the one issued this week by the nation's central bank, the Federal Reserve, while the latest median Wall Street forecast hovered close by. And in 2019, growth is expected to drop to 1.8 percent, Alec Phillips, chief United States political economist for Goldman, said Wednesday after the Senate vote.

"We note that the effect in 2020 and beyond looks minimal and could actually be slightly negative," the company said in a recent published summary.

Such projections are unlikely to deter Mr. Trump and Republican leaders from declaring success next year. Lower taxes and extra incentives to invest in 2018 are almost certain to encourage consumers to spend and businesses to expand.

Reduced rates mean most Americans will start taking home more money right away. Roughly three-quarters of taxpayers are expected to get a cut next year, according to the nonpartisan Tax Policy Center.

Employers may offer other sweeteners, even if they were not specifically spurred by the tax plan. AT&T announced Wednesday that it was giving more than 200,000 domestic employees a $1,000 bonus when the tax bill is signed. Fifth Third Bancorp, based in Cincinnati, also promised a $1,000 bonus and said it would raise the company's minimum wage to $15 an hour.

At the same time, the anticipated cut in the corporate rate to 21 percent from 35 percent and other business perks are lifting the stock market to new heights. In an earnings call this week, Alan B. Graf Jr., FedEx's chief financial officer, said the company planned to use part of its tax windfall to fatten dividends.

But like a shot of adrenaline, that initial burst of economic activity is likely to fade.

Some provisions of the bill were intended to be sharp and short. Next year, for example, businesses will be able to borrow money and deduct the cost of those loans at the current rate of 35 percent. But later on, when they reap the profits, they will pay a tax rate of only 21 percent. That could end up causing firms to simply shift the timing of investments they would have made regardless of a change in the tax code.

That initial burst of economic activity is likely to fade.

"The really hard question a year from now is going to be is how much of the miniboom we see is just an acceleration of stuff that was going to happen anyway or additional investment that is really going to spur the economy," said Mihir A. Desai, a professor of finance at Harvard Business School.

Tax cuts can provide an added incentive to invest. But as most chief executives acknowledge, they are generally not the crucial factor.

Investment decisions are much more closely linked to demand for goods and services or technological advancement. As it is, manufacturers are not making full use of the capacity in their existing facilities.

Mr. Graf of FedEx held out the possibility of more spending on capital investment and hiring next year. But he noted that the economy as a whole would first have to "increase materially."

Senator Bob Corker (R-Tenn.) is questioned by protesters during a demonstration on Capitol Hill against the G.O.P. Tax Bill, December 13, 2017.

Over time, most of the broad-based tax cuts will disappear. Although the richest sliver of Americans will continue to get a break, most people who earn less than $100,000 will see their taxes rise, which could slow the economy's primary engine, consumer spending.

Further tightening is likely if the Republicans follow through on sharply cutting Medicare, Medicaid, Social Security and other programs that tend to put extra cash into the pockets of lower and moderate-income households.

Either way, the deficit will continue to balloon. Over the last decade alone, the deficit has more than tripled. So far, the interest needed to cover that enormous loan has remained relatively small because interest rates have been at historically low levels.

But those costs are expected to soar. The Federal Reserve has indicated that it intends to slowly but surely raise the benchmark interest rate.

Some economists support such deficit spending during recessions, but they worry that offering stimulants when the economy is on fairly steady ground can backfire.

Although employers have resisted raising salaries by much, they continue to complain about the tightness of the labor market. The jobless rate has dipped to 4.1 percent while job openings have remained at record high levels.

Virtually no economists believe that the tax cuts will pay for themselves. Several studies have shown that they rarely cover more than a third of the cost. Others have questioned whether cuts produce any significant growth at all—even if they do encourage some individuals to work, save and invest. In a study that William G. Gale and Andrew Samwick did for the Tax Policy Center, they concluded that cuts that increase budget deficits "in the long term will reduce national saving and raise interest rates."

The pattern of short-term promise followed by disappointment is one that other presidents have experienced. President Ronald Reagan in 1981 and President George W. Bush in 2001 and 2003 both passed tax cuts that delivered temporary bumps to the economy followed by slowdowns and rising deficits.

"The clear consensus among independent economists is that the impact of the tax cuts on growth is nowhere close to what the administration is talking about," said Mr. Desai of Harvard. Whatever growth does occur, he added, will be "counteracted by the fiscal irresponsibility of the bill."

CHAPTER 4

RACE AND CIVIL RIGHTS

"If we do not get meaningful legislation out of this Congress, the time will come when we will not confine our marching to Washington. We will march through the South, through the streets of Jackson, through the streets of Danville ... through the streets of Birmingham. But we will march with the spirit of love and with the spirit of dignity that we have shown here today."

—Representative John Lewis (D-GA) (at the time, chairman of the Student Nonviolent Coordinating Committee), during the March on Washington, August 28, 1963

THE CIVIL WAR KILLED as many as 750,000 Americans and forced the Southern states to end slavery. But it did very little to resolve the wrenching arguments over race and racism that had tarnished the New World since its European settlers used fictitious definitions of race to justify their enslavement of dark-skinned Africans. The Jim Crow era of discrimination, subjugation and lynching made a mockery of the Union victory in the Civil War. Until 1953, no one could be naturalized as an American citizen unless they were classified as "free white men," and even the gains of the black rights and black power movements of the 1960s did not guarantee tolerance and equality. In the early 21st century, the country still suffers factions that refuse to acknowledge racial equality in society or the law. Native Americans, the victims of institutionalized hatred and genocide, continue to suffer massive discrimination.

OPPOSITE: Demonstrators at the March on Washington, August 28, 1963.

REPUBLICAN NATIONAL CONVENTION

JUNE 20, 1856

The convention met again this morning, and the hall was crowded to excess. Soon after 10 o'clock the convention was called to order, and prayer was offered by Rev. Mr. Levy, after which the president declared the first business in order in to be a consideration of the following resolution:

Resolved that a national convention of young men in favor of free soil, free Kansas, free speech, and Fremont, meet at New York in September next, under the call of the National Executive Committee.

The resolution was received with great enthusiasm and adopted unanimously.

A motion was then made and carried that the convention go into an informal ballot for a candidate for the vice presidency.

Mr. Whelplly, of New Jersey, proposed the name of Hon. W. L Dayton, of the same state, as candidate for the vice presidency, amid loud and reiterated cheering. With the consent of the convention he read the speech of Mr. Dayton, delivered at a recent Republican convention over which he was called to preside, which (the speech) contained an endorsement of the sentiments of the convention as to the repeal of the Missouri Compromise, and the character of the present administration. He read as follows:

After thanking the convention for the honor done him in his election as its president, he was glad to meet men of all parties assembled for the purpose of uniting in a movement to redeem the state and nation from political ruin. The debt of New Jersey has been excelled by mismanagement until it has quite reached almost the limit fixed by our constitution. The present national administration was installed under circumstances of peace and prosperity. But now there is strife and bloodshed and rapine, and freedom of speech is stricken down in the Senate. This has been foreseen since 1850 and is the result of the domineering spirit of slavery. The last compromise it was said healed the "five bleeding wounds," and all was to be peaceful when Pierce commenced his administration, the lion and the lamb laid down together, but only long enough for the one to get the other by the throat. The South, aided by Northern doughfaces, has abrogated the Missouri Compromise and opened again this strife in our country. We may not be able to restore the Missouri Compromise, but an executive and a Congress may be elected that will practically give effect to that enactment. He contended that freedom is national and slavery sectional. Slavery where it is, but it carries it nowhere. In conclusion, he urged harmonious action among the opponents of the present state and national administrations. If this is affected, it is of little consequence who may

JNº C. FREMONT. Wᵐ L. DAYTON.
THE CHAMPIONS OF FREEDOM.

An 1856 campaign poster for Republican candidates John C. Fremont and William L. Dayton.

come out of the Cincinnati convention; whether it be remembered, said that he had not a drop of Democratic blood in his veins. If we are united, we can vanquish our opponents. His speech was warmly applauded throughout.

Mr. Fisher, of Pennsylvania, said, "I take the liberty of naming a man as a candidate for the vice presidency, who is a tower of strength in Pennsylvania, I mean David L. Wilmot. If you nominate him I have no doubt about Pennsylvania. If you nominate him I have no doubt about Pennsylvania will ratify your nominations of November."

Hon. John Allison, of Pennsylvania, said he had been requested to present the name of Abraham Lincoln, of Illinois. All he had to say about him was that he was the prince of good fellows and had been an Old-Line Whig.

Col. Wm. B. Archer said he would not detain the convention but a moment. He had been acquainted with the man who had been named for 30 years. He had lived in Illinois 40 years. He had gone there when Illinois was a territory and had lived there until it had grown to be a populous and flourishing state. During 30 years of that time he had known Abraham Lincoln, and he knew him well. He was born in gallant Kentucky and was now in the prime of life—just about 55 years of age—and enjoying remarkably good health.

[Applause.] And, besides, the speaker knew him to be as pure a patriot as ever lived. He would give the convention to understand, that with him on the ticket, there was no danger of Northern Illinois, Illinois was safe with him, and he believed she was safe without him. [Laughter.] With him, however, she was doubly safe.

Governor Cleaveland, of Connecticut—Can he fight? The Speaker—Emphatically—"Yes! [Great applause.] Have I not told you that he was born in Kentucky? [Applause.] He's strong mentally—he's strong physically—he's strong every way."

Mr. Jay, of New Jersey, said he was an Old-Line Democrat. He had always been a Democrat, until the present administration, having thrown aside Democratic principles, he could remain with the party no longer. He had helped to elect Pierce, for which he hoped to be forgiven. [Applause.] With Dayton, of New Jersey, on the ticket with Fremont, he could work faithfully for its success, and he believed New Jersey would ratify the nominations with a large majority. He was not opposed to Judge Wilmot; he was a good man, but, then, was it policy to nominate him? They had nominated one who had been a Democrat for the presidency, and he thought it would be well to nominate a Whig for the vice presidency.

Hon. Judge Palmer, of Illinois, said: "I rise, like my friend from New Jersey. I, too, have been an Old-Line Democrat, and am very sorry for my last vote. [Applause.] I rise to second the presentation of the name of Abraham Lincoln for the vice presidency. I have known him long, and I know he is a good man and a hard worker in the field, although I have never heard him—for when he was on the stamp, I always dodged. He is my first choice; Dayton, of New Jersey, is the next and David Wilmot is the name next boy after him. [Laughter and applause.] We can lick Buchanan anyway, but I think we can do it a little easier if we have Lincoln on the ticket with John C. Fremont.

A delegate from Massachusetts said he had received a dispatch from Massachusetts concerning the feeling there about the nomination, which he would read if the convention wished to hear it. ["Cries of read it, read it."] He read as follows: "Great rejoicing—got a good company—give us a good vice president—clear the track."

The dispatch was received with cheers, and when order had been restored, Mr. Anthony J. Bleeker, of New York, rose and presented the name of John A. King, for the vice presidency.

NOTE: *This convention marked the birth of the Republican Party, which was formed largely around an antislavery platform and was centered in the industrial Northern states of the country.*

THE ELECTORAL TRIBUNAL;
OREGON BEFORE THE COMMISSION

FEBRUARY 22, 1877

Shortly after the two houses separated, the Electoral Commission went into session, and it was announced that Senator Kelly and Representative Jenks would appear as objectors on the part of the Democrats, and Senator Mitchell and Judge Lawrence, of the House, on the part of the Republicans. Before an audience the meagerness of which testified forcibly to the waning interest in the presidential question, Senator Kelly took the floor on behalf of the Democrats. He made an incoherent and blundering argument against the counting of the votes cast by the Hayes electors, and curiously enough, in view of his telegrams from Oregon to Tilden and Pelton, talked a great deal about honesty, truth, justice, &c. The principal, indeed the only point made by him, was that each state in the Union had the right to appoint presidential electors in its own way and according to its

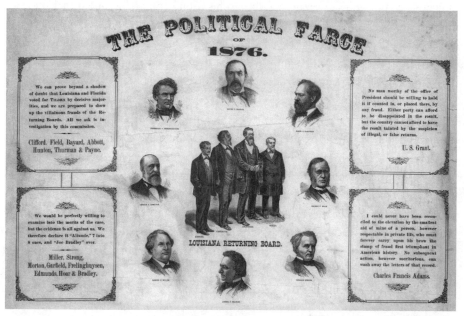

A circa 1877 political cartoon titled "The Political Farce of 1876," showing bust portraits of eight senators and court justices arrayed around a group of four standing men identified as the "Louisiana Returning Board." The cartoon includes four quotes regarding election fraud in the scandalous 1876 presidential election.

own laws. When it is remembered that this very fact was fully proved by the Republican counsel in the Louisiana case, it will be seen that Mr. Gobble Dispatch Kelly's one point was not a very original or important one.

Mr. Jenks was the next speaker on the part of the Democracy. He would not have a decision on any technical ground, he said. All he wanted was justice. Then Mr. Jenks went on to prove that in spite of the plainly expressed will of the people of Oregon, it would be justice to give the vote of that state to Tilden.

Senator Mitchell was the first speaker on the part of the Republicans. He made a very clear argument as to the facts of the case. He showed that while the governor had power to issue certificates, or at least had that duty to perform, he had no right and no power to determine as to the eligibility of electors.

Mr. Lawrence, of the House, was the next speaker on the part of the Republicans. He showed that the governor had no power to make a selection as between two contesting electors, and he cited numerous legal authorities to show that Cronin was clearly ineligible to the position of elector.

After the recess Judge Hoadley, of Cincinnati, who is the managing counsel in the Oregon case on the Democratic side, began his argument. He assumed that the commission had declined to exercise any judicial powers whatever, and on that assumption claimed they had no power except to count the returns certified by Gov. Grover. He claimed from first to last in his argument that the commission could act only with the narrowest ministerial powers, and that they had no judicial authority whatever.

He actually claimed that Grover's action was right and honest, and drew a most enchanting picture of the future renown of the commission and the reverence in which they would be held by posterity, if they would only count the vote of Cronin for Tilden.

It is not probable that the Democratic commissioners will contend for counting Cronin's vote. Mr. Thurman, particularly, is on record against the legality of such a vote, but they are likely to vote together, that there was no election, and that there was no legal filling of the vacancy, which would be the same effect as counting Cronin's vote, because it would throw the election into the House. A partisan vote on the Democratic side to take advantage of the Oregon fraud by throwing out one of the votes to which the state is entitled, is to be expected.

NOTE: *This election was a perfect example of backroom dealing and even outright fraud in American politics, and it is sometimes seen as a template for further deals of its kind. It also left the nation's African Americans under the oppression of racist policies. The Hayes-election's end inevitably came up in the coverage of the Supreme Court's decision to give the 2000 election to George W. Bush.*

CAPITAL IS OCCUPIED BY A GENTLE ARMY

By RUSSELL BAKER, AUGUST 29, 1963

N o one could remember an invading army quite as gentle as the 200,000 civil rights marchers who occupied Washington today. For the most part, they came silently during the night and early morning, occupied the great shaded boulevards along the Mall, and spread through the parklands between the Washington Monument and the Potomac. But instead of the emotional horde of angry militants that many had feared, what Washington saw was a vast army of quiet, middle-class Americans who had come in the spirit of the church outing. And instead of the tensions that had been expected, they gave this city a day of sad music, strange silences and good feeling in the streets.

It was apparent from early morning that this would be an extraordinary day. At 8 a.m. when rush-hour traffic is normally creeping bumper to bumper across the Virginia bridges and down the main boulevards from Maryland, the streets had the abandoned look of Sunday morning. From a helicopter over the city, it was possible to see caravans

The crowd at the Lincoln Memorial on August 28, 1963, where Martin Luther King Jr. would give his "I Have a Dream Speech" as part of the March on Washington.

of chartered buses streaming down New York Avenue from Baltimore and points North, but the downtown streets were empty. Nothing moved in front of the White House, nor on Pennsylvania Avenue.

A Day of Siege

For the natives, this was obviously a day of siege and the streets were being left to the marchers. By 9:30, the number of marchers at the assembly point by the Washington Monument had reached about 40,000, but it was a crowd without fire. Mostly, people who had traveled together sat on the grass or posed for group portraits against the monument, like tourists on a rare visit to the capital.

Here and there, little groups stood in the sunlight and sand. A group of 75 young people from Danville, Va., came dressed in white sweatshirts with crudely cut black mourning bands on their sleeves.

"We're mourning injustice in Danville," explained James Bruce, a 15-year-old who said he has been arrested three times for participating in demonstrations there.

Standing together, the group sang of the freedom fight in a sad melody. Other hymns came from groups scattered over the grounds, but there was no cohesion in the crowd. Instead, a fair-grounds atmosphere prevailed. Marchers kept straggling off to ride the elevators to the top of the monument. Women sat on the grass and concentrated on feeding babies.

Up on the slope near the monument's base, Peter Ottley, president of the Building Services International Union, Local 144, in New York City, was ignoring the loudspeaker and holding a press conference before about 100 of his delegates. He thought the march would "convince the legislators that something must be done, because it is the will of the people to give equality to all."

In the background, the amplifier was presenting Joan Baez, the folk singer.

One Note of Bitterness

In one section of the ground, a group from Americus and Albany, Ga., was gathered under its own placards singing its own hymn. The placards conveyed an uncharacteristic note of bitterness. "What is a state without justice but a robber band enlarged?" asked one. Another bore the following inscription: "Milton Wilderson—20 stiches. Emanuel McClendon—3 stiches (Age 67). James Williams—broken leg."

Charles Macken, 15, of Albany, explained the placard in a deep Georgia accent. "That's where the police beat these people up," he said.

Over the loudspeaker, Roosevelt Johnson was urged to come claim his lost son, Lawrence. From the monument grounds the loudspeaker boomed an announcement that the police had estimated that 90,000 marchers were already on the scene.

At 10:56 the loudspeaker announced desperately that "we are trying to locate Miss Lena Horne," and a group from Cambridge, Md., was kneeling while the Rev. Charles M. Bowne of Bethel A.M.E. Church prayed.

"We know truly that we will—we shall—overcome—some day," he was saying.

The Cambridge group rose and began a gospel hymn and clapped and swayed. The loudspeaker was saying, "Lena—wherever you are . . ."

Many were simply picnicking. They had brought picnic baskets and thermos jugs and camp stools, and lunched leisurely in the soft August sunshine. Some stretched out to doze on the grass.

Singer Introduced

At 11:10 Bobby Darin, the teenage pop singer, was being introduced over the amplifier. He was, he announced, "Here as a singer, and I'm proud and kind of choked up."

The marchers by this time, however, had had enough of the monument grounds. Spontaneously, without advice from the platform, they began to flow away, moving toward the Lincoln Memorial, where the official program was to begin at noon.

Thousands simply began to move out into Constitution Avenue, and in a few minutes it was tens of thousands. They trooped leisurely out into the boulevard and moved happily along in a strange mood of quiet contentment.

By 11:55, much of the crowd had regrouped at the Lincoln Memorial, where the speaker's platform was set on the top step under the Lincoln statue. This made an impressive stage for the star performers, but it was a bad theater for most of the audience, which was dispersed down the sides of the reflecting pool for a third of a mile. Still the crowd remained in good temper, and many who could not find comfortable space in the open with a clear view up to the memorial steps filtered back under the trees and sat down on their placards.

On the platform, Roy Wilkins, executive secretary of the National Association for the Advancement of Colored People, surveyed the sea of people and said, "I'm very satisfied. It looks like a Yankee game."

Photographers Busy

Inside, under the Lincoln statue, the photographers were deployed five deep around Burt Lancaster, Harry Belafonte and Charlton Heston. On metal chairs in the guest sections, Marlon Brando and Paul Newman were submitting to microphone interviewers.

As the crowd on the steps thickened and gradually became an impassable mass, the extraordinary politeness that characterized the day was dramatized every time an elbow was crooked. People excused themselves for momentarily obstructing a view, excused themselves for dropping cigarette ashes on shoeshines. When the marshals called for a clear path, hundreds hastened to fall aside with a goodwill rarely seen in the typical urban crowd. The sweetness and patience of the crowd may have set some sort of national high-water mark in mass decency.

The program at the memorial began with more music. Peter, Paul and Mary, a folk-singing trio, were there "to express in song what this meeting is all about," as Ossie Davis, the master of ceremonies, put it.

Then there was Josh White, in a gray short-sleeved sports shirt. And the Freedom Singers from Mississippi, a hand-clapping group of hot gospel shouters whom Mr. Davis introduced as "straight from one of the prisons of the South. They've been in so many, I forget which one it is."

At 1:19 p.m. there was the Rev. Fred L. Shuttlesworth, president of the Alabama Christian Movement for Human Rights and a leader of the Birmingham demonstrations.

At 1:28 p.m. Miss Baez was singing [while] Mayor Wagner of New York made his appearance, walking down the memorial steps.

Bunche Speaks

Miss Baez was followed by Dr. Ralph Bunche. "Anyone who cannot understand the significance of your presence here today," he said, "is blind and deaf." The crowd roared approval.

Then came Dick Gregory, the comedian. "The last time I saw this many of us," he said, "Bull Connor was doing all the talking." The reference was to Eugene (Bull) Connor, who was police commissioner of Birmingham during the spring demonstrations there.

To many of the marchers, the program must have begun to seem like eternity, and the great crowd slowly began dissolving from the edges. Mr. Lancaster read a lengthy statement from 1,500 Americans in Europe. They were in favor of the march. Mr. Belafonte read a statement endorsed by a large group of actors, writers and entertainers. They also favored the march.

Bob Dylan, a young folk singer, rendered a lugubrious mountain song about Medgar Evers. Mr. Lancaster, Mr. Belafonte and Mr. Heston found time dragging, stood up to stretch and chat, and set off pandemonium among the photographers. Mr. Brando submitted to another microphone interviewer.

Speaking Begins

At 1:59, the official speaking began. For those who listened it was full of noble statement about democracy and religious sincerity, but the crowd was dissolving fast now.

These [who left] missed two of the emotional high points of the day. One was Mahalia Jackson's singing, which seemed to bounce off the Capitol far up the mall. The other was the speech of the Rev. Dr. Martin Luther King Jr., president of the Southern Christian Leadership Conference.

Long before that, however, huge portions of the crowd had drifted out of earshot. Thousands had moved back into Constitution Avenue to walk dreamily in the sun. The grass for blocks around was covered with sleepers. Here and there, a man sat under a tree and sang to a guitar.

Mostly though, the "marchers" just strolled in the sunshine. Most looked contented and tired and rather pleased with what they had done.

ALABAMA POLICE USE GAS AND CLUBS TO ROUT NEGROES

By ROY REED, MARCH 8, 1965

A labama state troopers and volunteer officers of the Dallas County sheriff's office tore through a column of Negro demonstrators with tear gas, nightsticks and whips here [in Selma] today to enforce Gov. George C. Wallace's order against a protest march from Selma to Montgomery.

At least 17 Negroes were hospitalized with injuries and about 40 more were given emergency treatment for minor injuries and tear gas effects.

The Negroes reportedly fought back with bricks and bottles at one point as they were pushed back into the Negro community, far away from most of a squad of reporters and photographers who had been restrained by the officers.

A witness said that Sheriff James G. Clark and a handful of volunteer possemen were pushed back by flying debris when they tried to herd the angry Negroes into the church where the march had begun.

[In Washington the Justice Department announced that agents of the Federal Bureau of Investigation in Selma had been directed to make a full and prompt investigation and to gather evidence whether "unnecessary force was used by law officers and others" in halting the march.]

Dr. King in Atlanta

Some 200 troopers and possemen with riot guns, pistols, tear gas bombs and nightsticks later chased all the Negro residents of the Browns Chapel Methodist Church–area into their apartments and houses. They then patrolled the streets and walks for an hour before driving away.

The Rev. Dr. Martin Luther King Jr., who was to have led the march, was in Atlanta. After the attack on the marchers, Dr. King issued a statement announcing plans to begin another march Tuesday covering the 50 miles from Selma to Montgomery. He said he had agreed not to lead today's march after he had learned that the troopers would block it. Dr. King also said he would seek a court order barring further interference with the marchers.

John Lewis, chairman of the Student Nonviolent Coordinating Committee, was among the injured. He was admitted to the Good Samaritan Hospital with a possible skull fracture.

State troopers swing billy clubs to break up the civil rights voting march in Selma, Ala., March 7, 1965. John Lewis, chairman of the Student Nonviolent Coordinating Committee (in the foreground) is being beaten by a state trooper. Lewis, a future U.S. congressman, sustained a fractured skull.

Mr. Lewis and Hosea Williams, an aide to Dr. King, led the marchers back to the church after the encounter with the officers. Mr. Lewis, before going to the hospital, made a speech to the crowd huddled angry and weeping in the sanctuary.

Troops Are Sought

"I don't see how President Johnson can send troops to Vietnam—I don't see how he can send troops to the Congo—I don't see how he can send troops to Africa and can't send troops to Selma, Alabama," he said. The Negroes roared their approval.

"Next time we march," he said, "we may have to keep going when we get to Montgomery. We may have to go on to Washington."

The suppression of the march, which was called to dramatize the Negroes' voter-registration drive, was swift and thorough.

About 525 Negroes had left Browns Chapel and walked six blocks to Broad Street, then across Pettus Bridge and the Alabama River, where a cold wind cut at their faces and whipped their coats. They were young and old and they carried an assortment of packs, bedrolls and lunch sacks.

The troopers, more than 50 of them, were waiting 300 yards beyond the end of the bridge. Behind and around the troopers were a few dozen possemen, 15 of them on horses, and perhaps 100 white spectators. About 50 Negroes stood watching beside a yellow school bus well away from the troopers. The marchers had passed about three dozen more possemen at the other end of the bridge. They were to see more of that group.

The troopers stood shoulder to shoulder in a line across both sides of the divided four-lane highway. They put on gas masks and held their nightsticks ready as the Negroes approached, marching two abreast, slowly and silently.

When the Negroes were 50 feet away, a voice came over an amplifying system commanding them to stop. They stopped.

The leader of the troopers, who identified himself as Maj. John Cloud said, "This is an unlawful assembly. Your march is not condusive to the public safety. You are ordered to disperse and go back to your church or to your homes."

Mr. Williams answered from the head of the column.

"May we have a word with the major?" he asked.

"There is no word to be had," the major replied.

Two-Minute Warning

The two men went through the same exchange twice more, then the major said, "You have two minutes to turn around and go back to your church."

Several seconds went by silently. The Negroes stood unmoving.

The next sound was the major's voice. "Troopers, advance," he commanded.

The troopers rushed forward, their blue uniforms and white helmets blurring into a flying wedge as they moved. The wedge moved with such force that it seemed almost to pass over the waiting column instead of through it. The first 10 or 20 Negroes were swept to the ground screaming, arms and legs flying and packs and bags went skittering across the grassy divider strip and on to the pavement on both sides. Those still on their feet retreated.

Spectators Cheer

The troopers continued pushing, using both the force of their bodies and the prodding of their nightsticks.

A cheer went up from the white spectators lining the south side of the highway.

The mounted possemen spurred their horses and rode at a run into the retreating mass. The Negroes cried out as they crowded together for protection and the whites on the sideline whooped and cheered.

The Negroes paused in their retreat for perhaps a minute still screaming and huddling together. Suddenly there was a report, like a gunshot, and a gray cloud spewed over the troopers and the Negroes.

"Tear gas!" someone yelled. The cloud began covering the highway. Newsmen, who were confined by four troopers to a corner 100 yards away, began to lose sight of the action. But before the cloud finally hid it all, there were several seconds of unobstructed view. Fifteen or twenty nightsticks could be seen through the gas flailing at the heads of the marchers.

The Negroes Flee

The Negroes broke and ran. Scores of them streamed across the parking lot of the Selma Tractor Company. Troopers and possemen, mounted and unmounted, went after them.

Several more tear gas bombs were set off. One report was heard that sounded different. A white civil rights worker said later that it was a shotgun blast and that the pellets tore a hole in the brick wall of a hamburger stand five feet from him.

After about 10 minutes, most of the Negroes were rounded up. They began to move toward the city through the smell of the tear gas, coughing and crying as they stumbled onto Pettus Bridge.

Four or five women still lay on the grass strip where the troopers had knocked them down. Two troopers passed among them and ordered them to get up and join the others. The women lay still.

The two men then set off another barrage of tear gas and the women struggled to their feet, blinded and gasping, and limped across the road. One was Mrs. Amelia Boynton, one of the Selma leaders of the Negro movement. She was treated later at the hospital.

Lloyd Russell of Atlanta, a white photographer who had stayed at the other end of the bridge, said he saw at least four carloads of possemen overtake the marchers as they reentered Broad Street. He said the possemen jumped from the cars and began beating the Negroes with nightsticks.

Two other witnesses said they saw possemen using whips on the fleeing Negroes as they recrossed the bridge.

The other newsmen were finally allowed to follow the retreat. Ron Gibson, a reporter for *The Birmingham News*, reached Browns Chapel ahead of the other newsmen. He said later that he had seen Sheriff Clark lead a charge with about half a dozen possemen to try to force the Negroes from Sylvan Street into the church.

Mr. Gibson said the Negroes fell back momentarily, then surged forward and began throwing bricks and bottles. He said the officers had to retreat until reinforcements arrived. One posseman was cut under the eye with a brick, he said.

Mr. Gibson said that Wilson Baker, Selma's commissioner of public safety, intervened and persuaded the Negroes to enter the church. He said Captain Baker held back Sheriff Clark and his possemen, who were regrouping for another assault.

Mr. Gibson said that Sheriff Clark was struck on the face by a piece of brick but was not injured.

When the other newsmen arrived, more than 100 possemen were packed into Sylvan Street a block from the church. They were joined shortly by the 50 troopers, who had been called back to regroup after turning back the marchers.

The ground floor of the two-story patronage next to the church was turned into an emergency hospital for an hour and a half.

Negroes lay on the floors and chairs, many weeping and moaning. A girl in red slacks was carried from the house screaming. Mrs. Boynton lay semiconscious on a table. Doctors and nurses threaded feverishly through the crowd administering first aid and daubing a solution of water and baking soda on the eyes of those who had been in the worst of the gas.

From the hospital came a report that the victims had suffered fractures of ribs, heads, arms and legs, in addition to cuts and bruises.

Hundreds of Negroes, including many who had not been on the march, milled angrily in front of the church.

An old Negro who had just heard that officers had beaten a Negro on his own porch said to a friend, "I wish the bastard would try to come in my house."

The Negro leaders worked through the crowd urging calm and nonviolence.

At the end of the street the possemen and troopers could be seen grouping into a formation. The officers left after an hour, and tonight the Negroes emerged from their houses and poured into Browns Chapel for a mass meeting.

At the meeting Mr. Williams, who was not injured, told the 700 Negroes present about the plans for the Tuesday march.

"I fought in World War II," Mr. Williams said, "and I once was captured by the German army, and I want to tell you that the Germans never were as inhuman as the state troopers of Alabama."

NOTE: *The march on Selma and the furious rage directed against the marchers by the police helped spur the passage of landmark civil rights legislation, but that fell far short of solving the problem of racism in the United States, which persists to this day.*

MARTIN LUTHER KING IS SLAIN IN MEMPHIS; A WHITE IS SUSPECTED; GUARD CALLED OUT

By EARL CALDWELL, APRIL 5, 1968

The Rev. Dr. Martin Luther King Jr., who preached nonviolence and racial brotherhood, was fatally shot here last night by a distant gunman who raced away and escaped.

Four thousand National Guard troops were ordered into Memphis by Gov. Buford Ellington after the 39-year-old Nobel Prize–winning civil rights leader died.

A curfew was imposed on the shocked city of 550,000 inhabitants, 40 percent of whom are Negro.

But the police said the tragedy had been followed by incidents that included sporadic shooting, fires, bricks and bottles thrown at policemen, and looting that started in Negro districts and then spread over the city.

White Car Sought

Police Director Frank Holloman said the assassin might have been a white man who was "50 to 100 yards away in a flophouse."

Chief of Detectives W.P. Huston said a late model white Mustang was believed to have been the killer's getaway car. Its occupant was described as a bareheaded white man in his 30s, wearing a black suit and black tie.

The detective chief said the police had chased two cars near the motel where Dr. King was shot and had halted one that had two out-of-town men as occupants. The men were questioned but seemed to have nothing to do with the killing, he said.

Rifle Found Nearby

A high-powered 30.06-caliber rifle was found about a block from the scene of the shooting, on South Main Street. "We think it's the gun," Chief Huston said, reporting it would be turned over to the Federal Bureau of Investigation.

Dr. King was shot while he leaned over a second-floor railing outside his room at the Lorraine Motel. He was chatting with two friends just before starting for dinner.

Mourners at the funeral of Martin Luther King Jr., April 9, 1968. *The New York Times* **reported the following day that an estimated 50,000 people marched in the funeral procession with perhaps 100,000 more viewing from the sidelines.**

One of the friends was a musician, and Dr. King had just asked him to play a Negro spiritual, "Precious Lord, Take My Hand," at a rally that was to have been held two hours later in support of striking Memphis sanitation men.

Paul Hess, assistant administrator at St. Joseph's Hospital, where Dr. King died despite emergency surgery, said the minister had "received a gunshot wound on the right side of the neck, at the root of the neck, a gaping wound."

"He was pronounced dead at 7:05 p.m. Central standard time (8:05 p.m. New York time) by staff doctors," Mr. Hess said. "They did everything humanly possible."

Dr. King's mourning associates sought to calm the people they met by recalling his messages of peace, but there was widespread concern by law enforcement officers here and elsewhere over potential reactions.

In a television broadcast after the curfew was ordered here, Mr. Holloman said, "rioting has broken out in parts of the city" and "looting is rampant."

Dr. King had come back to Memphis Wednesday morning to organize support once again for 1,300 sanitation workers who have been striking since Lincoln's birthday. Just a week ago yesterday he led a march in the strikers' cause that ended in violence. A 16-year-old Negro was killed, 62 persons were injured and 200 were arrested.

Yesterday Dr. King had been in his second-floor room—Number 306—throughout the day. Just about 6 p.m. he emerged, wearing a silkish-looking black suit and white shirt.

Solomon Jones Jr., his driver, had been waiting to take him by car to the home of the Rev. Samuel Kyles of Memphis for dinner. Mr. Jones said later he had observed, "It's cold outside, put your topcoat on," and Dr. King had replied, "O.K., I will."

Two Men in Courtyard

Dr. King, an open-faced, genial man, leaned over a green iron railing to chat with an associate, Jesse Jackson, standing just below him in a courtyard parking lot:

"Do you know Ben?" Mr. Jackson asked, introducing Ben Branch of Chicago, a musician who was to play at the night's rally.

"Yes, that's my man!" Dr. King glowed.

The two men recalled Dr. King's asking for the playing of the spiritual. "I really want you to play that tonight," Dr. King said, enthusiastically.

The Rev. Ralph W. Abernathy, perhaps Dr. King's closest friend, was just about to come out of the motel room when the sudden loud noise burst out.

Dr. King toppled to the concrete second-floor walkway. Blood gushed from the right jaw and neck area. His necktie had been ripped off by the blast.

"He had just bent over," Mr. Jackson recalled later. "If he had been standing up, he wouldn't have been hit in the face.

Policemen "All Over"

"When I turned around," Mr. Jackson went on, bitterly, "I saw police coming from everywhere. They said, 'where did it come from?' And I said, 'behind you.' The police were coming from where the shot came."

Mr. Branch asserted that the shot had come from "the hill on the other side of the street.

"When I looked up, the police and the sheriff's deputies were running all around," Mr. Branch declared.

"We didn't need to call the police," Mr. Jackson said. "They were here all over the place."

Mr. Kyles said Dr. King had stood in the open "about three minutes."

Mr. Jones, the driver, said that a squad car with four policemen in it drove down the street only moments before the gunshot. The police had been circulating throughout the motel area on precautionary patrols. After the shot, Mr. Jones said, he saw a man "with something white on his face" creep away from a thicket across the street.

Someone rushed up with a towel to stem the flow of Dr. King's blood. Mr. Kyles said he put a blanket over Dr. King, but "I knew he was gone." He ran down the stairs and tried to telephone from the motel office for an ambulance.

Mr. Abernathy hurried up with a second larger towel.

Police with Helmets

Policemen were pouring into the motel area, carrying rifles and shotguns and wearing helmets. But the King aides said it seemed to be 10 or 15 minutes before a fire department ambulance arrived.

Dr. King was apparently still living when he reached the St. Joseph's Hospital operating room for emergency surgery. He was borne in on a stretcher, the bloody towel over his head.

It was the same emergency room to which James H. Meredith, first Negro enrolled at the University of Mississippi, was taken after he was ambushed and shot in June, 1965, at Hernando, Miss., a few miles south of Memphis. Mr. Meredith was not seriously hurt.

Outside the emergency room some of Dr. King's aides waited in forlorn hope. One was Chauncey Eskridge, his legal adviser. He broke into sobs when Dr. King's death was announced.

"A man full of life, full of love, and he was shot," Mr. Eskridge said. "He had always lived with that expectation- but nobody ever expected it to happen."

But the Rev. Andrew Young, executive director of Dr. King's Southern Christian Leadership Conference, recalled there had been some talk Wednesday night about possible harm to Dr. King in Memphis. Mr. Young recalled: "He said he had reached the pinnacle of fulfillment with his nonviolent movement, and these reports did not bother him."

FIRING STEPPED UP AT WOUNDED KNEE

By MARTIN WALDRON, MARCH 28, 1973

Negotiators stepped up efforts today to bring an end to the month-long takeover of Wounded Knee by dissident Indians as their confrontation with government forces became virtually open warfare.

Members of the Federal Community Relations Service spent most of the day at the Indian camp in Wounded Knee as United States marshals and Federal Bureau of Investigation agents on one side and Indians on the other fired rifles and machine guns at each other from trenchlike bunkers as close as 500 yards apart.

The firing continued sporadically through the day.

A United States marshal was shot in the chest last night, but there were no reports of any casualties today. A Justice Department spokesman said, however, that it would be only a matter of time before more casualties occurred.

Justice Department officials said tonight that as a cease-fire was being arranged with the Indians at Wounded Knee this afternoon, an airplane landed near the hamlet and unloaded weapons and ammunition for the rebellious Indians. Assistant Attorney General Kent Frizzell said that the small plane might have come from Canada. Its license number began

Members of the Oglala Sioux tribe march to the cemetery where their ancestors were buried following the 1890 massacre during the Wounded Knee standoff with federal authorities. March 10, 1973.

with an X, he said, an indication that it was of foreign registry. He added, however, that the number appeared to have been altered by masking tape. The government official said observers were unable to estimate how much ammunition and what type was unloaded. A government helicopter chased the plane when it took off but lost it.

Mr. Frizzell said that the Indians at Wounded Knee also made several forays toward government lines, coming within 150 yards at one point. "The fun and games are over," Mr. Frizzell said. "This is senseless. It has got to stop, one way or the other."

He said that the government had not yet set a deadline for the Indians holding Wounded Knee to surrender, but that further delay "invites further violence."

Leaders Reportedly Gone

The chairman of the Oglala Sioux Tribal Council, Richard Wilson, told reporters today that two key American Indian movement leaders, Russell Means and Dennis Banks, slipped through government lines last night while federal agents were pinned down by heavy gunfire.

Mr. Wilson, who has vowed to drive the militant Indians off the Sioux reservation, said he was told by a Justice Department official that Mr. Means and Mr. Banks had fled.

Mr. Frizzell said he could not confirm the escape of the two men, both of whom have been indicted by a federal grand jury for their part in the Wounded Knee takeover.

He said, however, that Community Relations Service negotiators, who were allowed through roadblocks to Wounded Knee this morning, did not see the two men.

Members of the movement seized Wounded Knee on Feb. 27 to dramatize their demands for government concessions to Indians.

4,000 Rounds Reported

Federal agents guarding the perimeter of Wounded Knee estimated that 4,000 or more rifle shots were exchanged last night. Deputy Chief United States Marshal William Hall of Marion, S.C., said that the Indians were firing at least one machine gun. He said that a meeting scheduled for this afternoon with leaders of the dissidents was canceled after the Indians objected to some of the proposed arrangements. Another attempt for such a meeting will be made tomorrow afternoon.

Mr. Frizzell said that he would meet with movement leaders at Rapid City tomorrow, but that he did not know if those attending the meeting could speak for the Indians at Wounded Knee.

The chief United States marshal for Nebraska, Lloyd Grimm, 50 years old, was seriously wounded last night as he and Mr. Frizzell were making an inspection of government positions.

Mr. Grimm, of Omaha, was paralyzed from the waist down by the bullet and was reported to be in serious condition in a Denver hospital today. He was flown there last night in a chartered aircraft.

Marshal Hall said that for the last several days, Indian patrols have been going into the mile-wide area between government roadblocks and the small town. F.B.I. agents have been prowling the area in armored personnel carriers borrowed from the army.

Chief of Marshals Wayne Coburn said he believed that the Indian patrols were trying to capture or set fire to one of the personnel carriers.

Government officials described the situation today as extremely dangerous and refused to issue passes to reporters trying to get through government roadblocks to Wounded Knee. The Oglala Sioux Indians set up their own roadblocks outside those of the government yesterday, and refused to let newsmen travel along Big Foot Trail to the main government roadblocks.

Mr. Wilson, as tribal chairman, ordered the roadblocks to prevent food from being taken to Wounded Knee. His forces last night seized a carload of food that lawyers representing the American Indian Movement had tried to bring in under a court order.

Judge Rescinds Action

The order, which had said that six carloads of food could be moved through government lines to Wounded Knee each day, was rescinded today by United States District Judge Andrew Bogue. Mr. Frizzell said, that the Justice Department believed that under Indian law, Mr. Wilson had the authority to order the roadblocks. Whether Mr. Wilson would have to obey a court order was between him and the courts, Mr. Frizzell said.

"I'm glad to see that they recognize that this is still Indian country," Mr. Wilson said.

The tribal chairman said that the Sioux roadblocks would stay up until Wounded Knee was recaptured. The Indians holding the town have vowed to die if necessary to force the federal government to live up to ancient Indian treaties.

Mr. Wilson and most of the Oglala Sioux leaders have denounced the American Indian Movement, saying that grievances should be handled through recognized tribal procedures and under the tribal constitution.

NOTE: *The radicalization of the American Indian Movement in the 1970s thrust the horrors inflicted on the continent's native populations to the forefront of public attention briefly, but it didn't last and the institutionalized racism against and oppression of indigenous people persists and remains a much-ignored catastrophe.*

RIOTS IN LOS ANGELES: THE BLUE LINE; SURPRISED, POLICE REACT SLOWLY AS VIOLENCE SPREADS

By ROBERT REINHOLD, MAY 1, 1992

The Los Angeles Police, apparently caught off guard by the violent reaction to the acquittal of four white officers in the beating of a black motorist, were slow to react, even after the scope of the anarchy sweeping the city had become apparent.

As unruly demonstrators threatened to invade police headquarters downtown early Wednesday evening, Chief of Police Daryl F. Gates was attending an event in the affluent Brentwood area, about 11 miles away, to raise money to fight a proposal on the June ballot to limit the term of the police chief. Matthew Hunt, the deputy chief in charge of the affected area, was attending a community meeting about 6 miles from the police command center.

It was hours before the police entered many of the areas in South Central Los Angeles where stores were being looted and motorists were being dragged from their cars and beaten.

Chief Resisted National Guard

As late as 11 p.m., with at least two dozen fires blazing out of control, Chief Gates resisted Mayor Tom Bradley's call for National Guard troops, telling Gov. Pete Wilson in a conference call with the mayor that he was not sure the police needed help handling the situation, according to someone who is close to Mayor Bradley and who spoke on the condition of anonymity.

The mayor prevailed with the governor, and by this morning Mr. Gates agreed that the guard was needed. But the first contingent, about 2,400 guardsmen, including 100 military police, was not deployed on the streets until midafternoon today. The governor traced the delay in part to a shortage of ammunition.

Fires Burned Unattended

Similarly, the Los Angeles Fire Department, had no special contingency plan apart from declaring a tactical alert, meaning engine companies moved in special teams. The department was forced to let many fires burn unattended, not because it lacked sufficient engines at first but because the police did not have enough officers to protect firefighters.

There were barely enough officers on hand to prevent Parker Center, the police head-quarters downtown, from being overrun.

The slow response was due in part to the fact that almost nobody, including the mayor, anticipated such a sweeping acquittal of all four officers and partly because the police department, as targets of minority animosity, tried to avoid seeming provocative.

The police apparently gambled that restraint would result in less violence than an aggressive show of force.

But by the time they mounted a more intense response, rioting, looting and burning had spread beyond containment. Mr. Gates today conceded that the police should have moved faster.

"Quite frankly, we were overwhelmed," he said at a news conference at city hall this morning. "I wish it had been much faster, but it was not. We think we were as ready as we ought to be. We did not want it to appear that we were overreacting. We were very, very careful not to show that provocativeness."

> *Nobody anticipated such a sweeping acquittal of all four officers.*

The police department had devised several contingency plans for the verdict's aftermath but apparently none that anticipated the speed and breadth of the violence. "We were overwhelmed from the beginning," said Jesse Brewer, a former deputy chief of police who is now a member of the Police Commission, the body appointed by the mayor to oversee police department policies. He fought the Watts riots in 1965 and said this one was vastly different because it broke out in so many places.

The police mobilization began slowly. After the first signs of unrest a tactical alert was issued at 6:45, meaning that all 18 police divisions were notified that they might have to provide up to half their force to combat disorders. The first thrown into the fray was the Metropolitan Division, an elite citywide unit with special training in crowd control. "They were suddenly used up," Chief Gates said today.

The full-scale mobilization did not start until 7:30, after demonstrators rushed Parker Center and started to vandalize buildings and vehicles downtown. Under a mobilization, officers are recalled from their homes and placed on 12-hour shifts; routine police tasks like taking accident reports are halted.

At city hall and Parker Center alike, the general assumption had been that the jury would return at least one or two guilty verdicts and that that would be enough to prevent unrest. In any case, it was assumed that trouble would start after dark, not during the afternoon.

"Drastic" Verdict Not Expected

"Given the sensitivity, there was the desire to avoid provoking," said Stanley K. Sheinbaum, president of the Police Commission. "And nobody in the first instance expected a verdict as drastic and extreme as this one."

Interestingly, it is Mr. Gates—whose critics accuse him of fostering a climate of police brutality and racism that led to the beating of Rodney G. King—who is in charge of quelling the riots. But even his detractors say Mr. Gates may have exactly the kind of experience needed for this kind of job, having cut his teeth as a commander in the Watts riot and having invented the Special Weapons and Tactics (S.W.A.T.) concept adopted by police departments nationwide to apply overwhelming force to dangerous situations.

"It is perhaps ironic he has to try to quell disturbances," said Mr. Brewer, who had criticized Mr. Gates before the official inquiry into last year's beating. "But he's doing a good job. He's a professional. I cannot criticize him."

Although Chief Gates announced plans to retire in June, he was described by associates today as very much in command of the force.

The chief conceded that he had underestimated the reaction. "I'll tell you quite frankly I did not expect it to break out that quickly," he said at the news conference, adding that he was dismayed at the pictures of random violence without police intervention.

"I asked the same question: where were the police?" he said. "Let me assure you we have looked at that very, very carefully." At one point, the police were forced to back off when an angry mob gathered as officers were arresting a suspect.

Sources on the mayor's staff said that Chief Gates's initial reluctance to call up the National Guard did not delay their deployment because the governor approved the activation shortly after the mayor declared a state of emergency at 8:55 p.m.

> *Between midnight and noon today, the fire department responded to 2,102 emergencies.*

With little police protection, firefighters came under siege. "They tried to kill them with axes, they tried to kill them with gunshots," said the fire chief, Donald O. Manning. "They tried to kill them in a number of ways." One firefighter was shot in the cheek and left partially paralyzed today after surgery, fire department officials said.

Between midnight and noon today, the fire department responded to 2,102 emergencies, 829 of them structure fires. It was aided by companies from Beverly Hills, Culver City, Santa Monica, Los Angeles County and numerous other nearby communities. Calls were coming in at the rate of four a minute, department officials said. At one time, the department was stretched so thin that it had only 21 engines covering the rest of the 420-square-mile city.

Under a tactical alert, fire engines moved around in "strike teams" of a hook-and-ladder and two engines, sometimes moving down streets without lights and sirens to avoid attracting attention, and returning to station houses by out-of-the-way routes.

At the height of the unrest early this morning, there were 30 major structural fires, more than half unattended because firefighters could not get police protection against angry aggressive mobs of youths. According to Stephen J. Ruda, a fire department spokesman, there was no animosity against the fire department. "This was a police matter. The people in the community do not have vengeance against us."

A top aide to Mayor Bradley said the fire department performed as well as could have been expected and that there had been no criticism of them.

The police, though, were in a difficult position. "We were the target," said Mr. Brewer. "That certainly put us at a disadvantage."

PRESIDENT OBAMA CONDEMNS BOTH THE BALTIMORE RIOTS AND THE NATION'S "SLOW-ROLLING CRISIS"

By JULIE HIRSCHFELD DAVIS AND MATT APUZZO, APRIL 28, 2015

President Obama responded with passion and frustration on Tuesday to the violence that has rocked Baltimore and other cities after the deaths of young black men in confrontations with the police, calling for a period of soul-searching about what he said had become a near-weekly cycle of tragedy.

Speaking from the White House Rose Garden, Mr. Obama condemned the chaos unfolding just 40 miles north of the White House and called for "full transparency and

Community members link arms in front of police Tuesday evening in Baltimore, April 28, 2015, with the intent of separating the police from demonstrators and preventing a replay of the previous night's violence.

accountability" in a Department of Justice investigation into the death of Freddie Gray, the young black man who died of a spinal cord injury suffered while in police custody.

He said that his thoughts were also with the police officers injured in Monday night's unrest in Baltimore, which he said "underscores that that's a tough job, and we have to keep that in mind."

But in a carefully planned 14-minute statement during a news conference with Prime Minister Shinzo Abe of Japan, Mr. Obama made clear that he was deeply dismayed not only by the recent unrest in several cities but also by the longstanding yet little-discussed racial and societal forces that have fed it.

"We have seen too many instances of what appears to be police officers interacting with individuals, primarily African American, often poor, in ways that raise troubling questions," Mr. Obama said. "This has been a slow-rolling crisis. This has been going on for a long time. This is not new, and we shouldn't pretend that it's new."

They have also raised difficult and familiar questions for Mr. Obama about whether he and his administration are doing enough to confront the problem, questions made all the more poignant because he is the first African American to occupy the White House.

The president struggled for balance in his remarks. He pushed back against critics who have said he should be more aggressive in his response to questionable practices by the police, saying: "I can't federalize every police department in the country and force them to retrain."

Mr. Obama also made clear that he had no sympathy for people rioting in the streets, calling them "a handful of people taking advantage of the situation for their own purposes," who should "be treated as criminals."

And he said that law enforcement officials and organizations that represent them must also admit that "there are some police who aren't doing the right thing."

But he emphasized that the problem went far beyond the police, who he said are too often deployed to "do the dirty work of containing the problems that arise" in broken urban communities where fathers are absent, drugs dominate, and education, jobs and opportunities are nonexistent.

The president had initially avoided commenting on the unrest in Baltimore, allowing only still photographers into the Oval Office on Monday afternoon as he held an unscheduled meeting with Ms. [Loretta] Lynch, thus denying reporters the chance to ask him questions about the chaos then unfurling one state away. The issue dominated Ms. Lynch's first day on the job [as attorney general], and her response to it will be watched closely. As he prepared to swear her in, Vice President Joseph R. Biden Jr. said that Ms. Lynch, the first black woman in the post, was uniquely qualified to bridge the divide between minority neighborhoods and police officers clashing over the use of deadly force. Within hours, Baltimore was in flames.

Ms. Lynch's predecessor, Eric H. Holder Jr., the first black attorney general, was the face of the Obama administration's response to unrest in Ferguson, Mo., last year after a white police officer killed an unarmed black teenager there, and he relished the opportunity to talk about policing and race relations.

It made him a hero of the civil rights movement, but drew sharp criticism from police groups who said the attorney general did not do enough to support them.

Ms. Lynch, a career prosecutor, came into office promising to strike a new tone and planned to visit police groups this summer. But the riots in Baltimore after the death of the 25-year-old Mr. Gray have overtaken that timeline. Almost as soon as she had taken her oath, there were signs that Baltimore was about to erupt.

As mourners gathered for Mr. Gray's funeral, the police announced that three street gangs had pledged to work together to "take out" police officers. The University of Maryland shut down its Baltimore campus early, saying it had been warned that the area could soon turn violent.

At the Justice Department, Ms. Lynch was met by Ms. [Vanita] Gupta [head of the department's Civil Rights Division] and Mr. [Ron] Davis [director of the Office of Community Oriented Policing Services] for a lengthy update on Baltimore. It was her first meeting as attorney general, and it led to the unscheduled trip to the White House to meet with Mr. Obama.

In one meeting on Tuesday, Ms. Lynch told officials that while in Baltimore, they should meet not only Mr. Gray's family but also the officers who were most seriously injured. "When officers get injured in senseless violence, they become victims as well," she said, a Justice Department official told reporters.

As night set in on Monday, chaos reigned on Baltimore's streets. Rioters burned and looted businesses. Others hurled rocks. Police officers were injured, and the police commissioner said his department was outnumbered in its own city.

Gov. Larry Hogan of Maryland activated the National Guard, sending hundreds of soldiers into the city after dawn on Tuesday.

Ms. Lynch issued a statement in which she condemned "the senseless acts of violence by some individuals in Baltimore that have resulted in harm to law enforcement officers, destruction of property and a shattering of the peace in the city."

It was a message that Mr. Obama echoed on Tuesday, as he bristled at what he argued was the news media's habit of focusing on dramatic images of brutality and chaos rather than on what have been mostly peaceful protests in Baltimore and other cities.

"One burning building will be looped on television over and over and over again, and thousands of demonstrators who did it the right way, I think, have been lost in the discussion," Mr. Obama said.

He said the that "overwhelming majority" in Baltimore protested peacefully and went back into the streets Tuesday to clean up after "a handful of criminals and thugs who tore up the place." Ms. Lynch, a child of the segregated South and the daughter of a local civil rights leader, has spoken of the need for police officers—because they wield the power—to repair broken relationships. But she has also spoken repeatedly about the police as a force for good in minority neighborhoods.

ONE SLOGAN, MANY METHODS:
BLACK LIVES MATTER ENTERS POLITICS

By JOHN ELIGON, NOVEMBER 18, 2015

When the Democratic National Committee recently rejected adding a presidential debate focusing exclusively on issues affecting black people, it got divergent responses from two groups widely associated with the Black Lives Matter movement.

Campaign Zero, whose agenda centers on ending police violence, quickly embraced the offer for a town hall forum instead and began working to arrange forums for Democratic and Republican candidates. But members of an organization named Black Lives Matter, which first asked for the debates, asserted that only a debate would demonstrate the Democrats' commitment to their cause.

Black Lives Matter began as a hashtag and grew into a protest slogan—after prominent police killings of blacks over the past year—and became an internet-driven civil rights movement. The phrase is as much a mantra as a particular organization, with the general public lumping numerous groups under the Black Lives Matter banner, even if they are not officially connected.

Yet amid the groups' different approaches has been a swirl of political activity. Local affiliates of the Black Lives Matter organization have disrupted numerous Democratic presidential campaign events, pushing the candidates to support policies to end mass incarceration and police brutality.

That organization now has 26 chapters, and 1 in Canada, that largely set their own direction. In Boston, that has meant protesting the city's short-lived Olympic bid, which activists said would have been harmful to black neighborhoods. The Grand Rapids, Mich., chapter has held workshops on nonviolent organizing and the prison industry. In St. Paul, Minn., organizers have held rallies to call for more minority vendors at the state fair and protested police shootings.

Yet as the rift over debates versus town halls underscores, the young and sometimes cacophonous movement is struggling to find its voice, as the activists who fly its banner wade into national politics.

Many of those activists and groups favor protest, distrust conventional politics and have no intention of supporting candidates. Others have begun lobbying candidates and elected officials on legislative issues. And still others are hoping to use money to make a difference in elections. Campaign Zero, whose founders gained prominence during protests in Ferguson, Mo., has issued a detailed policy platform on preventing police violence and increasing police accountability. It has also met with Hillary Rodham Clinton and Bernie Sanders to pressure them to embrace its racial justice platforms.

Two groups have started political action committees to back candidates who support ideas espoused by Black Lives Matter activists. One, Black Lives Matter Political Action Committee, started by a St. Louis radio host, plans to raise money for voter education in races for law enforcement–related offices, including for district attorney and judgeships. The second, Black Lives Matter Super PAC, was started by New York activists who hope to raise large donations from celebrities to influence campaigns for a variety of offices.

"At this point, marching and protesting, it's not going anywhere," said Tarik Mohamed, treasurer and a founder of the super PAC. "So we're trying to find new avenues of engaging people for change."

And, in a sign of its growing influence, the movement is attracting the attention of deep-pocketed Democratic donors, who met with activists in Washington this week to discuss how they can support the budding movement.

The diffuseness and decentralization of the movement is viewed by many activist leaders as a source of energy, with local organizations tailoring solutions to problems in their communities. The broader movement has also fomented a new brand of activism on college campuses, most notably at the University of Missouri. Reacting to what they saw as the administration's tepid response to racism, activists at the university organized marches, one held a hunger strike and the football team threatened a boycott, forcing the president and chancellor to resign.

"There's nothing wrong with being decentralized and dispersed," said Allen Kwabena Frimpong, an organizer with the New York chapter. "The problem is being disconnected. If we are going to build political power, we have to build connections."

Yet for all the movement's impact, even some of its sympathizers question whether it needs a clearer organization and more concrete plan of action.

"There has to be a reckoning, I agree with that," Mrs. Clinton told a group of Black Lives Matter activists after an August campaign event in New Hampshire. "But I also think there has to be some positive thing you can move people toward."

The name Black Lives Matter was born when Alicia Garza, a California-based activist, used it in a Facebook post after George Zimmerman was acquitted two years ago in the killing of Trayvon Martin, an unarmed black teenager, in Florida. She then teamed with two fellow activists to create the Black Lives Matter hashtag and social media pages. But the movement gained prominence after a white police officer killed Michael Brown, an unarmed black 18-year-old, in Ferguson last year, and the Black Lives Matter founders arranged a national "freedom ride" to Ferguson.

But the ubiquity of the name itself—and the fact that anyone can use it—has caused complications. At some protests, for instance, marchers' chants have called for violence against police officers. Critics, including several Republican presidential candidates, then equated Black Lives Matter to promoting attacks against the police.

"I don't believe that that movement should be justified when they're calling for the murder of police officers," Gov. Chris Christie of New Jersey said recently on CBS's *Face the Nation*. He repeated the charge in the fourth Republican debate last week.

But leaders within the movement said that they reject violence and that antipolice chants are the acts of individuals, not the movement.

"It's like saying, 'Because the Ku Klux Klan calls themselves Christian, Christianity has a problem and needs to answer for the Ku Klux Klan,'" said Kenneth Murdock, who hosts a political radio show in St. Louis.

Mr. Murdock, who has worked for politicians in Missouri, started the political action committee over the summer. He declined to disclose how much money he had raised, saying he hoped to endorse candidates in local races across the country.

The Black Lives Matter Super PAC, in addition to contributing to campaigns next year, hopes to capitalize on new technology, such as virtual reality software, to help people understand experiences like solitary confinement, Mr. Mohamed said.

Members of the Democracy Alliance, an influential club of liberal donors, met on Tuesday with groups allied under the Black Lives Matters banner—including ColorOfChange.org, Black Youth Project 100 and the Black Civic Engagement Fund—to discuss possibly directing funds to the movement, said Leah Hunt-Hendrix, an alliance member. The organizations represented only a sample of the groups that donors wanted to shed light on, she said.

"It was just a really real conversation about the complexities of funding movements and the need for more infrastructure, especially black-led infrastructure," said Ms. Hunt-Hendrix, who has inherited wealth from an oil company her grandfather started.

Specific funding commitments were not made, she said, and it would be up to individual donors to follow up with organizations they want to support.

"We don't want to raise expectations that this is a secretive group of donors hoping to raise tons of money," she said.

DeRay Mckesson, a founder of Campaign Zero, has been focusing much of his energy on trying to organize Black Lives Matter–themed forums for Democratic and Republican presidential candidates. Town hall forums are more in line with the spirit of the movement, Mr. Mckesson argued, because they allow ordinary people to ask questions. He said he has been in negotiations with television networks to broadcast the forums.

Mr. Mckesson got support for the town halls from an unexpected source recently when Senator Rand Paul of Kentucky, who is running for the Republican presidential nomination, said on NewsOne that Republicans would participate "if we were smart."

"They are drawing attention to issues that need to be drawn to," Mr. Paul said.

Some activists have criticized Campaign Zero as being too focused on legislative remedies for police violence, and were concerned the public would think of them as "a silver bullet" for injustices against blacks, Mr. Frimpong said.

Mr. Mckesson has responded by saying, "We acknowledge that this isn't the radical change required to rethink the system, but we can't discount or devalue the immediate, practical benefit this can have on people's lives."

While Campaign Zero has, among other things, called for investing in better police training and body cameras, other Black Lives Matter activists are demanding that public funds be used for antipoverty programs that could drive down crime.

When New York City officials sought to add 1,000 new police officers to the force this year, local Black Lives Matter members and other activists argued those funds would be better spent on youth summer jobs and transit access for low-income people, school social workers and teachers. Such programs would address the root causes of crime, the activists argued, but the city council voted for adding more officers.

Many members of the Black Lives Matter organization also continue to promote protests of presidential candidates in addition to more conventional political activities, such as voter registration or education. The tactic has proved effective with Democrats.

Activists disrupted a Clinton campaign event in Cleveland in August, calling for her to stop accepting contributions from groups affiliated with private prisons and investing in causes that help black transgender women. Months later, Mrs. Clinton said she would stop accepting those contributions. In August, activists took over a stage in Seattle when Mr. Sanders tried to speak, and the senator promptly released a racial justice platform.

"I think that it's not just about changing hearts and minds, it's not just about changing laws, it's about actually changing action," said Elle Hearns, a strategic adviser to the Black Lives Matter organization who is based in Ohio.

Khalil Gibran Muhammad, the director of the Schomburg Center for Research in Black Culture in New York and an observer of the movement, said that many Black Lives Matter activists seemed to be advocating change beyond laws, which they say are unfairly applied to blacks. But history, he said, suggested that activists might have to work within the traditional political system.

"They may have to accept that some people are going to have to sit at the table," he said, "and work this stuff out."

MAN CHARGED AFTER WHITE NATIONALIST RALLY IN CHARLOTTESVILLE ENDS IN DEADLY VIOLENCE

By SHERYL GAY STOLBERG AND BRIAN M. ROSENTHAL, AUGUST 12, 2017

The city of Charlottesville, Va., was engulfed by violence on Saturday as white nationalists and counterprotesters clashed in one of the bloodiest fights to date over the removal of Confederate monuments across the South.

White nationalists had long planned a demonstration over the city's decision to remove a statue of Robert E. Lee. But the rally quickly exploded into racial taunting, shoving and outright brawling, prompting the governor to declare a state of emergency and the National Guard to join the police in clearing the area.

Those skirmishes mostly resulted in cuts and bruises. But after the rally at a city park was dispersed, a car bearing Ohio license plates plowed into a crowd near the city's downtown mall, killing a 32-year-old woman. Some 34 others were injured, at least 19 in the car crash, according to a spokeswoman for the University of Virginia Medical Center.

The white separatist Unite the Right Rally in Charlottesville, Va. on August 12, 2017, quickly turned violent, with multiple skirmishes between marchers, protestors, and police, and a domestic-terrorism car attack that resulted in the death of 1 person and the wounding of 19.

Col. Martin Kumer, the superintendent of the Albemarle-Charlottesville Regional Jail, confirmed Saturday evening that an Ohio man, James Alex Fields Jr., 20, of Maumee, had been arrested and charged with second-degree murder, three counts of malicious wounding and failing to stop at the scene of a crash that resulted in a death. But the authorities declined to say publicly that Mr. Fields was the driver of the car that plowed into the crowd.

Witnesses to the crash said a gray sports car accelerated into a crowd of counterdemonstrators—who were marching jubilantly near the mall after the white nationalists had left—and hurled at least two people in the air. "It was probably the scariest thing I've ever seen in my life," said Robert Armengol, who was at the scene reporting for a podcast he hosts with students at the University of Virginia. "After that it was pandemonium. The car hit reverse and sped and everybody who was up the street in my direction started running."

The planned rally was promoted as "Unite the Right" and both its organizers and critics said they expected it to be one of the largest gatherings of white nationalists in recent times, attracting groups like the Ku Klux Klan and neo-Nazis and movement leaders like David Duke and Richard Spencer.

Many of these groups have felt emboldened since the election of Donald J. Trump as president. Mr. Duke, a former imperial wizard of the Ku Klux Klan, told reporters on Saturday that the protesters were "going to fulfill the promises of Donald Trump" to "take our country back."

Saturday afternoon, President Trump, speaking at the start of a veterans' event at his golf club in Bedminster, N.J., addressed what he described as "the terrible events unfolding in Charlottesville, Virginia."

In his comments, President Trump condemned the bloody protests, but he did not specifically criticize the white nationalist rally and its neo-Nazi slogans, blaming "hatred, bigotry and violence on many sides."

"It's been going on for a long time in our country, it's not Donald Trump, it's not Barack Obama," said Mr. Trump, adding that he had been in contact with Virginia officials. After calling for the "swift restoration of law and order," he offered a plea for unity among Americans of "all races, creeds and colors."

The president came under criticism from some who said he had not responded strongly enough against racism and that he failed to condemn the white nationalist groups by name who were behind the rally.

Among those displeased with Mr. Trump was the mayor of Charlottesville, Mike Signer. "I do hope that he looks himself in the mirror and thinks very deeply about who he consorted with during his campaign," he said.

Late on Saturday night, the Department of Justice announced that it was opening a civil rights investigation into "the circumstances of the deadly vehicular incident," to be conducted by the F.B.I., the United States attorney for the Western District of Virginia and the department's Civil Rights Division.

"The violence and deaths in Charlottesville strike at the heart of American law and justice," Attorney General Jeff Sessions said in a statement. "When such actions arise from racial bigotry and hatred, they betray our core values and cannot be tolerated."

The turmoil in Charlottesville began with a march Friday night by white nationalists on the campus of the University of Virginia and escalated Saturday morning as demonstrators from both sides gathered in and around the park. Waving Confederate flags, chanting Nazi-era slogans, wearing helmets and carrying shields, the white nationalists converged on the Lee statue inside the park and began chanting phrases like "You will not replace us" and "Jews will not replace us."

Hundreds of counterprotesters—religious leaders, Black Lives Matter activists and anti-fascist groups known as *antifa*—quickly surrounded the park, singing spirituals, chanting and carrying their own signs.

The morning started peacefully, with the white nationalists gathering in McIntire Park, outside downtown, and the counterdemonstrators—including Cornel R. West, the Harvard University professor and political activist—gathering at the First Baptist Church, a historically African American church here. Professor West, who addressed the group at a sunrise prayer service, said he had come "bearing witness to love and justice in the face of white supremacy."

At McIntire Park, the white nationalists waved Confederate flags and other banners. One of the participants, who gave his name only as Ted because he said he might want to run for political office someday, said he was from Missouri, and added, "I'm tired of seeing white people pushed around." But by 11 a.m., after both sides had made their way to Emancipation Park, the scene had exploded into taunting, shoving and outright brawling. Three people were arrested in connection with the skirmishes. Barricades encircling the park and separating the two sides began to come down, and the police temporarily retreated. People were seen clubbing one another in the streets, and pepper spray filled the air. One of the white nationalists left the park bleeding, his head wrapped in gauze.

Declaring the gathering an unlawful assembly, the police had cleared the area before noon, and the Virginia National Guard arrived as officers began arresting some who remained. But fears lingered that the altercation would start again nearby, as demonstrators dispersed in smaller groups.

Within an hour, politicians, including Gov. Terry McAuliffe, a Democrat, and the House speaker, Paul D. Ryan of Wisconsin, a Republican, had condemned the violence.

The first public response from the White House came from the first lady, Melania Trump, who wrote on Twitter: "Our country encourages freedom of speech, but let's communicate w/o hate in our hearts. No good comes from violence."

Former president Barack Obama responded to the violence on Twitter with a quote from Nelson Mandela: "No one is born hating another person because of the color of his skin or his background or his religion. . . . People must learn to hate, and if they can learn to hate, they can be taught to love."

After the rally was dispersed, its organizer, Jason Kessler, who calls himself a "white advocate," complained in an interview that his group had been "forced into a very chaotic situation." He added, "The police were supposed to be there protecting us and they stood down."

Both Mr. Kessler and Richard Spencer, a prominent white nationalist who was to speak on Saturday, are graduates of the University of Virginia. In an online video, titled "A Message to Charlottesville," Mr. Spencer vowed to return to the college town.

"You think that we're going to back down to this kind of behavior, to you and your little provincial town? No," he said. "We are going to make Charlottesville the center of the universe."

Later in the day, a Virginia State Police helicopter crashed near a golf course and burst into flames. The pilot, Lt. H. Jay Cullen, 48, of Midlothian, Va., and Berke M. M. Bates, 40, a trooper-pilot of Quinton, Va., died at the scene. Their Bell 407 helicopter was assisting with the situation in Charlottesville, the Virginia State Police said.

The violence in Charlottesville was the latest development in a series of tense dramas unfolding across the United States over plans to remove statues and other historical markers of the Confederacy. The battles have been intensified by the election of Mr. Trump, who enjoys fervent support from white nationalists.

In New Orleans, tempers flared this spring when four Confederate-era monuments were taken down. Hundreds of far right and liberal protesters squared off, with occasional bouts of violence, under another statue of Robert E. Lee. There were fisticuffs and a lot of shouting, but nothing like the violence seen in Charlottesville.

In St. Louis, workers removed a Confederate monument from Forest Park in June, ending a drawn-out battle over its fate. In Frederick, Md., a bust of Roger B. Taney, the chief justice of the United States who wrote the notorious 1857 Dred Scott decision denying blacks citizenship, was removed in May from its spot near city hall.

Here in Charlottesville, Saturday's protest was the culmination of a year and a half of debate over the Lee statue. A movement to withdraw it began when an African American high school student here started a petition. The city council voted 3 to 2 in April to sell it, but a judge issued an injunction temporarily stopping the move.

The city had been bracing for a sea of demonstrators, and on Friday night, hundreds of them, carrying lit torches, marched on the picturesque grounds of the University of Virginia, founded in 1819 by Thomas Jefferson.

"We're going to fulfill the promises of Donald Trump" to "take our country back," said Mr. Duke, a former imperial wizard of the Ku Klux Klan. Many of the white nationalist protesters carried campaign signs for Mr. Trump.

> ## *"We're going to fulfill the promises of Donald Trump."*

University officials said one person was arrested and charged Friday night with assault and disorderly conduct, and several others were injured. Among those hurt was a university police officer injured while making the arrest, the school said in a statement.

Teresa A. Sullivan, the president of the university, strongly condemned the Friday demonstration in a statement, calling it "disturbing and unacceptable."

Still, officials allowed the Saturday protest to go on—until the injuries began piling up.

Charlottesville declared a state of emergency around 11 a.m., citing an "imminent threat of civil disturbance, unrest, potential injury to persons and destruction of public and personal property."

Governor McAuliffe followed with his own declaration an hour later.

"It is now clear that public safety cannot be safeguarded without additional powers, and that the mostly-out-of-state protesters have come to Virginia to endanger our citizens and property," he said in a statement. "I am disgusted by the hatred, bigotry and violence these protesters have brought to our state."

The Republican candidate for governor in Virginia, Ed Gillespie, issued his own statement denouncing the protests as "vile hate" that has "no place in our Commonwealth."

Mr. Ryan agreed. "The views fueling the spectacle in Charlottesville are repugnant," he said on Twitter. "Let it only serve to unite Americans against this kind of vile bigotry."

NOTE: *President Trump shocked many Americans—but thrilled his base—when he said there were good people on both sides of the violence. Thus he created a moral equivalency between racism and those who fight it, which was a trademark of his defense against his critics on other issues and provided a justification for the racial rage that permeated his political base.*

CHAPTER 5
OTHER
HOT-BUTTON ISSUES

"No nation can have the policy that whole classes of people are immune from immigration law or enforcement. It was a simple decision by the administration to have a zero-tolerance policy for illegal entry, period."

—President Donald Trump's senior policy adviser Stephen Miller, to *The New York Times*, on the policy of separating families at the border, June 2018

AMERICAN POLITICS HAS BEEN marked by a series of debates over social issues that have roiled the country, from the Know Nothing movement of the 1860s to the antiwar protests of the 1960s and beyond. One of the most intractable of those arguments has historically been over immigration, a debate that is inextricably snarled in questions of skin color, religion and place of origin. Women's struggles for the vote and other rights equal to those of men have not yet ceased, with the country only recently grappling with questions of equal pay and sexual abuse in public and private spaces. Right-wing organizations used the legalization of marriage between same-sex partners to raise campaign money from their most loyal base. And in the early 21st century, the United States was one of the only developed nations that failed to regulate the epidemic of firearms.

OPPOSITE: Brothers, ages 4 and 3, from El Salvador, at a border patrol station in Brownsville, Tex., in 2014.

IMMIGRATION

AFTER 16 FUTILE YEARS, CONGRESS WILL TRY AGAIN TO LEGALIZE "DREAMERS"

By YAMICHE ALCINDOR AND SHERYL GAY STOLBERG, SEPTEMBER 5, 2017

For 16 years, advocates for legalizing young immigrants brought here illegally by their parents have tried to pass legislation to shield them from deportation. The bill was called the Dream Act, and in Congresses Democratic and Republican, and in the Bush and Obama administrations, whether by stand-alone bill or comprehensive immigration legislation, it failed again and again.

Now, with 800,000 lives in the balance and a fiercely anti-immigration current running through the Republican Party, lawmakers are being asked to try again—with a six-month deadline, to boot. The prospects for success after more than a decade of false starts would already be daunting, but President Trump may have made the odds even longer after he promised voters last year that Republicans would take a hard line on immigration, then punted the issue to Congress.

His invitation to lawmakers on Tuesday to "do something and do it right" for the so-called Dreamers will run into the headwinds of his own politics. On the other hand, lawmakers who for 16 years have been unwilling to grant legal status to a sympathetic group of unauthorized immigrants may find that taking their legal status away is even harder than conferring it.

"I'm hoping that this is a moment where we are forced to finally do something," said Senator Richard J. Durbin, Democrat of Illinois and an original author of the Dream Act—the letters stand for Development, Relief and Education for Alien Minors. "We want to call this bill for a vote on the floor of the House and the floor of the Senate. I am hoping that we will have enough votes to pass it."

Senator Susan Collins, Republican of Maine, said she believed there is "widespread bipartisan support for legislation that would provide some measure of protection to children who are brought to this country through no decision of their own."

DACA recipients Sofia Ruales, 24, her sister Erica Ruales, 23, and their cousin Marlon Ruales, 23, at a gathering in New York City, September 5, 2017, listen to Attorney General Jeff Sessions's announcement that the Deferred Action for Childhood Arrivals (DACA) program will be phased out. They were brought to the United States from Ecuador when they were small children. They later joined a group of Dreamers and supporters in a march to Trump Tower.

Before there was Deferred Action for Childhood Arrivals, or DACA, there was Mr. Durbin's Dream. In 2007, a version of the measure won the support of a majority of senators but fell victim to a bipartisan filibuster that included eight Democrats. Three years later, the bill passed the House but again did not get through the Senate.

And in 2013, language allowing Dreamers to stay in this country and work or attend school was included in a broader immigration package that passed the Senate with 68 votes—then failed in the House.

Frustrated after years of failings, President Barack Obama signed DACA as a temporary order in the hope that Congress would eventually pass the Dream Act and broader immigration changes. But with Republicans in control of both chambers of Congress, the Dream Act stalled once again.

The politics have clearly shifted on the issue—for both parties. With Mr. Trump scheduled to visit her state on Wednesday, Senator Heidi Heitkamp, a North Dakota Democrat who is facing a tough reelection bid, posted a lengthy statement on her Facebook page in which she echoed Mr. Obama's assertion on Tuesday that ending the program was "cruel."

Some Republicans have softened, as well. Representative Cathy McMorris Rodgers, a Washington Republican who chairs the House Republican Conference, said in a statement that while she has long said she did not agree with the way Mr. Obama enacted his program, Congress "must protect" the Dreamers who are currently shielded from deportation.

She added, "That principle is fundamental for me."

But hard-liners in the Republican conference remain unbowed. Representative Steve King of Iowa, one of the fiercest voices in his party against illegal immigration, tweeted that delaying an end to DACA so Republican leadership "can push Amnesty is Republican suicide."

The Dream Act's history is tortured. In 2001, a concerned guidance counselor for a frightened young woman whose family immigrated from South Korea reached out to Mr. Durbin for help. The young woman, Tereza Lee, was a pianist who was hoping to apply to top-ranked music schools, but the law said she would have to leave the United States for 10 years and apply for reentry. To help Ms. Lee, Mr. Durbin introduced the Dream Act.

Democrats had a hand in the legislation's historical futility. For years, they used the Dream Act as a bargaining chip to push for broader immigration legislation, hoping a sympathetic group of young immigrants could help win a pathway to citizenship for the far broader pool of 12 million unauthorized immigrants. Now, most Democrats say there is no time for comprehensive immigration changes.

But Republican leaders indicated that they will need sweeteners, perhaps funding for a border wall or other measures to bolster border security.

"The process of taking care of the kids will be a negotiated process," said Senator Lindsey Graham, Republican of South Carolina, who appeared with Mr. Durbin on Tuesday at a news conference to call for bipartisan action. "There are a lot of people who believe that a good marriage would be border security and Dream Act."

Both Mr. Graham and Mr. Durbin made clear they could support such a marriage— albeit reluctantly, in the case of Mr. Durbin—but negotiations look inevitable. Others agreed.

"I think it's an opportunity for us to deal with a myriad other issues that we need to deal with, with a broken immigration system," said Senator Bob Corker, Republican of Tennessee. Among those issues, he said, are border security, efforts by immigrants to overstay their visa and the so-called E-Verify system for employers to certify that their workers are in this country legally.

Senator John Cornyn of Texas, the number-two Republican, was definitive. "I think what President Trump did is appropriate, which is to kick it to Congress, and so we will take that up," he said. "But there's no way that it will stand alone."

In the House, Republican moderates say they are willing to work with Democrats to enshrine the program in legislation—and to force Republican leaders to abandon their customary strategy of passing bills only with overwhelming Republican support—a "majority of the majority."

"I believe the votes are there to pass some kind of a DACA program in the House," said Representative Charlie Dent, Republican of Pennsylvania and a chairman of the so-called Tuesday Group of House moderates. "I'm not saying a majority of the majority, but there are 218 votes."

Representative Mike Coffman, a Colorado Republican who represents a narrowly divided, heavily Latino district, said Monday that he planned to push a legislative maneuver to get a vote on a temporary extension of DACA that he wrote with Representative Luis V. Gutiérrez, Democrat of Illinois. The so-called discharge petition for the Bridge Act would force Republican leaders to bring the bill to the floor if it has 218 signatures.

"Democrats have to decide, O.K., do we allow the deportation of these young people because we don't like a Republican taking leadership on this issue? Or do we go with a Republican-led initiative?" said Mr. Coffman, a top target for Democrats in next year's midterm elections.

Mr. Gutiérrez weighed in for Mr. Coffman's efforts. "I don't care who gets the credit. There are 800,000 kids' futures at stake," Mr. Gutierrez said. "The only consideration we have is how do we legislatively fix this problem."

It remains unclear if Representative Nancy Pelosi of California, the House Democratic leader, would back the Bridge Act, which would extend DACA for three years, and rally others to do the same.

But she has requested a meeting with Speaker Paul D. Ryan, who has the power to bring the Dream Act to a vote at any time and who said Tuesday he hoped to find consensus to ensure "that those who have done nothing wrong can still contribute as a valued part of this great country."

NOTE: *Like all immigration-reform attempts in this period, the effort to find a legal answer for the Dreamers failed when conservative Republicans and the entire Democratic caucus rejected yet another compromise. Meanwhile, the Trump administration's hard-line policies on immigration led to an uproar over the government's decision to separate children from their undocumented immigrant parents and put them into literal cages in detention camps (see pages 235–237).*

NEW ORDER INDEFINITELY BARS ALMOST ALL TRAVEL FROM SEVEN COUNTRIES

By MICHAEL D. SHEAR, SEPTEMBER 14, 2017

President Trump on Sunday issued a new order indefinitely banning almost all travel to the United States from seven countries, including most of the nations covered by his original travel ban, citing threats to national security posed by letting their citizens into the country.

The new order is more far-reaching than the president's original travel ban, imposing permanent restrictions on travel, rather than the 90-day suspension that Mr. Trump authorized soon after taking office. But officials said his new action was the result of a deliberative, rigorous examination of security risks that was designed to avoid the chaotic rollout of his first ban. And the addition of non-Muslim countries could address the legal attacks on earlier travel restrictions as discrimination based on religion.

Starting next month, most citizens of Iran, Libya, Syria, Yemen, Somalia, Chad and North Korea will be banned from entering the United States, Mr. Trump said in a proclamation released Sunday night. Citizens of Iraq and some groups of people in Venezuela who seek to visit the United States will face restrictions or heightened scrutiny.

> *"As president, I must act to protect the security and interests of the United States and its people."*

Mr. Trump's original travel ban caused turmoil at airports in January and set off a furious legal challenge to the president's authority. It was followed in March by a revised ban, which expired on Sunday even as the Supreme Court is set to hear arguments about its constitutionality on Oct. 10. The new order—Chad, North Korea and Venezuela are new to the list of affected countries and Sudan has been dropped—will take effect Oct. 18.

"As president, I must act to protect the security and interests of the United States and its people," Mr. Trump said in the proclamation, which White House officials said had the same force as an executive order. He added that the restrictions will remain in effect until the governments of the affected nations "satisfactorily address the identified inadequacies."

For Mr. Trump, whose efforts on health care, infrastructure improvements and tax reform are gaining little steam, the new order is a third attempt to make good on his campaign promise to respond to terrorist threats by tightening entry at the nation's borders. In December 2015, he called for a complete ban on travel to the United States by Muslims "until our country's representatives can figure out what the hell is going on," though he later denied that he had sought a religious test on travel.

Officials described the new order as a much more targeted effort than the president's earlier one. Each of the countries will be under its own set of travel restrictions, though in most cases citizens of the countries will be unable to emigrate to the United States permanently and most will be barred from coming to work, study or vacation in America.

Iran, for example, will still be able to send its citizens on student exchanges, though such visitors will be subject to enhanced screening. Certain government officials of Venezuela and their families will be barred from visiting the United States. Somalis will no longer be allowed to emigrate to the United States but may visit with extra screening.

Administration officials said that the new rules would not apply to legal permanent residents of the United States, and that visitors who currently hold valid visas from the countries listed will not have their visas revoked. That means that students already in the United States can finish their studies and employees of businesses in the United States who are from the targeted countries may stay for as long as their existing visas remain valid. People whose visas expire will be subject to the travel ban, officials said.

People seeking access to the United States as refugees are not covered by the proclamation, officials said. Entry of refugees is currently limited by the president's original travel ban, and officials said the administration was preparing new rules for refugees that should be announced within days.

Reaction to the president's announcement was swift, as some critics of the original travel ban expressed similar concerns about the president's latest effort to bar potential terrorists and criminals.

"Six of President Trump's targeted countries are Muslim. The fact that Trump has added North Korea—with few visitors to the U.S.—and a few government officials from Venezuela doesn't obfuscate the real fact that the administration's order is still a Muslim ban," said Anthony D. Romero, the executive director of the American Civil Liberties Union.

"President Trump's original sin of targeting Muslims cannot be cured by throwing other countries onto his enemies list," Mr. Romero said.

But administration officials—who have long rejected the characterization of the president's travel restrictions as a "Muslim ban,"—noted that the latest effort also applies to non-Muslim countries and was based on a rigorous evaluation of each country's security capabilities.

One official who briefed reporters on Sunday evening insisted that the president's travel restrictions were "never, ever, ever" based on race, religion or creed.

In a statement released by the White House, Mr. Trump defended the new proclamation, saying that "we cannot afford to continue the failed policies of the past, which present an unacceptable danger to our country. My highest obligation is to ensure the safety and security of the American people, and in issuing this new travel order, I am fulfilling that sacred obligation."

The president's announcement comes after the administration conducted what it described as an in-depth, worldwide, 90-day review of the security measures in place in other countries to prevent terrorists or criminals from entering the United States by applying to emigrate or to visit with a tourist, work or education visa.

Mr. Trump called for the review—and a temporary ban on travel from several majority-Muslim countries—just days after being inaugurated. But a fierce legal challenge to the travel ban delayed the security assessment until the summer.

Officials said last week that most nations already met new, minimum standards for identifying and screening potential travelers and sharing investigative information with law enforcement agencies in the United States. Some nations that initially fell short of those standards agreed to implement changes to avoid travel restrictions.

But several countries either failed to meet those standards or flatly refused, officials said. Homeland Security officials recommended to Mr. Trump in a report last week that he impose the new travel restrictions on the residents of those countries. The president's 15-page proclamation accepted the recommendations, spelling them out in detail.

The proclamation imposes the most severe restrictions on Syria and North Korea, which Mr. Trump says fail to cooperate with the United States in any respect. All citizens from those countries will be denied visas to enter the United States once the proclamation goes into effect. Most citizens of Chad, Libya and Yemen will be blocked from emigrating to or visiting the United States because the countries do not have the technical capability to identify and screen their travelers, and in many cases have terrorist networks in their countries, officials said.

Officials said Somalia did, barely, meet the security standards set by the United States, but will still be subject to a ban on emigration and heightened scrutiny for travel because it is a safe haven for terrorists. Officials said that Iran was uncooperative and would be subject to a broad travel ban, but Mr. Trump made an exception for student and exchange visas.

In Venezuela, Mr. Trump restricted only the travel of government officials and their families, writing in the proclamation that the ban was focused on that group because they were "responsible for the identified inadequacies" in sharing information about travelers.

A mother and daughter embrace at Logan Airport in Boston, February 5, 2017. The daughter, a resident of Atlanta, was emotional after her mother disembarked from a Lufthansa flight from Frankfurt, Germany, one of the first flights allowing people into America from seven Muslim-majority countries that were banned from traveling to the U.S. Many travelers rushed to make it into the United States before a court ruling to stay the restraining order on the travel ban.

Mr. Trump's original travel ban prevented all travel from citizens of seven countries: Iraq, Iran, Libya, Somalia, Sudan, Syria and Yemen. Iraq was later removed from a second version of the travel ban in March after American officials said it had improved its ability to screen passengers and share information with the United States. In the new security review, Sudan was deemed to meet the security standards and was removed from the list of countries with travel restrictions.

Homeland Security officials had described the previous ban as a temporary pause on travel from certain countries to allow for the review of security measures.

By contrast, the new travel restrictions will be in place indefinitely, officials said. The United States will consider lifting the restrictions on those countries affected only if they meet the new minimum standards, they said.

The president's announcement could have a dramatic impact on the legal challenge to the previous travel ban, which is under consideration by the Supreme Court after the administration appealed lower court rulings that said the ban was unconstitutional and a breach of Mr. Trump's authority.

Oral arguments in the case are scheduled for Oct. 10, but legal experts said that parts of the case could be moot because of the president's decision to end that travel ban. Other parts of the case, including restrictions on refugees coming into the United States, were not affected by Sunday's announcement.

A spokeswoman for the Justice Department said Sunday that the solicitor general would be submitting an update to the Supreme Court about the latest travel restrictions on Sunday evening. The spokeswoman said the administration would continue to defend the president's "lawful authority to issue his executive order."

But lawyers who filed challenges to the president's previous travel ban left open the possibility that they would also challenge the new restrictions.

"This is an apparent effort to paper over the original sin of the Muslim ban, especially when just last week Trump said he wanted a 'larger, tougher, more specific' ban," Mr. Romero said.

The original travel ban was met with angry denunciations from civil rights activists and others who said the president was violating the Constitution by specifically targeting Muslims. They also criticized Mr. Trump's administration for abruptly imposing the ban, causing confusion at airports as visitors were turned away by border agents who had not been briefed on the new policy.

Administration officials said on Friday that the new policy was the result of months of deliberation that included the State Department, the Department of Homeland Security, the White House and other agencies involved in security and the border.

NOTE: *Despite the public outcry against his racist immigration policies, Trump held fast to his determination to stop the flow of Muslims into the United States, and ultimately the increasingly Republican, conservative Supreme Court, upheld his ban in a 5-to-4 vote in late June 2018.*

OPINION: THE TRUMP APOLOGISTS
AND THE CRYING CHILDREN

By MICHELLE GOLDBERG, JUNE 18, 2018

A pparently there are some people close to Donald Trump with the capacity for shame. Not decency or courage, of course, but at least furtive recognition that they're complicit in something vile.

Over the last few days, stories of bureaucratic sadism have poured forth from America's southern border. The Associated Press described a Texas warehouse where "hundreds of children wait in a series of cages" with up to 20 people inside. *The New York Times* reported on a mother deported to Guatemala without her eight-year-old son. In *The Washington Post,* the president of the American Academy of Pediatrics described a shelter for toddlers where staffers aren't allowed to hug or hold the bereft children. ProPublica obtained a recording of small children wailing for their parents in a U.S. Customs and Border Protection facility, while a Border Patrol agent joked, "We've got an orchestra here."

Migrants wait for asylum hearings outside the port of entry on the U.S. border in Tijuana, Mexico, June 2018.

As outrage has built nationally, several people associated with the White House stepped forward to dissemble. Kirstjen Nielsen, head of the Department of Homeland Security, sent out a series of tweets denying that the administration's policy was in fact the administration's policy. "We do not have a policy of separating families at the border. Period," she lied.

Melania Trump's spokeswoman put out a slippery statement distancing the first lady from the president's actions and sowing confusion about their cause. "Mrs. Trump hates to see children separated from their families and hopes both sides of the aisle can finally come together to achieve successful immigration reform," the statement said, as if her husband were not responsible for the separations.

On *Meet the Press* on Sunday, Kellyanne Conway, counselor to the president, claimed that "nobody" in the administration likes the policy. "You saw the president on camera, that he wants this to end," she said.

It's hard to tell if these women are engaged in deliberate gaslighting or frantic reputation maintenance. Perhaps Nielsen is worried about her post–White House prospects now that she's best known for the systematic traumatization of children. Maybe Melania Trump realizes that being the trophy wife of a child-torturer is bad for her brand. (#BeBest!) Conway, whose husband has already staked out a position as a Trump critic, may think she has a road back into decent society when this Grand Guignol regime finally ends.

> *"It was a simple decision by the administration to have a zero-tolerance policy for illegal entry, period."*

But no one should be able to squirm out of admitting that the evil practice of family separation is Donald Trump's doing, abetted by everyone who abets him. Indeed, part of the madness of this moment is that while some Trump apologists—as well as Trump himself—deny their role in tearing families apart, others in the administration boldly own it. "It was a simple decision by the administration to have a zero-tolerance policy for illegal entry, period," Trump's senior policy adviser Stephen Miller told *The Times*.

Some of the president's defenders insist he's bound by a legal settlement mandating that children be held in the least restrictive setting possible. The only alternative to the current policy, they say, is what they call "catch and release," a dehumanizing term borrowed from fishing to suggest that migrant families are simply being let go.

Senator Ben Sasse, a Nebraska Republican, dispatched this argument in a Facebook post on Monday. "The administration's decision to separate families is a new, discretionary choice. Anyone saying that their hands are tied or that the only conceivable way to fix the problem of catch-and-release is to rip families apart is flat wrong," he wrote. Some in the administration, he added, "have decided that this cruel policy increases their legislative leverage."

The administration's justifications and denials are meant to obscure that fact. Consider Nielsen's suggestion, during a speech on Monday, that the administration is worried about child smuggling: "We do not have the luxury of pretending that all individuals coming to this country as a family unit are, in fact, a family."

The government has made this argument before, in one of the first family separation cases to go to court. Last November, a Congolese woman known in court filings as Ms. L and her then-six-year-old daughter arrived at a port of entry near San Diego, presented themselves to border agents and asked for asylum. Officers separated them—according to a lawsuit, Ms. L could hear her daughter in the next room, screaming—and the girl was sent to Chicago while her mother was held in California.

When the A.C.L.U. sued on Ms. L's behalf, officials claimed they'd taken the girl because Ms. L couldn't prove she was her parent. The judge in the case ordered a DNA test, which quickly demonstrated Ms. L's relationship to her daughter. (In March, they were finally reunited.)

"The truth is they've been doing this all along for deterrence purposes, as sometimes they boldly said in the press," Lee Gelernt, an A.C.L.U. lawyer who argued the case, told me. "But when confronted in a federal lawsuit, they tried to retroactively justify it by saying they couldn't figure out whether it was the mother." It's hard to know who's worse—the sociopaths like Miller who glory in the administration's cruelty, or those who are abashed enough to lie about the filthy thing they're part of, but not to do anything else.

NOTE: *The policy of separating children from their parents was reversed by a federal judge in late June 2018, but the nation's anguish over immigration continues at the time of this writing (see pages 226–229).*

GUNS

END THE GUN EPIDEMIC IN AMERICA

By THE EDITORIAL BOARD, DECEMBER 4, 2015

All decent people feel sorrow and righteous fury about the latest slaughter of innocents, in California. Law enforcement and intelligence agencies are searching for motivations, including the vital question of how the murderers might have been connected to international terrorism. That is right and proper.

But motives do not matter to the dead in California, nor did they in Colorado, Oregon, South Carolina, Virginia, Connecticut and far too many other places. The attention and anger of Americans should also be directed at the elected leaders whose job is to keep us safe but who place a higher premium on the money and political power of an industry dedicated to profiting from the unfettered spread of ever more powerful firearms.

It is a moral outrage and a national disgrace that civilians can legally purchase weapons designed specifically to kill people with brutal speed and efficiency. These are weapons of war, barely modified and deliberately marketed as tools of macho vigilantism and even insurrection. America's elected leaders offer prayers for gun victims and then, callously and without fear of consequence, reject the most basic restrictions on weapons of mass killing, as they did on Thursday.

No right is unlimited and immune from reasonable regulation.

They distract us with arguments about the word *terrorism*. Let's be clear: These spree killings are all, in their own ways, acts of terrorism.

Opponents of gun control are saying, as they do after every killing, that no law can unfailingly forestall a specific criminal. That is true. They are talking, many with sincerity, about the constitutional challenges to effective gun regulation. Those challenges exist. They point out that determined killers obtained weapons illegally in places like France, England and Norway that have strict gun laws. Yes, they did.

But at least those countries are trying. The United States is not. Worse, politicians abet would-be killers by creating gun markets for them, and voters allow those politicians to keep their jobs. It is past time to stop talking about halting the spread of firearms, and instead to reduce their number drastically—eliminating some large categories of weapons and ammunition.

It is not necessary to debate the peculiar wording of the Second Amendment. No right is unlimited and immune from reasonable regulation.

Certain kinds of weapons, like the slightly modified combat rifles used in California, and certain kinds of ammunition, must be outlawed for civilian ownership. It is possible to define those guns in a clear and effective way and, yes, it would require Americans who own those kinds of weapons to give them up for the good of their fellow citizens.

What better time than during a presidential election to show, at long last, that our nation has retained its sense of decency?

FOR PARKLAND STUDENTS, A SURREAL JOURNEY FROM "NORMAL" TO A WORLDWIDE MARCH

By PATRICIA MAZZEI, MARCH 24, 2018

Little has returned to normal for the students of Marjory Stoneman Douglas High School since Feb. 14, when a gunman killed 14 of their classmates and three staff members. They juggle homework with activism. They wince at loud noises. Sometimes, they sleep.

But to the huge crowds that greeted them in Washington on Saturday at a march to protest gun violence, the students were fearless celebrities.

"We're here for you, Douglas!" a girl shrieked as five teenage boys from Stoneman Douglas and their history teacher made their way to the main stage.

"Go Douglas!" said the teacher, Greg Pittman.

As the crowd broke into applause, the boys remained stoic. They held up their poster boards—"It is a school zone, not a war zone," read one—and looked straight ahead.

They were part of a group of 200 people from Stoneman Douglas, in Parkland, Fla., who were sponsored by Giffords, the gun control advocacy group, to come to the Washington march. An alumni group raised enough money to get more than 550 additional students to the rally, a spokeswoman for the group said. Others traveled to Washington on their own, some of them rooming with family and friends.

Despite their numbers, their steady presence in the news, their unmistakable influence on the national debate over guns, some of them were trying to be teenagers again. It hasn't been easy.

The five boys did not organize the event on Saturday, called the March for Our Lives. They did not lose a relative in the shooting. They were not injured.

But their coach, Aaron Feis, was killed. Their school was forever changed. And now, they were in the nation's capital, feeling hundreds of eyes on them as they walked down Constitution Avenue.

"There's a lot of emotion," said one, Adrian Kauffman, 16.

The five boys, all sophomores, refrained from endorsing a specific policy proposal or calling out politicians they dislike. They arrived to show strength in numbers, "so nothing like this happens again," said Adam Hostig, 15.

"Most teenagers talk about drama about girlfriends and boyfriends," said Zach Cooper, 16. "And we're talking about bomb threats and guns."

Parkland protestors were joined by thousands of student marchers in Washington, D.C., shown here, and thousands more around the country, for the March for Our Lives, March 24, 2018.

"Nonstop," Adam said.

A police helicopter hovered overhead. Adam's eyes darted up suspiciously.

"Even coming to an event like this, it's scary," Zach said.

None of them paid much attention to the politics of guns before the shooting, they admitted. "We got more informed," said Evan Kuperman, 16.

The march will make it "feel like the people who died did not die in vain," added Josh Funk, 16.

Amid their newfound activism, they have tried to return to lives that resemble those they had before their high school turned into a mass-murder scene.

"You get a sense of guilt trying to have fun," Josh said. "But at the same time, you just want to be with friends and family all the time. To never miss a moment."

In Washington this week, the Florida visitors sponsored by Giffords went to museums and shared late-night ice cream sundaes in a hotel ballroom with foosball tables and a Pac-Man machine. But they also roved the hallways of the Capitol, meeting with lawmakers and lobbying for action on gun violence. The House minority leader, Nancy Pelosi, dropped in on their hotel. Some of them met former Vice President Joe Biden.

"I've gotten about nine hours of sleep in four days," Aly Sheehy, an 18-year-old senior, said near midnight on Friday. "But being around other people that understand what I've gone through just recharges me."

"On Sunday, we'll all be exhausted," she added. "But then we'll go back. For something this important, I'll make the time."

"They definitely think we're going to go away," Jose Iglesias, a 17-year-old senior, said of politicians and skeptical adults. "We know what we're doing. We have tactics. They think we're just children."

The students knew that interest in their cause might fade outside their own schools. They knew that for the grown-ups, the march, which was organized in a little more than a month, might seem like the culmination of their efforts. "It's just the beginning," Jose said.

On Saturday morning, he awoke early. "In my sleep, I called 911," he said. "Really it was my alarm that kept going off."

"I have flashbacks of running into a classroom," said Sarah Pierre, 17, a senior.

> *"We know what we're doing. We have tactics. They think we're just children."*

Over breakfast, students made last-minute signs with Crayola markers. Natasha Martinez, a 17-year-old junior, got on FaceTime with her mother, who was attending the march back home in Parkland. Her mother worried that Natasha was underdressed for the Washington cold. "I'm wearing the thermal, a turtleneck, this hoodie I bought, and a coat," Natasha insisted.

A friend sitting next to her, Isabel Chequer, a 16-year-old junior, waved at Natasha's mother. "She has a special pass," Natasha said, pointing at Isabel's neck. "Injured club!" said Isabel, who was twice grazed during the shooting. She was one of 17 people hurt.

Isabel fears the shooting will make it impossible for her to watch action movies anymore, despite her interest in film. "I feel like I can't see those movies again, like *Black Panther* or *Annihilation*, which makes me really sad, because I love movies so much," she said. "It's taken a little bit from myself."

"I feel weird doing normal things," her schoolmate Aly said.

Throngs of marchers soon took to the streets downtown. Students from Stoneman Douglas and other schools delivered speeches, some choked with emotion as they described living with violent memories, survivor's guilt and the ever-present shadow of fear.

Samantha Fuentes, an 18-year-old senior who was shot in both legs during the shooting, went on stage to read a poem. Halfway through it, she appeared to get nervous and quickly ducked behind the podium. She stood back up as people rushed from backstage to help her. "I just threw up on international television, and it feels great," she said with a laugh, before reading the rest of her poem.

It ended: "Will you give up? Or is enough enough?"

When the speeches—along with performances by Ariana Grande, Miley Cyrus and others—were finished, and the crowds began to disperse, the Stoneman Douglas students became tourists again, albeit ones who had moved thousands.

Amanda Lee, a 17-year-old junior who had been in one of the classrooms where shots were fired, left the rally with other students, pausing to snap pictures of the cherry blossoms that had started to bloom along the street.

Amanda said she had expected more of an actual march than speeches and a concert. But the magnitude of what they had accomplished in less than two months, she said, hit when she saw images of protests across the country and around the world.

"It sinks in," she said. "And then you feel that you've done the impossible."

NOTE: *The murders in Parkland are just one example of the spreading epidemic of mass shootings by gunmen in American schools, workplaces, and public spaces. The attack was remarkable for the way it drove young people to engage in political protest, agitation, and activity in numbers not seen in the country for decades. But the implacable opposition of the gun lobby to any reform of firearm laws continues to block congressional action, and no real progress had been made as of this writing.*

LGBTQ RIGHTS

THE SUPREME COURT: HOMOSEXUAL RIGHTS; JUSTICES, 6 TO 3, LEGALIZE GAY SEXUAL CONDUCT IN SWEEPING REVERSAL OF COURT'S '86 RULING

By LINDA GREENHOUSE, JUNE 27, 2003

The Supreme Court issued a sweeping declaration of constitutional liberty for gay men and lesbians today, overruling a Texas sodomy law in the broadest possible terms and effectively apologizing for a contrary 1986 decision that the majority said "demeans the lives of homosexual persons." The vote was 6 to 3.

Gays are "entitled to respect for their private lives," Justice Anthony M. Kennedy said for the court. "The state cannot demean their existence or control their destiny by making their private sexual conduct a crime."

Justice Kennedy said further that "adults may choose to enter upon this relationship in the confines of their homes and their own private lives and still retain their dignity as free persons."

While the result had been widely anticipated since the court agreed in December to hear an appeal brought by two Houston men who were prosecuted for having sex in their home, few people on either side of the case expected a decision of such scope from a court that only 17 years ago, in *Bowers v. Hardwick,* had dismissed the same constitutional argument as "facetious." The court overturned that precedent today.

In a scathing dissent, Justice Antonin Scalia accused the court of having "taken sides in the culture war" and having "largely signed on to the so-called homosexual agenda." He said that the decision "effectively decrees the end of all morals legislation" and made same-sex marriage, which the majority opinion did not discuss, a logical if not inevitable next step. Chief Justice William H. Rehnquist and Justice Clarence Thomas signed Justice Scalia's dissent.

While some gay rights lawyers said that there were still abundant legal obstacles to establishing a right either to gay marriage or to military service by gay soldiers, there was no doubt that the decision had profound legal and political implications.

A conservative Supreme Court has now identified the gay rights cause as a basic civil rights issue.

Ruth Harlow, legal director of the Lambda Legal Defense and Education Fund and the lead counsel for the two men, John G. Lawrence and Tyron Garner, called the decision "historic and transformative." Suzanne Goldberg, a professor at Rutgers Law School who had represented the men in the Texas courts, said that the decision would affect "every kind of case" involving gay people, including employment, child custody and visitation, and adoption.

"It removes the reflexive assumption of gay people's inferiority," Professor Goldberg said. *"Bowers* took away the humanity of gay people, and this decision gives it back."

The vote to overturn *Bowers v. Hardwick* was 5 to 4, with Justice Kennedy joined by Justices John Paul Stevens, David H. Souter, Ruth Bader Ginsburg and Stephen G. Breyer.

"Bowers was not correct when it was decided, and it is not correct today," Justice Kennedy said. "Its continuance as precedent demeans the lives of homosexual persons."

Justice Sandra Day O'Connor, who was part of the 5-to-4 majority in *Bowers v. Hardwick*, did not join Justice Kennedy in overruling it. But she provided the sixth vote for overturning the Texas sodomy law

Darren Nimnicht (left); his partner, Tom Cicero (right); and members of the National Gay and Lesbian Task Force and the NYC Gay & Lesbian Anti-Violence Project celebrate the Supreme Court decision to strike down sodomy laws. Sheridan Square, New York City, June 26, 2003.

in a forcefully written separate opinion that attacked the law on equal protection grounds because it made "deviate sexual intercourse"—oral or anal sex—a crime only between same-sex couples and not for heterosexuals.

"A law branding one class of persons as criminal solely based on the state's moral disapproval of that class and the conduct association with that class runs contrary to the values of the Constitution and the Equal Protection Clause," Justice O'Connor said.

Texas was one of only four states—Kansas, Oklahoma and Missouri are the others—to apply a criminal sodomy law exclusively to same-sex partners. An additional nine states—Alabama, Florida, Idaho, Louisiana, Mississippi, North Carolina, South Carolina, Utah and Virginia—have criminal sodomy laws on their books that in theory, if not in practice, apply to opposite-sex couples as well. As a result of the majority's broad declaration today that the government cannot make this kind of private sexual choice a crime, all those laws are now invalid.

Twenty-five states had such laws at the time the court decided *Bowers v. Hardwick*. The Georgia sodomy law the court upheld in that case was overturned by a state court ruling in 1998. Some of the other state laws have been repealed and others invalidated by state courts.

In the Texas case, Mr. Lawrence and Mr. Garner were discovered by the Houston police while having sex in Mr. Lawrence's apartment. The police entered through an unlocked door after receiving a report from a neighbor of a "weapons disturbance" in the apartment. The neighbor was later convicted of filing a false report.

The men were held in jail overnight. They later pleaded no contest, preserving their right to appeal, and were each fined $200. The Texas state courts rejected their constitutional challenge to the law.

Asked today for the Bush administration's reaction to the ruling, Ari Fleischer, the White House press secretary, noted that the administration had not filed a brief in the case. "And now this is a state matter," he said. In fact, the decision today, *Lawrence v. Texas*, No. 02-102, took what had been a state-by-state matter and pronounced a binding national constitutional principle.

The delicacy of the moment for the White House was apparent. Groups representing the socially conservative side of the Republican Party reacted to the decision with alarm and fury. On the other hand, important Libertarian groups had supported the challenge to the Texas law. Justice Thomas, who is often in sympathy with Libertarian arguments, wrote a brief separate dissenting opinion today with a nod in that direction.

He said he would vote to repeal the law if he were a member of the Texas Legislature. "Punishing someone for expressing his sexual preference through noncommercial consensual conduct with another adult does not appear to be a worthy way to expend valuable law enforcement resources," Justice Thomas said, but added that he could not overturn the law as a judge because he did not see a constitutional basis for doing so.

Charles Francis, cochairman of the Republican Unity Coalition, a group of gay and heterosexual Republicans seeking to defuse the issue within the party, said today, "I hope the giant middle of our party can look at this decision not as a threat but as a breakthrough for human understanding." The group includes prominent Republicans like former president Gerald R. Ford, David Rockefeller and Alan K. Simpson, the former senator from Wyoming, who is its honorary chairman. No member of the Bush administration has joined the group, Mr. Francis said.

As the court concluded its term today, the absence of any sign of a retirement meant that the issue was not likely to surface in judicial politics anytime soon. There was a tense and ultimately humorous moment in the courtroom this morning when, after the announcements of decisions, Chief Justice Rehnquist brought the term to a close with his customary words of thanks to the court staff.

"The court today notes the retirement," he then said drily as those in the audience caught their breath, "of librarian Shelley Dowling." A collective sigh and audible chuckles followed as the marshal, Pamela Talkin, banged her gavel and the nine justices left the bench, all of them evidently planning to return when the court meets on Sept. 8 for arguments in the campaign finance case.

Earlier, as Justice Kennedy was reading excerpts from his decision, the mood in the courtroom went from enormous tension and then—on the part of the numerous gay and lesbian lawyers seated in the bar section—to visible relief. By the time he referred to the dignity and respect to which he said gays were entitled, several were weeping, silently but openly.

The majority opinion was notable in many respects: its critical dissection of a recent precedent; its use of a decision by the European Court of Human Rights, supporting gay rights, to show that the court under *Bowers v. Hardwick* was out of step with other Western countries; and its many citations to the court's privacy precedents, including the abortion rights cases.

The citations to *Roe v. Wade* and *Planned Parenthood v. Casey* appeared particularly to inflame Justice Scalia. If *Bowers v. Hardwick* merited overruling, he said, so too did *Roe v. Wade*. He also said that laws against bigamy, adultery, prostitution, bestiality and obscenity were now susceptible to challenges. The majority opinion did not precisely respond to that prediction, noting instead that the right claimed by Mr. Lawrence and Mr. Garner did not involve prostitution, public behavior, coercion or minors.

The fundamental debate on the court was over the meaning of the Constitution's due process guarantee, which Justice Kennedy said was sufficiently expansive so that "persons in every generation can invoke its principles in their own search for greater freedom."

SENATE REPEALS BAN AGAINST OPENLY GAY MILITARY PERSONNEL

By CARL HULSE, DECEMBER 18, 2010

The Senate on Saturday struck down the ban on gay men and lesbians serving openly in the military, bringing to a close a 17-year struggle over a policy that forced thousands of Americans from the ranks and caused others to keep secret their sexual orientation.

By a vote of 65 to 31, with 8 Republicans joining Democrats, the Senate approved and sent to President Obama a repeal of the Clinton-era law, known as "don't ask, don't tell," a policy critics said amounted to government-sanctioned discrimination that treated gay and lesbian troops as second-class citizens.

Mr. Obama hailed the action, which fulfills his pledge to reverse the ban. "As commander in chief, I am also absolutely convinced that making this change will only underscore the professionalism of our troops as the best-led and best-trained fighting force the world has ever known," Mr. Obama said in a statement after the Senate, on a 63 to 33 vote, beat back Republican efforts to block a final vote on the repeal bill.

The vote marked a historic moment that some equated with the end of racial segregation in the military.

It followed a comprehensive review by the Pentagon that found a low risk to military effectiveness despite greater concerns among some combat units and the Marine Corps. The review also found that Pentagon officials supported Congressional repeal as a better alternative than a court-ordered end. Supporters of the repeal said it was long past time to end what they saw as an ill-advised practice that cost valuable personnel and forced troops to lie to serve their country.

"We righted a wrong," said Senator Joseph I. Lieberman, the independent from Connecticut who led the effort to end the ban. "Today we've done justice."

Before voting on the repeal, the Senate blocked a bill that would have created a path to citizenship for certain illegal immigrants who came to the United States at a young age, completed two years of college or military service and met other requirements including passing a criminal background check.

The 55 to 41 vote in favor of the citizenship bill was 5 votes short of the number needed to clear the way for final passage of what is known as the Dream Act. The outcome effectively kills it for this year, and its fate beyond that is uncertain since Republicans who will assume control of the House in January oppose the measure and are unlikely to bring it to a vote.

The Senate then moved on to the military legislation, engaging in an emotional back and forth over the merits of the measure as advocates for repeal watched from galleries crowded with people interested in the fate of both the military and immigration measures. "I don't care who you love," Senator Ron Wyden, Democrat of Oregon, said as the debate opened. "If you love this country enough to risk your life for it, you shouldn't have to hide who you are."

Mr. Wyden showed up for the Senate vote despite saying earlier that he would be unable to do so because he would be undergoing final tests before his scheduled surgery for prostate cancer on Monday.

The vote came in the final days of the 111th Congress as Democrats sought to force through a final few priorities before they turn over control of the House of Representatives to the Republicans in January and see their clout in the Senate diminished.

It represented a significant victory for the White House, Congressional advocates of lifting the ban and activists who have pushed for years to end the Pentagon policy created in 1993 under the Clinton administration as a compromise effort to end the practice of banning gay men and lesbians entirely from military service. Saying it represented an emotional moment for members of the gay community nationwide, activists who supported repeal of "don't ask, don't tell" exchanged hugs outside the Senate chamber after the vote.

> *Repeal will "finally end a policy which has burdened our armed services."*

"Today's vote means gay and lesbian service members posted all around the world can stand taller knowing that 'don't ask, don't tell' will soon be coming to an end," said Aubrey Sarvis, an army veteran and executive director for Servicemembers Legal Defense Network.

The executive director of the Log Cabin Republicans, a gay group that challenged the policy in federal court, thanked Republicans senators for participating in a historic vote. The director, R. Clarke Cooper, who is a member of the army reserve, said repeal will "finally end a policy which has burdened our armed services for far too long, depriving our nation of the talent, training and hard-won battle experience of thousands of patriotic Americans."

A federal judge had ruled the policy unconstitutional in response to the Log Cabin suit, but that decision had been stayed pending appeal.

Aaron Belkin, director of the Palm Center in California, a research institute at the University of California in Santa Barbara that studies issues surrounding gays and lesbians in the military, said that the vote "ushers in a new era in which the largest employer in the United States treats gays and lesbians like human beings."

In a statement on the group's website, Mr. Belkin said: "It has long been clear that there is no evidence that lifting the ban will undermine the military, and no reason to fear the transition to inclusive policy. Research shows that moving quickly is one of the keys to a successful transition. If the president and military leadership quickly certify the end of 'don't ask, don't tell,' they will ensure an orderly transition with minimal disruption."

Organizations that opposed repeal of the ban assailed the Republican senators who defied their party majority.

The Center for Military Readiness, a group that specializes in social issues in the military and has opposed repeal, said the new legislation "will impose heavy, unnecessary burdens on the backs of military men and women." It said the Senate majority voted with "needless haste" by not waiting for hearings into a recent Department of Defense study of the "don't ask, don't tell" policy. Elaine Donnelly, president of the group, said that the Pentagon's survey indicated that 32 percent of Marines and 21.4 percent of Army combat troops would leave the military sooner than planned if "don't ask, don't tell" were repealed.

Kris Mineau, president of the Massachusetts Family Institute, said senators like Scott Brown, a Republican from Massachusetts, "broke trust with the people" by voting on repeal before the federal budget was resolved and "have put the troops at risk during wartime."

During the debate, Senator John McCain, Republican of Arizona and his party's presidential candidate in 2008, led the opposition to the repeal and said the vote was a sad day in history. "I hope that when we pass this legislation that we will understand that we are doing great damage," Mr. McCain said. "And we could possibly and probably, as the commandant of the Marine Corps said, and as I have been told by literally thousands of members of the military, harm the battle effectiveness vital to the survival of our young men and women in the military."

He and other opponents of lifting the ban said the change could harm the unit cohesion that is essential to effective military operations, particularly in combat, and deter some Americans from enlisting or pursuing a career in the military. They noted that despite support for repealing the ban from Defense Secretary Robert M. Gates and Adm. Mike Mullen, chairman of the Joint Chiefs of Staff, other military commanders have warned that changing the practice would prove disruptive.

"This isn't broke," Senator James M. Inhofe, Republican of Oklahoma, said about the policy. "It is working very well."

Other Republicans said that while the policy might need to be changed at some point, Congress should not do so when American troops are fighting overseas.

"In the middle of a military conflict, is not the time to do it," said Senator Saxby Chambliss, Republican of Georgia.

Only a week ago, the effort to repeal the "don't ask, don't tell" policy seemed to be dead and in danger of fading for at least two years with Republicans about to take control of the House. The provision eliminating the ban was initially included in a broader Pentagon policy bill, and Republican backers of repeal had refused to join in cutting off a filibuster against the underlying bill because of objections over the ability to debate the measure.

In a last-ditch effort, Mr. Lieberman and Senator Susan Collins of Maine, a key Republican opponent of the ban, encouraged Democratic Congressional leaders to instead pursue a vote on simply repealing it. The House passed the measure earlier in the week.

The repeal will not take effect for at least 60 days while some other procedural steps are taken. In addition, the bill requires the defense secretary to determine that policies are in place to carry out the repeal "consistent with military standards for readiness, effectiveness, unit cohesion, and recruiting and retention."

Because of the uncertainty, Mr. Sarvis appealed to Mr. Gates to suspend any investigations into military personnel or discharge proceedings under the policy to be overturned in the coming months.

Mr. Lieberman said the ban undermined the integrity of the military by forcing troops to lie. He said 14,000 members of the armed forces had been forced to leave the ranks under the policy.

"What a waste," he said.

NOTE: *It took longer for the Pentagon to lift its discriminatory ban on transgender Americans serving in uniform (announced June 2016) once Donald Trump tried and failed to reverse the move—although transgender people who have tried to enlist continue to experience delays and obstacles in the acceptance of their applications.*

G.O.P. HOPEFULS
DENOUNCE MARRIAGE-EQUALITY RULING

By JEREMY W. PETERS, JUNE 26, 2015

A cross the country, among people of all ages and religions, the acceptance of same-sex marriage has grown with stunning speed. But not in the leadership of the Republican Party.

There is a striking unanimity among the candidates who are running for the party's presidential nomination in 2016: Not one supports allowing gay and lesbian couples to marry. And after the Supreme Court ruled on Friday that the Constitution guarantees a right to marriage for all couples, regardless of their sexual orientation, the degree of difference among the candidates was largely a matter of how aggressively they would continue to resist.

Many pledged to fight on, using language that was both biblical and bellicose, framing the debate over marriage rights as a choice between surrender and retreat, between the divine and the profane. Others vowed to keep the debate alive in a more measured and indirect way, by advocating for the rights of Christians and others who worry the ruling could force them to violate their religious beliefs.

But either way, the clash over same-sex marriage seems likely to smolder well into the 2016 primary season, despite the hopes of many less hard-line Republicans that

Stacey Allen and Sean Allen celebrate their wedding in Cincinnati, the day the Supreme Court ruled in favor of same-sex marriage, June 26, 2015.

a Supreme Court decision would allow the party finally to move past one of the most divisive aspects of the culture wars.

Mike Huckabee, the former governor of Arkansas, said that while he was certain that "some cowardly politicians will wave the white flag," he was determined not to bow to a decision he saw as illegitimate. "I will not acquiesce to an imperial court," he said Friday.

Gov. Scott Walker of Wisconsin said he would push for a constitutional amendment that would allow states to continue prohibiting same-sex marriage. "No one wants to live in a country where the government coerces people to act in opposition to their conscience," he said. "We will continue to fight for the freedoms of all Americans."

Others tried to shift the debate to the safer terrain of religious tolerance.

Jeb Bush, the former governor of Florida, was brief and more tempered. In a statement that ran just 82 words, he said that while he believed the court had erred, he urged respect for all couples, "including those making lifetime commitments." He then said it was crucial "to protect religious freedom and the right of conscience and also not discriminate."

Senator Marco Rubio of Florida also criticized the decision but added, "We live in a republic and must abide by the law." The next president, he said, must focus on protecting "the First Amendment rights of religious institutions and millions of Americans whose faiths hold a traditional view of marriage." (Mr. Bush and Mr. Rubio, unlike Mr. Walker, have said they do not support a constitutional amendment to reverse the court's ruling.)

The varied reactions reflected the priorities of the Republicans seeking the presidency. Some, like Mr. Bush, are eyeing a general election in which hostility to same-sex marriage could present difficulties in winning competitive states. Others, like Mr. Huckabee, Mr. Walker and Gov. Bobby Jindal of Louisiana—who said Friday that marriage was ordained by God "and no earthly court can alter that"—are focused on winning over social conservatives in early nominating states like Iowa and South Carolina. A few, like Mr. Rubio, seem equally mindful of both.

Overheated language on gay rights may rally a socially conservative base whose confidence deflated as one court after another, then finally the highest court, declared that banning same-sex marriage was unconstitutional. But it also ignores a reality on the ground in the states where the presidential contest will take shape next year.

Same-sex marriage has been legal in both Iowa and New Hampshire, which hold the first two nominating contests, since 2009. Yet resistance movements, to the extent that there ever were serious ones, have had no success. And many conservatives appear to have moved on.

"It's not an issue anymore because we've evolved," said John Reagan, a Republican state senator in New Hampshire.

"We saw nothing happened," he added. "Our lives didn't get worse. And we began to see people we knew in that situation and it made it more acceptable."

With public opinion moving so unambiguously away from support for restricting marriage to heterosexual couples, the Republican National Committee has acknowledged that the party stands to continue to lose favor with voters, especially younger people who are overwhelmingly in favor of same-sex marriage. Its 2012 postelection assessment warned that if Republicans appear intolerant on gay rights, "voters will continue to tune us out."

Yet acceptance of same-sex marriage inside the party continues to be outside the norm. The official party platform states that marriage between a man and a woman "must be upheld as the national standard, a goal to stand for, encourage and promote."

There are no members of the senior Republican leadership in Congress who publicly support same-sex marriage. There is not a single openly gay or lesbian Republican lawmaker in the House or the Senate. Just one Republican governor, Charlie Baker of Massachusetts, signed a brief urging the Supreme Court to overturn laws banning same-sex marriage.

"I would have expected there to be at least one candidate who's in favor," said Mary Cheney, a daughter of former vice president Dick Cheney, who is a lesbian and has pushed Republicans to be more inclusive on gay rights. "At this point, I'm not really sure it's an act of bravery to support marriage equality. The horse has already left the barn."

Absent a surprise change of heart by one of the Republicans, the Democrats will look to use same-sex marriage to their advantage. Democrats see the issue as one that allows them to hold up their nominee as empathetic and compassionate, while portraying the Republican as retrogressive and out of touch. Hillary Rodham Clinton hinted at the party's line of attack on Friday when she said, "As love and joy flood our streets today, it is hard to imagine how anyone could deny the full protection of our laws to any of our fellow Americans—but there are those who would."

Many Republican strategists privately say they believe 2016 will be the last year their nominee can get away with not supporting gay marriage rights. The key question, they say, is whether by 2020 the damage to the party will already be done.

"It may be a fatal problem for them as the generation turns," said Charles Francis, who served as chairman of the Republican Unity Coalition, an alliance of gay and straight Republicans that worked with the administration of President George W. Bush. But after Mr. Bush decided in 2004 to support a constitutional amendment banning same-sex marriage, Mr. Francis resigned.

"Republicans have had a few opportunities, a few exit ramps," Mr. Francis said, "and they've steadfastly failed."

WOMEN'S RIGHTS

ANOTHER AMENDMENT RATIFIED

AUGUST 19, 1920

There is still a bare possibility that the Tennessee legislature may reconsider its ratification of the suffrage amendment. It is probable, too, that the legality of its action—the Constitution of the state distinctly forbidding ratification in the way followed—will be challenged in the courts. But there is no doubt that its vote of yesterday will be almost universally taken as ending the long struggle for woman suffrage in this country. In the main, the result will be accepted in good American fashion. The minority will submit to what it does not like and has fought, and will try to make the best of it. What has now come about has long been felt, even by opponents of woman suffrage, to be certain, to be achieved in time. Already 16 of the 48 states had granted the full rights of voters

Governor Edwin P. Morrow of Kentucky, surrounded by a group of women wearing "Votes for Women" sashes, signs the 19th Amendment, January 6, 1920. Kentucky was the 24th state to ratify.

to women. In addition, 24 states had by law given to women presidential suffrage. A movement gathering such momentum was bound to succeed in time.

It cannot be said that the Tennessee Legislature decided the question on its merits. The members were not swayed by suffrage arguments pure and simple. The contest became a competition between parties. Tremendous pressure from the outside was brought to bear upon the luckless legislature, and it was pressure of a partisan sort. President Wilson and Governor Cox made appeals in the name of the Democratic Party; Senator Harding and Chairman Hays sent messages to the Republican members of the legislature. It certainly is a tribute to the shrewdness of the women managing the campaign that they were able thus to induce the two parties to bid against each other for the honor—or partisan advantage—of having settled the suffrage question. And there was the adroit allurement dangled before Tennessee to become "the 36th state "and win all the glory of passing the suffrage amendment. Strictly speaking, of course, Tennessee's decision was no more vital than the ratification by the first states, Wisconsin and Michigan, which acted more than a year ago. But the clever lady politicians made use of this and every other weapon upon which they could lay their hands and showed that they, at least, are not innocent of the wiles of politics. Veteran male political manipulators will take off their hats to them, in both admiration and envy.

There will naturally be an outburst of jubilation by suffragists over their hard-won victory. But that mood ought not to be lasting or dominant. It is a great experiment upon which the nation is entering. Its difficulties and dangers should be uppermost in the thoughts of serious-minded citizens of either sex. In winning over the country to woman suffrage a concrete state of facts has probably had more influence than abstract arguments about the inalienable rights of the individual, or about the nature of a democracy. We had a large and growing body of citizens who were dissatisfied with their political conditions. And in a democratic government it is expedient to eliminate such dissatisfaction, if it can be done without violating any vital principle. That, it would seem, has been the chief moving cause in bringing America round to the idea of woman suffrage. But discontent does not necessarily become intelligent by the act of being enfranchised, and the new political privileges now bestowed upon women carry with them the gravest responsibilities. It is no longer a question of sex, but of country and the common weal. And Americans, whatever their doubts and fears in all this matter have been, will hope that the new voters may blend easily in the already great electorate. For a time, our elections will be made more dubious and cumbrous, as they certainly will be more costly. But we do not doubt that the cheerful and indomitable American spirit will apply itself to making our institutions "work" as Gladstone phrased it, even under novel and arduous and what may almost seem revolutionary conditions.

SENATORS BAR WEAKENING OF EQUAL RIGHTS PROPOSAL

By EILEEN SHANAHAN, MARCH 22, 1972

The Senate, by unexpectedly large margins, defeated today attempts to dilute a constitutional amendment that would bar all legal forms of discrimination based on sex.

The key vote came on a proposal by Senator Sam J. Ervin Jr., Democrat of North Carolina, to permit continued exemption of women from the draft. It was defeated, 73 to 18. Other proposals failed by similar margins.

Ratification by three-quarters, or 38, of the states will be the next step if, as expected, the Senate passes the amendment tomorrow in a version identical with the one passed by the House last year.

The president's signature is not required on a constitutional amendment. President Nixon, however, was believed to have contributed to the lopsidedness of today's votes. Breaking an official silence of years on the subject, he endorsed the amendment over the weekend in a letter to Senator Hugh Scott of Pennsylvania, the Republican floor leader.

The debate over exempting women from the draft was the most serious and prolonged of the day.

Despite the margins by which he was defeated today on all three of his proposed changes in the amendment, Senator Ervin served notice that he would propose more changes tomorrow.

It was not clear whether he hoped to win approval of one of his changes or possibly to delay a final vote until there were enough absentees to block passage of the amendment, which requires a two-thirds margin.

The two other changes that were voted on today would have barred women from assignment to combat units of the armed forces and would have kept on the statute books all laws "which extend protections or exemptions to women."

The latter proposal is regarded by feminist groups as a virtual nullification of the equal rights amendment. It was rejected, 75 to 11. The vote on the combat proposal was 71 to 18.

The debate over exempting women from the draft was the most serious and prolonged of the day. No significant challenge was made to Senator Ervin's argument that, once the amendment as in effect, women would have to be drafted if men were. Senator

Birch Bayh of Indiana, the chairman of the constitutional amendments subcommittee who is the chief sponsor of the amendment, conceded that the draft issue "is one of the most difficult with which to deal."

But he argued that, at present levels of draft calls, fewer than 10 percent of the men in the draft pool are inducted and that the proportion of women would probably be even smaller. That would be the case, he said, because "sex-neutral" physical standards for draftees might exclude more women than men.

Women in Combat

Out of the present relatively small group of draftees, only 15 percent are assigned to combat, Senator Bayh argued. Woman draftees could be sent into combat if they met all the qualifications, he continued, but he said he felt their proportion would be even smaller.

Senator Bayh also argued that many women were serving in dangerous areas now.

"Ask a nurse in a hospital in Danang whether she is in combat zone," he challenged.

If the time comes when larger numbers of draftees are needed than at present, he said, "I think most American women would say, 'Count me in if my country needs me.'"

Senator Bayh also argued that being drafted was "not all a minus." He pointed to educational and other benefits that veterans get and said the amendment would help more women become eligible for these benefits by putting an end to higher requirements for women volunteers for the armed forces than for men. For example, women are usually required to be high school graduates, and men are not.

Senator Ervin spoke of the hardships, dangers and horrors that women would face if they were drafted and sent into combat. He pleaded with the Senate not to pass the amendment without his provision "for the sake of gratifying the demands of a few business and professional women who think God made a serious mistake when He created two sexes instead of one."

PENTAGON IS SET TO LIFT COMBAT BAN FOR WOMEN

By ELISABETH BUMILLER AND THOM SHANKER, JANUARY 23, 2013

Defense Secretary Leon E. Panetta is lifting the military's official ban on women in combat, which will open up hundreds of thousands of additional front-line jobs to them, senior defense officials said Wednesday.

The groundbreaking decision overturns a 1994 Pentagon rule that restricts women from artillery, armor, infantry and other such combat roles, even though in reality women have frequently found themselves in combat in Iraq and Afghanistan; according to the Pentagon, hundreds of thousands of women have deployed in those conflicts. As of last year, more than 800 women had been wounded in the two wars and more than 130 had died.

Defense officials offered few details about Mr. Panetta's decision but described it as the beginning of a process to allow the branches of the military to put the change into effect. Defense officials said Mr. Panetta had made the decision on the recommendation of the Joint Chiefs of Staff.

U.S. Marine Captain Emily Naslund, who commanded the Female Engagement Teams (F.E.T.s) throughout Helmand Province, aiming her weapon after shots were fired on the patrol of the FETs attached to the 2nd Battalion, 6th Marine Regiment, in Southern Marja, Afghanistan, September 15, 2010.

Women have long chafed under the combat restrictions and have increasingly pressured the Pentagon to catch up with the reality on the battlefield. The move comes as Mr. Panetta is about to step down from his post and would leave him with a major legacy after only 18 months in the job.

The decision clearly fits into the broad and ambitious liberal agenda, especially around matters of equal opportunity, that President Obama laid out this week in his inaugural address. But while it had to have been approved by him, and does not require action by Congress, it appeared Wednesday that it was in large part driven by the military itself. Some midlevel White House staff members were caught by surprise by the decision, indicating that it had not gone through an extensive review there.

> *"The time has come to rescind the direct combat exclusion rule for women."*

Mr. Panetta's decision came after he received a Jan. 9 letter from Gen. Martin E. Dempsey, the chairman of the Joint Chiefs of Staff, who stated in strong terms that the armed service chiefs all agreed that "the time has come to rescind the direct combat exclusion rule for women and to eliminate all unnecessary gender-based barriers to service."

A military official said the change would be implemented "as quickly as possible," although the Pentagon is allowing three years, until January 2016, for final decisions from the services.

Each branch of the military will have to come up with an implementation plan in the next several months, the official said. If a branch of the military decides that a specific job should not be opened to a woman, representatives of that branch will have to ask the defense secretary for an exception.

"To implement these initiatives successfully and without sacrificing our war-fighting capability or the trust of the American people, we will need time to get it right," General Dempsey wrote.

It will be carried out during what the administration describes as the end of the American combat role in Afghanistan, the nation's longest war.

A copy of General Dempsey's letter was provided by a Pentagon official under the condition of anonymity. The letter noted that this action was meant to ensure that women as well as men "are given the opportunity to succeed."

It was unclear why the joint chiefs acted now after examining the issue for years, although in recent months there has been building pressure from high-profile lawsuits.

In November 2012 the American Civil Liberties Union filed a federal lawsuit challenging the ban on behalf of four service women and the Service Women's Action Network, a group that works for equality in the military. The A.C.L.U. said that one of the plaintiffs, Maj. Mary Jennings Hegar, an Air National Guard helicopter pilot, was shot down, returned fire and was wounded while on the ground in Afghanistan, but could not seek combat leadership positions because the Defense Department did not officially acknowledge her experience as combat.

In the military, serving in combat positions like the infantry remains crucial to career advancement. Women have long said that by not recognizing their real service, the military has unfairly held them back.

The A.C.L.U. embraced Mr. Panetta's decision with cautious optimism. Ariela Migdal, an attorney with the A.C.L.U.'s Women's Rights Project, said in a statement that the organization was "thrilled" by the decision, but added that she hoped it would be implemented "fairly and quickly."

By law Mr. Panetta is able to lift the ban as a regulatory decision, although he must give Congress a 30-day notice of his intent. Congress does not need to approve the decision before it goes into effect. If Congress disagrees with the action, members would have to pass new legislation prohibiting the change, which appeared highly unlikely.

Although in the past some Republican members of the House have balked at allowing women in combat, on Wednesday there appeared to be bipartisan endorsement for the decision, which was first reported by the Associated Press and CNN in midafternoon.

"It reflects the reality of 21st-century military operations," Senator Carl Levin, Democrat of Michigan and chairman of the Senate Armed Services Committee, said in a statement.

Senator Patty Murray, Democrat of Washington and the chairwoman of the Senate Veterans Affairs Committee, called it a "historic step for recognizing the role women have, and will continue to play, in the defense of our nation."

Senator Kelly Ayotte, a New Hampshire Republican and a member of the Armed Services Committee, said in a statement that she was pleased by the decision and said that it "reflects the increasing role that female service members play in securing our country."

Representative Loretta Sanchez, the California Democrat who has long pressed to have women's role in combat recognized, said that she was pleased that Mr. Panetta was removing what she called "the archaic combat exclusion policy."

Senator Kirsten E. Gillibrand, a New York Democrat who has pushed for lifting the ban, called it "a proud day for our country" and an important step in recognizing "the brave women who are already fighting and dying."

But the leadership of a conservative Christian group, the Family Research Council, immediately weighed in with its opposition, sending out a statement from Jerry Boykin, a retired three-star general with a long career in Special Operations Forces.

General Boykin said that "the people making this decision are doing so as part of another social experiment." He especially criticized the concept of placing women into special forces units where "living conditions are primal in many situations with no privacy for personal hygiene or normal functions." It remains unclear if women will be permitted to fight in special forces and other commando units.

Public opinion polls show that Americans generally agree with lifting the ban. A nationwide Quinnipiac University poll conducted a year ago found that three-quarters of voters surveyed favored allowing military women to serve in units that engaged in close combat, if the women wanted to.

Policy experts who have pushed the military to lift the ban said that it was striking that much of the impetus appeared to come from joint chiefs, indicating that the top military leadership saw that the time had come to open up to women.

"It's significant that the change came from the uniformed side, rather than being forced on the uniformed side by the civilian leadership," said Greg Jacob, the policy director of the Service Women's Action Network.

Under current rules, a number of military positions are closed to women—and to open them, the services have to change the rules. Under Mr. Panetta's new initiative, the situation is the opposite: Those combat positions would be open to women, and they could only be closed through specific action.

Capt. Emily Naslund, a marine officer who saw ground combat in Afghanistan in 2010, said Wednesday that she embraced the decision. "This is awesome," she said.

NATIONAL GUIDELINES SET BY 7-TO-2 VOTE

By WARREN WEAVER JR., JANUARY 23, 1973

The Supreme Court overruled today all state laws that prohibit or restrict a woman's right to obtain an abortion during her first three months of pregnancy. The vote was 7 to 2.

In a historic resolution of fiercely controversial issue, the court drafted a new set of national guidelines that will result in broadly liberalized antiabortion laws in 46 states but will not abolish restrictions altogether.

Establishing an unusually detailed timetable for the relative legal rights of pregnant women and the states that would control their acts, the majority specified the following:

For the first three months of pregnancy the decision to have an abortion lies with the woman and her doctor, and the state's interest in her welfare is not "compelling" enough to warrant any interference.

For the next six months of pregnancy a state may "regulate the abortion procedure in ways that are reasonably related to maternal health," such as licensing and regulating the persons and facilities involved.

For the last 10 weeks of pregnancy, the period during which the fetus is judged to be capable of surviving if born, any state may prohibit abortions, if it wishes, except where they may be necessary to preserve the life or health of the mother.

Today's action will not affect existing laws in New York, Alaska, Hawaii and Washington, where abortions are now legally available in the early months of pregnancy. But it will require rewriting of statutes in every other state.

The basic Texas case decided by the court today will invalidate strict antiabortion laws in 31 states; a second decision involving Georgia will require considerable rewriting of more liberal statutes in 15 others.

Justice Harry A. Blackmun wrote the majority opinion in which Chief Justice Warren E. Burger and Justices William O. Douglas, William J. Brennan Jr., Potter Stewart, Thurgood Marshall and Lewis F. Powell Jr. joined.

Dissenting were Justices Byron R. White and William H. Rehnquist.

Justice White, calling the decision "an exercise of raw judicial power," wrote that "the court apparently values the convenience of the pregnant mother more than the continued existence and development of the life or potential life which she carries."

The court's decision was at odds with the expressed views of President Nixon. Last May, in a letter to Cardinal Cooke, he opposed "liberalized abortion policies" and spoke

A group of anti-abortion demonstrators pose beside a bank of funeral flowers delivered to the assembly at the New York State Capitol in Albany, May 5, 1972.

out for "the right to life of literally hundreds of thousands of unborn children."

But three of the four Justices Mr. Nixon has appointed to the Supreme Court voted with the majority, with only Mr. Rehnquist dissenting.

The majority rejected the idea that a fetus becomes "person" upon conception and is thus entitled to the due process and equal protection guarantees of the Constitution. This view was pressed by opponents of liberalized abortion, including the Roman Catholic Church.

Justice Blackmun concluded that "the word 'person,' as used in the 14th Amendment, does not include the unborn," although states may acquire, "at some point in time" of pregnancy, an interest in the "potential human life" that the fetus represents, to permit regulation.

It is that interest, the court said, that permits states to prohibit abortion during the last 10 weeks of pregnancy, after the fetus has developed the capacity to survive.

In both cases decided today, the plaintiffs had based their protest on an assertion that state laws limiting the availability of abortion had circumscribed rights and freedoms guaranteed them by the Constitution: due process of law, equal protection of the laws, freedom of action and a particular privacy involving a personal and family matter. In its decision on the challenge to the Georgia abortion law, the high, court majority struck down several requirements that a woman seeking to terminate her pregnancy in that state would have to meet.

Decision for Doctors

Among them were a flat prohibition on abortions for out-of-state residents and requirements that hospitals be accredited by a private agency, that applicants be screened by a
hospital committee and that two independent doctors certify the potential danger to the
applicant's health.

The Georgia law permitted abortions when a doctor found in "his best clinical
judgment" that continued pregnancy would threaten the woman's life or health, that the
fetus would be likely to be born defective or that the pregnancy was the result of rape.

The same Supreme Court majority, with Justice Blackmun writing the opinion again,
emphasized that this medical judgment should cover all relevant factors—"physical, emotional, psychological familial and the woman's age."

In some of the 15 states with laws similar to Georgia's, doctors have tended to take relatively narrow view of what constituted a woman's health in deciding whether an abortion
was legally justified.

The Texas law that the court invalidated entirely was typical of the criminal statutes
passed in the last half of the 19th century prohibiting all abortions except those to save
a mother's life. The Georgia law, approved in 1972 and altered by the court today, was
patterned after the model penal code of the American Law Institute.

In the Texas case, Justice Blackmun wrote that the constitutional right of privacy,
developed by the court in a long series of decisions, was "broad enough to encompass a
woman's decision whether or not to terminate her pregnancy.

He rejected, however, the argument of women's rights groups that this right was
absolute "and she is entitled to terminate her pregnancy at whatever time, in whatever way
and for whatever reason she alone chooses."

"With this we do not agree," the justice declared.

"A state may properly assert important interests in safeguarding health in main-
taining medical standards and in protecting potential life," Mr. Blackmun observed. "At
some point in pregnancy, these respective interests become sufficiently compelling to
sustain regulation of the factors that govern the abortion decision."

The majority concluded that this "compelling" state interest arose at the end of the
first three months of pregnancy because of the "now established medical fact" that until
then, fewer women die from abortions than from normal childbirth.

During this three-month period, the court said, a doctor can recommend an abortion
to his patient "without regulation by the state" and the resulting operations can be conducted "free of interference by the state."

The "compelling state interest" in the fetus does not arise, however, until the time of "viability," Justice Blackmun wrote, when it has "the capability of meaningful life outside the mother's womb." This occurs about 10 weeks before delivery.

In reading an abbreviated version of his two opinions to the court this morning, Justice Blackmun noted that most state legislatures were in session now and would thus be able to rewrite their states' abortion laws to conform to the court's decision.

Both of today's cases wound up with anonymous parties winning victories over state officials. In the Texas case, "Jane Roe," an unmarried pregnant woman who was allowed to bring the case without further identity, was the only plaintiff after the Supreme Court disqualified a doctor and a childless couple who said that the wife's health would be endangered by pregnancy.

In the Georgia case, the surviving plaintiff was "Mary Doe," who, when she brought the action, was a 22-year-old married woman 11 weeks pregnant with her fourth child.

SENATE REJECTS MEASURE TO BAN ABORTION AFTER 20 WEEKS OF PREGNANCY

By SHERYL GAY STOLBERG, JANUARY 29, 2018

The Senate rejected a bill on Monday to ban most abortions after 20 weeks of pregnancy, a largely symbolic vote aimed at forcing vulnerable Democrats to take a stand that could hurt their prospects for reelection in states won by President Trump.

By a vote of 51 to 46, the measure fell well short of the 60-vote threshold required for the Senate to break a Democratic filibuster. The outcome was not a surprise, and the vote fell mostly along party lines.

The Senate voted on a similar measure in 2015. At that time three Democrats—Senators Bob Casey of Pennsylvania, Joe Donnelly of Indiana and Joe Manchin of West Virginia—voted in favor of it. All three are up for reelection this year in states that Mr. Trump carried, and all of them voted in favor of the measure again on Monday. Two Republicans—Senators Susan Collins of Maine and Lisa Murkowski of Alaska—voted against it.

The bill, which has the strong backing of the Trump administration, is identical to one that passed the House in October and similar to legislation that has been adopted in 20 states. It would make nearly all abortions after 20 weeks illegal; anyone who performed the procedure could face a potential prison term of five years, fines or both, though exceptions could be made when the life of the mother was at risk, or in cases of rape or incest.

> *"You're on the right side of history. You're where America will be. It's just a matter of time before we get there."*

"To those who believe in this issue, we will be back for another day," Senator Lindsey Graham, Republican of South Carolina and the chief sponsor of the bill, said in advance of the vote. To his colleagues who supported the measure, he said: "You're on the right side of history. You're where America will be. It's just a matter of time before we get there."

The Senate floor debate offered supporters and opponents of abortion rights an opportunity to speak expansively about *Roe v. Wade*, the landmark 1973 Supreme Court decision legalizing abortion—and they took it.

"Forty-five years after *Roe v. Wade,* abortions are safer today than getting your tonsils out," declared Senator Elizabeth Warren, Democrat of Massachusetts. "A lot of women are alive today because of *Roe.*" She called the ban "part of a broad and sustained assault by Republican politicians on women's rights to make decisions about their own bodies."

But Senator Thom Tillis, Republican of North Carolina, said it was time for the Senate to act.

"The life of the unborn is a precious life, and we as members of the United States Senate and the U.S. Congress are tasked with making sure we protect all lives in America," Mr. Tillis said, adding, "This is just a very important, precious, helpless part of the population."

The 20-week ban, named the Pain-Capable Unborn Child Protection Act, is central to the strategy of the antiabortion movement, which is newly emboldened under Mr. Trump. The president's election in 2016 ushered in a wave of antiabortion victories in states like Ohio, where lawmakers adopted a 20-week abortion ban in December of that year.

"Forty-five years after Roe v. Wade, abortions are safer today than getting your tonsils out."

Abortion foes say that if enough states pass such bans, Congress will be more likely to follow. They note that it took their movement 15 years to persuade Congress to outlaw the procedure that opponents call partial-birth abortion. They see the 20-week abortion ban on a similar trajectory.

"We are building momentum for eventual federal legislation," said Mallory Quigley, a spokeswoman for Susan B. Anthony List, a group that works to elect antiabortion candidates. She added, "We want to get vulnerable Democrats who are up for reelection this year on the record once again."

Abortion rights advocates, meanwhile, say the opponents are badly misreading the political climate. In the era of the #MeToo movement, they say, Republicans will face a backlash for supporting a bill that prevents women from taking control of their own health care decisions.

"I think they fail to recognize the context of the moment and what they're contending with," said Ilyse Hogue, the president of NARAL Pro-Choice America, an abortion rights advocacy group. "We are seeing a rising up of women, unprecedented in my lifetime, and women who recognize that the role of abortion rights is so crucially important for women's health."

Jennifer Duffy, who tracks Senate races for the nonpartisan Cook Political Report, said vulnerable Republicans—she cited Dean Heller in Nevada—might have as much to lose in voting for the measure as vulnerable Democrats had in voting against it.

"Since when's the last time we saw a Democrat pay for what is essentially a pro-choice vote?" Ms. Duffy asked. "It's been a long time."

Polling by the Pew Research Center shows that backing for abortion is as high as it has been in two decades. As of 2017, 57 percent of Americans said abortion should be legal in all or most cases, while 40 percent said it should be illegal in all or most cases. But the issue animates social conservatives; 71 percent of conservative Republicans said abortion should be illegal in all or most cases, the Pew poll found.

The United States is one of just seven countries—including China and North Korea—that permit elective abortion after 20 weeks, a fact that backers of the failed measure brought up repeatedly on Monday.

"The United States keeps the company of countries like China and North Korea. They deny unborn children the most basic of protections," Senator Joni Ernst, Republican of Iowa, said on the Senate floor Monday. "This, folks, is not who we are as a nation."

Supporters of the ban cite medical studies suggesting that fetuses can feel pain at 20 weeks. But the science surrounding fetal pain is complex. In a July 2013 memo, the American Congress of Obstetricians and Gynecologists wrote that "the fetus does not even have the physiological capacity to perceive pain until at least 24 weeks of gestation."

DEMOCRATS MAKE HILLARY CLINTON A HISTORIC NOMINEE

By PATRICK HEALY AND JONATHAN MARTIN, JULY 26, 2016

The Democratic convention formally nominated Hillary Clinton for president on Tuesday, making history by choosing a woman to be the first standard-bearer of a major political party, a breakthrough underscored by a deeply personal speech by Bill Clinton calling her "the best darn change-maker I have ever known."

At 6:39 p.m., the hall erupted in cheers and joyful tears as South Dakota cast the decisive 15 votes to put Mrs. Clinton over the threshold of 2,382 delegates required to clinch the nomination.

A sea of delegates waved multicolored signs with Mrs. Clinton's "H" campaign logo, while others fell into hugs and several women jumped up and down with elation.

Vince Insalaco, the chairman of the Democratic Party of Arkansas, where the Clintons built their public profile over two decades, said the choice of the first female presidential nominee was a historic moment. "I'm so proud to be a Democrat tonight," Mr. Insalaco said, "and so proud that we can call this woman one of our own."

Hillary Clinton at the Democratic National Convention in Philadelphia, July 28, 2016; she is the first female presidential nominee of a major party.

Mrs. Clinton's primary rival, Senator Bernie Sanders of Vermont, played a symbolic role in hopes of unifying the party behind her. After Vermont arranged to go last in the roll call, Mr. Sanders joined its delegation to roars of "Bernie, Bernie" and called on the party to rally behind Mrs. Clinton.

But it was the appearance of Mr. Clinton, shortly after 10 p.m., that stirred the crowd most, as he set out to share a more personal side of the sometimes-reserved former secretary of state.

Unspooling memories of their 45 years together, Mr. Clinton used warm and detailed anecdotes to argue that the couple's political enemies had spent decades creating a "cartoon" of his wife that he was now determined to puncture. Mrs. Clinton is among the most unpopular presidential nominees in modern history, and the former president appealed to the audience to see through the political attacks on her.

"One is real," Mr. Clinton said of the divergent portrayals of his wife, "the other is made up." He recalled the affection of Mrs. Clinton's old friends, her empathy for those in need and the praise she had won from Republicans as a senator and as secretary of state.

"You nominated the real one," Mr. Clinton said to a long burst of applause. Seeming to realize that he had been speaking for 38 minutes, he added in classically loquacious Bill Clinton fashion, "We have to get back on schedule."

Mr. Clinton's testimony was so personal that he even appeared to obliquely invoke problems in the couple's marriage. "She'll never quit when the going gets tough," he said. "She'll never quit on you."

Earlier in the evening, several dozen Sanders delegates paraded off in a coordinated demonstration against Mrs. Clinton's nomination. Some of them said beforehand that they were attending their first Democratic convention and felt no party loyalty or compulsion to fall in line behind Mrs. Clinton, whom they described as insufficiently progressive on new banking regulations, a $15 minimum wage, a ban on fracking and other issues.

"I'm just not there yet in terms of supporting Hillary, because her words are only her words, and I don't fully trust that she'll act on our agenda," said Ingrid Olson, 38, a delegate from Iowa.

The final delegate count was 2,842 for Mrs. Clinton, 1,865 for Mr. Sanders and 56 "no votes."

The scenes in the hall, and the huge street protests that continued through Tuesday night, were more fractious than those at the party's gathering in Denver in 2008. Back then, Mrs. Clinton, defeated for the nomination, moved to stop the roll call and nominate Barack Obama. Her gesture, aimed at soothing the bitterness of the primary fight, helped her supporters make peace with Mr. Obama and embrace his barrier-breaking candidacy.

Mr. Sanders and Mrs. Clinton had their own brutal competition this year, and their policy differences were greater than those between Mrs. Clinton and Mr. Obama—part of why many of Mr. Sanders's supporters are reluctant to get behind her.

Mr. Clinton's task was clear: to humanize his wife but also energize Democrats by flattering those in the hall and villainizing Donald J. Trump, the Republican nominee.

"She never made fun of people with disabilities," Mr. Clinton said, referring to Mr. Trump's mocking of a disabled reporter last year. "She tried to empower them based on their abilities."

Yet as Mr. Clinton recounted his wife's well-chronicled professional accomplishments, he also tried to paint a portrait of a mother who is not as well known. Recounting the day they moved their daughter, Chelsea, into her freshman dorm at Stanford University, Mr. Clinton recounted how Mrs. Clinton kept looking for "one more drawer to put that liner paper in," reluctant to say goodbye to her only child.

The speech was extraordinary in its intimacy and in Mr. Clinton's willingness to use their much-scrutinized marriage as a testament to her character. He began by recalling how he first met his future wife in 1971 at Yale Law School—he so nervous, she full of confidence—and spent almost 15 minutes describing courting her and proposing marriage three times before she said yes. At one point, trying to play a mind game, Mr. Clinton told her that she should move to Illinois or New York and run for office rather than marry him and have other young Democrats eclipse her.

"They mean well, and they speak well, but none of them are as good as you are," Mr. Clinton told her about their political generation. "She said: 'Are you out of your mind? Nobody would ever vote for me.'"

The convention underwent a notable shift as the evening went on: Mr. Sanders was barely mentioned, a deliberate decision by the Clinton campaign officials who organized the lineup of speakers. Advisers said that, with Mrs. Clinton now the nominee, they wanted to focus on her character and political record, and on taking the fight to Mr. Trump, rather than continuing to nod to Mr. Sanders and his primary fight.

The crowd was subdued for much of the evening, but in the most searing part, nine African American mothers whose children were killed by gun violence or in encounters with the police took the stage to chants of "Black lives matter." The women, who have been campaigning for Mrs. Clinton for months, described how she had sat with them privately to hear their stories and worked with them to promote gun-control measures.

One of the mothers, Lucia McBath—whose 17-year-old son, Jordan Davis, was fatally shot after playing loud music in his car in 2012—said Mrs. Clinton "isn't afraid to say black lives matter," a phrase Mr. Trump and other Republicans have derided by saying that all lives matter. But Ms. McBath also said Mrs. Clinton knew that Americans needed to come together to keep children safe.

"We're going to keep building a future where police officers and communities of color work together in mutual respect," she said.

Convention organizers, apparently seeking a balance with the mothers, invited the Pittsburgh police chief, Cameron McLay, to speak earlier in the evening. But as Chief McLay spoke of fallen officers and called for a criminal justice overhaul, many in the hall carried on their conversations.

Democrats used Tuesday to appeal to some of their traditional constituencies, but they also highlighted Mrs. Clinton's faith. A video was played in which she asked for a prayer and then joined a prayer circle, and an image on one of the screens for part of the evening showed a group of people laying hands on her.

It was a striking, and surely not accidental, contrast to the Republican convention last week, in which appeals to the faithful were somewhat muted and Mr. Trump scarcely mentioned faith in his acceptance speech. The hosannas for Mrs. Clinton were in marked contrast to the steady stream of boos that rained down at the mention of her name on Monday. Still, the party's divisions remained in plain sight.

Many states announced that they had split their delegates by having representatives of Mrs. Clinton and Mr. Sanders speak separately. And it was clear that some Sanders supporters were not ready to give up. Tim Vandeveer, the chairman of the Hawaii Democratic Party, announced that Mr. Sanders had won a majority of the state's delegates, calling him "the leader of our revolution, which shall continue."

Later, as the convention wound down after 11 p.m., black and white images of every previous president flashed on the screen, which finally seemed to crack as a smiling Mrs. Clinton suddenly appeared by video connection.

The hall broke out in applause and shouts of excitement as Mrs. Clinton acknowledged breaking the glass ceiling.

"If there are any little girls out there who stayed up late to watch," she said, "let me just say, I may become the first woman president, but one of you is next."

NOTE: *It was not until 2008 that the Republican Party put a woman on its presidential ticket— Sarah Palin—and until 2016 that any party nominated a woman for president, Hillary Clinton. While there were many reasons for Clinton's defeat as a candidate, the persistent sexism in American life was an important one.*

HARVEY WEINSTEIN PAID OFF SEXUAL HARASSMENT ACCUSERS FOR DECADES

By JODI KANTOR AND MEGAN TWOHEY, OCTOBER 5, 2017

Two decades ago, the Hollywood producer Harvey Weinstein invited Ashley Judd to the Peninsula Beverly Hills hotel for what the young actress expected to be a business breakfast meeting. Instead, he had her sent up to his room, where he appeared in a bathrobe and asked if he could give her a massage or she could watch him shower, she recalled in an interview.

"How do I get out of the room as fast as possible without alienating Harvey Weinstein?" Ms. Judd said she remembers thinking.

In 2014, Mr. Weinstein invited Emily Nestor, who had worked just one day as a temporary employee, to the same hotel and made another offer: If she accepted his sexual advances, he would boost her career, according to accounts she provided to colleagues who sent them to Weinstein Company executives. The following year, once again at the Peninsula, a female assistant said Mr. Weinstein badgered her into giving him a massage while he was naked, leaving her "crying and very distraught," wrote a colleague, Lauren O'Connor, in a searing memo asserting sexual harassment and other misconduct by their boss.

"There is a toxic environment for women at this company," Ms. O'Connor said in the letter, addressed to several executives at the company run by Mr. Weinstein.

An investigation by *The New York Times* found previously undisclosed allegations against Mr. Weinstein stretching over nearly three decades, documented through interviews with current and former employees and film industry workers, as well as legal records, emails and internal documents from the businesses he has run, Miramax and the Weinstein Company.

During that time, after being confronted with allegations including sexual harassment and unwanted physical contact, Mr. Weinstein has reached at least eight settlements with women, according to two company officials speaking on the condition of anonymity. Among the recipients, *The Times* found, were a young assistant in New York in 1990, an actress in 1997, an assistant in London in 1998, an Italian model in 2015 and Ms. O'Connor shortly after, according to records and those familiar with the agreements.

In a statement to *The Times* on Thursday afternoon, Mr. Weinstein said: "I appreciate the way I've behaved with colleagues in the past has caused a lot of pain, and I sincerely apologize for it. Though I'm trying to do better, I know I have a long way to go."

He added that he was working with therapists and planning to take a leave of absence to "deal with this issue head on."

Lisa Bloom, a lawyer advising Mr. Weinstein, said in a statement that "he denies many of the accusations as patently false." In comments to *The Times* earlier this week, Mr. Weinstein said that many claims in Ms. O'Connor's memo were "off base" and that they had parted on good terms.

He and his representatives declined to comment on any of the settlements, including providing information about who paid them. But Mr. Weinstein said that in addressing employee concerns about workplace issues, "my motto is to keep the peace."

Ms. Bloom, who has been advising Mr. Weinstein over the last year on gender and power dynamics, called him "an old dinosaur learning new ways." She said she had "explained to him that due to the power difference between a major studio head like him and most others in the industry, whatever his motives, some of his words and behaviors can be perceived as inappropriate, even intimidating."

Though Ms. O'Connor had been writing only about a two-year period, her memo echoed other women's complaints. Mr. Weinstein required her to have casting discussions with aspiring actresses after they had private appointments in his hotel room, she said, her description matching those of other former employees. She suspected that she and other female Weinstein employees, she wrote, were being used to facilitate liaisons with "vulnerable women who hope he will get them work."

The allegations piled up even as Mr. Weinstein helped define popular culture. He has collected six best-picture Oscars and turned out a number of touchstones, from the films *Sex, Lies, and Videotape, Pulp Fiction* and *Good Will Hunting* to the television show *Project Runway*. In public, he presents himself as a liberal lion, a champion of women and a winner of not just artistic but humanitarian awards.

In 2015, the year Ms. O'Connor wrote her memo, his company distributed *The Hunting Ground*, a documentary about campus sexual assault. A longtime Democratic donor, he hosted a fund-raiser for Hillary Clinton in his Manhattan home last year. He employed Malia Obama, the oldest daughter of former president Barack Obama, as an intern this year, and recently helped endow a faculty chair at Rutgers University in Gloria Steinem's name. During the Sundance Film Festival in January, when Park City, Utah, held its version of nationwide women's marches, Mr. Weinstein joined the parade.

"From the outside, it seemed golden—the Oscars, the success, the remarkable cultural impact," said Mark Gill, former president of Miramax Los Angeles when the company was owned by Disney. "But behind the scenes, it was a mess, and this was the biggest mess of all," he added, referring to Mr. Weinstein's treatment of women.

Dozens of Mr. Weinstein's former and current employees, from assistants to top executives, said they knew of inappropriate conduct while they worked for him. Only a handful said they ever confronted him.

Mr. Weinstein enforced a code of silence; employees of the Weinstein Company have contracts saying they will not criticize it or its leaders in a way that could harm its "business reputation" or "any employee's personal reputation," a recent document shows. And most of the women accepting payouts agreed to confidentiality clauses prohibiting them from speaking about the deals or the events that led to them.

Charles Harder, a lawyer representing Mr. Weinstein, said it was not unusual to enter into settlements to avoid lengthy and costly litigation. He added, "It's not evidence of anything."

At Fox News, where the conservative icons Roger E. Ailes and Bill O'Reilly were accused of harassment, women have received payouts well into the millions of dollars. But most of the women involved in the Weinstein agreements collected between roughly $80,000 and $150,000, according to people familiar with the negotiations.

In the wake of Ms. O'Connor's 2015 memo, some Weinstein Company board members and executives, including Mr. Weinstein's brother and longtime partner, Bob, 62, were alarmed about the allegations, according to several people who spoke on the condition of anonymity. In the end, though, board members were assured there was no need to investigate. After reaching a settlement with Mr. Weinstein, Ms. O'Connor withdrew her complaint and thanked him for the career opportunity he had given her.

"The parties made peace very quickly," Ms. Bloom said.

Through her lawyer, Nicole Page, Ms. O'Connor declined to be interviewed. In the memo, she explained how unnerved she was by what she witnessed or encountered while a literary scout and production executive at the company. "I am just starting out in my career, and have been and remain fearful about speaking up," Ms. O'Connor wrote. "But remaining silent is causing me great distress."

In speaking out about her hotel episode, Ms. Judd said in a recent interview, "Women have been talking about Harvey amongst ourselves for a long time, and it's simply beyond time to have the conversation publicly."

A Common Narrative

Ms. Nestor, a law and business school student, accepted Mr. Weinstein's breakfast invitation at the Peninsula because she did not want to miss an opportunity, she later told colleagues. After she arrived, he offered to help her career while boasting about a series

Harvey Weinstein is escorted into Manhattan Criminal Court on Centre Street, New York, for his arraignment on charges of rape and sexual assault, May 25, 2018.

of famous actresses he claimed to have slept with, according to accounts that colleagues compiled after hearing her story and then sent on to company executives.

"She said he was very persistent and focused though she kept saying no for over an hour," one internal document said. Ms. Nestor, who declined to comment for this article, refused his bargain, the records noted. "She was disappointed that he met with her and did not seem to be interested in her résumé or skill set."

The young woman chose not to report the episode to human resources personnel, but the allegations came to management's attention through other employees.

Across the years and continents, accounts of Mr. Weinstein's conduct share a common narrative: Women reported to a hotel for what they thought were work reasons, only to discover that Mr. Weinstein, who has been married for most of three decades, sometimes seemed to have different interests. His home base was New York, but his rolling headquarters were luxury hotels: the Peninsula Beverly Hills and the Savoy in London, the Hôtel du Cap-Eden-Roc near the Cannes Film Festival in France and the Stein Eriksen Lodge near the Sundance Film Festival.

Working for Mr. Weinstein could mean getting him out of bed in the morning and doing "turndown duty" late at night, preparing him for sleep. Like the colleague cited in Ms. O'Connor's memo, some junior employees required to perform those tasks said they were disturbing.

In interviews, eight women described varying behavior by Mr. Weinstein: appearing nearly or fully naked in front of them, requiring them to be present while he bathed or repeatedly asking for a massage or initiating one himself.

The women, typically in their early or middle 20s and hoping to get a toehold in the film industry, said he could switch course quickly—meetings and clipboards one moment, intimate comments the next. One woman advised a peer to wear a parka when summoned for duty as a layer of protection against unwelcome advances.

Laura Madden, a former employee who said Mr. Weinstein prodded her for massages at hotels in Dublin and London beginning in 1991, said he had a way of making anyone who objected feel like an outlier. "It was so manipulative," she said in an interview. "You constantly question yourself—am I the one who is the problem?"

NOTE: *Harvey Weinstein was arrested in May 2018 and indicted on first- and third-degree rape charges. Although many women went public with accusations against him, because of the statute of limitations, as of this writing criminal charges are confined to those filed by three women. Currently Mr. Weinstein continues to deny all allegations of nonconsensual sex, and has pled not guilty.*

The accounts of the women who said he threatened, intimidated, abused, and raped them spawned what is popularly known as the #MeToo movement and started to force Hollywood and other industries to confront decades of unfair and abusive treatment of women. Dozens of prominent men were suddenly called to account for behavior that had previously gone unpunished, losing their jobs and sometimes facing criminal charges. It was the biggest moment in decades in women's battles for equal rights and legal protections, creating a political momentum that energized women's groups and women candidates in the 2018 midterm elections. At this writing, the long-term results are still very much in doubt.

GLOBAL WARMING

HOW G.O.P. LEADERS CAME TO VIEW CLIMATE CHANGE AS FAKE SCIENCE

By CORAL DAVENPORT AND ERIC LIPTON, JUNE 3, 2017

The campaign ad appeared during the presidential contest of 2008. Rapid-fire images of belching smokestacks and melting ice sheets were followed by a soothing narrator who praised a candidate who had stood up to President George W. Bush and "sounded the alarm on global warming."

It was not made for a Democrat, but for Senator John McCain, who had just secured the Republican nomination.

It is difficult to reconcile the Republican Party of 2008 with the party of 2017, whose leader, President Trump, has called global warming a hoax, reversed environmental policies that Mr. McCain advocated on his run for the White House, and this past week announced that he would take the nation out of the Paris climate accord, which was to bind the globe in an effort to halt the planet's warming.

> *"The entire climate change debate has now been caught up in the broader polarization of American politics."*

The Republican Party's fast journey from debating how to combat human-caused climate change to arguing that it does not exist is a story of big political money, Democratic hubris in the Obama years and a partisan chasm that grew over nine years like a crack in the Antarctic shelf, favoring extreme positions and uncompromising rhetoric over cooperation and conciliation.

"Most Republicans still do not regard climate change as a hoax," said Whit Ayres, a Republican strategist who worked for Senator Marco Rubio's presidential campaign. "But the entire climate change debate has now been caught up in the broader polarization of American politics."

"In some ways," he added, "it's become yet another of the long list of litmus test issues that determine whether or not you're a good Republican."

Since Mr. McCain ran for president on climate credentials that were stronger than his opponent Barack Obama's, the scientific evidence linking greenhouse gases from fossil fuels to the dangerous warming of the planet has grown stronger. Scientists have for the first time drawn concrete links between the planet's warming atmosphere and changes that affect Americans' daily lives and pocketbooks, from tidal flooding in Miami to prolonged water shortages in the Southwest to decreasing snow cover at ski resorts.

That scientific consensus was enough to pull virtually all of the major nations along. Conservative-leaning governments in Britain, France, Germany and Japan all signed on to successive climate change agreements.

Constituents were genuinely threatened by policies that would raise the cost of burning fossil fuels.

Yet when Mr. Trump pulled the United States from the Paris accord, the Senate majority leader, the speaker of the House and every member of the elected Republican leadership were united in their praise.

Those divisions did not happen by themselves. Republican lawmakers were moved along by a campaign carefully crafted by fossil fuel industry players, most notably Charles D. and David H. Koch, the Kansas-based billionaires who run a chain of refineries (which can process 600,000 barrels of crude oil per day) as well as a subsidiary that owns or operates 4,000 miles of pipelines that move crude oil.

Government rules intended to slow climate change are "making people's lives worse rather than better," Charles Koch explained in a rare interview last year with *Fortune*, arguing that despite the costs, these efforts would make "very little difference in the future on what the temperature or the weather will be."

Republican leadership has also been dominated by lawmakers whose constituents were genuinely threatened by policies that would raise the cost of burning fossil fuels, especially coal. Senator Mitch McConnell of Kentucky, always sensitive to the coal fields in his state, rose through the ranks to become majority leader. Senator John Barrasso of Wyoming also climbed into leadership, then the chairmanship of the Committee on Environment and Public Works, as a champion of his coal state.

Mr. Trump has staffed his White House and cabinet with officials who have denied, or at least questioned, the existence of global warming. And he has adopted the Koch language, almost to the word. On Thursday, as Mr. Trump announced the United States' withdrawal, he at once claimed that the Paris accord would cost the nation millions of jobs and that it would do next to nothing for the climate.

Beyond the White House, Representative Lamar Smith of Texas, chairman of the House Science Committee, held a hearing this spring aimed at debunking climate science, calling the global scientific consensus "exaggerations, personal agendas and questionable predictions."

A small core of Republican lawmakers—most of whom are from swing districts and are at risk of losing their seats next year—are taking modest steps like introducing a nonbinding resolution in the House in March urging Congress to accept the risks presented by climate change.

But in Republican political circles, speaking out on the issue, let alone pushing climate policy, is politically dangerous. So for the most part, these moderate Republicans are biding their time, until it once again becomes safe for Republicans to talk more forcefully about climate change. The question is how long that will take.

"With 40 percent of Florida's population at risk from sea-level rise, my state is on the front lines of climate change," said Representative Carlos Curbelo, Republican of Florida. "South Florida residents are already beginning to feel the effects of climate change in their daily lives."

"The Turning Point"

It was called the *No Climate Tax* pledge, drafted by a new group called Americans for Prosperity that was funded by the Koch brothers. Its single sentence read: "I will oppose any legislation relating to climate change that includes a net increase in government revenue." Representative Jim Jordan, Republican of Ohio, was the first member of Congress to sign it in July 2008.

The effort picked up steam the next year after the House of Representatives passed what is known as cap-and-trade legislation, a concept invented by conservative Reagan-era economists.

The idea was to create a statutory limit, or cap, on the overall amount of a certain type of pollution that could be emitted. Businesses could then buy and sell permits to pollute, choosing whether to invest more in pollution permits or in cleaner technology that would then save them money and allow them to sell their allotted permits. The administration of the first President George Bush successfully deployed the first national cap-and-trade system in 1990 to lower emissions of the pollutants that cause acid rain. Mr. McCain pushed a cap-and-trade proposal to fight climate change.

"I thought we could get it done," recalled Henry A. Waxman, a retired House Democrat who led the cap-and-trade push in 2009. "We just had two candidates from the Republican and Democratic parties who had run for president and agreed that climate change was a real threat."

Conservative activists saw the legislative effort as an opportunity to transform the climate debate. With the help of a small army of oil-industry-funded academics like Wei-Hock Soon of Harvard-Smithsonian and think tanks like the Competitive Enterprise Institute, they had been working to discredit academics and government climate change scientists. The lawyer and conservative activist Chris Horner, whose legal clients have included the coal industry, gathered documents through the Freedom of Information Act to try to embarrass and further undermine the climate change research. Myron Ebell, a senior fellow with the Competitive Enterprise Institute, worked behind the scenes to make sure Republican offices in Congress knew about Mr. Horner's work—although at the time, many viewed Mr. Ebell skeptically, as an extremist pushing out-of-touch views.

> *They had been working to discredit academics and government climate change scientists.*

In 2009, hackers broke into a climate research program at the University of East Anglia in England, then released the emails that conservatives said raised doubts about the validity of the research. In one email, a scientist talked of using a statistical "trick" in a chart illustrating a recent sharp warming trend. The research was ultimately validated, but damage was done.

As Congress moved toward actually passing climate change legislation, a fringe issue had become a part of the political mainstream.

"That was the turning point," Mr. Horner said.

The House passed the cap-and-trade bill by seven votes, but it went nowhere in the Senate—Mr. Obama's first major legislative defeat.

Unshackled by the Supreme Court's Citizens United decision and other related rulings, which ended corporate campaign finance restrictions, Koch Industries and Americans for Prosperity started an all-fronts campaign with television advertising, social media and cross-country events aimed at electing lawmakers who would ensure that the fossil fuel industry would not have to worry about new pollution regulations.

Their first target: unseating Democratic lawmakers such as Representatives Rick Boucher and Tom Perriello of Virginia, who had voted for the House cap-and-trade bill, and replacing them with Republicans who were seen as more in step with struggling Appalachia, and who pledged never to push climate change measures.

But Americans for Prosperity also wanted to send a message to Republicans. Until 2010, some Republicans ran ads in House and Senate races showing their support for green energy.

"After that, it disappeared from Republican ads," said Tim Phillips, the president of Americans for Prosperity. "Part of that was the polling, and part of it was the visceral example of what happened to their colleagues who had done that."

What happened was clear. Republicans who asserted support for climate change legislation or the seriousness of the climate threat saw their money dry up or, worse, a primary challenger arise. "It told Republicans that we were serious," Mr. Phillips said, "that we would spend some serious money against them."

By the time Election Day 2010 arrived, 165 congressional members and candidates had signed Americans for Prosperity's No Climate Tax pledge. Most were victorious.

"The midterm election was a clear rejection of policies like the cap-and-trade energy taxes that threaten our still-fragile economy," said James Valvo, then Americans for Prosperity's government affairs director, in a statement issued the day after the November 2010 election. Eighty-three of the 92 new members of Congress had signed the pledge.

Even for congressional veterans, that message was not missed. Representative Fred Upton, a Michigan Republican who once called climate change "a serious problem" and cosponsored a bill to promote energy-efficient light bulbs, tacked right after the 2010 elections as he battled to be chairman of the powerful House Energy and Commerce Committee against Joe Barton, a Texan who mocked human-caused climate change.

Mr. Upton deleted references to climate change from his website. "If you look, the last year was the warmest year on record, the warmest decade on record. I accept that," he offered that fall. "I do not say that it's man-made."

Mr. Upton, who has received more than $2 million in campaign donations from oil and gas companies and electric utilities over the course of his career, won the chairmanship and has coasted comfortably to reelection since.

Two years later, conservative "super PACs" took aim at Senator Richard G. Lugar of Indiana, a senior Republican who publicly voiced climate concerns, backed the creation of a Midwestern cap-and-trade program and drove a Prius. After six Senate terms, Mr. Lugar lost his primary to a Tea Party challenger, Richard E. Mourdock. Although Mr. Lugar says other reasons contributed, he and his opponents say his public views on climate change played a crucial role.

"In my own campaign, there were people who felt strongly enough about my views on climate change to use it to help defeat me, and other Republicans are very sensitive to that possibility," Mr. Lugar said in an interview. "So even if they privately believe we ought to do something about it, they're reticent, especially with the Republican president taking the views he is now taking."

Obama Feeds the Movement

After winning reelection in 2012, Mr. Obama understood his second-term agenda would have to rely on executive authority, not legislation that would go nowhere in the Republican-majority Congress. And climate change was the great unfinished business of his first term.

To finish it, he would deploy a rarely used provision in the Clean Air Act of 1970, which gave the Environmental Protection Agency the authority to issue regulations on carbon dioxide.

"If Congress won't act soon to protect future generations, I will," he declared in his 2013 State of the Union address.

The result was the Clean Power Plan, which would significantly cut planet-warming emissions by forcing the closing of hundreds of heavy-polluting coal-fired power plants.

The end run around Congress had consequences of its own. To Republican (and some Democratic) critics, the Clean Power Plan exemplified everything they opposed about Mr. Obama: He seemed to them imperious, heavy-handed, pleasing to the elites on the East and West Coasts and in the capitals of Europe, but callous to the blue-collar workers of coal and oil country.

"It fed into this notion of executive overreach," said Heather Zichal, who advised Mr. Obama on climate policy. "I don't think there was a good enough job on managing the narrative."

Republicans who had supported the climate change agenda began to defect and have since stayed away.

"On the issue of climate change, I think it's happening," Mr. McCain said in a CNN podcast interview last April. But, he said, "The president decided, at least in the last couple years if not more, to rule by edict."

Mr. Obama's political opponents saw the climate rules as a ripe opportunity. "When the president went the regulatory route, it gave our side more confidence," Mr. Phillips said. "It hardened and broadened Republican opposition to this agenda."

Starting in early 2014, the opponents of the rule—including powerful lawyers and lobbyists representing many of America's largest manufacturing and industrial interests—regularly gathered in a large conference room at the national headquarters of the U.S. Chamber of Commerce, overlooking the White House. They drafted a long-game legal strategy to undermine Mr. Obama's climate regulations in a coordinated campaign that brought together 28 state attorneys general and major corporations to form an argument that they expected to eventually take to the Supreme Court.

They presented it not as an environmental fight but an economic one, against a government that was trying to vastly and illegally expand its authority.

"This is the most significant wholesale regulation of energy that the United States has ever seen, by any agency," Roger R. Martella Jr., a former E.P.A. lawyer who then represented energy companies, said at a gathering of industry advocates, making an assertion that has not been tested.

Attorneys General Step In

Republican attorneys general gathered at the Greenbrier resort in West Virginia in August 2015 for their annual summer retreat, with some special guests: four executives from Murray Energy, one of the nation's largest coal mining companies. Murray was struggling to avoid bankruptcy—a fate that had befallen several other coal mining companies already, given the slump in demand for their product and the rise of natural gas, solar and wind energy.

The coal industry came to discuss a new part of the campaign to reverse the country's course on climate change. Litigation was going to be needed, the industry executives and the Republican attorneys general agreed, to block the Obama administration's climate agenda—at least until a new president could be elected.

West Virginia's attorney general, Patrick Morrisey, led the session, The Dangerous Consequences of the Clean Power Plan & Other E.P.A. Rules, which included, according to the agenda, Scott Pruitt, then the attorney general of Oklahoma; Ken Paxton, Texas' attorney general; and Geoffrey Barnes, a corporate lawyer for Murray, which had donated $250,000 to the Republican attorneys general political group.

That same day, Mr. Morrissey would step outside the hotel to announce that he and other attorneys general would sue in federal court to try to stop the Clean Power Plan, which he called "the most far-reaching energy regulation in this nation's history, drawn up by radical bureaucrats."

Mr. Pruitt quickly became a national point person for industry-backed groups and a magnet for millions of dollars of campaign contributions, as the fossil fuel lobby looked for a fresh face with conservative credentials and ties to the evangelical community.

"Pruitt was instrumental—he and A.G. Morrisey," said Thomas Pyle, a former lobbyist for Koch Industries, an adviser to Mr. Trump's transition team and the president of a pro–fossil fuel Washington research organization, the Institute for Energy Research. "They led the charge and made it easier for other states to get involved. Some states were keeping their powder dry, but Pruitt was very out front and aggressive."

After the litigation was filed—by Mr. Morrissey and Mr. Pruitt, along with other attorneys general who attended the Greenbrier meeting—Murray Energy sued in the federal court case as well, just as had been planned.

In February 2016, the Supreme Court indicated that it would side with opponents of the rule, moving by a 5 to 4 vote to grant a request by the attorneys general and corporate players to block the implementation of the Clean Power Plan while the case worked its way through the federal courts.

Trump Stokes the Fires

When Donald J. Trump decided to run for president, he did not appear to have a clear understanding of the nation's climate change policies. Nor, at the start of his campaign, did he appear to have any specific plan to prioritize a huge legal push to roll those policies back.

Mr. Trump had, in 2012, said on Twitter, "The concept of global warming was created by and for the Chinese in order to make U.S. manufacturing non-competitive." But he had also, in 2009, joined dozens of other business leaders to sign a full-page ad in *The New York Times* urging Mr. Obama to push a global climate change pact being negotiated in Copenhagen, and to "strengthen and pass United States legislation" to tackle climate change.

However, it did not go unnoticed that coal country was giving his presidential campaign a wildly enthusiastic embrace, as miners came out in full force for Mr. Trump, stoking his populist message.

And the surest way for Mr. Trump to win cheers from coal crowds was to aim at an easy target: Mr. Obama's climate rules. Hillary Clinton did not help her cause when she said last spring that her climate policies would "put a lot of coal miners and coal companies out of business."

In May 2016, Mr. Trump addressed one of the largest rallies of his campaign: an estimated crowd of over 10,000 in Charleston, W.Va., where the front rows were crammed with mine workers.

"I'm thinking about miners all over the country," he said, eliciting cheers. "We're going to put miners back to work."

"They didn't used to have all these rules and regulations that make it impossible to compete," he added. "We're going to take it all off the table."

Then an official from the West Virginia Coal Association handed the candidate a miner's hat.

As he put it on, giving the miners a double thumbs-up, "The place just went nuts, and he loved it," recalled Barry Bennett, a former adviser to Mr. Trump's presidential campaign. "And the miners started showing up at everything. They were a beaten lot, and they saw him as a savior. So he started using the 'save coal' portions of the speech again and again."

Mr. Trump's advisers embraced the miners as emblematic of the candidate's broader populist appeal.

"The coal miners were the perfect case for what he was talking about," Mr. Bennett said, "the idea that for the government in Washington, it's all right for these people to suffer for the greater good—that federal power is more important than your little lives."

Mr. Trump took on as an informal campaign adviser Robert E. Murray—chief executive of the same coal company that had been working closely for years with the Republican attorneys general to unwind the Obama environmental legacy.

Mr. Murray, a brash and folksy populist who started working in coal mines as a teenager, is an unabashed skeptic of climate science. The coal magnate and Mr. Trump had a natural chemistry, and where Mr. Trump lacked the legal and policy background to unwind climate policy, Mr. Murray was happy to step in.

"I thank my lord, Jesus Christ, for the election of Donald Trump," Mr. Murray said soon after his new friend won the White House.

Mr. Trump appointed Mr. Ebell, the Competitive Enterprise Institute fellow who had worked for years to undermine the legitimacy of established climate science, to head the transition team at E.P.A. Mr. Ebell immediately began pushing for an agenda of gutting the Obama climate regulations and withdrawing from the Paris Agreement.

When it came time to translate Mr. Trump's campaign promises to coal country into policy, Mr. Murray and others helped choose the perfect candidate: Mr. Pruitt, the Oklahoma attorney general.

Mr. Trump, who had never met Mr. Pruitt before his election, offered him the job of E.P.A. administrator—putting him in a position to dismantle the environmental rules that he had long sought to fight in court.

Meanwhile, Mr. Trump wanted to be seen delivering on the promises he had made to the miners. As controversies piled up in his young administration, he sought comfort in the approval of his base.

In March, Mr. Trump signed an executive order directing Mr. Pruitt to begin unwinding the Clean Power Plan—and he did so at a large public ceremony at the E.P.A., flanked by coal miners and coal executives. Mr. Murray beamed in the audience.

Meanwhile, a battle raged at the White House over whether to withdraw the United States from the Paris Agreement. Mr. Trump's daughter Ivanka and his secretary of state, Rex W. Tillerson, urged him to remain in, cautioning that withdrawing could be devastating to the United States' foreign policy credentials.

Murray Energy—despite its enormous clout with Mr. Trump and his top environmental official—boasts a payroll with only 6,000 employees. The coal industry nationwide is responsible for about 160,000 jobs, with just 65,000 directly in mining, according to the federal Energy Information Administration.

By comparison, General Electric alone has 104,000 employees in the United States, and Apple has 80,000. Their chief executives openly pressed Mr. Trump to stick with Paris, as did dozens of other major corporations that have continued to support regulatory efforts to combat climate change.

But these voices did not have clout in Washington, either in Congress or at the White House, when it comes to energy policy.

Mr. Trump's senior adviser, Stephen K. Bannon, backed by Mr. Pruitt, told the president that pulling out of the deal would mean a promise kept to his base.

"It is time to put Youngstown, Ohio; Detroit, Michigan; and Pittsburgh, Pennsylvania along with many, many other locations within our great country—before Paris, France," Mr. Trump said in his Rose Garden speech on Thursday. "It is time to make America great again."

The Science Gets Stronger

The recognition that human activity is influencing the climate developed slowly, but a scientific consensus can be traced to a conference in southern Austria in October 1985. Among the 100 or so attendees who gathered in the city of Villach, nestled in the mountains along the Drava River, was Bert Bolin, a Swedish meteorologist and a pioneer in using computers to model the climate.

Dr. Bolin helped steer the conference to its conclusion: "It is now believed that in the first half of the next century a rise of global mean temperature could occur which is greater than any in man's history," he wrote in the conference's 500-page report.

While the politics of climate change in the United States has grown more divided since then, the scientific community has united: Global warming is having an impact,

scientists say, with sea levels rising along with the extremity of weather events. Most of the debate is about the extent of those impacts—how high the seas may rise, or how intense and frequent heavy storms or heat waves may be.

In recent years, many climate scientists have also dropped their reluctance to pin significant weather events on climate change. Studies have shown that certain events—a 2015 Australian heat wave, floods in France last year and recent high temperatures in the Arctic—were made more likely because of global warming.

But in Congress, reluctance to embrace that science has had no political downsides, at least among Republicans.

"We don't yet have an example of where someone has paid a political price being on that side of it," said Michael Steel, who served as press secretary for the former House speaker John A. Boehner, the Republican presidential candidate Jeb Bush and the current House speaker, Paul D. Ryan, during his 2012 run as Mitt Romney's vice-presidential choice. Instead, the messages of Mr. Pruitt still dominate.

"It is now believed that in the first half of the next century a rise of global mean temperature could occur which is greater than any in man's history."

"This is an historic restoration of American economic independence—one that will benefit the working class, the working poor and working people of all stripes," Mr. Pruitt said on Thursday, stepping to the Rose Garden lectern after Mr. Trump. "We owe no apologies to other nations for our environmental stewardship."

American voters—even many Republicans—recognize that climate change is starting to affect their lives. About 70 percent think global warming is happening, and about 53 percent think it is caused by human activities, according to a recent study by the Yale Program on Climate Change Communication. About 69 percent support limiting carbon dioxide emissions from coal-fired power plants.

But most public opinion polls find that voters rank the environment last or nearly last among the issues that they vote on. And views are divided based on party affiliation. In 2001, 46 percent of Democrats said they worried "a great deal" about climate change, compared with 29 percent of Republicans, according to a Gallup tracking poll on the issue. This year, concern among Democrats has reached 66 percent. Among Republicans, it has fallen, to 18 percent.

Until people vote on the issue, Republicans will find it politically safer to question climate science and policy than to alienate moneyed groups like Americans for Prosperity

The U.S. Coast Guard Cutter *Healy* encountered only small patches of sea ice in the Chukchi Sea off the coast of Alaska during the final days collecting ocean data for NASA's 2011 ICESCAPE mission, which studied how changing conditions in the Arctic affect the ocean's chemistry.

There will be exceptions. The 2014 National Climate Assessment, a report produced by 14 federal agencies, concluded that climate change is responsible for much of the flooding now plaguing many of the Miami area's coastal residents, soaking homes and disrupting businesses, and Representative Curbelo is talking about it.

"This is a local issue for me," Mr. Curbelo said. "Even conservatives in my district see the impact. It's flooding, and it's happening now."

Mr. Curbelo helped create the House Climate Solutions Caucus, 20 Republicans and 20 Democrats who say they are committed to tackling climate change. Mr. Curbelo is confident that as the impact of climate change spreads, so will the willingness of his Republican colleagues to join him.

Outside of Congress, a small number of establishment conservatives, including a handful of leaders from the Reagan administration, have begun pushing Washington to act on climate change. Earlier this year, James A. Baker III, one of the Republican Party's more eminent senior figures, met with senior White House officials to urge them

to consider incorporating a carbon tax as part of a broader tax overhaul package—a way to both pay for proposed cuts to corporate tax rates and help save the planet. A Reagan White House senior economist, Art Laffer; a former secretary of state, George P. Shultz; and Henry M. Paulson Jr., George W. Bush's final Treasury secretary, have also pushed the idea.

"There are members from deep-red districts who have approached me about figuring out how to become part of this effort," Mr. Curbelo said. "I know we have the truth on our side. So I'm confident that we'll win eventually."

NOTE: *President Donald Trump and his team systematically dismantled the environmental protections put into place in previous decades. Trump pulled the United States out of global efforts to combat climate change and named first one, then another, staunch allies of the fossil fuels industry to head the Environmental Protection Agency, which they proceeded to gut.*

CHAPTER 6

THE RISE
OF THE RIGHT

"[Moral Majority] will not be deterred from our constitutional right and duty to speak out on the great issues of the day."

—Reverend Jerry Falwell, September 1981

ONE OF THE MOST consequential movements of American history—in its impacts on economics, society, foreign affairs and religious observance—was the rise of modern right-wing political groups within the Republican Party. Defined at first by Barry Goldwater's notions of small government and an aggressive foreign policy, Republican economic thought was later dominated by the Reagan philosophy of trickle-down economics, deregulation and "family values." In the 1970s and 1980s, the ascendance of the religious right, which was hotly denounced by Goldwater himself, began to redefine Republican conservatism along increasingly moral and religious lines. In the early 21st century, the nihilistic Tea Party movement upended the G.O.P. once again, paving the way for the election of Donald Trump, the ultimate insider who found a way to style himself as the ultimate outsider.

OPPOSITE: President Donald Trump enters the East Room of the White House for a joint news conference with Prime Minister Stefan Löfven of Sweden, March 6, 2018.

GOLDWATER VOWS TO FIGHT TACTICS OF "NEW RIGHT"

By JUDITH MILLER, SEPTEMBER 16, 1981

S enator Barry Goldwater, Republican of Arizona, accused Moral Majority and other members of the "new right" today of undermining the basic American principle of separation of church and state by using the "muscle of religion towards political ends."

"The uncompromising position of these groups is a divisive element that could tear apart the very spirit of our representative system if they gain sufficient strength," Mr. Goldwater warned in remarks offered for the record on the Senate floor. In those remarks and at a breakfast meeting with reporters, Mr. Goldwater contended that members of what he termed "special issue religious groups" were uncompromising and unconcerned about upholding the integrity of the Constitution. He said they were also "diverting" Congress from what he termed such "vital" issues as the economy and national defense toward concerns of "secondary" importance such as abortion, busing, the proposed equal rights amendment to the Constitution and pornography.

Names Helms, East and Denton

Mr. Goldwater's speech did not identify groups other than Moral Majority as members of the new right, but at breakfast he listed among its ranks the Rev. Jerry Falwell, leader of Moral Majority, along with Republican Senators Jesse Helms and John P. East of North Carolina and Jeremiah Denton of Alabama.

Saying that the religious issues of the new right had "little or nothing to do with liberal or conservative politics," Mr. Goldwater vowed to "fight them every step of the way if they try to dictate their moral convictions to all Americans in the name of conservatism."

Mr. Goldwater previously expressed anger at Mr. Falwell when Moral Majority announced its opposition to the Supreme Court nomination of Judge Sandra Day O'Connor, a fellow Arizonan. But today's criticism constituted a broadside attack on the political goals and tactics of the new right.

While A. Bartlett Giamatti, president of Yale University, recently issued a similar critique of Moral Majority and other conservative groups, Mr. Goldwater's remarks represent the first major assault on the "new conservatives" by a Republican who for many years has, in his own words, "carried the flag of the old conservatism."

Mr. Goldwater maintained that the birth of the new right was "a direct reaction to years of increasing social activism by the liberal side of the religious house." At breakfast, for example, he accused the National Council of Churches of engaging in activities that went far beyond religious concerns.

He noted, moreover, that he shared many of the positions held by Senator Helms and other members of the new right. For instance, he said that he, too, opposed abortion.

However, Mr. Goldwater said he was "sick and tired of the political preachers across this country telling me as a citizen that if I want to be a moral person, I must believe in 'A,' 'B,' 'C' and 'D.' Just who do they think they are?"

The 72-year old senator, who has acquired a reputation of late for unpredictable public statements, said he prepared his remarks some time ago and had been waiting for an opportunity to express them. Instead of delivering his speech on the floor, he asked that it be

Senator Barry Goldwater at the Republican National Convention in San Francisco, July 1964.

inserted into the Congressional Record. None of the colleagues he criticized offered any comment on Mr. Goldwater's challenge to their conservative credentials.

Mr. Falwell responded, however, that Mr. Goldwater's statement "would make one wonder whether time has passed him by." Mr. Falwell also asserted that his group "will not be deterred from our constitutional right and duty to speak out on the great issues of the day."

At breakfast, Mr. Goldwater said he did not believe that Moral Majority and the new right would damage the Republican Party "unless they become too demanding." He likened the new right to the labor movement, which he said had "petered out and lost clout" because it pressed for political goals that were unrelated to employment issues.

Finally, he derided specific legislative proposals offered by the new right, including a measure proposed by Senator Denton that would establish federal programs to discourage teenage promiscuity.

"Oh God," Mr. Goldwater said. "There's no way. How the hell could you regulate that?"

NOTE: *In retrospect, Goldwater seems almost moderate by comparison with the religious and social right-wingers who would come to take control of the Republican Party, and his legacy now represents a period of honest disagreement over big issues—a discourse that has vanished from the nation's political landscape.*

G.O.P. CELEBRATES ITS SWEEP TO POWER; CLINTON VOWS TO FIND COMMON GROUND

By ADAM CLYMER, NOVEMBER 10, 1994

Republicans today declared a political revolution, promised to balance the federal budget and generally reveled in winning control of both the House and the Senate for the first time in 40 years.

The depth of their victory was sounded by the fact that no sitting Republican governor, senator or representative was defeated.

Behaving more like striped-pants diplomats than the cranky, feuding politicians who had exchanged insults in the final days of the campaign, President Clinton and the Republican Congressional leaders, Senator Bob Dole of Kansas and Representative Newt Gingrich of Georgia, promised to look for areas where they could work together.

President Clinton told a White House news conference, "I am going to do my dead level best" to work with Republicans, and identified welfare reform as an area where "I think we will get an agreement."

Representative Gingrich, in line to become Speaker in a House where not one member has ever served under a Republican, said in an interview that he hoped his party could find a way to deal with Mr. Clinton and "package some things he can sign while he is vetoing others." He identified welfare reform, allowing the president to veto specific spending items and not just entire bills, and increasing the tax benefits for parents with children as matters that "fit rhetorically" with the president's aims.

Senator Dole, who will be Senate majority leader again, said he had called the president to tell him, "I wanted to let you know right up front that we want to work together where we can." But he offered fewer specifics, saying he would work with Mr. Clinton to secure approval of the new international trade agreement, but that he expected Mr. Clinton to explain the pact to the nation.

With eight of the House races not yet decided, the Republican landslide produced a gain of at least 49 Representatives—for a total of 227, to 199 for the Democrats and one independent. The Democratic casualties included the speaker of the House, Thomas S. Foley, the former Ways and Means chairman, Dan Rostenkowski, and the Judiciary chairman, Jack Brooks.

In the Senate, Republicans won eight additional seats, and their edge went to 53–46 when Senator Richard C. Shelby of Alabama, who was elected eight years ago as a Democrat but who votes with Republicans on major issues, made an anticlimactic announcement this morning that Southern conservatives were no longer welcome in the Democratic Party and joined the new majority. The California Senate race between the Democratic incumbent, Dianne Feinstein, and the Republican Michael Huffington, remained undecided today, although Ms. Feinstein claimed victory.

Their gains were most dramatic among governors, where they held California, won New York and Texas, and gained eight overall, so there are now 31 Republicans, 18 Democrats and 1 independent.

Haley Barbour, the chairman of the Republican National Committee, said the success of Republican officeholders showed the mood was not anti-incumbent, or anti-Washington.

He said it was a "historic victory," with voters embracing Republican ideas of smaller government, lower taxes "and more individual freedom and personal responsibility, instead of more government power and government responsibility."

David Wilhelm, the chairman of the Democratic National Committee, did not offer any complicated excuses. He said: "Well, we made history last night. Call it what you want: an earthquake, a tidal wave, a blowout. We got our butts kicked. We're bruised and battered, but we're still standing."

The front page of *The New York Times* of November 10, 1994, featured a photograph of President Bill Clinton at a news conference the day before, "looking somewhat chastened" by the "devastating defeats suffered by Democrats in Congress."

President Clinton offered three explanations for the results. He said that first, the public was dismayed at Washington business as usual, from lobbying to campaign spending to partisanship, and was saying, "Democrats are in charge—we're holding you responsible, and we hope you hear this, Mr. President."

The second message he discerned was skepticism about whether the administration had really done what it claimed about crime and the deficit, but that even if it had: "We still feel insecure. We don't feel that our incomes are going up, that our jobs are more stable, that our neighborhoods are safer, that the fabric of American life is growing more civilized and more law-abiding."

Finally, he said the public was saying, "We don't think the government can solve all the problems, and we don't want the Democrats telling us from Washington that they know what is right about everything."

> *The public was dismayed at Washington business as usual, from lobbying to campaign spending to partisanship.*

The legislative leaders avoided discussions of how their cooperation, and confrontation, could affect Mr. Clinton's likely bid for reelection in 1996. Mr. Dole, asked again if he intended to run himself, replied, "I've thought about it."

Mr. Gingrich said the Republicans on the House would move swiftly after the new Congress convenes, on Jan. 4, to adopt the legislation specified in their Contract with America, which was signed by at least 219 Republican candidates who won election yesterday.

The first day the House meets, he said, it would adopt a bill to require Congress to operate under laws relating to working conditions and the environment that it imposes on others. Other major items in the "contract" are cutting the number of House committees and reducing their staffs by one-third; passing a constitutional amendment to require a balanced federal budget; the line-item veto, and an income tax credit of $500 a child, called the American Dream Restoration Act.

Mr. Dole identified his priorities as the balanced budget amendment, "welfare reform, maybe a vote on term limits." He said many efforts would focus on Congress, from staff reductions to lobbying laws.

"We can't let somebody say, 'Well, we won the election and we don't have to worry about that for a couple of years." He said the public had elected Republicans because they had made these promises, and "If we don't do some of these things, they are going to cancel our lease."

There are plainly some items on this short list on which Mr. Clinton and the Republicans can agree. One is the line-item veto, which he campaigned for, but soft-pedaled because of the intense opposition of Senator Robert C. Byrd, the West Virginia Democrat who headed the Senate Appropriations Committee and who regards the proposal as a betrayal of hundreds of years of democratic tradition. As a ranking minority member, Mr. Byrd may no longer be an impenetrable obstacle, although his skill with Senate procedures will still be a major hurdle.

A constitutional amendment to require a balanced federal budget has had almost enough support in recent Congresses to get the required two-thirds majorities. It is likely to have it now, with the departure of such powerful, skilled opponents as Speaker Foley and Senator George J. Mitchell of Maine, the majority leader, who retired.

And legislation to limit lawsuits over how manufacturers of equipment are liable for damages when users are injured, known as "product liability legislation," seems likely to escape the Democratic filibuster that killed it this year. Five of the 41 senators who voted for the filibuster are gone, along with Mr. Brooks, an implacable House foe.

But other things on this list are much more difficult. Both the president and the Republicans say they want to change welfare so that people do not spend their lives on it.

Republicans tend to favor automatic time limits after which recipients are cut off, while most Democrats are reluctant to cut people off if no job is available. Senator Phil Gramm of Texas, for example, said Republicans would push for reform that saved money and said of recipients: "If they work hard, we'll help them. If they don't work hard, they will have to work hard."

Nor is it clear just what strategy Senate Democrats will pursue.

As Mr. Dole and the Republicans demonstrated again and again, a strong minority can block action on many measures in the Senate. It only takes 41 senators to prolong a filibuster, so if Democrats are unified, they can find that strength among their 47-member minority.

But the retiring Senator Mitchell said at a news conference, "I do not recommend confrontation." He said, "The fact that it worked for the Republicans this time doesn't mean that it will work for Democrats or others in the future."

There is also some question of how well Mr. Dole and Mr. Gingrich will work with each other. Mr. Dole has often been critical of his colleague's firebrand tactics, and Mr. Gingrich once called Mr. Dole the "tax collector for the welfare state."

But today each spoke of how Mr. Gingrich would have a different role now. Mr. Gingrich compared being Speaker of the whole House of Representatives with being a head coach. As deputy minority leader, he said, using a football metaphor, he was more of an aggressive "middle linebacker" for the partisan minority. (The leader, Robert H. Michel of Illinois, retired.) Mr. Dole said, "Newt understands—in fact he has asked me if I would meet with and sit down and talk to him about being in the majority."

Mr. Dole said he anticipated no difficulties with transforming some of his party's more contentious senior minority members into chairmen. He said Strom Thurmond, the 91-year-old senator from South Carolina, would head the Armed Services Committee, Senator Alfonse M. D'Amato of New York would head Banking, and Jesse Helms of North Carolina would head Foreign Relations.

Most of the Senate Republicans who will advance to chairmanships are known quantities. But presumptive House chairmen like Representative Floyd D. Spence of South Carolina at Armed Services, or Carlos J. Moorhead of California at Energy and Commerce, are largely unknown, because House Republicans have had limited legislative roles.

One ranking member who will not progress to a chairmanship is Representative Joseph M. McDade of Pennsylvania, who is under indictment for bribery. Mr. Gingrich said he had told Mr. McDade in July "he would not be chairman" and intended to take the Democrats' approach of barring indicted members from chairmanships.

Otherwise, Mr. Gingrich said, ranking members would not automatically become chairmen.

IN POWER PUSH, MOVEMENT SEES BASE IN G.O.P.

By KATE ZERNIKE, JANUARY 14, 2010

The Tea Party movement ignited a year ago, fueled by antiestablishment anger. Now, Tea Party activists are trying to take over the establishment, ground up.

Across the country, they are signing up to be Republican precinct leaders, a position so low-level that it often remains vacant, but which comes with the ability to vote for the party executives who endorse candidates, approve platforms and decide where the party spends money.

A new group called the National Precinct Alliance says it has a coordinator in nearly every state to recruit Tea Party activists to fill the positions and has already swelled the number of like-minded members in Republican Party committees in Arizona and Nevada.

Its mantra is this: take the precinct, take the state, take the party—and force it to nominate conservatives rather than people they see as liberals in Republican clothing.

Tea Party activists are trying to take over the establishment, ground up.

Here in Holland, Pa., a perennial battleground district outside Philadelphia, Tea Party activists are trying to strip the local committee of its influence in choosing the Republican nominee to run against Representative Patrick J. Murphy, a Democrat who won the seat in 2006 by about1,500 votes.

After the local party said it would stick to its custom of endorsing a candidate rather than holding an open primary, Tea Party groups decided to hold their own candidate forum where people could cast a ballot. If the party does not yield, the groups say they will host a debate, too.

"We kind of changed the rules," said Anastasia Przybylski, one of the organizers.

The Tea Party movement, named after the original tax revolt in 1773, might be better described as a diverse, rambunctious and internet-connected network of groups, powered by grass-roots anxiety about the economy, bailouts and increasing government involvement in health care. At one extreme are militia members who have shown up at meetings wearing guns and suggesting that institutions like the Federal Reserve be eliminated. At the other are those like Ms. Przybylski, who describes herself as "just a stay-at-home mom" who became agitated about the federal stimulus package.

And if the Democrats are big-government socialists, the Republicans, in the Tea Party mind, are enablers.

In some recent polls, a hypothetical Tea Party wins more support than Democrats or Republicans, and the most antiestablishment Tea Party activists push to fight as a third party. But as the movement looks toward the midterm elections in November, a growing number of activists argue that the best way to translate anger into influence is to infiltrate the Republican establishment (Democrats being, for the average Tea Partier, beyond redemption).

"If you want to have revenge against the Republican Party for using you for so many years, the best way is to turn around and use the Republican Party to your advantage," said Eric Odom, a Tea Party activist in Chicago who recently started a political action committee, and on his blog urged Tea Partiers to stop complaining about the Republican Party and "move in and take it over."

Republican leaders have been trying to harness the Tea Party energy—Michael Steele, the chairman of the Republican National Committee, recently called the Tea Parties "a revelatory moment."

"It puts in stark relief where the American people are, how they feel and what they feel," Mr. Steele said. "It's important for our party to appreciate and understand that so we can move toward it and embrace it."

Not all Republicans agree. Some say the party needs to broaden its reach, not cater to the fringe.

The defining experience for many Tea Party groups was the special election in the 23rd Congressional District of New York in November, where party leaders chose a candidate whom conservatives viewed as a Republican in name only—she supported same-sex marriage, abortion rights and the federal stimulus package. After activists flooded the district to support a conservative third-party candidate, the Republican dropped out and endorsed the Democrat, who won.

Conservatives took the Republican retreat as a victory, but also saw the power of the party structure in deciding who the candidates will be. The rallying cry for more local involvement has been "No more NY-23s."

"We don't want to see what happened in New York happen here," Ms. Przybylski said.

The forum here drew nine candidates and a standing-room crowd in an auditorium built for 1,200. The questions organizers had drawn up for the candidates hinted at the issues important to so called Teapublicans.

Will you pledge to vote against tax increases, even hidden taxes like those in health care reform? Should corporate executives who encourage illegal immigrants to stay

Candidate hopefuls line up onstage along with moderator Steve Highsmith (far left) for a congressional forum held by the Kitchen Table Patriots, a nonprofit grass roots political organization, on January 11, 2010, Holland, Pa.

because it is good for business be hauled off to jail? Do you believe manmade pollution is a significant contributor to global warming? ("I don't necessarily think there's been global warming," one candidate objected.)

Each was asked to define the 10th Amendment, and to cite examples of where it "might have been violated." "It's my favorite amendment in the Constitution," exclaimed one candidate, Ira Hoffman. "I can't believe it!"

The amendment declares that powers not granted to the federal government by the Constitution are reserved to the states or the people, and Tea Party activists hold that Congress has overstepped its bounds, particularly by legislating health care. So candidates were asked whether they would support efforts to nullify the health care bill.

Finally, the moderator asked them if 2010 would be "the year of the Tea Party." The candidates, and many in the audience, said it would, but only if the Tea Party advocates worked the system.

"I think we can do greater things working in a system that's established than we ever can being a bunch of anarchists," said Jennifer Turner Stefano, a vice president of a local Tea Party group who is contesting her local Republican committeeperson.

Ms. Stefano, a stay-at-home mother and former television reporter, will have to get 10 signatures and put her name on the ballot to run. But the National Precinct Alliance estimates that about 60 percent of the roughly 150,000 local Republican committee seats are vacant and can be filled by essentially showing up.

"Even if you've got a slight majority, you just need maybe 26 states, then you can have your say in how the party goes," said Philip Glass, a former commercial mortgage banker in Cincinnati who is the national director of the precinct alliance.

The precinct strategy, like the Tea Party movement itself, has spread via the internet, on sites like Resistnet.com. A National Tea Party Convention in Nashville next month will feature seminars on how to take over starting at the precinct level.

Advocates hold up the example of Las Vegas, where a group of about 30 people who had become friendly at Tea Party events last spring met to discuss how they could turn their crowds into political influence. One mentioned that there were about 500 open precinct committee positions in the local Republican Party.

They recruited other activists and flooded the committee—the Republican Party says it now has 780 committee people, up from about 300. In July, they approved a new executive committee, and Tony Warren, one of the organizers and a new precinct committeeman himself, said six out of seven executives are "constitutional conservatives," in keeping with Tea Party ideology.

With the bulk of Nevada's population in the Las Vegas area, the local committee was able to elect a conservative slate to the state party in December, including a state chairman who has said he wants to make the party "safe" for conservatives.

As recently as last spring, Mr. Warren said, "we didn't even know how the darn party worked."

ELECTION RESULTS: REPUBLICANS WIN
SENATE CONTROL WITH AT LEAST SEVEN NEW SEATS

By JONATHAN WEISMAN AND ASHLEY PARKER, NOVEMBER 4, 2014

————

Resurgent Republicans took control of the Senate on Tuesday night, expanded their hold on the House and defended some of the most closely contested governors' races in a repudiation of President Obama that will reorder the political map in his final years in office.

Propelled by economic dissatisfaction and anger toward the president, Republicans grabbed Democratic Senate seats in North Carolina, Colorado, Iowa, West Virginia, Arkansas, Montana and South Dakota to gain their first Senate majority since 2006.

Senator Mitch McConnell of Kentucky, a shrewd Republican tactician, cruised to reelection and stood poised to achieve a goal he has pursued for years—Senate majority leader.

An election that started as trench warfare, state by state and district by district, crested into a sweeping Republican victory. Contests that were expected to be

> *The uneven character of the economic recovery added to a sense of anxiety, leaving voters in a punishing mood.*

close were not, and races expected to go Democratic broke narrowly for the Republicans. The uneven character of the economic recovery added to a sense of anxiety, leaving voters in a punishing mood, particularly for Democrats in Southern states and the Mountain West, where political polarization deepened.

The biggest surprises of the night came in North Carolina, where the Republican, Thom Tillis, came from behind to beat Senator Kay Hagan, and in Virginia. There, Senator Mark Warner, a former Democratic governor of the state, was thought to be one of the safest incumbents in his party, and instead found himself clinging to the narrowest of leads against a former Republican Party chairman, Ed Gillespie.

Those contests were measures of how difficult the terrain was for Democrats in an election where Republicans put together their strategy as a referendum on the competence of government, embodied by Mr. Obama.

House seats where Democrats had fought off Republican encroachment for years were finally toppled. Gov. Scott Walker, a Republican, was easily reelected in Wisconsin, a state that voted twice for Mr. Obama. In Florida, Gov. Rick Scott, once considered endangered, finished the night on top. And states that had seemingly been trending Democratic, like Colorado and Iowa, fell into Republican hands.

With at least a nine-seat gain and most likely more, House Republicans will have close to 245 seats, the largest Republican majority since the Truman administration.

"Barack Obama has our country in a ditch, and many of his lieutenants running for the Senate were right there with him," said Reince Priebus, chairman of the Republican National Committee. "The punishment is going to be broad, and it's going to be pretty serious."

The breadth of the Republican victories also reset the political landscape ahead of the 2016 presidential campaign. And it left Mr. Obama with a decision to make: Will he move toward Republicans in his final years in areas of common interest, such as tax reform and trade, or will he dig in and hope Republican overreach will give his party a lane for a comeback?

"Just because we have a two-party system doesn't mean we have to be in perpetual conflict," vowed Mr. McConnell, in a victory speech.

White House officials accepted the overture and said Mr. Obama had invited the bipartisan leadership of Congress to the White House on Friday.

For Republicans, the victories piled up, winning not only Senate Democratic seats they were expected to take—Montana, West Virginia, South Dakota and Arkansas—but also in states that were supposed to be close. Representative Cory Gardner, a Republican, crushed Senator Mark Udall in Colorado. In Georgia, the Democrat Michelle Nunn, daughter of former Senator Sam Nunn, was widely expected to force David Perdue, a Republican businessman, into a runoff for the Senate seat of Saxby Chambliss, a retiring Republican.

Instead, Mr. Perdue won more than half the vote to take the race outright.

Senator Pat Roberts, a Kansas Republican, also fended off the independent challenger Greg Orman, who just weeks ago appeared headed to victory.

And for Democrats, it could get worse. Votes were still being tallied in Alaska, where Senator Mark Begich, a Democrat, was trying to hold back the wave. Senator Mary L. Landrieu of Louisiana was able to force her strongest Republican foe, Representative Bill Cassidy, into a Dec. 6 runoff. But the combined vote of the top two Republicans in the race easily eclipsed hers.

"I think it's a message from the American people about their concern about the direction of the country, and the competency of the current administration," said Senator Rob Portman of Ohio, vice chairman of the National Republican Senatorial Committee. "Most people have voted to end the dysfunction and to get back to legislating on issues that will help them and their families, and I think that's something that both parties need to listen to."

One bright spot for Democrats came in New Hampshire, where Senator Jeanne Shaheen, the Democratic incumbent, fended off Scott Brown, the former Republican senator from Massachusetts, according to projections by the Associated Press. In Pennsylvania, Tom Wolf, a Democrat and political novice, easily defeated the Republican governor, Tom Corbett.

And in the panhandle of Florida, Gwen Graham, daughter of a former Democratic senator and governor, defeated Representative Steve Southerland, a Tea Party favorite.

But those high notes were swamped by the lows for the president's party. In Arkansas, Representative Tom Cotton, a freshman Republican and an Iraq War veteran, defeated Senator Mark Pryor, despite the efforts of former president Bill Clinton.

In Colorado, Mr. Udall tried to replicate the storied ground game that helped propel his Democratic colleague, Senator Michael Bennet, to an unexpected victory in 2010. He was not even close, and drew further criticism for running a campaign that some felt was too focused on abortion rights and contraception.

Supporters react as U.S. Senate candidate Joni Ernst attends a Republican Party of Iowa election-night party in West Des Moines, Ia., November 4, 2014.

And in West Virginia, Representative Shelley Moore Capito, a Republican, won the Senate seat long held by Jay Rockefeller, a Democrat, to become that state's first female senator and the first Republican elected to the Senate from West Virginia since 1956. In Iowa, Joni Ernst also made history by becoming the first woman to be elected in that state's congressional delegation.

Two years after handing Democrats broad victories, voters again seemed to be reaching for a way to end Washington inertia. Yet the results on Tuesday may serve only to reinforce it. Voters appeared unsure of just what they wanted, according to surveys. Among those who voted for a Democrat, only one out of eight expressed an unfavorable opinion of the Democratic Party. Republican voters were more conflicted; among those who voted Republican, one of four viewed the party unfavorably.

Mr. Obama is left with the prospect of finding a new path to work with Republicans, something for which he has shown little inclination, and Republicans must find a way to demonstrate they are more than the party of "no."

Even though a record $4 billion poured into the election—from the campaigns, parties and outside groups for advertising and other candidate support—the money did little to stir enthusiasm as the campaign set a more dubious mark for its low levels of voter interest.

For their part, Democrats were hindered by their inability to persuade members of the coalition that delivered the White House to Mr. Obama—young voters, women and minorities—to turn out at levels seen in presidential elections. Decisions like Mr. Obama's delay of executive action on behalf of illegal immigrants also angered crucial constituencies.

Even the president conceded the steep climb his allies faced.

"This is possibly the worst possible group of states for Democrats since Dwight Eisenhower," Mr. Obama told a Connecticut public radio station on Tuesday. "There are a lot of states that are being contested where they just tend to tilt Republican."

SUDDENLY, THE G.O.P. REMEMBERS ALL ITS DOUBTS ON TRUMP

By CARL HULSE, MARCH 7, 2018

O ver the past week, congressional Republicans have gotten a glimpse of the President Trump they hoped to never see.

On gun safety and, more significantly to many of them, trade, the president has loudly broken with longstanding party orthodoxy and reminded Republican leaders on Capitol Hill that they can never be 100 percent certain of what they are going to get with the onetime New York Democrat.

Despite such worries, Mr. Trump's first-year actions on policy and personnel—particularly judicial nominees—provided substantial reassurance to congressional Republicans. They concluded that Mr. Trump was really one of them when it came to bedrock issues and that the anti-Washington, drain-the-swamp cries from the raucous campaign rallies were only so many applause lines.

> *[Republicans] don't want to do anything that could threaten economic gains.*

In the chaos of the early weeks of his administration, Mr. Trump provoked a sigh of relief from Senator Mitch McConnell, Republican of Kentucky and the majority leader, that the president seemed to actually be conservative. "If you look at the steps that have been taken so far, looks good to me," Mr. McConnell said.

Now here comes Mr. Trump with his sudden proposal to rebuild the country's steel and aluminum industries through steep tariffs on imports from leading trading partners. Most congressional Republicans fundamentally disagree with that approach, which they consider a backdoor tax that could easily touch off a calamitous trade war, hurt their local businesses and overwhelm any gains from their hard-won, Republican-only tax bill.

Already facing a harsh political climate heading toward the November midterm elections, Republicans fear that moving ahead with the tariffs could send the party—not to mention the economy—spiraling in the wrong direction. Republicans are banking on a robust economy that they can attribute to their tax cuts and regulatory rollbacks to overcome the deep public disapproval of Mr. Trump exhibited in multiple elections last year. They don't want to do anything that could threaten economic gains.

"The economy is moving in the right direction; that is what we are working on," Senator John Thune of South Dakota, the chamber's number-three Republican, told reporters on Tuesday. "We are going to stay focused on a pro-growth, pro-jobs agenda."

Mr. McConnell had remained quiet about the tariffs since Mr. Trump unexpectedly announced them last week. But on Tuesday, he made it very clear that he, and almost all of his colleagues, have major problems with them.

"There's a high level of concern about interfering with what appears to be an economy that's taking off in every respect," Mr. McConnell said. "I think the best way to characterize where I am, and where our members are, is we are urging caution that this [not] develop into something much more dramatic that could send the economy in the wrong direction."

This major policy divide goes to a disconnect between the president and congressional Republican leaders that has been papered over by fights with Democrats over the past year as well as the party unity behind the tax bill.

Most of the Republican leaders on Capitol Hill remain firmly aligned with big business and want to retain the strong support of advocacy groups such as the U.S. Chamber of Commerce and organizations affiliated with David H. and Charles G. Koch. Those business factions, always important to Republicans in a campaign year, do not like new tariffs.

Mr. Trump, on the other hand, has for years preached about the dangers and disadvantages of free trade and the harm it has done to once-leading American industries. Republicans now hoping to talk the president down from his tariff stance may find that his campaign promises about protectionism are ones he truly wants to keep.

It is a similar situation with gun safety. Mr. Trump has in the past backed the idea of an assault weapons ban. But congressional Republicans figured that his strong campaign embrace of the National Rifle Association would keep him securely in the anti-gun-control corner.

Then, in last week's extraordinary public White House meeting after the Parkland, Fla., school massacre, Mr. Trump embraced multiple aspects of the gun control agenda. He even uttered the words "take the guns first"—a phrase previously unthinkable for a top Republican politician given the party's history on gun rights.

Republicans were aghast. They also figured that, under pressure from his allies at the N.R.A., Mr. Trump would quickly return to the fold and let his enthusiasm for gun control wane. More important, congressional Republicans also knew that gun control legislation was really in their hands, not the administration's, and that they could easily bottle up any proposal.

But tariffs are a completely different matter, with the president given wide latitude to act on international trade policy. Republicans, who say they have little legislative recourse, are now engaged in a furious effort to pull the president back from making too sweeping a decision.

They are also treading carefully to avoid antagonizing a mercurial figure whose mind they still hope to change as they have in previous cases where he drifted from the party line, such as on immigration.

Speaker Paul D. Ryan, for instance, was careful to credit Mr. Trump on Tuesday for exposing that some countries do take advantage of the trade rules.

"The president's right to point out that there are abuses," Mr. Ryan said. "There clearly is dumping and transshipping of steel and aluminum."

Referring to any trade restrictions, Mr. Ryan said that Republicans simply "want to make sure that it's done in a prudent way that's more surgical, so we can limit unintended consequences."

As for Mr. McConnell, he said that "we need to wait and see what the White House finally decides to do on this."

Mr. McConnell would no doubt prefer that Mr. Trump revert to the conventional conservative principles the senator found so comforting last year. But this break could prove to be real, putting Mr. Trump and his Republican allies at cross-purposes at an inauspicious moment on the political calendar.

CHAPTER 7

POLITICAL SCANDALS

"Until this moment, Senator, I think I never really gauged your cruelty or your recklessness."

— U.S. Army counsel Joseph Welch to Senator Joseph McCarthy, June 9, 1954, during the Army-McCarthy hearings

---

WASHINGTON BREEDS SCANDAL. Most every president and Congress has had scandals—whether brought on by policy decisions, like George Washington's granting of most-favored-nation status to Great Britain, or by personal failings, like Richard Nixon's paranoia or Bill Clinton's libido. The Communist witch hunts of Senator Joe McCarthy during the Eisenhower era bathed the Capitol in an especially harsh light until the special counsel for the army, Joseph Welch, asked McCarthy if he had any "sense of decency."

For President Donald Trump, scandal has been an almost daily occurrence, or so it seems at times: the firing of F.B.I. Director James Comey, the investigation into Russian meddling in the 2016 election, his former campaign manager Paul Manafort's indictment on fraud charges, and the criminal investigation of Michael Cohen, his lawyer, who, among other things, arranged payments to women—including both a porn star and a *Playboy* model—to silence their accusations against Trump.

OPPOSITE: Senator Joseph McCarthy (right) and Joseph Welch, U.S. Army counsel (center) during the Army-McCarthy hearings in Washington, D.C., June 1954.

DEMANDS OIL REGULATION—LA FOLLETTE COMMITTEE SUGGESTS EIGHT IMMEDIATE REMEDIES

MARCH 5, 1923

Startling charge with respect to the oil industry in the United States are made in a report submitted to the Senate shortly before its adjournment today by Senator La Follette, Chairman of the Senate Committee on Manufactures, giving the results of its special investigation into the high cost of gasoline and other petroleum products.

The report charges that the oil industry today is under the complete control of the Standard companies, notwithstanding the decree of the United State Supreme Court in 1911 ordering the dissolution of the so-called Standard Oil Trust, and asserts that a careful examination of the evidence taken in the Senate investigation will show that in respect to the matter which "led to the outlawing of the Standard oil monopoly the same conditions exist as existed when the decree of the Supreme Court was entered." The report further goes on to declare that "in some respects the industry as a whole, as well as the public, are more completely at the mercy of the Standard interest now than they were when the decree of dissolution was entered in 1911."

"This point," says the report, "cannot be too strongly emphasized for the reason that the intolerable conditions in the oil industry, which are established in the investigation, cannot be corrected while Standard Oil dominates the business as it does today."

Warns of Dollar Gasoline

The report warns that if a "few great companies are permitted to manipulate prices for the next few years as they have since 1920," the people of the country must be prepared before long to pay "at least $1 a gallon for gasoline."

Besides the alleged Standard Oil control of the industry the La Follette report deals with the division of marketing territory between the Standard Oil companies, profits and prices, the effect of price changes, pipeline transportation, the situation in California, the so-called cracking process in the production of gasoline, alleged combinations among Standard companies, government concessions to oil companies, railway freight rates on oil, refinery operations, and gives detailed data relative to prices and stocks of crude and refined oil, gasoline and by-products, and concludes with the suggestion of eight suggested remedies.

That the report will be vigorously challenged by the oil industry was indicated tonight when Colonel Robert W. Stewart of Chicago, chairman of the board of directors of the Standard Oil Company of Indiana, before leaving Washington stated that in his opinion the La Follette report was "unjust" to his company and to the oil industry generally and "not based even on the testimony brought out during the hearings."

Eight Remedies Are Suggested

Senator La Follette informed the Senate that it would be useless in the closing days of the session to present a bill—which there was no time to consider much less to pass—attempting to regulate the oil industry in any comprehensive manner, but he said the Senate committee suggests eight "immediate remedies," adding that "their suggestions here made of certain remedies does not imply that other and more drastic ones may not later be found necessary."

The "immediate" remedies suggested by the La Follette committee are:

1. A uniform system of bookkeeping in all oil companies doing an interstate business, which will show at any time in detail the costs and profits of the business so that reasonableness of the prices charged for any petroleum products can be ascertained on a cost basis.

2. A compulsory system of reports to a government bureau every month showing the operations of each oil company engaged in interstate business and particularly the quantities of crude oil and its products in storage or transportation.

3. That pipelines "must be made real common carriers," with a view to divorcing the ownership of pipelines from the ownership of oil transported.

4. Changes in freight rates on petroleum products so as to permit the mid-continent refineries "once more to find a market" for their products through Michigan, Indiana, Ohio, Pennsylvania and the New England states.

Harry F. Sinclair of Mammoth Oil (left) and his counsel Martin W. Littleton during the Teapot Dome hearing, 1924. In 1922, Sinclair leased oil rights to a field near Teapot Rock in Wyoming directly from Interior Secretary Albert Fall, leading to the Teapot Dome Scandal.

5. That exportation of petroleum and its products should be either prohibited or so regulated as not to permit the export from this country of those products for which there is pressing demand in this country, the view of the committee being that it is extreme folly to permit our resources of crude oil, gasoline and similar products to be drained out of this country.

6. That any attempt at price manipulation, such as the La Follette report alleges occurred during the past three years, should be made the basis of grand jury investigation in every state where such prices were made, and if existing laws are insufficient for this, then "such legislation should be speedily enacted."

7. All parties to "implied" contracts or agreements, forbidden by the decree of the Supreme Court, should be cited by the court for contempt of the decree made when the dissolution of the Standard Oil trust was directed by the Court.

8. That the Department of Justice should immediately institute a rigid investigation into all claims for basic patents on pressure-still processes used in the production of gasoline.

Declares Change Is Imperative

"It must be obvious from the facts in this report," Senator La Follette informed the Senate, "that the business cannot go on as at present organized and conducted. It is essential to the life of the industry and vital to the public also that neither the public nor the small independent producers and refiners shall not be left as at present to the mercy of a combination which advances or depresses prices as it pleases. Unless some means can be found to prevent the manipulation of prices by the large companies, and particularly the Standard group, it is as certain as any future event can be that gasoline prices in the near future will be so advanced as to put gasoline beyond the reach of the public generally as a motor fuel."

Refers to Teapot Dome

"No greater concessions," says the report, "have ever been bestowed upon oil companies in any land than that which the government of the United States has bestowed upon the oil companies in this country. It must be borne in mind that the vast oil-producing area in Wyoming now dominated by the Midwest Refining Company, owned by the Standard Oil of Indiana, was entered upon and wells drilled while the order of the president of Sept. 27, 1909, withdrawing the lands from location and settlement was well known. Not only were the lands so withdrawn, but in 1914 the Supreme Court decided that they had been validly withdrawn and that claims to location thereon arising since the president's withdrawal order of 1909 were void.

WELCH ASSAILS MCCARTHY'S "CRUELTY" AND "RECKLESSNESS" IN ATTACK ON AIDE; SENATOR ON STAND, TELLS OF RED HUNT

By W. H. LAWRENCE, JUNE 10, 1954

The Army-McCarthy hearings reached a dramatic high point today in an angry, emotion-packed exchange between Senator Joseph R. McCarthy and Joseph N. Welch, special counsel for the Army.

Irritated by Mr. Welch's persistent cross-examination of Roy M. Cohn, Senator McCarthy suddenly injected into the hearings a charge that one of Mr. Welch's Boston law firm associates, Frederick G. Fisher Jr., had been a member of the National Lawyers Guild "long after it had been exposed as the legal arm of the Communist party."

Mr. Welch, almost in tears from this unexpected attack, told the Wisconsin Republican that "until this moment, Senator, I think I never really gauged your cruelty or your recklessness." He asked Senator McCarthy if any "sense of decency" remained in him.

> *"If there is a God in heaven, it will do neither you nor your cause any good."*

"If there is a God in heaven, it [the attack on Mr. Fisher] will do neither you nor your cause any good," Mr. Welch declared.

Spectators Break into Applause

The crowded hearing room burst into applause for Mr. Welch as he abruptly broke off his conversation with Senator McCarthy. Mr. Welch refused to address any more questions to Mr. Cohn, counsel to the McCarthy subcommittee, and suggested to Karl E. Mundt, South Dakota Republican who is acting committee chairman, that he call another witness.

Senator McCarthy thereupon was called and took the stand on the thirtieth day of the hearing.

Senator McCarthy had interrupted Mr. Welch's cross-examination of Mr. Cohn to denounce Mr. Fisher. He asserted, despite contradictions by Senator Mundt, that Mr. Welch had tried to get Mr. Fisher employed as "the assistant counsel for the committee" so he could be in Washington "looking over the secret and classified material."

Senator Mundt said Mr. Welch never had recommended Mr. Fisher or anyone else for a subcommittee job. Mr. Welch explained that he had planned to have Mr. Fisher, a leader in the Young Republican League of Newton, Mass., as one of his own assistants in this case until Mr. Fisher told him that he had belonged to the National Lawyers Guild while at Harvard Law School "and for a period of months after."

The violent, unforeseen character of Senator McCarthy's attack seemed to upset Mr. Cohn, himself, whose facial expressions and grimaces caused Senator McCarthy to comment: "I know Mr. Cohn would rather not have me go into this."

Senator Mundt has daily cautioned the audience to refrain from "audible expressions of approval or disapproval" of the proceedings on pain of being expelled from the hearing room. But he made no effort to control or admonish the crowd that applauded Mr. Welch's retort to Senator McCarthy.

Disputes Obscure the Issues

The McCarthy-Welch exchange, and another hot battle between Senators McCarthy and Stuart Symington, Missouri Democrat, served to divert attention from the basic issues in this controversy. The army initially charged that Senator McCarthy and Mr. Cohn had sought by improper means to obtain preferential treatment for Pvt. G. David Schine, who until he was drafted, was an unpaid committee consultant.

Senator McCarthy and Mr. Cohn, in turn, have charged that the army held Private Schine as a "hostage" and tried to "blackmail" the committee out of investigating the army.

Other Highlights:

· Senator Symington specified that Senator McCarthy agree to explain whether, among other things, it had been proper for him to accept $10,000 from the Lustron Corporation for a pamphlet on housing, whether funds supplied to fight Communism were diverted to Senator McCarthy's own use and whether he had violated state and federal tax laws and banking laws over a period of years.

· Charging that Senator Symington's offer demonstrated "how low an alleged man can sink," Senator McCarthy said he would give a firm commitment, but sign no letter, agreeing to testify before such a committee "if the Vice President or the Senate want to appoint a committee to investigate these smears."

· Calling the exchanges divisionary and "mid-morning madness," Senator Mundt tried to halt the personal feud between the two senators, but not until Senator McCarthy had denied that Senator Symington, while in private industry, had dealt with a Communist, one William Sentner, and paid him money to settle a strike.

The army and McCarthy sides are willing to end the hearings after Senator McCarthy and his subcommittee staff director, Frances P. Carr, have testified fully and been cross-examined. The Republican members and Senator McCarthy are seeking a specific date as a time limit, but Mr. Welch has thus far resisted that proposal. He has said he is willing instead to accept a stated number of turns in ten-minute cross-examination periods. The Democrats, on the other hand, have been fighting against an arbitrary time limit, and have insisted that other witnesses whose testimony may be material to the controversy may not be refused the right to appear.

Mr. Welch mixed humor with persistency in his cross-examination of Mr. Cohn early in the day. He made Senator McCarthy angry when he chided "these Communist hunters" for "sitting on a document for month after month" while they waited for committee hearings instead of telling Secretary Stevens about alleged Reds at Fort Monmouth.

He brought out that the altered F.B.I. report "purloined" from the army's files had been given to Senator McCarthy last spring, but that not during March, April, May, June or July did Mr. Cohn or Senator McCarthy convey the information in it to Mr. Stevens. The crowd in the room roared with laughter as Mr. Welch added: "I think it is really dramatic to see how these Communist hunters will sit on this document when they could have brought it to the attention of Bob Stevens in twenty minutes, and they let month after month go by without going to the head and saying, 'Sic 'em, Stevens.'"

> *"He knows it is ridiculous. He is wasting time doing it."*

Angrily Senator McCarthy said Mr. Welch was being unfair. "That may sound funny as all get-out here," Senator McCarthy said. "It may get a laugh. He knows it is ridiculous. He is wasting time doing it. He is trying to create a false impression. I would like to suggest that after this long series of ridiculous questions, talking about why he wouldn't go over to the Pentagon and yell out 'Sic 'em, Stevens,' that Mr. Cohn should be able to tell what happened after the document was received. That is the only fair thing, Mr. Chairman."

Just before Mr. Cohn was excused abruptly, Mr. Welch created something of a stir in the committee room by disclosing he had obtained hotel and night club records indicating Mr. Cohn's expenditures for dinners and parties in New York and Trenton at times when Private Schine was on leave from Fort Dix.

Some of them concerned the Stork Club, but Mr. Cohn swore that Private Schine, had not been there during the time he was assigned to Fort Dix. Some of the other expenditures, he said, represented occasions when he had dined with Private Schine, and, on one occasion, when they had been accompanied by girls.

NOTE: *McCarthy was ultimately censured by Congress for his witch hunts, but the atmosphere of suspicion, distrust and guilt by association persists in Washington.*

VIETNAM ARCHIVE: PENTAGON STUDY TRACES THREE DECADES OF GROWING U. S. INVOLVEMENT

By NEIL SHEEHAN, JUNE 13, 1971

A massive study of how the United States went to war in Indochina, conducted by the Pentagon three years ago, demonstrates that four administrations progressively developed a sense of commitment to a non-Communist Vietnam, a readiness to fight the North to protect the South and an ultimate frustration with this effort—to a much greater extent than their public statements acknowledged at the time.

The 3,000-page analysis, to which 4,000 pages of official documents are appended, was commissioned by Secretary of Defense Robert S. McNamara and covers the American involvement in Southeast Asia from World War II to mid-1968—the start of the peace talks in Paris after President Lyndon B. Johnson had set a limit on further military commitments and revealed his intention to retire. Most of the study and many of the appended documents have been obtained by *The New York Times* and will be described and presented in a series of articles beginning today.

Though far from a complete history, even at 2.5 million words, the study forms a great archive of government decision-making on Indochina over three decades. The study led its 30 to 40 authors and researchers to many broad conclusions and specific findings, including the following:

- That the Truman administration's decision to give military aid to France in her colonial war against the Communist-led Vietminh "directly involved" the United States in Vietnam and "set" the course of American policy.

- That the Eisenhower administration's decision to rescue a fledgling South Vietnam from a Communist takeover and attempt to undermine the new Communist regime of North Vietnam gave the administration a "direct role in the ultimate breakdown of the Geneva settlement" for Indochina in 1954.

- That the Kennedy administration, though ultimately spared from major escalation decisions by the death of its leader, transformed a policy of "limited-risk gamble," which it inherited, into a "broad commitment" that left President Johnson with a choice between more war and withdrawal.

· That the Johnson administration, though the president was reluctant and hesitant to take the final decisions, intensified the covert warfare against North Vietnam and began planning in the spring of 1964 to wage overt war, a full year before it publicly revealed the depth of its involvement and its fear of defeat.

· That this campaign of growing clandestine military pressure through 1964 and the expanding program of bombing North Vietnam in 1965 were begun despite the judgment of the government's intelligence community that the measures would not cause Hanoi to cease its support of the Vietcong insurgency in the South, and that the bombing was deemed militarily ineffective within a few months.

· That these four succeeding administrations built up the American political, military and psychological stakes in Indochina, often more deeply than they realized at the time, with large-scale military equipment to the French in 1950; with acts of sabotage and terror warfare against North Vietnam beginning in 1954; with moves that encouraged and abetted the overthrow of President Ngo Dinh Diem of South Vietnam in 1963; with plans, pledges and threats of further action that sprang to life in the Tonkin Gulf clashes in August, 1964; with the careful preparation of public opinion for the years of open warfare that were to follow, and with the calculation in 1965, as the planes and troops were openly committed to sustained combat, that neither accommodation inside South Vietnam nor early negotiations with North Vietnam would achieve the desired result.

The Pentagon study also ranges beyond such historical judgments. It suggests that the predominant American interest was at first containment of Communism and later the defense of the power, influence and prestige of the United States, in both stages irrespective of conditions in Vietnam.

And it reveals a great deal about the ways in which several administrations conducted their business on a fateful course, with much new information about the roles of dozens of senior officials of both major political parties and a whole generation of military commanders.

MOTIVE IS BIG MYSTERY IN RAID ON DEMOCRATS

By WALTER RUGABER, JUNE 26, 1972

oving through the basement after midnight, the guard found strips of tape across the latches of two doors leading to the underground garage.

It was an altogether fit beginning for a first-rate mystery—the raid on the Democratic National Committee headquarters.

In the eight days since, the White House and the Republican party have been embarrassed, the Democrats have sensed a big election-year issue and a major federal investigation has begun. The mystery has involved Republican officials, former agents of the Central Intelligence Agency, White House aides and bewildering assortments of anti-Castro Cubans.

Guard Not Alarmed

There has been talk of telephone taps, spy cameras and stolen files; of obscure corporations and large international financial transactions; of an unsolved raid on a chancery office and on an influential Washington law firm.

The guard, Frank Wills, a tall, 24-year-old bachelor who earned $80 a week patrolling one of the office buildings in the Watergate complex for General Security Services, Inc., was not greatly alarmed when he found the tape.

The high-priced hotel rooms, prestigious offices and elegant condominium apartments within the Watergate development had been favorite targets of Washington's burglars and sneak thieves for several years.

Along with three present or former cabinet officers and various other Republican leaders, the tenants included the Democratic National Committee. Its offices had been entered at least twice within the last six weeks. But Mr. Wills assumed that the office building's maintenance men had immobilized the latches. He tore off the strips of tape, allowing the two doors to lock, and returned to his post in the lobby.

"Somebody was taping the doors faster than I was taking it off."

Ten minutes later, acting on what he now calls a "hunch," he returned to the basement. The latches were newly taped. So were two others, on a lower level, that had been unobstructed only minutes before.

"Somebody was taping the doors faster than I was taking it off," Mr. Wills said in an interview later. "I called the police." His alarm was logged at the central station at 1:52 a.m. on Saturday, June 17.

It took less than 48 hours for the authorities to clamp a fairly tight lid on things. Much of the information that emerged afterward, even on the most pedestrian points, was unofficial or leaked by unnamed sources.

And none of it established motive. Washington went on a speculative binge, but even those running the investigation were said to be confused and uncertain. The available facts offered many possible interpretations.

More Tape Found

First to reach the Watergate were plainclothes members of the Second District Tactical Squad. They went first to the eighth and top floor, where tape was found on a stairway door. Nothing else was amiss, however.

Working their way down, they found more tape on the sixth floor. With guns drawn, they entered the darkened offices of the Democratic National Committee. Crouched there were five unarmed men, who surrendered quietly.

"They didn't admit what they were doing there," said John Barret, one of the plainclothes men who handcuffed the five and lined them up against a wall. "They were very polite, but they wouldn't talk."

Presumably, there was plenty to talk about—the taped latches, for example.

For one thing, taping the doors was a dead giveaway. Ordinarily, burglars use wooden match sticks. Also, why did anyone bother with the door on the eighth floor?

Furthermore, once the tampering had been discovered, it was risky in the extreme to repeat it. Who did it? And why were two separate basement entrances taped the second time?

Why, in fact, were any? All of the doors open freely from the inside, and once entrance to the building had been gained, an intruder could have left without keys and without setting off an alarm.

Too Many Men

Five men were found in the Democratic offices, which struck those informed in such matters as three or four too many. The five men were charged with burglary and led off to the District of Columbia jail, where they all gave false names to the booking officer. After a routine fingerprint check, they were identified as follows:

Bernard L. Barker, 55 years old, a native of Havana who fled the Fidel Castro regime and became an American citizen. He is president of Barker Associates, a Miami real estate concern.

James Walter McCord Jr., 53, a native of Texas. He is now president of McCord Associates, Inc. of suburban Rockville, Md., a private security agency.

Frank Sturgis, 48, who lost his American citizenship for fighting in the Castro army but regained it later. He has changed his name from Frank Fiorini but is still known under both names. He works at the Hampton Roads Salvage Company, Miami.

Eugenio R. Martinez, 51, a man with $7,199 in his savings account and who works as a notary public and as a licensed real estate operator. He now works for Mr. Barker's agency and is said to earn $1,000 a month.

Virgilio R. Gonzalez, 45, a locksmith at the Missing Link Key Shop, Miami. He is reported to have been a housepainter and a barber in Cuba, which he fled after Mr. Castro's takeover in 1959.

All except Mr. McCord left Miami Friday afternoon, apparently on Eastern Airlines flight 190, which arrived at Washington National Airport at 3:59 p.m. Mr. Barker used his American Express credit card to rent a car at that time.

The four men checked into two rooms—214 and 314—at the Watergate Hotel. They are understood to have dined that evening in the hotel restaurant. The hotel connects with the office building through the underground garage.

What Police Seized

The police collected what the five men had with them at the time of their arrest and obtained warrants to search the two hotel rooms and the rented automobile. An inventory included:

- Two 35-mm cameras equipped with close-up lens attachments, about 40 rolls of unexposed 35-mm film, 1 roll of film from a Minox "spy" camera and a high-intensity lamp—all useful in copying documents.

- Two or three microphones and transmitters. Two ceiling panels had been removed in an office adjacent to that of the party chairman, Lawrence F. O'Brien, and it was theorized that the equipment was being installed, replaced or removed.

- An assortment of what were described as lock picks and burglary tools, two walkie-talkie radios, several cans and pen-like canisters of Chemical Mace and rubber surgical gloves, which all five men had been wearing.

- Nearly $6,000 in cash. The money, found in the possession of the five and in the two hotel rooms, included some $5,300 in $100 bills bearing consecutive serial numbers.

Parts of the Democratic headquarters had been ransacked. Mr. O'Brien subsequently said that the party's opponents could have found an array of sensitive material, but no pattern to the search has been disclosed.

Last Sunday, the Associated Press discovered from Republican financial records filed with the government that Mr. McCord worked for both the Committee to Re-Elect the President and the Republican National Committe.

"Security Coordinator"

The records showed that since January Mr. McCord had received $1,209 a month as "security coordinator" for the Nixon organization, and that since October he was paid more than $600 a month for guard services for the Republican unit.

The following day it was learned that in address books taken by the police from Mr. Barker and Mr. Martinez the name of E. (for Everette) Howard Hunt appeared. Mr. Hunt had worked, as recently as March 29, as a White House consultant.

The police also turned up in the belongings of the five suspects an unmailed envelope that contained Mr. Hunt's check for $6, made out to the Lakewood Country Club in Rockville, and a bill for the same amount.

> *The records showed that since January Mr. McCord had received $1,209 a month as "security coordinator" for the Nixon organization.*

Both Mr. Hunt and Mr. McCord were members of the Rockville Club, and there were published reports that Mr. Hunt met with Mr. Barker in Miami two weeks before the break-in. The White House said that Mr. Hunt worked 87 days in 1971 and 1972 under Charles W. Colson, special counsel to the president. Mr. Colson has frequently handled sensitive political assignments.

The consultant, who is the author of 42 novels under several pen names, works full time as a writer for Robert R. Mullen & Co., a Washington public relations firm with long-standing Republican connections. The firm's president, Robert F. Bennett, quoted Mr. Hunt as saying he "was nowhere near that place [the Watergate] Saturday." The writer has declined public comment, however, and Mr. Bennett has suspended him.

Security Man Dropped

The Republicans quickly discharged Mr. McCord as their security man and denied emphatically that they had had any connection with the raid on the Democratic headquarters.

"We want to emphasize that this man [Mr. McCord] and the other people involved were not operating either on our behalf or with our consent," said John N. Mitchell, the former attorney general who is now head of the Nixon committee.

Ronald L. Ziegler, the White House press secretary, said that "a third-rate burglary attempt" was unworthy of comment by him and asserted that "certain elements may try to stretch this beyond what it is."

The White House pointed out that there was no evidence that either Mr. Colson or Mr. Hunt had been involved in any way in the raid on the Democrats, and several high-ranking police officials privately advanced the same view.

The Democratic National Committee, however, filed a $1-million civil suit against the five accused raiders and against the Committee to Re-Elect the President, charging that the Democrats' civil rights and privacy had been violated.

Mr. Mitchell described this as "another example of sheer demagoguery on the part of Mr. O'Brien." Mr. O'Brien said that there was "a developing clear line to the White House.

Stories about Spies

More or less simultaneously with the political exchanges, the reports about former spies began to come in. All five of the arrested men were said to have had ties to the Central Intelligence Agency.

Mr. Hunt, operating under the code name Eduardo, was described as the man in direct charge of the abortive invasion of the Bay of Pigs in Cuba in 1961. He is known to have worked for the C.I.A. from 1949 to 1970.

Mr. Barker also worked for the C.I.A. He was reported to have been Mr. Hunt's "pay master" for the Cuban landing and, under the code name Macho, to have established the secret invasion bases in Guatemala and Nicaragua.

Mr. McCord, too, was a C.I.A. agent. After three years with the Federal Bureau of Investigation, he joined the intelligence unit in 1951 and resigned in 1970. His role in the Bay of Pigs was understood to be relatively minor.

The spy angles led directly to the Cuban refugee angle. It was disclosed that on the weekend of May 26–29, eight men who described themselves as representatives of an organization called Ameritas registered at the Watergate Hotel.

The eight included those arrested in Democratic headquarters except Mr. McCord. It was also disclosed that during that May weekend there was a burglary of the Democratic offices. Ameritas turned out to be an obscure real estate concern in Miami. One of the principals was a close friend of Mr. Barker but none of the arrested men ever owned an interest in the company. A man who does, Miguel A. Suarez, a prominent lawyer in the Cuban community, said that Mr. Barker had made "unauthorized" use of the Ameritas letterheads in making reservations at the Watergate for the eight men.

Search Is on for Four

The F.B.I. began a nationwide search for the four others who stayed there, and the theory grew that if Ameritas was not, as the police had speculated, a right-wing, anti-Castro paramilitary unit, there must be one somewhere.

The Chilean chancery, representing a left-wing government, was mysteriously searched during the night of May 13–14, and the door of a law firm with several prominent Democrats as members was tampered with on the night of May 15–16.

Some of the $100 bills found by the police appear to have been withdrawn from Mr. Barker's Miami bank. The money had been deposited there in the form of checks drawn on the Banco Internacional, S.A., Mexico City.

There are countless anti-Castro organizations in the Miami area, ranging in size from one member to hundreds, and many of them are devoted to plotting. Among those cited in connection with the break-in was one involving veterans of the Bay of Pigs.

While it was conjectured that a Cuban group might have been seeking to curry favor with the Republicans or to battle leftists, this theory, like all the others, was uncertain.

TEARS AT PARTING

By JAMES T. WOOTEN, AUGUST 10, 1974

Richard M. Nixon, his face wet with tears, bade an emotional farewell to the remnants of his broken administration today, urging its members to be proud of their record in government and warning them against bitterness, self-pity and revenge.

"Always remember, others may hate you," he told members of his cabinet and staff in a final gathering at the White House, "but those who hate you don't win unless you hate them—and then you destroy yourself."

Shortly thereafter, for the last time as president of the United States, he strode up the ramp of the plane that had taken him to the capitals of the world and was flown home to California, where his career in American politics began nearly 30 years ago.

It was 11:35 a.m. here when President Nixon's letter of resignation was delivered to the office of Secretary of State Kissinger. This is what it said:

"Dear Mr. Secretary: I hereby resign the office of President of the United States. Sincerely, Richard Nixon."

Richard Nixon waves goodbye to members of his staff as he boards a helicopter, August 9, 1974, the day after resigning the presidency following the Watergate scandal.

Greeted by 5,000

Soon after his departure, while the giant jet was soaring high above the heartland of the country, Gerald R. Ford was sworn in here as the nation's president.

Despite that new status, 5,000 people greeted his arrival in his native state at El Toro Marine Base. They cheered and applauded when, with his wife, Pat, standing nearby, Mr. Nixon stepped to a waiting microphone, squinted into the brilliant midday heat and said, "We're home."

After a few more remarks, a helicopter whisked the former president, Mrs. Nixon, their daughter Tricia and her husband, Edward F. Cox, to La Casa Pacifica, the sprawling seaside villa near San Clemente.

Mr. Nixon's day began in the mist and rain of a humid Washington morning, when Manolo Sanchez, his long-time valet, laid out the clothes he would wear during the final hours of his tenure as president.

He had determined that he would leave the city as president and, after saying goodbye to the White House servants, he and Mrs. Nixon and their two daughters and son-in-law went downstairs to the spacious East Room, where the men and women who had worked for him were waiting for his farewell remarks.

"You are here to say goodbye to us," he began, "and we don't have a good word for it in English. The best is au revoir. We will see you again."

Then, with his family standing behind him, Mr. Nixon began to speak of many things—of the White House itself, the faithfulness and loyalty of his subordinates there, of his parents, and of the vagaries of human existence.

"This house has a great heart," he said, "and that heart comes from those who serve."

He stated his pride in the cabinet he had appointed and the staff he had named, and he conceded that "we have done some things wrong in this administration, and the top man always takes the responsibility—and I have never ducked it."

"We Can Be Proud"

He went on: "But, I want to say one thing: We can be proud of it—five and a half years—no man or no woman came into this administration and left it with more of this world's goods than when he came in."

While he spoke, Mr. Nixon's eyes brimmed with tears that glistened in the glare of the television lights, and although he occasionally smiled, his remarks were tinted with the sadness his friends say now plagues him.

There was also a moment of irony, when, in discussing vocational integrity, he said that among other craftsmen, the country needs "good plumbers."

The ornate room, crowded with those who had watched the Watergate scandals grow from a small group of "plumbers" commissioned by Mr. Nixon to find and stop leaks to the media, was quiet except for a scraping chair or two and scattered coughing.

Unlike his quiet, controlled demeanor in his television appearance last night, when he announced to the nation that he would resign, Mr. Nixon was animated in his last White House appearance, moving energetically behind the wooden lectern, gesturing and nodding in punctuation of his remarks.

To Pay His Taxes

The lightest moment in his remarks came when he told the audience that he would like to compensate them monetarily for their services.

"I only wish that I were a wealthy man," he said. "At the present time, I have got to find a way to pay my taxes."

There was laughter in the East Room, and some of the quiet but heavy tension was temporarily relieved.

He was calm, though, as he remembered his father, "my old man," but as he reminisced, his voice grew thick and approached the breaking point.

"I think they would have called him sort of a little man," he said. "Common man— but he didn't consider himself that way. . . . He was a great man because he said his job, and every job, counts up to the hilt, regardless of what happens."

His mother, he said, was a saint about whom no books would ever be written.

Then, Mr. Cox, his son-in-law, stepped over and handed him an open copy of a book. Mr. Nixon pulled a pair of glasses from his coat pocket, put them on and began to read from President Theodore Roosevelt's diary. The passage he cited was written after the death of his first wife, an event that, according to the diary, "took the light from my life forever."

Served His Country

"But," said Mr. Nixon, "he went on, and he not only became president, but as an ex-president he served his country—always in the arena: tempestuous, strong, sometimes wrong, sometimes right, but he was a man."

At the end of his remarks, he paused and began his, farewell:

"And so, we leave with high hopes, in good spirit and with deep humility, and with very, much gratefulness in our hearts.

"And I can only say to each and every one of you, we come from many faiths, we pray perhaps to different gods, but really the same God in a sense, but I wish to say to each and every one of you, not only will we always remember you, not only will we always be grateful to you, but always you will be in our hearts and you will be in our prayers."

As they had, when he had entered the room a quarter hour before, the audience stood and applauded. Mr. Nixon and his family stepped down from the curved platform and walked outside to the South Lawn, where Mr. and Mrs. Ford and another crowd of well-wishers were waiting.

The Last Ride

At the end of a scarlet carpet and a corridor of honor guards from the military services, an olive-drab helicopter stood waiting for the last ride from the White House out to Andrews Air Force base and the big, silver-and-blue plane he had dubbed the *Spirit of '76*.

Julie Eisenhower kissed her father. David Eisenhower and Mr. Ford kissed Mrs. Nixon. Mrs. Ford kissed Mr. Nixon, and at the last moment, the president reached out for the vice president's hand, shook it warmly, and then touched Mr. Ford's elbow with his left hand, like a coach sending in a substitute.

Mr. Nixon mounted the steps to the helicopter, turned and jerked a wave and then lifted his arm in the familiar "victory" gesture.

Several hundred people were at the airport outside Washington to see the president depart. He made no comments there, but once again waved and smiled from the ramp just before disappearing inside.

The engines whined and then screamed and then roared as the plane turned on the tarmac and began moving slowly away from the waving group along the wire fence.

Onboard with Mr. and Mrs. Nixon were Mr. and Mrs. Cox and Ronald L. Ziegler, the press secretary and presidential adviser.

The jet wheeled onto the runway, paused momentarily and then began its takeoff roll toward the west.

THE PRESIDENT'S ACQUITTAL: THE WHITE HOUSE; PRESIDENT SAYS HE IS SORRY AND SEEKS RECONCILIATION

By JAMES BENNET AND JOHN M. BRODER, FEBRUARY 13, 1999

Teetering between remorse and anticipation, President Clinton said today that he felt humbled and "profoundly sorry," as he pledged to make the most of his latest second chance.

Bill Clinton has survived, again. After the Senate found him not guilty on two articles of impeachment, he tried today to contend with two inescapable questions: At what cost, and for what purpose?

"I want to say again to the American people how profoundly sorry I am for what I said and did to trigger these events and the great burden they have imposed on the Congress and on the American people," Mr. Clinton said. But, he said, the outcome of his trial presented an opportunity: "This can be and this must be a time of reconciliation and renewal for America."

Hoping to betray no hint of smugness, the president spent part of Thursday evening in the White House residence working on his five-sentence statement, barely longer than a sound bite. His aides said he revised it this morning in the residence, where he remained until early afternoon.

As a strong southerly wind rustled the magnolia trees and puffed into the microphone, Mr. Clinton walked alone from the Oval Office two hours after the Senate finished voting. Speaking slowly

President Clinton apologizes to the nation during a press conference in the White House Rose Garden on February 12, 1999, several hours after his acquittal in the impeachment trial.

and shaking his head for emphasis, he kept his statement short and bittersweet; its essential elements reflected those in a statement of regret he made on Dec. 11, before the House impeached him.

Mr. Clinton took one shouted question, pausing to consider it after he had started walking away: Could he forgive and forget?

He smiled slightly after he turned back to the crowd of reporters, jostling on a springlike day that would later turn stormy and cold. "I believe any person who asks for forgiveness has to be prepared to give it," he said. Then he left.

Hoping to mold history's judgment, Mr. Clinton is bent on remaking his protean presidency once again, his friends and advisers say. As of today, it had become something no one could have imagined at his second inaugural two years ago, when he laid his hand on a biblical passage declaring, "Thou shalt be called the repairer of the breach."

Over 13 months of investigations, revelations and political venom, the president has put his family through misery, taxed the loyalty of his cabinet and his aides, and admitted outright lies to the nation about his affair with Monica S. Lewinsky. The political breach in Washington is gaping.

But for all the personal damage done, Mr. Clinton has prospered politically and his Republican foes have suffered. The president remains firmly in office and resoundingly popular, while Speaker Newt Gingrich and the man who was to succeed him, Robert L. Livingston, are departing for private life.

> *"I believe any person who asks for forgiveness has to be prepared to give it."*

Besides apologizing again to the country, Mr. Clinton expressed remorse and gratitude today to his staff. Not a single member of Mr. Clinton's cabinet or staff resigned to protest his behavior.

Via electronic mail, the president's chief of staff, John Podesta, forwarded to the White House staff an apology from Mr. Clinton, who for all his praise of information technology does not use a computer.

"Your dedication and loyalty have meant more to me than you can ever know," the message read, in part. "The best way I can repay you is to redouble my own efforts on behalf of the ideals we share, and to make the most of every day we are here."

After leaving the Rose Garden, Mr. Clinton telephoned several Democratic senators to thank them. Then, in a display of the business-as-usual briskness that carried him through his yearlong crisis, he met with his foreign policy team to begin preparing for an overnight trip to Mexico on Sunday.

Later, Mr. Clinton met in the Oval Office with his public and private lawyers to thank them, and then received a visit from the Rev. Jesse L. Jackson, who has counseled him and supported him politically during his ordeal.

As he told House Democrats at a retreat this week, Mr. Clinton wants to score legislative gains on Social Security, health care and education—even as he fights to win back Congress for the Democrats in 2000. He wants to work with the Republicans who voted to eject him from office, while he tries to eject some of them from office. Some of his allies think that Mr. Clinton has gained the upper hand and will be able to do both.

"This thing has empowered him," said James Carville, the president's former campaign manager and informal adviser. "His own party is unified, and the opposition party desperately needs him to get some things done before the election. He's become stronger and his opponents have become weaker."

Other Clinton advisers worry that his approval ratings may slide once a public urge to rally around him subsides. They fret that today's unity might crumble if House Democrats prove less interested in agreement than in fighting Republicans on issues like raising the minimum wage.

Mr. Clinton's history—as college politician, Arkansas governor, presidential campaigner and president—is a stuttering series of reversals and political fresh starts. Some of his aides divide his presidential terms into as many as five distinct periods of governance and politics, since the Clintons arrived here as bright-eyed outsiders promising intelligence, integrity and compassion. That was only six years ago.

First came a burst of energy and innovation, culminating in the Clintons' politically disastrous health care proposal and the first Republican Congress in 40 years. There followed a period of drift and despondency, some officials recalled, as Mr. Clinton publicly insisted on his relevance and privately wondered what to do.

By appearing firm and compassionate after the Oklahoma City bombing and then standing up to the Republicans during the government shutdown, Mr. Clinton regained his political footing. Under the influence of his sometime adviser, Dick Morris, he took the initiative again, this time with smaller proposals tested to insure their popularity.

Those ideas carried him to reelection in 1996, but the administration seemed to run out of gas after his second inaugural. Then, as he began to regain his bearings, the disclosures about Ms. Lewinsky swamped him.

Mr. Clinton's advisers say there is no mystery about what comes next. Mr. Clinton unrolled his policy wish list in his State of the Union message, and he is hoping that success in shoring up Social Security will counterbalance the weight of impeachment.

Some of his aides suspect that the Republicans who tried to remove him will be more scarred by their votes than he is.

"Their votes on impeachment will be in the first paragraph of their obituaries," said one senior White House official. Mr. Clinton, he said, "will try to get impeachment erased from the first paragraph of his—or at least make it a very, very long paragraph."

Mr. Clinton did not watch the Senate vote today, his aides said. Instead, Mr. Podesta telephoned him after each ballot to report the outcome. A group of senior aides had gathered in the chief of staff's office, confident of acquittal but worried that the second charge, obstruction of justice, might draw a majority. "There was a good bit of suspense," said one who was present.

But, cautioned by Mr. Podesta at the senior staff meeting this morning, Mr. Clinton's aides avoided any celebration. Only his legal team permitted themselves public grins, as they strolled from the White House to an Indian restaurant for lunch. But even they deferred to appearances, declining a bottle of champagne offered by well-wishers.

"I think, given the circumstances of this matter that's gone on for this long, we can be relieved it's over," said Joe Lockhart, the White House press secretary. "But there's really nothing to celebrate."

FIRING FUELS CALLS FOR INDEPENDENT INVESTIGATOR, EVEN FROM REPUBLICANS

By DAVID E. SANGER, MATTHEW ROSENBERG AND MICHAEL S. SCHMIDT,
MAY 9, 2017

President Trump's decision on Tuesday to fire the F.B.I. director, James B. Comey, immediately fueled calls for an independent investigator or commission to look into Russia's efforts to disrupt the election and any connections between Mr. Trump's associates and the Russian government.

Calls to appoint an independent prosecutor have simmered for months, but until now, they had been voiced almost entirely by Democrats. Mr. Comey's insistence that he was pressing ahead with the Russia investigation, and would go wherever the facts took him, had deflected those calls—especially because he was in such open defiance of a president who said the charges were "fake."

Mr. Comey's firing upended the politics of the investigation, and even Republicans were joining the call for independent inquiries.

Senator John McCain, Republican of Arizona, who is among the most hawkish members of Congress on Russia, said that he was "disappointed in the president's decision" and that it bolstered the case "for a special congressional committee to investigate Russia's interference in the 2016 election."

He got support from the chairman of the Senate Intelligence Committee, Richard M. Burr of North Carolina, a Republican leading what appears to be the most active congressional investigation on Russia. "I am troubled by the timing and reasoning of Jim Comey's termination," Mr. Burr said in a statement. It "further confuses an already difficult investigation by our committee," he said, adding that Mr. Comey had been "more forthcoming with information" than any of his predecessors.

The Democratic vice chairman of the Senate panel, Mark Warner of Virginia, said in a brief interview that Mr. Comey's firing "means the Senate Intelligence investigation has to redouble its efforts, has to speed up its timeline, because we've got real questions about the rule of law." Even before Mr. Comey was fired, the committee was pressing forward with its investigation. Late last month, it asked a number of high-profile Trump campaign associates to hand over emails and other records of dealings with Russians. Mr. Warner said the committee planned to announce on Wednesday who had complied and who had not.

Officials familiar with the investigation say the committee is prepared to issue subpoenas to get the records. Mr. Warner would not say when, or if, those might come.

Earlier in the evening, he told CNN the committee had sent the Treasury Department a request for financial records of Mr. Trump and a number of associates.

The Justice Department insisted the dismissal had nothing to do with the Russia investigation. Rather, it said, it was a response to how Mr. Comey handled the investigation of Hillary Clinton, and his decision to declare last summer that there was no reason to prosecute her for using a private email server. Yet Mr. Trump's letter to Mr. Comey made an oblique reference to the Russia investigation that has consumed the early months of his presidency.

James Comey, Director of the F.B.I., is sworn in during the Senate Judiciary Committee hearing at the Dirksen Senate Office building on Capitol Hill in Washington, D.C. on May 3, 2017.

"While I greatly appreciate you informing me, on three separate occasions, that I am not under investigation, I nevertheless concur with the judgment of the Department of Justice that you are not able to effectively lead the bureau," Mr. Trump wrote.

The letter "doesn't pass any legitimate smell test," Mr. Warner said.

For weeks, Mr. Trump has turned to his Twitter account to denounce the investigations as a waste of taxpayer money, including in the hours before Mr. Comey testified to Congress last week. His Twitter posts appeared to be direct challenges to an open F.B.I. investigation, a subject presidents have traditionally tried to avoid commenting on publicly.

Whether Mr. Trump was seeking to affect the Russia investigation will now become a subject of argument and a new partisan battle. Some in the White House feared that Mr. Comey's inquiry, first publicly acknowledged nearly two months ago, could harm the president even if no charges were brought.

At the core of the concern about Mr. Trump's motive for firing Mr. Comey is whether the White House is trying to delay or derail the F.B.I.'s investigation into Mr. Trump's associates. Among the former advisers to the president now under investigation are his campaign chairman Paul Manafort, and Roger Stone, a longtime confidant.

Mr. Stone predicted last year that there would be major, embarrassing revelations about Democratic officials, which proved prescient when WikiLeaks published emails from John D. Podesta, Mrs. Clinton's campaign chairman.

The emails had been stolen by Russian hackers months earlier.

Appearing before Congress in March, Mr. Comey described the F.B.I. inquiry as a counterintelligence investigation, indicating that one question was whether Russia's government had tried to recruit Mr. Trump's associates. He said explicitly that one focus was possible collusion between Trump associates and the Russian officials behind interference in the election. Investigations of this type can go on for years, and some Republicans were increasingly concerned that it was creating a cloud over the president and the party that they could not dispel.

Democrats said they had little doubt of what had motivated Mr. Trump to fire his F.B.I. director. Representative Adam B. Schiff of California, the top Democrat on the House Intelligence Committee, said the firing "raises profound questions about whether the White House is brazenly interfering in a criminal matter."

When Mr. Trump was preparing for the presidency after his election, there was no immediate sign that he would seek to oust Mr. Comey. The F.B.I. director came to brief him at Trump Tower with other intelligence officials, carrying a detailed intelligence report, ordered by President Barack Obama, on Russia's actions and the intelligence supporting the conclusion that President Vladimir V. Putin was behind them.

Afterward, Mr. Trump said briefly in public that he was persuaded by the evidence.

During that same session, Mr. Comey briefed Mr. Trump on a dossier compiled by a former British intelligence officer that alleged a broad conspiracy between Mr. Trump and Russian officials. None of those charges have been proven, but the briefing immediately associated Mr. Comey with an investigation Mr. Trump has dismissed as a politically motivated witch hunt.

The firing also raised questions about the role of Attorney General Jeff Sessions, a former senator from Alabama and one of Mr. Trump's earliest supporters. Mr. Sessions recused himself from the Russia investigation in March, after it was revealed that he had provided inaccurate information to Congress about his meetings with the Russian ambassador to the United States, Sergey I. Kislyak. On Tuesday, however, he wrote a letter to Mr. Trump endorsing a memorandum by his deputy, Rod Rosenstein, and making the case for Mr. Comey's immediate ouster. In that letter, Mr. Sessions did not describe his specific concerns but said, "A fresh start is needed at the leadership of the F.B.I."

NOTE: *President Donald Trump hoped the firing of James Comey as F.B.I. director would quash the investigation into whether or not his campaign conspired with the Kremlin to interfere in the 2016 election, but it had the opposite effect. The stunning move led to the appointment of a special counsel, former F.B.I. chief Robert Mueller, to head an investigation that, as of this writing, continues well into his presidency and which is an object of almost daily public rants by Trump on Twitter and in his speeches.*

ACKNOWLEDGMENTS

I would like to thank the people and institutions that made this book possible, starting, naturally, with *The New York Times* itself, which has been part of my life since I was born. The Annenberg Public Policy Center at the University of Pennsylvania gave me time and space to delve into the history of political journalism. The Shorenstein Center on Media, Politics and Public Policy at the Harvard Kennedy School, gave me the opportunity to teach, and thus learn, about the press, politics and race.

The great political journalists I've worked with at *The Times*—Maureen Dowd, R. W. "Johnny" Apple, Howell Raines, Robin Toner, Adam Nagourney, Adam Clymer, Michael Kelly, Gail Collins and others—not only taught me lessons beyond measure or price, but also inspired me to view politics as fun, sport and entertainment.

Alex Ward of *The Times* and Barbara Berger, executive editor of Sterling Publishing, put up with my breaking of virtually every deadline and provided invaluable reactions and suggestions about the contents of this collection. Cecilia Bohan, a longtime colleague from *The Times* newsroom, edited the photos and illustrations with her great skill and wise experience. At Sterling, I am also grateful to Lorie Pagnozzi, art director; David Ter-Avanesyan, cover designer; Linda Liang, photo editor; Elizabeth Lindy, senior art director, covers; Michael Cea, production editor; Terence Campo, production manager, and at Tandem Books, Ashley Prine and Katherine Furman.

Most of all, I need to express my gratitude to my children, Gabriel and Natasha, who tolerated my endless talk about political reporting and gave me their own insights, and to my wife, Mary Beth Rosenthal, a former Capitol Hill staffer and Washington lawyer/lobbyist who understands politics and politicians better than anyone I know. She urged me to take on this project and helped me with it at every step—from the creation of the book's outline to the selection of the articles.

—Andrew Rosenthal

CONTRIBUTORS

Yamiche Alcindor, a former national reporter for *The Times*, is now a White House correspondent for the *PBS NewsHour*.

Edmund L. Andrews is a former economics reporter for *The Times*.

R. W. Apple Jr. (1934–2006) was a *Times* correspondent for more than 40 years, reporting on war, revolution, politics and government, food and drink.

Matt Apuzzo, a two-time Pulitzer Prize–winning reporter for *The Times* based in Washington, has covered law enforcement and security matters for more than a decade.

Peter Baker, the chief White House correspondent for *The Times*, covered the presidencies of Bill Clinton and George W. Bush for *The Washington Post*, and Barack Obama and Donald Trump for *The Times*.

Russell Baker, a columnist for *The Times* for more than 20 years, won a Pulitzer Prize for distinguished commentary in 1979.

Michael Barbaro is the host and editor of *The Times*'s podcast *The Daily*.

Felix Belair Jr. (1907–1978) was a correspondent in *The Times*'s Washington bureau who covered the administrations of seven presidents.

James Bennet is the editor for *The Times*'s editorial page. He was previously the Jerusalem bureau chief, a White House correspondent and a political reporter at the paper, and was the editor in chief of *The Atlantic*.

Gerald M. Boyd (1950–2006) covered the administration of George H. W. Bush for *The Times* before becoming the paper's metropolitan editor and then managing editor.

John M. Broder, who has been *The Times*'s White House correspondent, Washington editor, Los Angeles bureau chief and director of polling, is now an associate editor for the editorial page.

Elisabeth Bumiller is the Washington bureau chief of *The Times* and has also been the paper's City Hall bureau chief in New York as well as a White House and Pentagon correspondent.

Earl Caldwell is a former national correspondent for *The Times* who was later a columnist for *The New York Daily News*.

Adam Clymer was a national political correspondent, chief Washington correspondent and polling editor at *The Times*.

Patricia Cohen is a national economics correspondent for *The Times* who has written extensively about the theater, books and the arts.

Edward Cowan was an editor and correspondent at *The Times* from 1962 to 1986.

Coral Davenport is a reporter in *The Times*'s Washington bureau, covering energy and environmental policy with a focus on climate change.

Julie Hirschfeld Davis is a White House correspondent for *The Times* who frequently covers immigration issues.

Maureen Dowd, an Op-Ed page columnist for *The Times*, won a Pulitzer Prize for distinguished commentary in 1999.

John Eligon is a national correspondent for *The Times* covering race issues.

Stephen Engelberg, who was an editor and reporter for *The Times*, is now editor in chief of ProPublica.

George Esper (1932–2012) spent a decade covering the Vietnam War for the Associated Press.

Matt Flegenheimer covers national politics for *The Times*.

Michelle Goldberg, an Op-Ed columnist for *The Times*, was part of a 2018 Pulitzer Prize–winning team that reported on sexual harassment in the workplace.

Linda Greenhouse, a longtime Supreme Court correspondent for *The Times*, is now a contributing Op-Ed page writer for the paper.

Bernard Gwertzman, a former national and foreign correspondent for *The Times*, is the foreign editor and editor of *The New York Times* online.

Patrick Healy, a national political correspondent for *The Times* during the 2016 presidential campaign, is the paper's politics editor.

Harold B. Hinton (1898–1954), a reporter in *The Times*'s Washington bureau for more than 30 years, covered the White House, Congress, the State Department and the Pentagon.

Carl Hulse, *The Times*'s chief Washington correspondent, has reported from the capital for more than 30 years.

Jodi Kantor, a reporter for *The Times*, was part of the 2018 Pulitzer Prize–winning team that exposed sexual harassment and misconduct in the workplace.

E. W. Kenworthy (1909–1993) worked at *The Times* for nearly 30 years in both New York and Washington.

John Kifner is a former senior foreign correspondent for *The Times*.

Arthur Krock (1886–1974) was an editorial writer, correspondent and columnist for the paper.

W. H. Lawrence (1916–1972) reported for *The Times* on World War II, the Korean War and the White House. He was later with ABC News.

Neil A. Lewis was a *Times* correspondent for 20 years, covering presidential campaigns, the Justice Department and Apartheid-era South Africa.

Eric Lichtblau is a former reporter in *The Times*'s Washington bureau. He and James Risen won a 2006 Pulitzer Prize for their coverage of the secret eavesdropping program approved by President George W. Bush.

Eric Lipton, a Washington-based investigative reporter for *The Times*, is a three-time Pulitzer Prize winner.

Jonathan Martin is a national political correspondent for *The Times*.

Patricia Mazzei is *The Times*'s Miami bureau chief, covering Florida and Puerto Rico.

Judith Miller, a former correspondent for *The Times*, is now a commentator for Fox News.

CONTRIBUTORS

Adam Nagourney, a former chief political correspondent for *The Times*, is now the paper's Los Angeles bureau chief.

James M. Naughton (1938–2012) was a White House and national correspondent for *The Times* during the Nixon, Ford and Carter administrations.

Ashley Parker, formerly a Washington-based political reporter for *The Times*, covers the White House for *The Washington Post*.

Jeremy W. Peters is a reporter in *The Times*'s Washington bureau reporting on politics.

Howell Raines was executive editor of *The New York Times* from 2001 to 2003. Prior to that he was *The Times*'s bureau chief in Atlanta and Washington.

Roy Reed (1930–2017) covered the civil rights movement in the South for *The Times* from 1965 to 1978.

Robert Reinhold (1941–1996) was a science reporter and national correspondent for *The Times* and later an editorial writer at *The Los Angeles Times*.

James Reston (1909–1995) was a columnist, Washington correspondent, executive editor at *The Times* and winner of two Pulitzer Prizes.

James Risen won a Pulitzer Prize while at *The Times* for uncovering the warrantless eavesdropping program approved by President George W. Bush. He now reports for *The Intercept*.

Matthew Rosenberg covers intelligence and national security for *The Times*, and he was part of a 2018 Pulitzer Prize–winning team that reported on connections between Donald Trump's advisors and Russia.

Andrew Rosenthal is the former editorial page editor for *The Times*.

Brian M. Rosenthal is a reporter on *The Times*'s metropolitan desk.

Walter Rugaber was a correspondent in *The Times*'s Detroit, Atlanta and Washington bureaus.

Harrison E. Salisbury (1908–1993) was a foreign correspondent for *The Times* and its first Op-Ed page editor. He won a Pulitzer Prize in 1955 for his articles from Moscow.

David E. Sanger is a national security correspondent and senior writer at *The Times*, and he was part of three Pulitzer Prize–winning teams for the paper.

Robert B. Semple Jr. was a White House correspondent, deputy national editor, London bureau chief, foreign editor, Op-Ed page editor and associate editor for the editorial page at *The Times*. He won a Pulitzer Prize in 1996 for his editorials on the environment.

Sidney Shalett (1911–1965) was an author and journalist who worked for *The New York Times* and *The Chattanooga Times*.

Eileen Shanahan (1924–2001) was an economics reporter for *The Times* from 1962 to 1977.

Thom Shanker, an assistant Washington editor for *The Times*, was the paper's Pentagon correspondent for 13 years.

Michael S. Schmidt is a Washington correspondent for *The Times* who was part of two Pulitzer Prize–winning teams in 2018.

CONTRIBUTORS

Michael D. Shear is a White House correspondent for *The Times* with a focus on domestic policy, the regulatory state and life at 1600 Pennsylvania Avenue.

Neil Sheehan, who covered the war in Vietnam for *The Times* and United Press International, obtained the Pentagon Papers, the publication of which won *The Times* a Pulitzer Prize.

Edwin M. Stanton (1814–1869) was secretary of war in the Lincoln administration.

Sheryl Gay Stolberg, formerly a science and national correspondent for *The Times*, reports on Congress for the paper.

Robin Toner (1954–2008), the first woman to be the national political correspondent of *The Times*, covered five presidential elections and innumerable congressional and gubernatorial campaigns.

Megan Twohey, an investigative reporter, was part of *The Times* team that won a 2018 Pulitzer Prize for exposing sexual harassment and misconduct in the workplace.

Martin Waldron (1925–1981) was a national correspondent and bureau chief in Houston and Trenton, N.J., for *The Times*.

Warren Weaver Jr. (1923–1997) was a reporter in *The Times*'s Washington bureau for 27 years, covering Congress and the Supreme Court, among other beats.

Jonathan Weisman is a deputy Washington editor at *The Times*, in charge of congressional coverage and politics, health care and education policy.

Tom Wicker (1926–2011) was *The Times*'s Washington bureau chief and political columnist.

James T. Wooten is a former national reporter and White House correspondent for *The Times* who became a correspondent for ABC News.

Kate Zernike, who covers women and politics for *The Times*, is the author of *Boiling Mad: Inside Tea Party America*.

INDEX

PICTURE CREDITS